HNC HND BUSINESS

Core Unit 6:

The Legal and Regulatory Framework

Course Book

BPP PUBLISHING

EDEXCEL HNC & HND BUSINESS

First edition August 2000
ISBN 0 7517 7036 1

British Library Cataloguing-in Publication Data
A catalogue record for this book is available from the British Library

Printed in Great Britain by Ashford Colour Press, Gosport, Hants

Published by
BPP Publishing Limited
Aldine House, Aldine Place
London W12 8AW

www.bpp.com

We are grateful to the Institute of Chartered Secretaries and Administrators for permission to reproduce past examination papers. The suggested solutions have been prepared by BPP Publishing Ltd

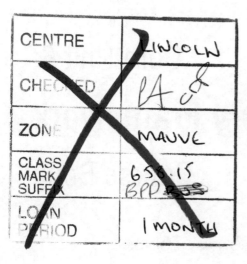

CONTENTS

INTRODUCTION

The HNC and HND qualifications in Business are very demanding. The suggested content, set out by Edexcel in guidelines for each unit, includes topics which are normally covered at degree level. Students therefore need books which get straight to the core of these topics, and which build upon the student's existing knowledge and experience. BPP's series of Course Books have been designed to meet that need.

This book has been written specifically for Unit 6: *The Legal and Regulatory Framework*. It covers the Edexcel guidelines and suggested content in full, and includes the following features.

- The Edexcel guidelines
- A study guide explaining the key features of the book and how to get the most from your studies
- A glossary and index

Each chapter contains:

- An introduction and study objectives
- Summary diagrams and signposts, to guide you through the chapter
- Numerous activities, topics for discussion, definitions and examples
- A chapter roundup, a quick quiz with answers, answers to activities and an assignment (with answer guidelines at the end of the book.)

BPP Publishing are the leading providers of targeted texts for professional qualifications. Our customers need to study effectively. They cannot afford to waste time. They expect clear, concise and highly-focused study material. This series of Course Books for HNC and HND Business has been designed and produced to fulfil those needs.

BPP Publishing
August 2000

Other titles in this series:

Core Unit 1	Marketing
Core Unit 2	Managing Financial Resources
Core Unit 3	Organisations and Behaviour
Core Unit 4	Organisations, Competition and Environment
Core Unit 5	Quantitative Techniques for Business
Core Unit 6	Legal and Regulatory Framework
Core Unit 7	Management Information Systems
Core Unit 8	Business Strategy
Option Units 9-12	Business & Finance (1/01)
Option Units 13-16	Business & Management (1/01)
Option Units 17-20	Business & Marketing (1/01)
Option Units 21-24	Business & Personnel (1/01)

For more information, or to place an order, please call 020 8740 2211, or fill in the order form at the back of this book.

If you would like to send in your comments on this book, please turn to the review form on the last page.

EDEXCEL GUIDELINES FOR CORE UNIT 6: LEGAL AND REGULATORY FRAMEWORK

Description of unit

This unit provides an introduction to basic principles of law relating to business. It develops students' knowledge of general principles of contract and criminal law, and the more specific statutory provisions relating to consumer and employee protection. It also provides an introduction to business units - their formation, management and dissolution. The student is encouraged to analyse and evaluate legal provisions and to adopt a practical approach to problem solving.

Summary of outcomes

To achieve this unit a student must:

1. Discuss the **prinicples of law** relating to the formation and discharge of commercial and customer contracts
2. Identify key provisions contained in **consumer protection legislation**
3. Explain the legal provisions concerned with the **formation, management and dissolution** of business units
4. Explain key provisions relating to **employment protection legislation**

Content

1 Principles of law

Definition of contract

Essentials for a valid contract

Rules of offer and acceptance

Vitiating factors: misrepresentation, fundamental mistake

Classification of terms: express/implied, conditions/warranties/innominate

Discharge of contract: performance, agreement, breach, frustration

Specialist terms: exclusion, force majeure, price variation, retention of title, liquidated damages

Remedies for breach

Sales of goods: transfer of property, risk and title, delivery, real and personal remedies

2 Consumer protection legislation

Key provisions relating to protection given to the buyer/debtor/user from the following legal sources:

- Sale of Goods Act 1979, eg implied rights of buyer (ss 12-15, ss 21-26)
- Supply of Goods and Services Act 1982 (Parts 1 & 2)
- Unfair Contract Terms Act 1977

- Consumer Credit Act 1974, eg rights re information, copies, cancellation, early termination, defaulting
- Consumer Protection Act 1987 (Part 1)
- Data Protection Act 1984
- Relevant European Directives and domestic regulations, eg Unfair Terms in Consumer Contracts Regulations 1994

Role of the main regulatory agencies concerned with consumer protection.

3 Formation, management and dissolution of business units

Legal considerations influencing choice of business unit

Legal requirements relating to the formation of sole traders, partnerships and registered companies

General provisions relating to the running/management of the above business units, eg statutory and common law rights/duties of partners, shareholders, directors and creditors

Dissolution of business units - voluntary/compulsory

Role of the main regulatory agencies relating to company formation and management, eg Registrar of Companies, DTI

4 Employment protection legislation

Key statutory provisions relating to the protection of full-time and part-time employees and independent contractors:

- Employment Rights Act 1996 (written particulars of main terms, time off work, unlawful deductions from pay, maternity rights, minimum notice, unfair dismissal, redundancy payments)
- Directives and Domestic Regulations relating to the above areas, eg Collective Redundancies Regulations 75/129/EEC; Transfer of Undertakings Directive 77/187/EEC

Key statutory provisions relating to health and safety at work:

- Health & Safety at Work Act 1974 (the general provisions contained in ss 2-9)
- The role of European Community Directives, Domestic Regulations and Codes of Practice

The role of the main regulatory agencies relating to health and safety, ie Health and Safety Commission, Health and Safety Executive, local authorities.

Outcomes and assessment criteria

The learning outcomes and the criteria used to assess them are shown in the table below.

Outcomes	Assessment criteria **To achieve each outcome a student must demonstrate the ability to:**
1 Discuss the **principles of law** relating to the formation and discharge of commercial and customer contracts	• identify on what basis a contract can be made • explain the significance of specialist terms contained in a specimen contract • assess the validity of at least two contractual clauses contained in a specimen contract
2 Identify key provisions contained in **consumer protection legislation**	• identify the source and content of the key statutory provisions relating to consumer protection • assess the effectiveness of a provision found in the different acts • apply relevant legislation on consumer protection to a case study and present findings
3 Explain the legal provisions concerned with the **formation, management and dissolution** of business units	• identify the relevant legal principles which can influence choice of business unit • explain the differences in the regulatory approach adopted for partnerships and registered companies with regard to their management • describe the procedures for the dissolution of business units
4 Explain key provisions relating to **employment protection legislation**	• identify the source and content of the key statutory provisions relating to employer protection • describe limitations to their availability • apply relevant law on employment protection to a case study and present findings

GUIDANCE

Generating evidence

Evidence of outcomes may be in the form of:

- group work examining a contractual negotiation case study, and using specimen 'terms and conditions' documentation to decide rights and duties
- case studies which evaluate the effectiveness of at least two statutory provisions relating to consumer protection found in different Acts
- group research assignment which considers the legal implications relating to choice of business unit
- time-constrained assessment involving advanced case study reading material relating to termination of employment

Links

The unit does not include discrimination law nor trade union law. These topics are addressed in 'Managing Human Resources Issues' (Unit 22) and 'Employee Relations' (Unit 24).

There is clearly common ground between some of the content in this unit and that of other units, eg health and safety issues covered in 'Managing Human Resources Issues' (Unit 22), terms and conditions of employment issues considered in 'Human Resource Management' (Unit 21).

This unit offers opportunities for demonstrating Common Skills in Communicating and Managing Tasks and Solving Problems.

Resources

Students need access to a library with the key texts and to case studies.

World wide web sites can be useful in providing information and case studies (eg http://www.bized.co.ac.uk which provides business case studies appropriate for educational purposes).

Delivery

It is anticipated that much of the material in this unit lends itself to active methods of learning and delivery. Extensive use of case studies and specimen documentation is to be encouraged both as a means of assessment and as part of the normal learning process.

Suggested reading

There are a large number of textbooks available covering the areas contained within the unit.

Dobson P and Schmitthoff C, *Charlesworth's Business Law* (Sweet and Maxwell, 1997)

Kelly D and Holmes A, *Principles of Business Law* (Cavendish Publishing, 1997)

Keenan D, *Smith and Keenan's Advanced Business Law* (Pitman Publishing, 1997)

STUDY GUIDE

This text gives full coverage of the Edexcel guidelines. This text also includes features designed specifically to make learning effective and efficient.

(a) Each chapter begins with a summary diagram which maps out the areas covered by the chapter. There are detailed summary diagrams at the start of each main section of the chapter. You can use the diagrams during revision as a basis for your notes.

(b) After the main summary diagram there is an introduction, which sets the chapter in context. This is followed by learning objectives, which show you what you will learn as you work through the chapter.

(c) Throughout the text, there are special aids to learning. These are indicated by symbols in the margin,

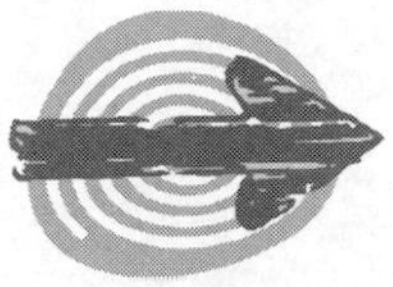

Signposts guide you through the text, showing how each section connects with the next.

Definitions give the meanings of key terms. The *glossary* at the end of the text summarises these.

Activities help you to test how much you have learnt. An indication of the time you should take on each is given. Answers are given at the end of each chapter.

Topics for discussion are for use in seminars. They give you a chance to share you views with your fellow students. They allow you to highlight holes in your knowledge and to see how others understand concepts. If you have time, try "teaching" someone the concepts you have learnt in a session. This helps you to remember key points and answering their questions will consolidate your knowledge.

Examples relate what you have learnt to the outside world. Try to think up your own examples as you work through the text.

Chapter roundups present the key information from the chapter in a concise format. Useful for revision.

(d) The wide **margin** on each page is for your notes. You will get the best out of this book if you interact with it. Write down your thoughts and ideas. Record examples, question theories, add references to other pages in the text and rephrase key points in your own words.

(e) At the end of each chapter, there is a **chapter roundup**, a **quick quiz** with answers and an **assignment**. Use these to revise and consolidate your knowledge. The chapter roundup summarises the chapter. The quick quiz tests what you have learnt (the answers often refer you back to the chapter so you can look over subjects again). The assignment (with a time guide) allows you to put your knowledge into practice. Answer guidelines for the assignments are at the end of the text.

(f) At the end of the text, there is a glossary of key terms and an index.

PART A

COMMERCIAL AND CONSUMER CONTRACTS

Chapter 1 :
INTRODUCTION TO THE LAW

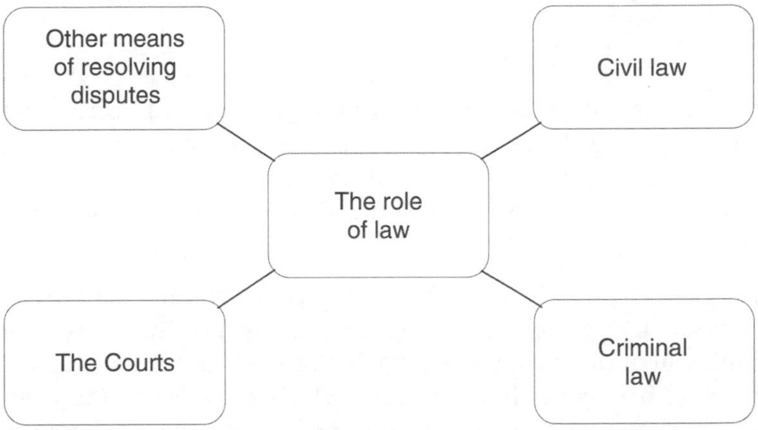

Introduction

A quick look at the syllabus and outcomes for this Unit will show you that the main elements are the various types of contract and the problems which can arise with them, and some basic aspects of business and company law. However, in order fully to understand those topics it is vital that you have an appreciation of the background to the English legal system and are familiar with the terminology used. This means that when you come to study the fine detail of the law in later chapters of this book you will be able to put into context the legal rules and decisions which you encounter.

Your objectives

In this chapter you will learn about the following.

(a) The role of law within society

(b) The difference between civil and criminal law

(c) How disputes may be resolved by the courts, by tribunals and by arbitration

(d) The sources of English law which are applied today

You should appreciate that the first two chapters of this book are for background reading, and the subject matter would not be covered in the assignments that you are expected to sit as part of your course. It is important, however, that you understand the legal background underpinning the law you will cover later.

NOTES

1 THE ROLE OF LAW WITHIN SOCIETY

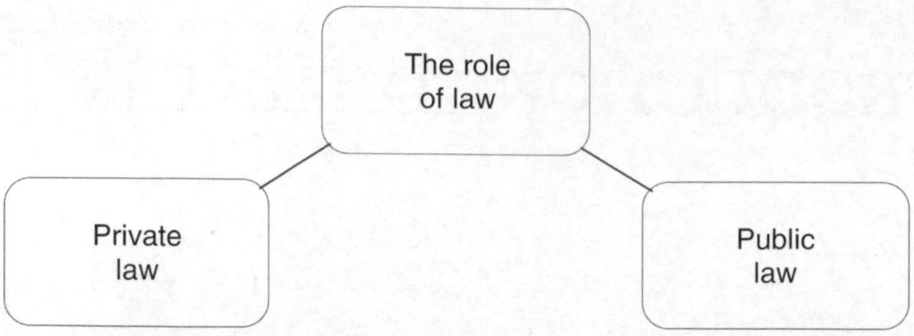

Law can be summarised as a body of rules for the guidance of human conduct, imposed upon and enforced among the members of a particular state in order to enable the state to function. If there is no legal system it is likely that chaos will ensue, as can sometimes be seen in countries where civil war causes the system of law and order to be abused and ultimately to break down.

We are all subject to the law. Its consequences affect us all on a daily basis, whether we are buying a house, buying goods in a shop (ie entering a consumer contract) entering a contract of employment or driving a car, in which case criminal penalties apply if we fail to do that properly. It is not only individuals who are subject to the law: the different types of law, much of which is specific to them, also govern companies and other business units.

1.1 Public and private law

One basic division of law is between public and private.

Public law governs relations between an individual citizen and the state. Examples include:

(a) the criminal law, which will be discussed in greater detail shortly;

(b) constitutional law, which is the law governing matters such as the operation of Parliament and the frequency with which general elections must be held;

(c) administrative law.

Private law, which is also known as civil law, is the law governing relations between citizens themselves. Examples include:

(a) the law of contract, which you will cover in some depth later in this book;

(b) the law of tort, which is the law covering the legal duty of people towards each other, such as the law of negligence

(c) the law of trusts, dealing with the disposal of a person's property according to their wishes;

(d) property law, that is the rules on the buying, selling and holding of property; and

(e) family law, concerned with issues such as divorce, custody of children and wards of court.

1.2 The developing nature of law

The law is not static but changes and develops, reflecting the values and institutions of each era. Any study of English law as it now is (for the time being) requires a brief explanation of the process of historical development which has made it what it is. Until Parliament was reformed in the nineteenth century the main purpose and effect of English law was to define and safeguard rights of property and to uphold public order. Since that time there has been an increasing flow of new laws designed, for example, to deal with social problems and to develop the national economy. Many old laws have been repealed; for instance, a broken promise of marriage was formerly actionable by the jilted woman as a breach of contract, but this is no longer so.

Although English law has many features which are common to other national legal systems, it also has some distinctive features of its own. It differs from the law of many Western European countries (and also Scotland) in having absorbed only a small amount of Roman law. Secondly, English law is case law made by decisions of the courts to a much greater extent than the law of many other countries.

2 CIVIL AND CRIMINAL LAW

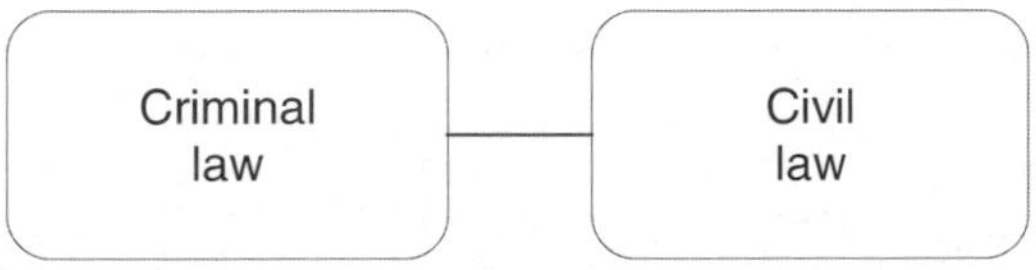

The distinction between criminal and civil liability is central to the legal system and to the way in which the court system is structured. The objectives of each category of the law, although closely connected, are different.

2.1 Criminal law

A crime is conduct prohibited by the law. The State (in the form of the Crown Prosecution Service) is the usual prosecutor in a criminal case because it is the community as a whole which suffers as a result of the law being broken. However, private individuals may also prosecute (although this is rare). Persons guilty of crimes are punished by fines or imprisonment.

In a criminal trial, the burden of proof to convict the accused rests with the prosecution, which must prove its case beyond reasonable doubt. A criminal case might be referred to as *R v Shipman 2000*. The prosecution is brought in the name of the Crown (R signifying Regina, or the Queen). Shipman is the name of the accused or defendant.

2.2 Civil proceedings

Civil law exists to regulate disputes over the rights and obligations of persons dealing with each other. The State has no role in a dispute over, for instance, a breach of contract. It is up to the persons involved to settle the matter in the courts if they so wish. The general purpose of such a course of action is to impose a settlement, sometimes using financial compensation in the form of the legal remedy of damages, sometimes using equitable remedies such as injunctions or other orders. There is no concept of punishment; it is more a case of righting a wrong.

In civil proceedings, the case must be proved on the balance of probability. The party bearing the burden of proof is not required to produce absolute proof, nor prove the issue beyond reasonable doubt. He must convince the court that it is more probable than not that his assertions are true.

Terminology is different from that in criminal cases; the claimant sues the defendant, and the burden of proof may shift between the two.

The main areas of civil liability are contract and tort. Both are forms of relationship between persons.

(a) A contract is a legally binding agreement, breach of which infringes one person's legal right given by the contract to have it performed.

(b) A tort is a wrong committed by one person against another (such as a libel), infringing general rights given by the law. Hence for there to be liability there need not have been any pre-existing personal relationship before the tort was committed.

Definition

> Standard of proof: the extent to which the court must be satisfied by the evidence presented.

> **Activity 1** **(5 minutes)**
>
> Why do you think that the standard of proof in criminal trials does not have to be beyond *all* doubt?

> **Activity 2** **(10 minutes)**
>
> While driving, Martin exceeded the speed limit and crashed into the wall of Andrew's house, causing damage worth £5,000. What legal actions, either criminal or civil, may arise as a result of his actions?

3 RESOLUTION OF DISPUTES

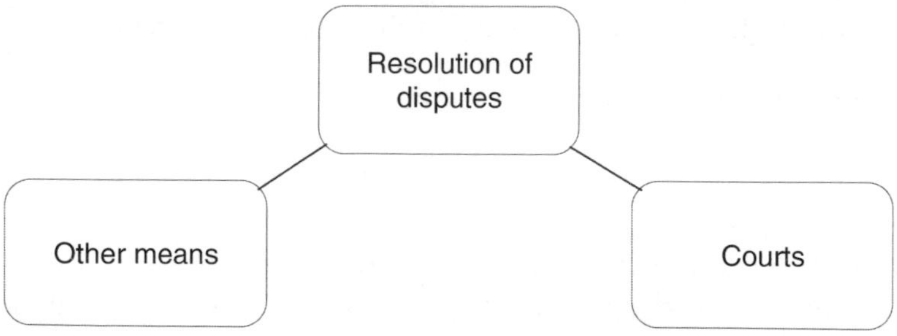

Most people think that legal disputes are resolved purely by going to court. It is true that there is a well-established hierarchy of courts, the precise structure of which depends on whether the matter is dealt with under civil or criminal procedures, but other means of resolving disputes are becoming increasingly popular. The use of tribunals and arbitration is often seen as quicker, cheaper and more focused than the traditional routes through the Courts, although recent reforms to the conduct of civil proceedings have helped to streamline the procedure.

NOTES

4 THE STRUCTURE OF THE COURTS

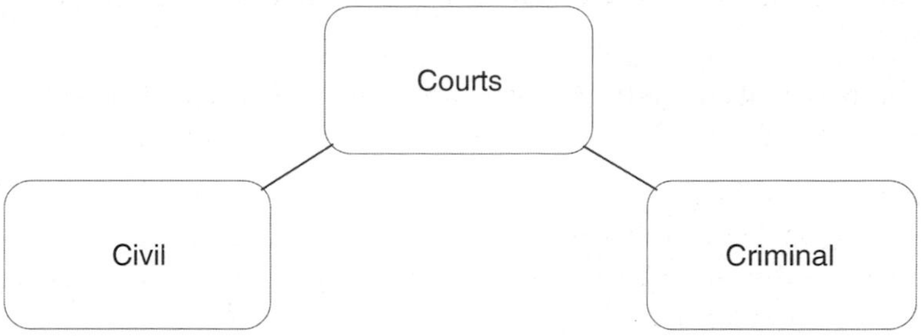

The diagrams below set out the basic structure of the courts within the civil and the criminal hierarchy. They are then discussed in further detail below.

4.1 The civil courts

The diagram below sets out the English civil court structure.

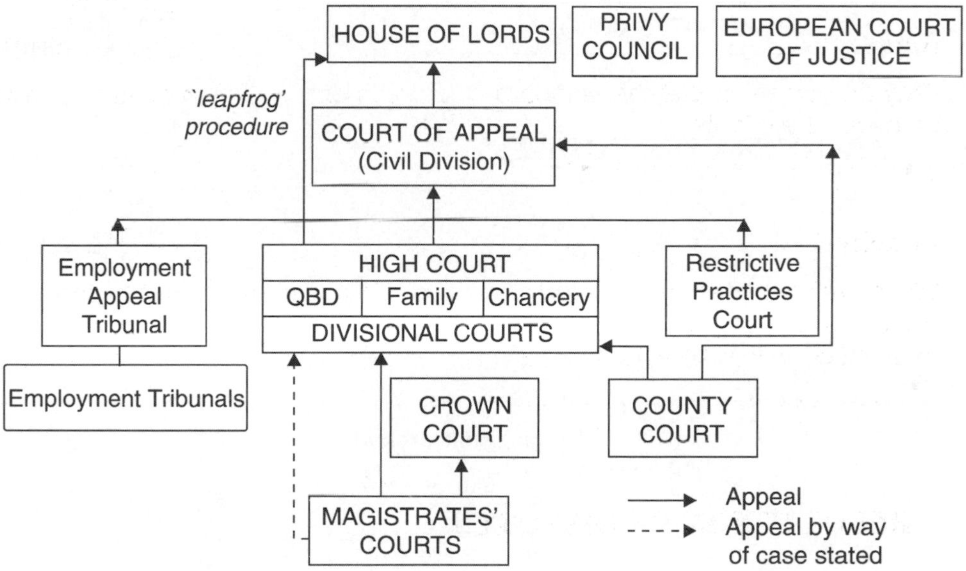

4.2 The criminal court structure

The diagram below sets out the English criminal court structure.

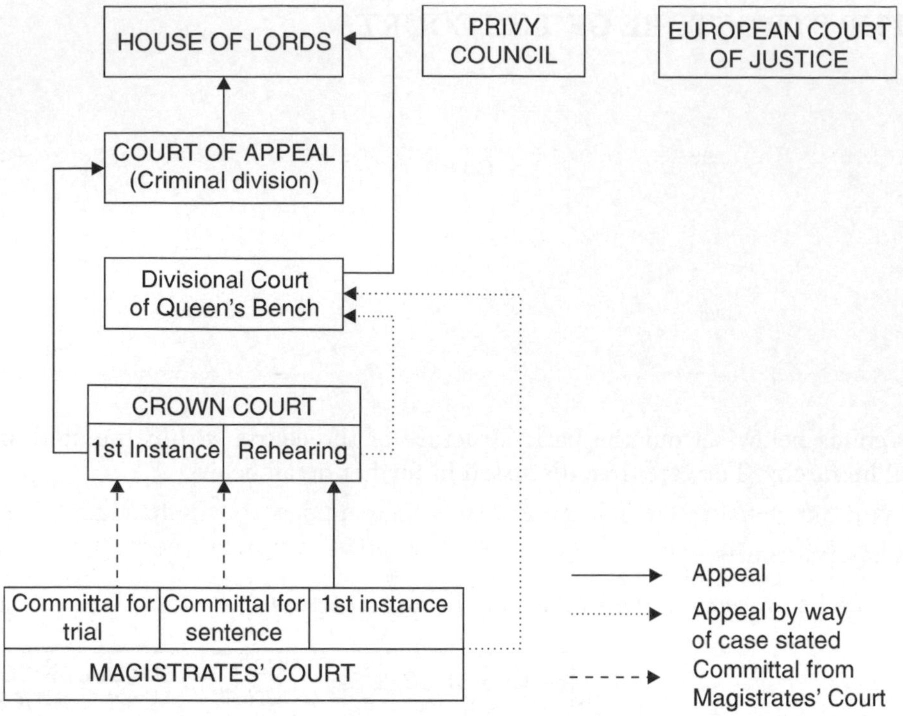

5 MAGISTRATES' COURTS

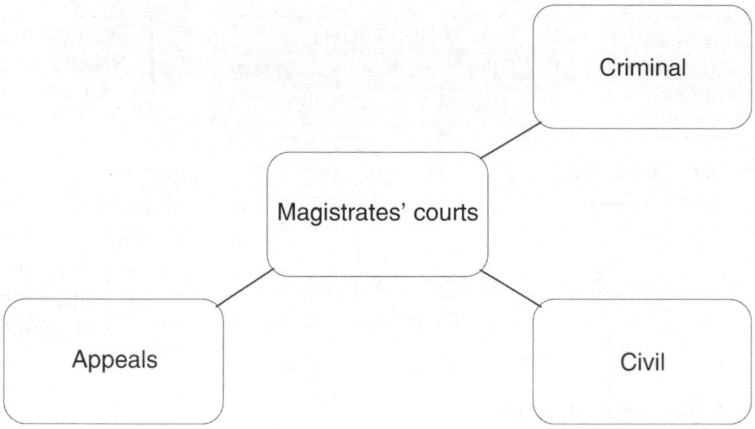

Magistrates' courts are the inferior criminal courts. In addition they exercise certain family law, administrative law and minor civil functions.

5.1 Criminal jurisdiction

Magistrates' courts deal with criminal cases as follows.

(a) They try summarily (without a jury) all minor offences.

(b) They conduct **committal proceedings**, which are preliminary investigations of the prosecution case, when the offence is triable only on **indictment** (by a Crown Court).

Definitions

Summary offences are minor crimes, only triable summarily in magistrates' courts.

Indictable offences are more serious offences that can only be heard in a Crown Court. Some offences are '**triable either way**'. This means that the defendant can choose whether to be tried summarily by the magistrates, or by a jury in the Crown Court.

Penalties

The maximum penalties which **magistrates** may impose on a defendant convicted summarily of a criminal offence are **six months' imprisonment** or a **fine (or compensation to victim) of up to £5,000**. However, they can commit a person convicted of a summary offence to Crown Court for sentencing, so that a larger penalty may be imposed.

5.2 Civil jurisdiction

Magistrates' civil jurisdiction includes family proceedings (financial provision for parties to a marriage and children, the custody or supervision of children and guardianship, and adoption orders), various types of licensing and enforcement of local authority charges and rates.

5.3 Appeals

Criminal cases

A defendant convicted on a criminal charge in a magistrates' court has a general right to a rehearing by a Crown Court.

A '**case stated' appeal** is based on the idea that magistrates or the Crown Court have wrongly interpreted the law. If not, then the case may be sent back to the lower court with instructions as to how it should be decided.

Civil cases

On family matters, appeals are to a divisional court of the Family Division of the High Court.

5.4 Staffing

Lay magistrates are not legally qualified and they sit part-time. They are appointed by the Lord Chancellor and are assisted by a legally qualified clerk, who must be a solicitor or barrister of at least five years' standing. **Stipendiary magistrates** must be solicitors or barristers of at least seven years' standing. Lay magistrates sit two or three to a court, while stipendiary magistrates sit alone.

Activity 3 **(10 minutes)**

Agatha is being prosecuted for an offence that is triable either way. She elects to be tried summarily in the magistrates' court, as she thinks that this will ensure that she cannot be sentenced to more than six months imprisonment or fined more than £5,000. Is she right?

Give reasons for your answer. Look at the table at paragraph 4.2 if you need help.

6 THE COUNTY COURT

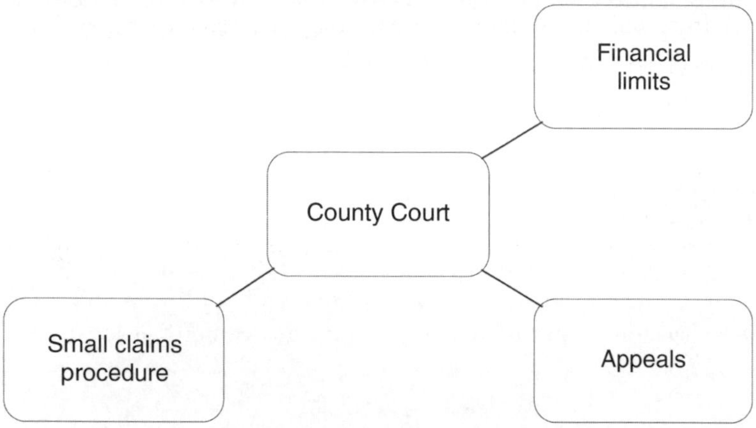

6.1 Jurisdiction

County courts have **civil jurisdiction** only but deal with almost every kind of civil case. The practical importance of the county courts is that they deal with **the majority of the country's civil litigation**.

The county court is involved in:

(a) **Contract and tort** claims

(b) **Equitable matters** concerning trusts, mortgages and partnership dissolution up to £30,000, unless the parties waive the limit

(c) Disputes concerning land where the capital value of the land is less than £30,000

(d) **Undefended matrimonial cases**

(e) **Probate matters** where the estate of the deceased is estimated to be less than £30,000

(f) **Miscellaneous matters** conferred by various statutes, for example the Consumer Credit Act 1974 (no limit on jurisdiction)

(g) Some **bankruptcy**, company winding-up and admiralty cases

(h) 'Small claims' of up to £5,000

Actions in contract and tort worth **less than £25,000** must normally be tried in a **county** court and those worth **£50,000 or more** must normally be tried in the **High Court**, with those in between going either way, depending on the case itself and the importance of the law attached to it.

6.2 The small claims procedure

To assist litigants who decide to conduct their case in person the county court registrar may, if the amount involved **does not exceed £5,000** or if the parties agree, refer a case to an arbitrator to hear and decide informally under the small claims procedure.

(a) The arbitrator is usually the district judge himself but may be another person chosen by the parties. The arbitrator's award is recorded as a county court judgement.

(b) This is a cheaper and quicker way of settling small claims in an informal atmosphere.

(c) Personal injury claims, claims for possession of land, housing disrepair claims and harassment claims may be dealt with by the small claims procedure only if they fall below £1,000.

FOR DISCUSSION

In 1996 a survey by the National Audit Office found that although 94 per cent of claimants in the Small Claims Court obtained judgement in their favour, only 54% recovered all or part of their claim and 36% recovered nothing.

6.3 Appeals

From the county court there is a right of appeal direct to the Civil Division of the Court of Appeal. In bankruptcy cases an appeal goes to the Chancery Division of the High Court.

6.4 Staffing

A **circuit judge** presides, being a barrister of at least ten years' standing. A **recorder** is a solicitor or barrister of at least ten years' standing and may be appointed as a circuit judge after three years' experience as a recorder. A **district judge**, who must be a solicitor or barrister of at least seven years' standing, assists the circuit judge.

Activity 4 **(10 minutes)**

Penny sues Desmond for breach of contract, asking for and obtaining damages of £10,000. In which court would this case be heard? Suppose the sum involved was £3,000. Would that make any difference to your answer?

NOTES

7 THE CROWN COURT

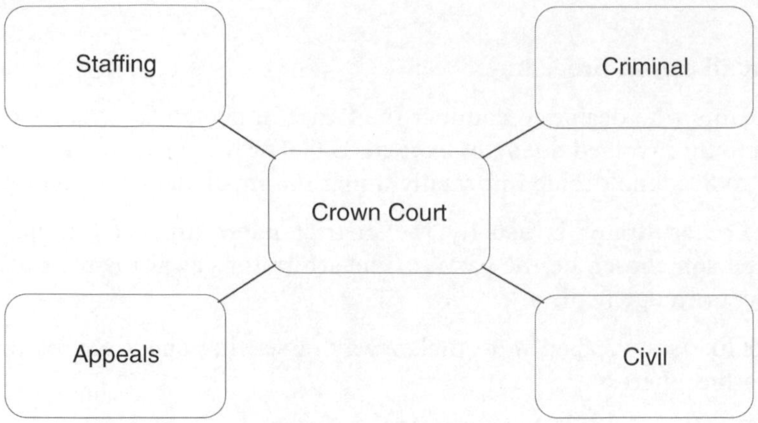

The Crown Courtis theoretically a single court forming part of the **Supreme Court**, but in fact it comprises **local courts** in large towns and also the **Central Criminal Court** (the Old Bailey) in London.

7.1 Criminal jurisdiction

It tries all indictable offences with a jury and hears appeals and deals with committals for sentencing from magistrates' courts.

There are four classes of offence triable in the Crown Court.

(a) **Class 1 offences** are the **most serious offences** such as murder and treason. A High Court judge must preside.

(b) **Class 2 offences** include **serious** offences such as rape and manslaughter. Cases are usually presided over by a High Court judge.

(c) **Class 3 offences** are **less serious** offences which must be tried on indictment. Examples are robbery and grievous bodily harm. A High Court judge, circuit judge or recorder may preside.

(d) **Class 4 offences** are those offences which may be tried on **indictment or summarily** (triable either way) such as burglary and reckless driving. Usually a circuit judge or recorder presides, though a High Court judge may do so.

7.2 Civil jurisdiction

The Crown Court deals with a few types of civil cases, being appeals from the magistrates' court on matters of betting, gaming and licensing.

7.3 Appeals

From the Crown Court there is a right of appeal on criminal matters to the Criminal Division of the Court of Appeal. An appeal by way of 'case stated' on a point of law may also be made to a Divisional Court of the Queen's Bench Division.

7.4 Staffing

A High Court Judge, a circuit judge or a recorder may sit in the Crown Court, depending on the nature of the offence being tried. Sometimes lay magistrates also sit. All indictable offences will be heard by a judge with a jury of between 10 and 12 persons.

NOTES

8 THE HIGH COURT

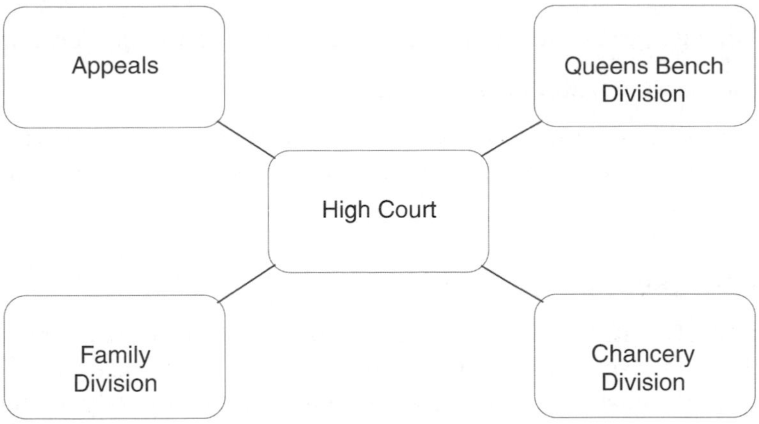

The **High Court** is organised into three divisions.

- Queen's Bench
- Chancery Division
- Family Division

8.1 Queen's Bench Division

(a) *Civil jurisdiction*

The Queen's Bench Division (QBD) deals mainly with common law matters such as actions based on contract or tort. It also has a supervisory role over other courts. It is the largest of the three divisions, having 54 judges. It includes a separate **Admiralty Court** to deal with shipping matters, and a **Commercial Court** which specialises in commercial cases.

(b) *Supervisory role*

It may issue a writ of **habeas corpus**, which is an order for the release of a person wrongfully detained, and also prerogative orders against inferior courts, tribunals and other bodies such as local authorities. There are three types of **prerogative order.**

(i) **Mandamus** requires the court or other body to carry out a public duty.

(ii) **Prohibition** prevents a court or tribunal from exceeding its jurisdiction (before it has done so).

(iii) **Certiorari** orders a court or tribunal which has taken action to submit the record of its proceedings to the High Court for review.

(c) *Criminal (appellate) jurisdiction*

The division hears appeals by way of case stated from the magistrates' courts and the Crown Courts.

8.2 Chancery Division

This division deals with traditional equity matters.

- Trusts and mortgages

BPP PUBLISHING

- Revenue matters
- Bankruptcy (though outside London this is a county court subject)
- Disputed wills and administration of estates of deceased persons
- Partnership and company matters

There is a separate **Companies Court** within the division which deals with liquidations and other company proceedings, and a Patents Court established under the Patents Act 1977.

8.3 Family Division

This division deals with matrimonial cases, family property cases, and proceedings relating to children (wardship, guardianship, adoption, legitimacy etc. The division hears appeals from magistrates' courts and the county court on family matters.

8.4 Appeals

Appeals are made from the High Court as follows.

(a) *Civil cases*

Appeals may be made to the **Court of Appeal (Civil Division)** or to the **House of Lords**, under what is known as the (rarely used) **'leapfrog'** procedure. For the leapfrog procedure to be followed, all parties must give their consent to it, and the case must involve a point of law of general public importance.

(b) *Criminal cases*

Appeals are made direct to the House of Lords where the case has reached the High Court on appeal from a magistrates' court or from the Crown Court.

8.5 Staffing

The High Court is staffed by no more than 98 puisne judges, who must be barristers of at least ten years' standing. QBD is presided over by the Lord Chief Justice. Chancery has 13 judges and is presided over by the Lord Chancellor. Family Division has 16 judges and its President presides.

9 THE COURT OF APPEAL

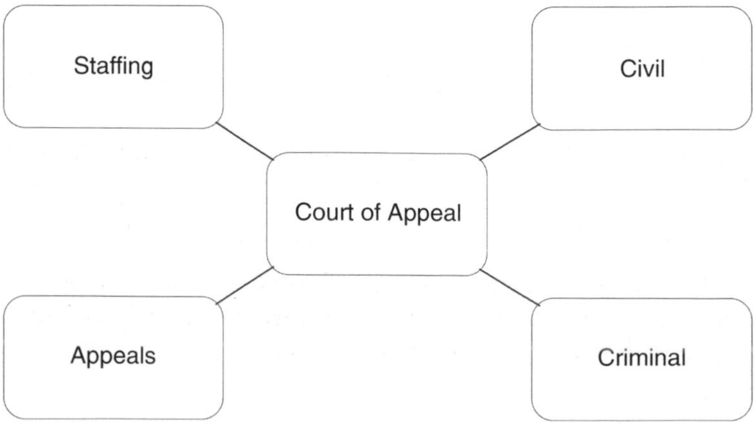

NOTES

9.1 Civil Division

The Civil Division of the Court of Appeal can hear appeals from the High Court, county courts, and from certain other courts and special tribunals. It reviews the record of the evidence in the lower court and the legal arguments put before it. It may uphold or reverse the earlier decision or order a new trial.

9.2 Criminal Division

The Criminal Division of the Court of Appeal hears appeals from the Crown Court. It may also be invited to review a criminal case by the Home Secretary or to consider a point of law at the request of the Attorney General.

9.3 Appeals

Appeals lie to the House of Lords, with the leave of the House of Lords or the Court of Appeal, on a point of law.

9.4 Staffing

There are 29 **Lord Justices of Appeal**, promoted from the High Court. Three judges normally sit together. In the Criminal Division, the **Lord Chief Justice** presides. In the Civil Division the **Master of the Rolls** presides.

> **Activity 5** **(15 minutes)**
>
> Find out the names of the current Lord Chief Justice and the Master of the Rolls.

10 THE HOUSE OF LORDS

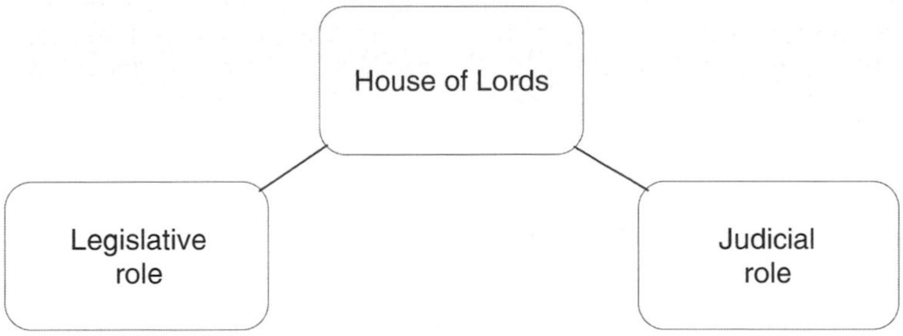

The House of Lords has two separate roles, and it is important that these are not confused.

(a) It has a **legislative role**, as one of the two Houses of Parliament.

(b) It has a **judicial role**, as the highest appeal court of the legal system, hearing appeals from both the civil and criminal divisions of the Court of Appeal.

Judges are usually promoted from the Court of Appeal to be members of the House of Lords. They are known as **Lords of Appeal in Ordinary**, or **Law Lords**. Five judges normally sit together, though there may only be three.

Activity 6 **(10 minutes)**

List the court (or courts) to which an appeal may be made from each of the following:

(a) The county court
(b) The High Court (civil cases)

(Refer to the court structure diagram in section 4.1)

11 THE WOOLF REFORMS

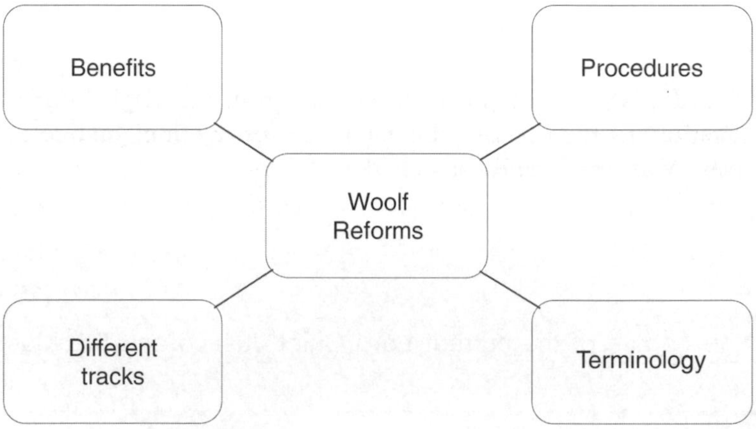

Major changes to the system of civil justice in England and Wales took effect from 26 April 1999, bringing in new **procedure rules** for the High Court and County Courts. The reform of civil justice was first proposed by Lord Woolf in his 1996 report *Access to Justice*.

Under the reforms, the Courts have the power to control every aspect of the litigation process, shifting responsibility away from the litigants and their advisers. This affects a wide range of commercial disputes.

The new procedures are designed to lead to **quicker and less confrontational** settlement of disputes at the beginning of a case, to encourage parties to consider **alternative methods** of dispute resolution, and to avoid the excessive expense of litigation, which Lord Bingham has called “a cancer eating at the heart of the administration of justice”.

FOR DISCUSSION

A recent survey of 217 cases by a firm of solicitors acting for claimants in personal injury cases found average costs to be £836, whilst damages recovered were on average only £694.

11.1 Examples of some of the changes

(a) The court allocates cases to 'tracks' – the **small claims track**, the **fast track** or the **multi-track**.

(b) The small claims track deals with claims of not more than £5,000.

(c) The fast track limit is £15,000. This is a strictly limited procedure, designed to take cases to trial within a short but reasonable timescale. Trials should take only half a day. The fast track is likely to include personal injury, building, consumer and neighbour dispute cases.

(d) Larger claims are allocated to the multi-track. This spans both High Court and county court cases, and covers most commercial claims. There is an initial 'case management conference' to encourage parties to settle the dispute or to consider alternative dispute resolution (such as mediation or arbitration).

(e) The trial judge in a multi-track trial sets a budget and a final timetable for the trial.

11.2 Benefits of the reforms

The court's management of a case is achieved by the setting up of **codes of practice** with which the parties must comply, and which will ensure effective exchange of information **before the proceedings begin**.

Litigants will have to be much better prepared before going to court. One consequence of this is that costs of litigation will be largely known in advance. For example, the court's permission will now be needed to call expert witnesses, and the court can compel the parties to use a single joint witness. The names of court documents and applications are being changed to make them more user friendly. A new procedure will allow for quick disposal of inadequate cases.

The Court of Appeal has recently upheld a trial judge's decision to debar an expert witness from giving evidence for a defendant, because the witness failed to follow the procedures required by the new rules *(Stevens v Gullis 1999)*. The **overriding duty of an expert witness is to the court**, rather than the party who instructed him. Those holding themselves out as expert witnesses should be prepared to arrange their affairs so that they can meet the court's timetable (*Matthews v Tarmac Bricks and Tiles Ltd 1999*).

There will be a new senior judge with overall responsibility for civil justice, to be known as the **Head of Civil Justice**. His appointment is designed to raise the status of civil justice, which has long been in the shadow of the criminal justice system.

FOR DISCUSSION

The detail presented here on the Woolf reforms is mainly included for your background information, so that you are aware of the principles involved. You should note that the changes are mainly procedural (ie how cases are to be conducted). The main point to be aware of is that the reforms hope to encourage speedy dispute resolution without recourse to the courts, by forcing litigants to be much better prepared in advance and to really think about what they are getting themselves into.

The phrase "I'll see you in court" may now be less frequently heard.

12 OTHER MEANS OF RESOLVING DISPUTES

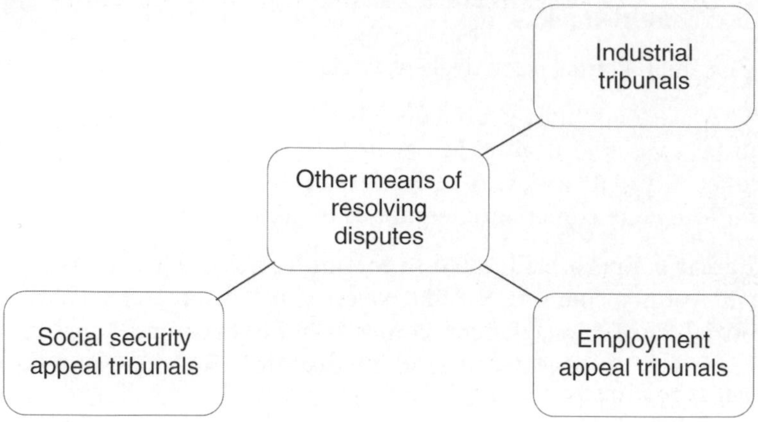

There is a number of other courts and tribunals which feature prominently in the English legal system, either because they have a relatively important status (for example, the Employment Appeal Tribunal is of equal status with the High Court) or because they have a heavy caseload.

12.1 Industrial tribunals

Industrial tribunals were established by the Industrial Training Act 1964. They have a wide jurisdiction over most disputes between **employee and employer**. They are now called **employment tribunals**. Each tribunal is staffed by a legally qualified **chairman** and two other persons, one representing the employer and one representing the employee. Here are some examples of typical cases.

- Disputes about redundancy pay
- Complaints of unfair dismissal
- Questions as to terms of contracts of employment
- Equal pay claims
- Appeals against health and safety notices
- Complaints about sex and race discrimination

There is a right of appeal to the **Employment Appeal Tribunal**.

12.2 Employment Appeal Tribunal

This is a court of equal status with the High Court. It was established by the Employment Protection Act 1975. It hears appeals from tribunals mainly on employment matters.

A **High Court judge** and two **lay assessors** from a panel appointed on the Lord Chancellor's recommendation sit. From the EAT there is a right of appeal to the Court of Appeal.

12.3 Social security appeal tribunals

A variety of cash benefits are available under the Social Security Act 1975 (including unemployment benefit, invalidity and sickness benefit and retirement pensions) and the Social Security Act 1986 (including income support, family credit and housing benefit). Questions may arise in the administration of these benefits.

NOTES

The Social Security appeal tribunals hear appeals arising from the adjudication process. Either party may appeal from the decision of the tribunal to the Social Security Commissioners. On a point of law there is a further right of appeal to the High Court.

12.4 Lands Tribunal

This tribunal deals with disputes over the value of property, for example for compulsory purchase. It is usually composed of three members, being experienced lawyers and qualified valuation experts.

12.5 The Restrictive Practices Court

This is equal in status with the High Court. Appeals from it go to the Court of Appeal. It investigates the merits of agreements registered under the Competition Act 1998. In these functions it is required to have regard to EC law.

Usually a **High Court judge** and two **lay assessors** from a panel appointed on the Lord Chancellor's recommendation sit.

12.6 Supervision of tribunals

The working of the system of tribunals is supervised by a **Council on Tribunals**. In many instances there is a statutory right to appeal from a tribunal to a higher court on points of law. The High Court may also make prerogative orders to prevent or remedy errors and injustices.

13 ARBITRATION

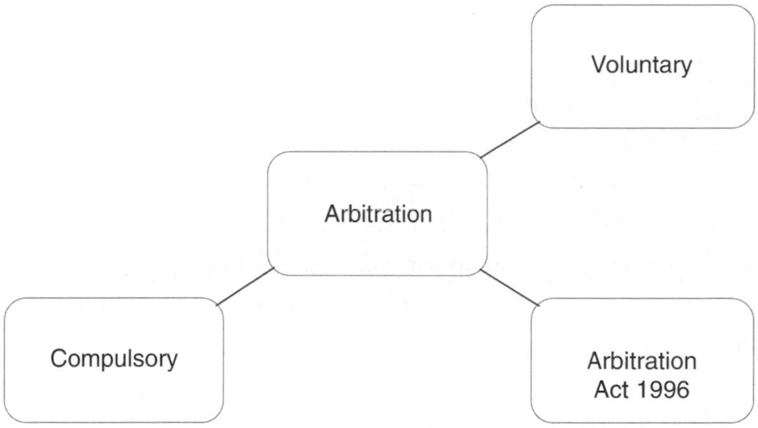

This is increasingly becoming a popular alternative to litigation in the courts, and it is now quite common for contracts, especially large commercial contracts, to contain provision for arbitration in the event of a dispute arising between the parties to the contract. This can be very helpful, for example in the case of a complex shipping contract (an extremely complicated area of commercial law) as referring the dispute to arbitration means that it will be handled by an independent expert on shipping who fully understands the legal ramifications. It also provides advantages such as privacy for the parties involved.

Proceedings in arbitration are less adversarial in nature than court hearings (where one party is 'opposed' to the other) so it is more likely that a compromise will be found, meaning that the concept of 'winners and losers' is less pronounced.

13.1 Voluntary agreements

It is common practice to include in commercial contracts a clause providing that any dispute is to be settled by arbitration under the relevant legislation. There is therefore a growing tendency for business people to settle disagreements using alternative methods of dispute resolution, in particular forms of **arbitration.**

An **arbitrator is usually an expert** in the field of dispute. The parties may name their arbitrators or provide that some other person, say the President of the Law Society, shall appoint him. The High Court has power to appoint an arbitrator.

Unless otherwise agreed, a hearing before an arbitrator follows the same essential procedure as in a court of law. However, following the Arbitration Act 1996, the arbitrators and parties can settle on the **form** of the arbitration.

13.2 The Arbitration Act 1996

The Arbitration Act 1996 aimed to introduce **greater speed and flexibility** into the arbitration process, in particular by conferring upon the parties the right to make their own agreement on virtually all aspects of the arbitration (s 1). It contains provisions for the **appointment and removal** of arbitrators, and the power to appoint **experts** (s 37), advisers and assessors. It turned the courts' role into a **supervisory** rather than an interventionist one. Under this Act, the parties may choose to dispense with formal hearings and strict rules of evidence and procedure (s 46).

Under the 1996 Act, an arbitration agreement is a **separate agreement** which can outlive the original contract that gave rise to the arbitration proceedings.

The main advantage of the arbitration procedure is **privacy**, since the public and the press have no right to attend a hearing before an arbitrator.

13.3 Compulsory arbitration

In addition to voluntary arbitration as described above, compulsory arbitration may be enforced in the following circumstances.

(a) Certain statutes (Acts of Parliament) provide for arbitration on disputes arising out of the provision of the statute.

(b) The High Court may order that a case of a technical nature shall be tried (or investigated with report back to the court) by an Official Referee or other arbitrator.

(c) A county court may order that a small claim (not exceeding £5,000) shall be referred to arbitration, under the small claims court procedure.

Chapter roundup

- Law is a fundamental part of a civilised society and governs the relationships between individuals among themselves and between individuals and the state.
- People are prosecuted under the criminal law for offences committed against the state, and a penalty is imposed.
- Individuals (or companies) sue each other under the civil law to receive compensation for some kind of loss or damage suffered. The purpose is not punishment but the righting of a wrong.
- There is a hierarchy of civil and criminal courts. In broad terms those lower down in the hierarchy have a right to appeal to those above. The operation of the civil courts depends largely on the financial value of the case under consideration.
- Sweeping reforms were introduced to the civil court procedure in 1999 under the recommendations of the Woolf Report. The purpose is to enable justice to be dispensed more quickly, more cheaply and more efficiently.
- Going to court is not the only means of resolving a dispute. Tribunals deal with specific cases involving employment and other specialised areas, and arbitration provides a highly effective alternative to litigation.

Quick quiz

1 Give two examples each of public and private law.

2 What degree of proof is required in a civil case?

3 In which court will a criminal case start to go through the legal process?

4 What is the difference between a summary offence and an indictable offence?

5 What matters are dealt with by the Small Claims Court?

6 Which court hears appeals arising from decisions of the Court of Appeal?

7 What are the main purposes of the Woolf reforms?

8 What are the advantages of arbitration over court action?

Answers to quick quiz

1 Public law: criminal law
constitutional law
Private law: contract law
law of tort (see para 1.1)

2 Proof on the balance of probability. (para 2.2)

3 Magistrate's court. (para 5.1)

4 Summary offences: minor crimes, only triable by magistrates.

Indictable offences: serious offences which must be tried in the Crown Court. (para 5.1)

5 Small contract and other claims worth less than £5,000. (para 6.2)

6 The House of Lords. (para 10)

7 Better preparation
Advanced knowledge of costs
Speedier justice (para 11.2)

8 Reference to detail
Use of experts
Privacy
Compromise (para 13)

Answers to activities

1 Nothing can be proved beyond **all** doubt

2 Martin could be prosecuted under the criminal law for speeding, and also sued by Andrew under the civil law for damages for the damage caused to Andrew's house.

3 This will not ensure a lower sentence, as Agatha could be convicted in the magistrates' court but then committed to the Crown Court for sentencing.

4 The case for £10,000 would probably be heard in the County Court. If the amount involved was £3,000 it would probably be dealt with under the small claims procedure.

5 At the time of writing, the Lord Chief Justice is Lord Woolf and the Master of the Rolls is Lord Phillips of Worth Matravers.

6 (a) The Court of Appeal (Civil Division) or the High Court
(b) The Court of Appeal (Civil Division) or the House of Lords

Assignment

Since the content of this chapter is introductory background reading, and you will not be tested in detail on the contents in any assignment, we do not include a specific assignment for this chapter.

However, remember that you will encounter many of the terms and concepts introduced here in your later studies, and you may be expected to apply them in assignments at that stage.

Chapter 2 :
SOURCES OF LAW

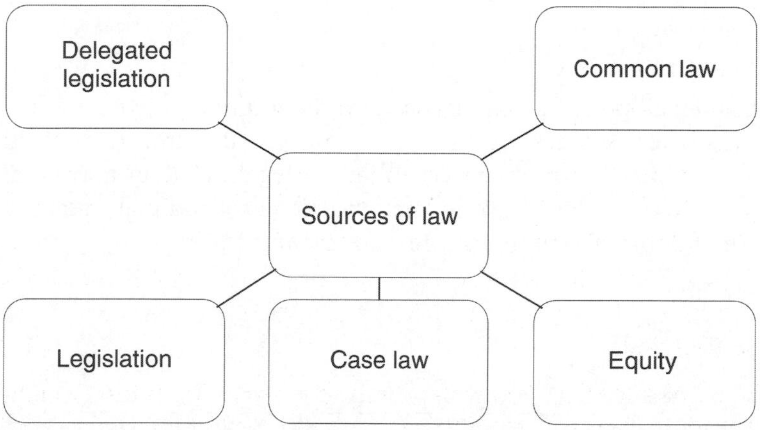

Introduction

There are two main sources of law with which you need to be familiar if you are fully to understand the detailed areas of the law which are covered in the forthcoming chapters. The first is case law, which is the law that is created as a result of the decisions of the courts. The second is statute, which is the law created by Acts of Parliament.

Throughout this textbook, you will find references to cases (shown for example as *Donoghue v Stevenson*) to illustrate the legal principles and rules which you will learn, and also to statute (shown for example as *Companies Act 1985 S368*). Therefore it is helpful for you to understand these two sources of law.

Case law and statute are often referred to as the *legal* sources of law. There are also two important *historical* sources of law, common law and equity, from which much of case law springs, and we shall consider these first.

Your objectives

In this chapter you will learn about the following.

(a) The development of the common law

(b) The development of equity

(c) The doctrine of judicial precedent and when it is not applied

(d) The importance of legislation

(e) How legislation is made

(f) The importance of delegated legislation

As with the previous chapter, you should regard this as background reading. You will not be tested on this in your assignments.

1 COMMON LAW

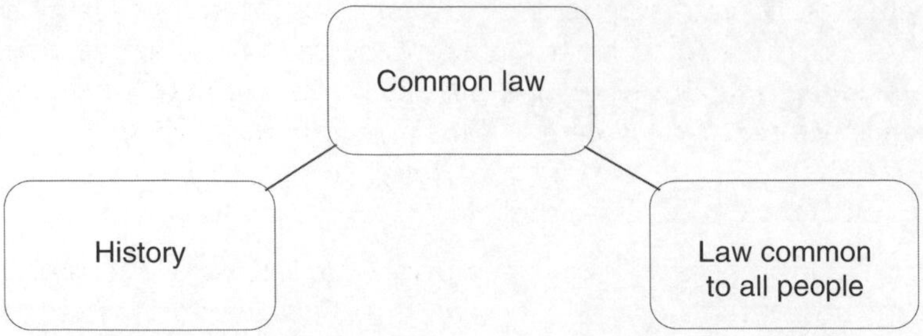

English law has developed in an unbroken progression over a period of some 900 years. English law's historical sources are those procedures, rules and ways of thinking which have given rise to today's current sources of law. A legal problem may be decided on the rules of the legal sources, but these in turn (particularly judicial precedent) have been derived from the historical sources of common law and equity.

1.1 Common law

Definition

> Common Law: the body of legal rules developed by the common law courts and now embodied in legal decisions.

At the time of the Norman Conquest in 1066 there was no system of law common to the whole country. Rules of local custom were applied by local manorial courts. To improve the system, the King sent royal commissioners on tour (circuit) to different parts of the realm to deal with crimes and civil disputes. These commissioners, who often heard their cases with the assistance of a local jury, at first applied the local customary law of the neighbourhood. On their return from circuit the commissioners sat in the royal courts at Westminster to try cases there. In time the commissioners developed rules of law, selected from the differing local customs which they had encountered, as a common law (ius commune) which they applied uniformly in all trials (before the King's courts) throughout the kingdom.

Definitions

> Claimant: the person who complains or brings an action asking the court for relief (used to be called the plaintiff).
>
> Defendant: the person against whom a civil action is brought or who is prosecuted for a criminal offence.
>
> Statement of claim: a written command issued under the King's authority (used to be called a writ). It is now the document which sets the ball rolling in a civil case.

To commence an action before any of these courts, the claimant obtained from the main royal office, the Chancery, an order (a statement of claim) issued under the King's authority and addressed to the Sheriff of the county in which the defendant resided, by which the Sheriff was required to ensure that the defendant appeared for the trial. The statement of claim specified the ground of complaint and gave a brief summary of the facts on which the claimant required judgement. Statements of claim could only be issued in one of the established forms, which were grounds of action. If there were no appropriate statement of claim it was not possible to have one of a new type in order to bring a grievance before the royal courts. This principle was slightly relaxed in 1285 but the common law system, based on the availability of standard statements of claim, was still very rigid and hence an inadequate means of providing justice.

The procedure of common law courts was also unsatisfactory. A claimant might lose his case owing to a minor technicality of wording or be frustrated by specious defences, deliberate delay or corruption, or find himself unable to enforce a judgement given in his favour because there was no suitable common law remedy.

2 EQUITY

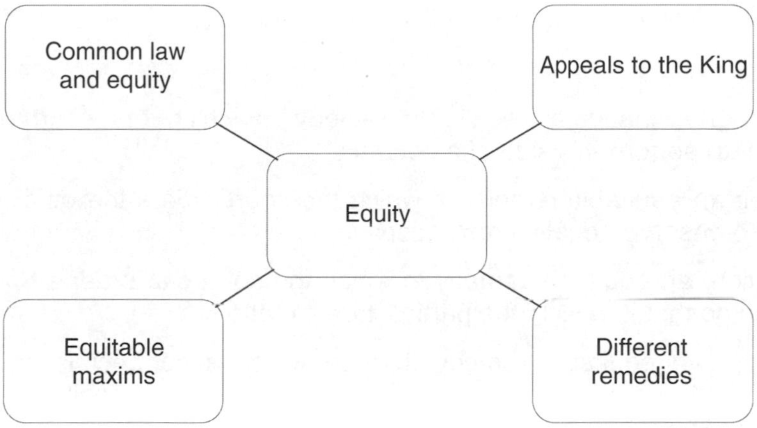

Definition

> Equity: a source of English law consisting of those rules which emerged from the Court of Chancery.

2.1 Development of equity

Citizens who could not obtain redress for grievances in the common law courts petitioned the King to obtain relief by direct royal intervention. These petitions came before the King in Council and by custom were referred to the principal civil minister, the Chancellor. In dealing with each petition his concern was to establish the truth of the matter and then to impose a just solution without undue regard for technicalities or procedural points.

Because the principles on which the Chancellor decided points were based on fair dealing between two individuals as equals, these principles became known as equity. The system of equity, developed and administered by the Court of Chancery, was not an alternative to the common law, but a method of adding to and improving on the common law. This interaction of common law and equity produced three major changes.

(a) New rights. Equity recognised and protected rights for which the common law gave no safeguards. If, for example, Sam transferred property to the legal ownership of Tom to pay the income of the property to Ben (in modern law Tom is a trustee for Ben), the common law simply recognised that Tom was the owner of the property and ignored Tom's obligations to Ben. Equity recognised that Tom was the owner of the property at common law but insisted, as a matter of justice and good conscience, that Tom must comply with the terms of the trust imposed by Sam (the settlor) and pay the income to Ben (the beneficiary).

(b) Better procedure. Equity could be more effective than common law in bringing a disputed matter to a decision.

(c) Better remedies. The standard common law remedy for the successful claimant was the award of monetary compensation, damages, for his loss. Equity was able to order the defendant to do what he had agreed to do (specific performance), to abstain from wrongdoing (injunction), to alter a document so that it reflected the parties' true intentions (rectification) or to restore the pre-contract status quo (rescission).

Definitions

Specific performance: an equitable remedy in which the court orders the defendant to perform his side of a contract.

Injunction: an equitable remedy in which the court orders the other party to a contract to observe negative restrictions.

Rectification: an equitable remedy in which the court can order a document to be altered so that it reflects the parties' true intentions.

Rescission: an equitable remedy through which a contract is cancelled or rejected and the parties are restored to their pre-contract condition, as if it had never been entered into.

2.2 Equitable maxims

The development of equity was based on a number of equitable maxims (or principles).

These are still applied today if an equitable remedy is sought. The following are examples.

(a) *He who comes to equity must come with clean hands*. To be fairly treated, the claimant must have acted fairly himself. For example, in the case *D and C Builders v Rees 1966* the defendant could not plead a defence of equitable estoppel because she had tried to take advantage of the claimant's financial difficulties.

(b) *Equality is equity*. The law attempts to play fair and redress the balance; hence what is available to one person must be available to another. As an example, equity does not allow the remedy of specific performance to be granted against a minor (ie a person under the age of 18), and it does not allow a minor to benefit from the remedy either.

(c) *Equity looks at the intent, not the form*. However a person may try to pretend that he is doing something in the correct form, equity will look at what he is actually trying to achieve. For example, if an agreed damages clause in a contract is not a genuine estimate of likely loss, equity will treat the clause as a penalty clause, and it is less likely to be awarded to the injured party.

2.3 The relationship between common law and equity

Until the 1870's, common law and equity as sources of law had to be administered in separate courts. However, the Judicature Acts of the 1870's enabled them to be administered in the same court, and a judge is able to apply whichever principles he thinks fit.

In the case of a conflict between the two, however, equity will prevail. It is sometimes described as 'a gloss on the common law' in that where a common law decision would produce an unfair, or inequitable, result, equity can be applied to avoid that outcome.

3 CASE LAW

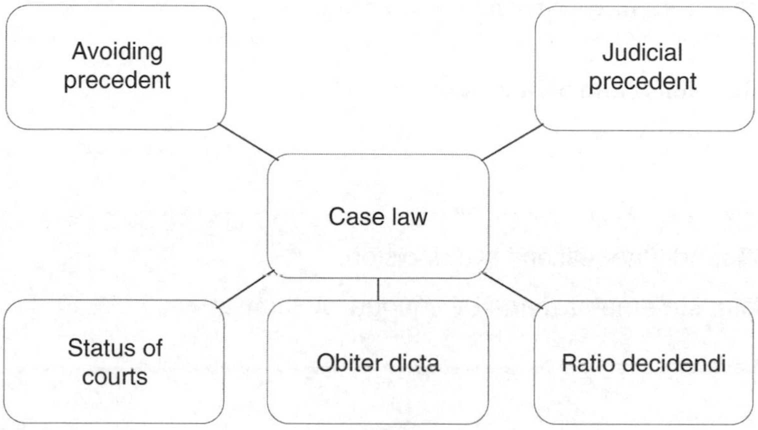

As noted above, the development of common law and equity has led to one of the main legal sources of law, case law, and has an influence on much of the other main source, legislation.

3.1 Judicial precedent

Both common law and equity are the product of decisions in the courts. They are judge-made law but based on a principle of consistency. Once a matter of principle has been decided (by one of the higher courts) it becomes a precedent. In any later case to which that principle is relevant the same principle should (subject to certain exceptions) be applied. This doctrine of consistency, following precedent, is expressed in the maxim stare decisis, 'to stand by a decision'.

Judges inevitably create law. Sometimes an Act of Parliament will deliberately vest a wide discretion in the judiciary. In other cases there may be no statutory provision and no existing precedent relevant to the particular dispute. Even so, the doctrine of judicial precedent is based on the view that it is not the function of a judge to make law, but to decide cases in accordance with existing rules.

It is generally accepted that consistency is an important feature of a good decision-making process. Similar cases should be treated in the same way. However, the passage of time, or changing circumstances, may cause a case to offer a solution which no longer appears just. One of the main functions of the higher courts is to give an authoritative decision on disputed questions of law. A court's decision is expected to be consistent (or at least not unjustifiably inconsistent) with previous decisions and to provide an opinion which the parties, and others, can use to direct their future relationships. This is the basis of the system of judicial precedent.

Judicial precedent depends on the following.

(a) There must be adequate and reliable reports of earlier decisions.

(b) There must be rules for extracting from an earlier decision on one set of facts the legal principle to be applied in reaching a decision on a different set of facts.

  (i) The principle must be a proposition of law.

  (ii) It must form part of the ratio decidendi of the case.

  (iii) The material facts of each case must be the same.

(c) Precedents must be classified into those which are binding and those which are merely persuasive. This depends primarily on the respective status of the preceding court and the later one.

3.2 Ratio decidendi and obiter dicta

Definitions

Ratio decidendi: the reason for a decision.

Obiter dicta: statements made by a judge 'by the way'.

A judgement will start with a description of the facts of the case and probably a review of earlier precedents and possible alternative theories. The judge will then make statements of law applicable to the legal problems raised by the material facts. Provided these statements are the basis for the decision, they are known as the ratio decidendi of the case. The ratio decidendi (reason for deciding) is the vital element which binds future judges.

If a judge's statements of legal principle do not form the basis of the decision, or if his statements are not based on the existing material facts but on hypothetical facts, they are known as obiter dicta (said by the way). A later court may respect such statements, but it is not bound to follow them. They are only of persuasive authority.

It is not always easy to identify the ratio decidendi. The same judgement may appear to contain contradictory views of the law in different passages. In decisions of appeal courts, where there are three or even five separate judgements, the members of the court may reach the same conclusion but give different reasons. The ratio may also be mingled with obiter statements. Many judges help by indicating in their speeches which comments are ratio and which are obiter.

Activity 1 **(10 minutes)**

A case hinges upon whether clementines are oranges. The judgement contains the remark 'clementines are oranges, just as peanuts are nuts'. How does this remark illustrate the distinction between ratio decidendi and obiter dicta?

3.3 Distinguishing the facts

Although there may arguably be a finite number of legal principles to consider when deciding a case, there are necessarily an infinite variety of facts which may be presented. Apart from identifying the ratio decidendi of an earlier case, it is also necessary to consider how far the facts of the previous and the latest case are similar. Facts are never identical. If the differences appear significant the court may 'distinguish' the earlier case on the facts and thereby avoid following it as a precedent.

3.4 The status of courts

A court's status has a significant effect on whether its decisions are binding, persuasive or disregarded.

(a) The Judicial Committee of the House of Lords stands at the apex of the judicial system. Its decisions are binding on all other English courts. The House of Lords generally regards itself as bound by its own earlier decisions but it reserves the right to depart from its own precedents in exceptional cases.

(b) The Court of Appeal's decisions are binding on all English courts except the House of Lords. It is bound by its own previous decisions and by those of the House of Lords.

(c) A single High Court judge is bound by decisions of higher courts but not by a decision of another High Court judge sitting alone (though he would treat it as strong persuasive authority). When two or more High Court judges sit together as a Divisional Court, their decisions are binding on any other Divisional Court (and on a single High Court judge sitting alone).

(d) Lower courts (the Crown Court, county courts and magistrates' courts) do not make precedents, and their decisions are not usually reported. They are bound by decisions of the higher courts.

(e) If, in a case before the House of Lords there is a dispute about a point of European Community (EC) law, it must be referred to the Court of Justice (of the EC) for a ruling. English courts are also required to take account of principles laid down by the Court of Justice in so far as these are relevant. The Court of Justice does not, however, create or follow precedents as such.

Apart from binding precedents as described above, reported decisions of any court (even if lower in status) may be treated as persuasive precedents: they may be (but need not be) followed in a later case.

Overruling a precedent

A court of higher status is not only free to disregard the decision of a court of lower status in an earlier case. It may also deprive it of authority and expressly overrule it. This does not affect the outcome as regards the defendant and claimant in the earlier decision; it only affects the precedents to be applied in later cases.

3.5 Avoidance of a binding precedent

Even if a precedent appears to be binding, a court may decline to follow it:

(a) by distinguishing the facts (as described above);

(b) by declaring the ratio decidendi obscure, particularly when a decision by three or five judges gives as many different ratios;

(c) by declaring that the previous decision was made per incuriam, that is without taking account of some essential point of law, such as an important precedent;

(d) by declaring the precedent to be in conflict with a fundamental principle of law;

(e) by declaring the precedent to be too wide;

(f) because the earlier decision has been subsequently overruled by another court or by statute.

Activity 2 **(10 minutes)**

A brings an action against B and the case is finally settled in favour of B in the Court of Appeal. Fifteen years later C brings an action against D on similar but slightly different facts and the case of A v B is the only relevant precedent. If C v D reaches the House of Lords, consider whether the case of A v B is binding.

3.6 The advantages and disadvantages of precedent

Many of the strengths of judicial precedent also indicate some of its weaknesses. Generally the arguments revolve around the principles of consistency, clarity, flexibility and detail.

Consistency. The whole point of following binding precedent is that the law is decided fairly and predictably. In theory therefore it should be possible to avoid litigation because the result is a foregone conclusion. However, judges are often forced to make illogical distinctions to avoid an unfair result which, combined with the wealth of reported cases, serves to complicate the law.

Clarity. Following only the reasoning in ratio statements should lead to statements of principle for general application. In practice, however, the same judgement may be found to contain propositions which appear inconsistent with each other or with the precedent which the court purports to follow.

Flexibility. The real strength of the system lies in its ability to change with changing circumstances since it arises directly out of the actions of society. The counter argument is that the doctrine limits judges' discretion and they may be unable to avoid deciding in line with a precedent which produces an unfair result. Often the deficiency may only be remedied by passing a statute to correct the law's failings.

Detail. Precedents state how the law applies to facts, and it should be flexible enough to allow for details to be different, so that the law is all-encompassing. However, judges often distinguish cases on facts to avoid following a precedent. The wealth of detail is also a drawback in that it produces a vast body of reports which must be taken into account; again, though, statute can help by codifying rules developed in case law.

NOTES

4 LEGISLATION

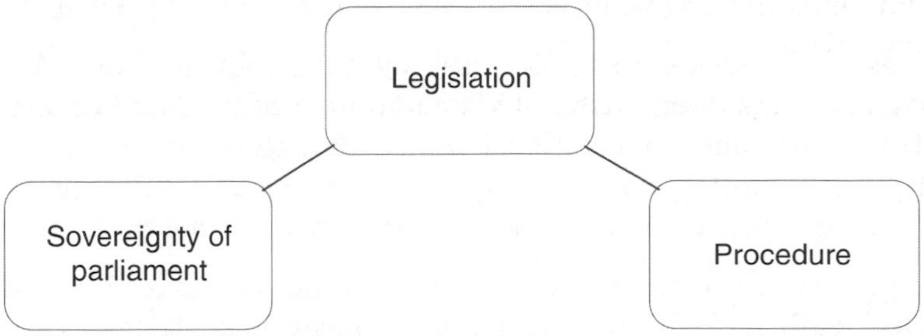

Legislation is enacted by Parliament. Until the UK entered the European Community (the EC) in 1973 the UK Parliament was completely sovereign: its law-making powers were unfettered.

Parliamentary sovereignty means that:

(a) Parliament is able to make the law as it sees fit. It may repeal earlier statutes, overrule case law developed in the courts or make new law on subjects which have not been regulated by law before.

(b) no Parliament can legislate so as to prevent a future Parliament changing the law:

(c) judges are bound to apply the relevant statute law however distasteful to them it may be. But judges have to interpret statute law, and they may find a meaning in a statutory rule which those members of Parliament who promoted the statute did not intend.

In practice, Parliament usually follows certain conventions which limit its freedom. It does not usually enact statutes which alter the law with retrospective effect or deprive citizens of their property without compensation.

4.1 Parliamentary procedure

A proposal for legislation is originally aired in public in a Government green paper. After comments are received a white paper is produced, which sets out the aim of the legislation. It is then put forward in draft form as a bill, and may be introduced into either the House of Commons or the House of Lords, the two Houses of Parliament. When the bill has passed through one House it must then go through the same stages in the other House.

In each House the successive stages of dealing with the bill are as follows.

(a) First reading: publication and introduction into the agenda: no debate.

(b) Second reading: debate on the general merits of the bill but no amendments at this stage.

(c) Committee stage: the bill is examined by a standing committee of about 20 members, representing the main parties and including some members at least who specialise in the relevant subject. The bill is examined section by section and may be amended. If the bill is very important all or part of the committee stage may be taken by the House as a whole sitting as a committee.

(d) Report stage: the bill as amended in committee is reported to the full House for approval. If the Government has undertaken in committee to reconsider various points it often puts forward its final amendments at this stage.

(e) Third reading: this is the final approval stage at which only verbal amendments may be made.

When it has passed through both Houses it is submitted for the Royal Assent which in practice is given on the Queen's behalf by a committee of the Lord Chancellor and two other peers. It then becomes an act of Parliament (or statute). It comes into effect at the start of the day on which Royal Assent is given, or (if the act itself so provides) at some other time or on a commencement date set by statutory instrument.

Most bills are public bills of general application, whether introduced by the Government or by a private member. They are referred to as Government bills or private members' bills respectively. An example of the latter is the Abortion Act 1967, sponsored by David Steel MP. Private members' bills are often brought on matters of conscience such as fox hunting.

If the House of Commons and the House of Lords disagree over the same bill, the House of Lords may delay the passing of the bill for a maximum of one year (except for financial measures, such as the annual Finance Act). It may veto any bill which tries to extend the life of Parliament beyond five years, and it may veto any private bill.

Activity 3 **(10 minutes)**

Many countries have a bill of rights, which cannot be changed by normal legislative procedures. What aspect of Parliamentary sovereignty would make it difficult to give a bill of rights for the UK such a secure position?

5 DELEGATED LEGISLATION

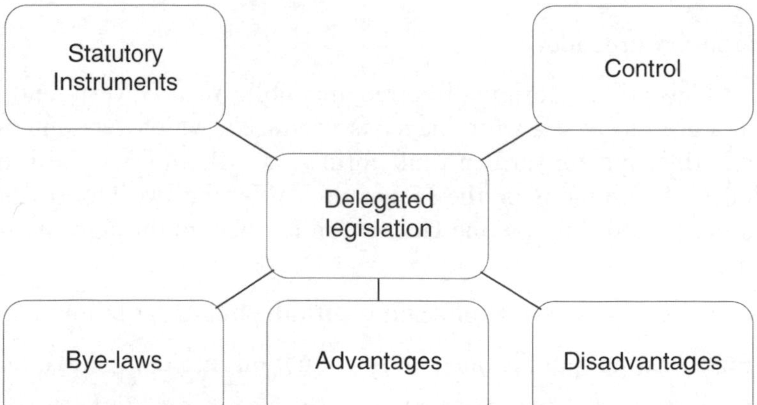

Definition

Delegated legislation: rules of law made by subordinate bodies to whom the power to do so has been given by statute.

To save time in Parliament it is usual to set out the main principles in the body of an act as numbered sections and to relegate the details to schedules (at the end of the act) which need not be debated, though they are visible and take effect as part of the act. But even with this device there is a great deal which cannot conveniently be included in acts. It may, for example, be necessary, after an act has been passed, for the Government to consult interested parties and then produce regulations, having the force of the law, to implement the act, to fix commencement dates to bring the act into operation or to prescribe printed forms for use in connection with it. To provide for these and other matters a modern act usually contains a section by which power is given to a minister, or a public body such as a local authority, to make subordinate or delegated legislation for specified purposes only.

Delegated legislation appears in various forms. Ministerial powers are exercised by statutory instrument (including emergency powers of the Crown exercised by Orders in Council). Local authorities are given statutory powers to make bye-laws, which apply within a specific locality.

Definition

> Bye-law: a type of delegated legislation made by local authorities.

5.1 Advantages and disadvantages

This procedure is unavoidable for various reasons.

(a) Parliament has no time to examine these matters of detail.

(b) Much of the content of delegated legislation is technical and is better worked out in consultation with professional, commercial or industrial groups outside Parliament.

(c) If new or altered regulations are required later, they can be issued in a much shorter time than is needed to pass an amending act.

The disadvantages of delegated legislation are that Parliament loses control of the law-making process and that a huge mass of detailed law appears piecemeal each year. It is difficult for persons who may be affected by it to keep abreast of the changes. Yet ignorance of the law is not accepted as an excuse for infringing it.

5.2 Control

Parliament does exercise some control over delegated legislation by restricting and defining the power to make rules and by keeping the making of new delegated legislation under review. Some statutory instruments do not take effect until approved by affirmative resolution of Parliament. Most other statutory instruments must be laid before Parliament for 40 days before they take effect. During that period members may propose a negative resolution to veto a statutory instrument to which they object.

There are standing scrutiny committees of both houses whose duty it is to examine statutory instruments with a view to raising objections if necessary, usually on the grounds that the instrument is obscure, expensive or retrospective.

As explained above, the power to make delegated legislation is defined by the Act which confers the power. A statutory instrument may be challenged in the courts on the ground that it is ultra vires, that is that it exceeds the prescribed limits, or on the ground that it has been made without due compliance with the correct procedure. If the objection is valid the court declares the statutory instrument to be void.

Definition

Ultra vires: beyond their powers. In company law this term is used in connection with transactions which are outside the scope of the objects clause and therefore, in principle, unenforceable.

Activity 4 **(10 minutes)**

An act of Parliament gives the Chancellor of the Exchequer power to fix the rate of tax on land values by statutory instrument. The Chancellor issues a statutory instrument extending the tax to the values of shareholdings. Consider whether the statutory instrument could be challenged.

Chapter roundup

- Laws are rules enforced by the State. English law is largely case law, with little Roman law.
- Common law developed after the Norman Conquest, but became too rigid to give just results in many cases.
- Equity gave more discretion to do justice than common law, and new rights and remedies, but fair dealing was expected from litigants expecting to be treated fairly themselves.
- Common law and equity remain separate, although both are applied in all courts. Equity prevails over common law.
- Case law is the application of reported cases to later cases.
- Decided cases can fix the law for the purposes of future cases heard before certain courts, through the doctrine of precedent.
- The binding element in an earlier decision is the ratio decidendi, not the obiter dicta.
- The House of Lords binds all courts except itself. The Court of Appeal and a Divisional Court of the High Court bind themselves and all lower courts.
- A court can avoid following a precedent on several grounds.
- Statute law is made by Parliament, which, subject to the UK's membership of the European Community, has unfettered legislative powers.
- A bill goes through two readings, a committee stage, a report stage and a third reading in each House of Parliament before receiving the Royal Assent.
- Much detailed legislation is delegated to Government departments exercising powers conferred by Acts of Parliament.

Quick quiz

1 How was the common law first developed?

2 Give some examples of equitable maxims.

3 Can obiter dicta in a case have any influence on the outcome of subsequent cases?

4 What does it mean to say that a court's decision was taken per incuriam?

5 What is meant by Parliamentary sovereignty?

6 Why is delegated legislation essential?

Answers to quick quiz

1 Through justices sent by the King to administer the same law to everyone. (see para 1.1)

2 'He who comes to equity must come with clean hands'

'Equality is equity'

'Equity looks to the intent rather than the form' (para 2.2)

3 It can be persuasive, but it is not binding. (para 3.2)

4 Without taking some essential point into account. (para 3.5)

5 Parliament can make any law, but cannot prevent a future parliament from changing the law. Judges are bound by parliament. (para 4)

6 To enable governments to introduce all legislation needed, otherwise there would not be enough time. (para 5)

Answers to activities

1 'Clementines are oranges' is the ratio decidendi (ie the decision in the case). 'Peanuts are nuts' is an obiter dictum, an additional comment which is not central.

2 The House of Lords in C v D could disregard the Court of Appeal decision in A v B or even over-rule it. Alternatively the case A v B might be distinguished on its facts.

3 No Parliament can bind its successors.

4 It would be ultra vires (ie beyond the powers of the Chancellor).

Assignment

Since the content of this chapter is introductory background reading, and you will not be tested in detail on the contents in any assignment, we do not include a specific assignment for this chapter.

However, remember that you will encounter many of the terms and concepts introduced here in your later studies, and you may be expected to apply them in assignments at that stage.

Chapter 3 :

INTRODUCTION TO THE LAW OF CONTRACT

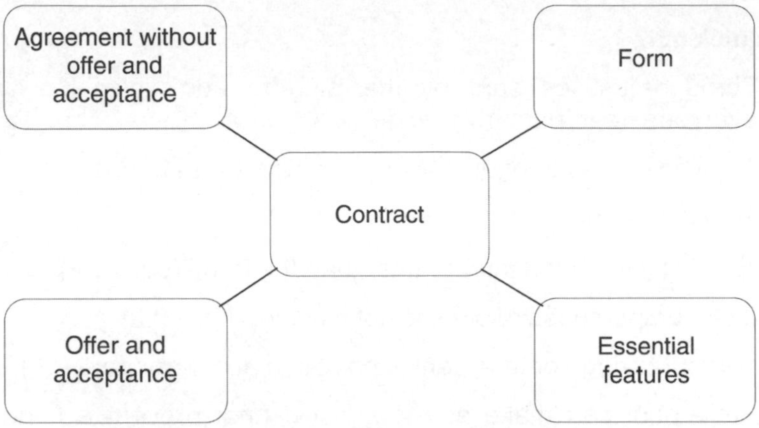

Introduction

A contract is an agreement which legally binds the parties to it. Consider the contracts that you may have entered into as an individual, when buying a house for example, or starting work. Similarly, a business will enter into contracts when it deals with property or takes on new staff.

Most contracts do not have to be in writing. Consider what happens when you go shopping. Clearly, in most cases, the retailer and purchaser do not draw up and sign a written contract, and yet a contract is formed. This is an important point.

However restrictions on the individual's freedom to make contracts have been developed to protect the disadvantaged, particularly in their dealings with large or monopolistic organisations. An example is the Sale of Goods Act 1979, which implies certain terms into contracts for the sale of goods, which cannot be excluded in consumer sales. A seller is bound by these terms even though he has never agreed to them, or may never have even thought of them.

Your objectives

In this chapter you will learn about the following.

(a) The nature of a contract

(b) The classification of contracts

(c) The essentials of a valid contract

(d) The rules governing offer and acceptance in contract law

From this point onwards, you are dealing with precise topics within the Edexcel guidelines, rather than background reading.

NOTES

1 DEFINITION OF A CONTRACT

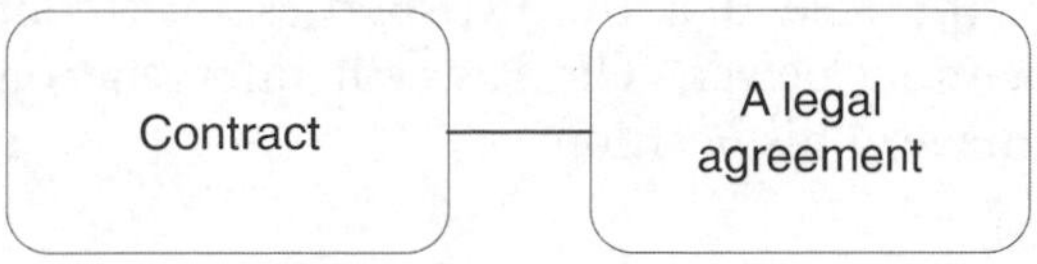

A contract may be defined as an agreement which legally binds the parties.

A party to a contract is bound because he has **agreed** to be bound. The underlying theory, then, is that a contract is the outcome of 'consenting minds'. Parties are not judged by what is in their minds, but by what they have said, written or done.

Contracts are sometimes referred to as **enforceable agreements**. This too is somewhat misleading. English law will not usually allow one party to force the other to fulfil his part of the bargain. He will usually be restricted to the remedy of damages.

FOR DISCUSSION

You may like to think what kinds of contract you have entered into as an individual. If you have bought a house, you will have signed a contract of purchase and 'exchanged' it with the vendor. You should have a signed contract of employment, setting out such matters as your hours of work, your holiday entitlement and the period of noticc required to be given by either party.

Similarly, a business will enter into and usually sign a contract when it buys or sells property or when it takes on new staff. What happens if an employee goes to the local stationery store to buy some paperclips? Clearly the retailer and the purchaser do not draw up and sign a written contract, and yet a contract *is* formed. The former agrees to sell, and the latter agrees to buy, the goods. This is an important point. Most contracts do not have to be in writing.

---

2 FACTORS AFFECTING THE MODERN CONTRACT

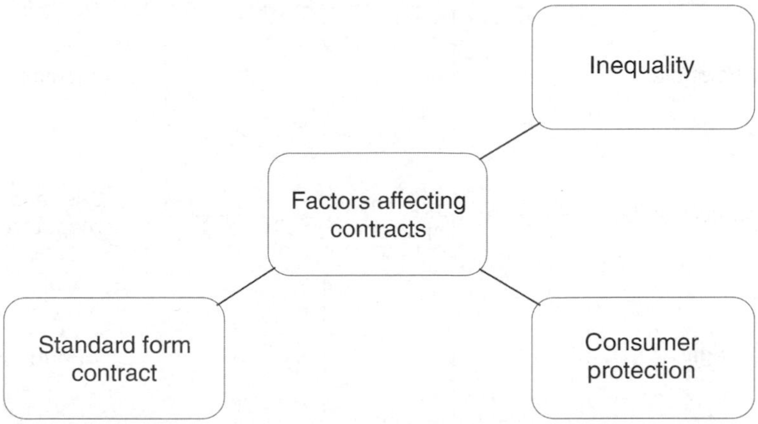

Many principles of modern contract law are strongly influenced by the events and important cases of the nineteenth century. However, a number of **developments in the twentieth century** should be brought into consideration.

2.1 Inequality of bargaining power

It is almost invariably the case that the two parties to a contract bring with them differing levels of bargaining power. The law will intervene only where the stronger party takes unfair advantage of his position.

2.2 The standard form contract

Mass production and nationalisation have led to the standard form contract.

Definition

> The **standard form** contract is a standard document prepared by many large organisations and setting out the terms on which they contact with their customers. The individual must usually take it or leave it: he does not really 'agree' to it. For example, a customer has to accept his supply of electricity on the electricity board's terms; individuals cannot negotiate discounts.

2.3 Consumer protection

In the second half of the twentieth century, there was a surge of interest in **consumer matters** mainly because of mass production and aggressive marketing. There is a greater need for **consumer protection**. Consumer interests are now served by consumer protection agencies, which include government departments (the **Office of Fair Trading**) and independent bodies (the **Consumers Association**) and legislation.

Public policy sometimes requires that the freedom of contract should be modified. For example, the Consumer Credit Act 1974 and the Unfair Contract Terms Act 1977 both regulate the extent to which contracts can contain certain terms.

Consumer protection is covered in detail in later chapters.

3 THE ESSENTIALS OF A CONTRACT

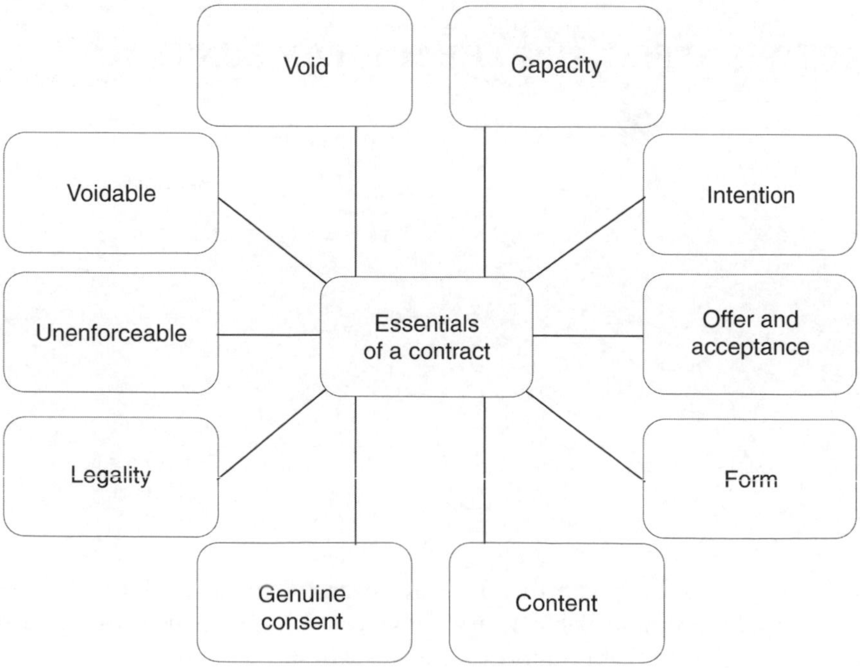

In order to be valid and enforceable by the law, a contract must contain certain key elements. If one of them is missing then the contract may be described as void, voidable or unenforceable.

3.1 The essential elements of a contract

These are as follows.

(a) The parties must have an **intention to create legal relations** between themselves.

(b) There is an agreement made by **offer and acceptance**.

(c) The obligations assumed by each party are supported by **consideration** given by the other.

3.2 Factors affecting the validity of a contract

Even if these essential elements can be shown, a contract may not necessarily be valid. The **validity** of a contract may also be affected by the following factors.

(a) **Form**. Some contracts must be made in a particular form (for example in writing) or supported by written evidence.

(b) **Content**. A contract can only be enforced if it is sufficiently complete and precise in its terms. Some terms which the parties do not express may be implied and some terms which the parties do express are overridden by statutory rules.

(c) **Genuine consent**. A misrepresentation made by one party to the contract may affect the validity of a contract.

(d) **Legality**. The courts will not enforce a contract which is deemed to be illegal or contrary to public policy.

(e) **Capacity**. Some persons have only restricted capacity to enter into contracts The most important category of such persons are minors (persons under the age of 18).

3.3 Void, voidable and unenforceable contracts

A contract which does not satisfy the relevant tests may be either **void, voidable** or **unenforceable**.

Definitions

(a) A **void** contract is **not a contract** at all. The parties are not bound by it and if they transfer property under it they can sometimes (unless it is also an illegal contract) recover their goods even from a third party.

For example, A sells goods to B, who sells them on to C. B then fails to pay A for the goods and disappears without trace. If A can demonstrate that he was genuinely mistaken as to the identity of B and would not have dealt with him had he known who B really was, then A can recover the goods which were subject to the original contract from C. This is because the law takes the view in such a situation that the original contract between A and B was no contract at all and of no effect.

Therefore C, who was an innocent third party acting in good faith, has to return the goods to A and either bear the loss or find and sue B.

(b) A **voidable** contract is a **contract which one party may avoid**, that is terminate at his option. The contract is treated as valid unless and until it is avoided. Property transferred before avoidance is usually irrecoverable from a third party.

For example A sells goods to B on 1st June. On 8th June B sells them onto C. On 10th June, it is discovered that B had made a misrepresentation in the original contract between A and B and A seeks to recover the goods. Given these dates, A cannot do so, as the goods have been sold on to C *before* A tries to avoid the original contract, and at the time that B sells them he (B) still has good title.

If on the other hand, B did not sell the goods on to C until 12th June, which is after A seeks to avoid the original contract with B, that original contract has already been avoided, and B would not be able to pass good title on to C.

(c) An **unenforceable** contract is a **valid contract** and property transferred under it cannot be recovered even from the other party to the contract. If either party refuses to perform the contract, the other party cannot compel him to do so. A contract is usually unenforceable when the required evidence of its terms, for example, written evidence of a contract relating to land, is not available. Unenforceable contracts are only problematic if a dispute over the contract arises.

3.4 The life of a contract

Once a valid contract has been formed, it remains in existence until **discharged**, usually in one of four ways. The most common means of discharge is **performance**, where both parties fulfil their contractual obligations.

4 THE FORM OF A CONTRACT

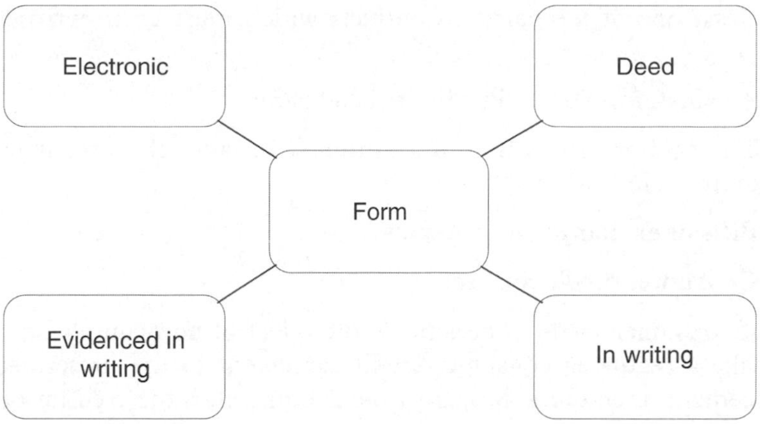

One of the most widely held misapprehensions about contracts is that they have to be in writing and signed by both parties.

FOR DISCUSSION

A binding contract does not need to be in writing. As a general rule, a contract may be made in any form. It may be written, or oral, or inferred from the conduct of the parties.

For example, a customer in a self-service shop may take his selected goods to the cash desk, pay for them and walk out without saying a word. The three essential elements of a contract (offer, acceptance, consideration and the intention to create legal relations) are present and a contract of sale has been formed.

Writing makes it easier to prove the contents of the contract, but it is not usually necessary unless related to one of the following:

- Some contracts must be by **deed**
- Some contracts must be in **writing**
- Some contracts must be **evidenced in writing**

4.1 Contracts by deed

Under s 1 Law of Property (Miscellaneous Provisions) Act 1989, contracts relating to the transfer of land must be by deed, **in writing, signed and witnessed**. Delivery is conduct indicating that the parties intend to be bound by the contract.

Contracts which must be by deed include the following.

(a) **Leases** for three years or more

(b) A **conveyance** or transfer of a legal estate in land (including a mortgage). This is the 'completion' on the sale of a house.

(c) A **promise not supported by consideration** (such as a covenant to make annual payments to a charity)

Contracts made by deed are also referred to as specialty contracts.

4.2 Contracts which must be in writing

Some types of contract are required to be in the form of a written document, usually signed by at least one of the parties. Contracts which must be in writing include the following.

- A **transfer of shares** in a limited company
- The **sale** or **disposition of an interest in land** (the 'exchange of contracts' on the sale of a house)
- **Bills of exchange** and **cheques**
- **Consumer credit** contracts

In the case of consumer credit transactions, the effect of non-compliance by the seller (failure to make a regulated consumer credit agreement in the prescribed form) is to make the agreement unenforceable against the debtor unless the creditor obtains a court order.

4.3 Contracts which must be evidenced in writing

Certain contracts may be made orally, but are not enforceable in a court of law unless there is written evidence of their terms. The most important contract of this type is the contract of guarantee. A signed note of the material terms of the contract is sufficient.

4.4 The electronic contract

English law has been concerned with formulating the rules for oral and written contracts for centuries. Business conducted **on-line** creates a new category of contract: the **electronic contract**.

The law in this area is still in its infancy. Below is a summary of the **basic contract principles** which will need to be considered.

(a) **In writing**? There are two main reasons why contracts need to be in writing.

    (i) A written contract provides evidence of the terms of the contract.

    (ii) The requirement of formality allows a weaker party to 'think twice' before entering into a transaction.

    An electronic contract meets the reasoning behind the requirement for writing, and can thus be said to be in writing.

(b) **Signed**? In early 1999 the UK government unveiled a new legal framework for electronic commerce, designed to boost public confidence in using the Internet. The courts are to be allowed to recognise electronic signatures as legally binding, removing any discrimination between electronic and traditional forms of doing business.

(c) **Timing of acceptance**. A contract comes into existence when an offer is accepted; in the case of acceptance by letter, this is when the letter is posted (more on this in the next chapter). Internet e-mail shares many of the qualities of conventional mail - it is not usually instantaneous and may be subject to delay. Therefore the postal rule probably applies, although the point has not been tested. There is also the problem of failure of delivery of an e-mail.

(d) **Consideration**. Difficulties and concern about the security of credit card payments have slowed the growth of electronic commerce.

5 OFFER AND ACCEPTANCE

OFFER + ACCEPTANCE = AGREEMENT

The first essential element of a binding contract is **agreement**. To determine whether or not an agreement has been reached, the courts will consider whether one party has made a firm offer which the other party has accepted.

In most contracts, **offer and acceptance** may be made orally or in writing, or they may be implied by the conduct of the parties. The person making an offer is the **offeror** and the person to whom an offer is made is the **offeree**.

The particular significance of offer and acceptance is that a **binding contract** is thereby formed, so that new terms cannot thereafter be introduced into the contract unless both parties agree. From this moment on, the terms of the contract appear from the offer and acceptance, rather than from the unexpressed intentions of the parties.

6 OFFER

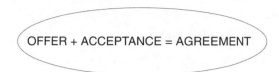

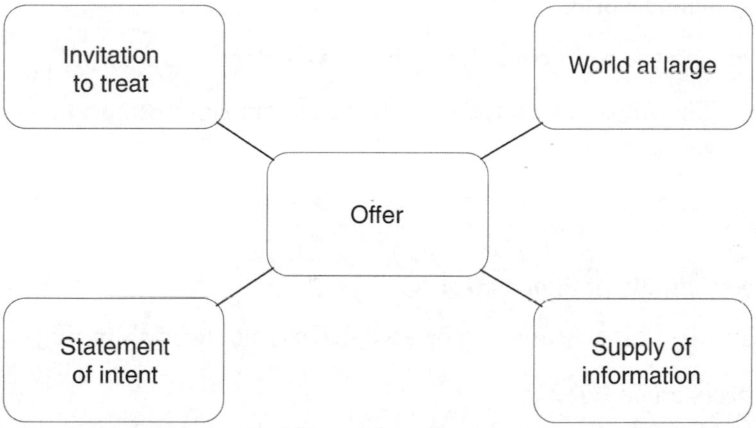

An **offer** is a definite promise to be bound on specific terms.

6.1 Certainty of the offer

An apparently vague offer can be made certain by reference to the parties' previous dealing.

Gunthing v Lynn 1831

The facts: the offeror offered to pay a further sum for a horse if it was 'lucky'.

Decision: the offer was too vague and no contract could be formed by any purported acceptance.

Hillas & Co Ltd v Arcos Ltd 1932

The facts: the claimants agreed to purchase from the defendants '22,000 standards of softwood goods of fair specification over the season 1930'. The agreement contained an option to buy a further 100,000 standards in 1931. The 1930 transaction took place but the sellers refused to supply any wood in 1931, saying that the agreement was too vague to bind the parties.

Decision: the wording used, and the previous transactions, showed a sufficient intention to be bound. There was therefore a valid contract.

6.2 An offer made to the world at large

A definite offer may be made to a class of persons or to the world at large.

The case below is very important. Learn it before you learn any of the others.

Carlill v Carbolic Smoke Ball Co 1893
The facts: the manufacturers of a patent medicine published an advertisement by which they undertook to pay '£100 reward ... to any person who contracts ... influenza ... after having used the smoke ball three times daily for two weeks'. The advertisement added that £1,000 had been deposited at a bank 'showing our sincerity in this matter'. The claimant read the advertisement, purchased the smoke ball and used it as directed. She contracted influenza and claimed her £100 reward. The manufacturers argued a number of defences, including the following.

(a) The offer was so vague that it could not form the basis of a contract as no time limit was specified.

(b) It was not an offer which could be accepted since it was offered to the whole world.

Decision: the court considered these two defences as follows.

(a) The smoke ball must protect the user during the period of use. The offer was not vague.

(b) An offer to the public can be accepted so as to form a contract.

6.3 The mere supply of information

Only an offer in the proper sense may be accepted so as to form a binding contract.

Harvey v Facey 1893
The facts: the claimant telegraphed to the defendant 'Will you sell us Bumper Hall Pen? Telegraph lowest cash price'. The defendant telegraphed in reply 'Lowest price for Bumper Hall Pen, £900'. The claimant telegraphed to accept what he regarded as an offer; the defendant made no further reply.

Decision: the defendant's telegram was merely a statement of his minimum price if a sale were to be agreed. It was not an offer and no contract had been made.

If, in the course of negotiations for a sale, the vendor states the price at which he will sell, that statement may be an offer which can become accepted eventually.

Bigg v Boyd Gibbons 1971
The facts: in the course of correspondence the defendant rejected an offer of £20,000 by the claimant and added 'for a quick sale I would accept £26,000 .... if you are not interested in this price would you please let me know immediately'. The claimant accepted this price of £26,000 and the defendant acknowledged his acceptance, stating that he had given instructions for the sale to his solicitor.

Decision: in this context the defendant must be treated as making an offer (at £26,000) which the claimant had accepted.

Reference to a more detailed document will not necessarily protect one party.

Bowerman and Another v Association of British Travel Agents Ltd 1996
The facts: the case arose out of the insolvency in 1991 of a tour operator through whom a school party had booked a holiday. The party claimed a full refund under the ABTA scheme of protection, which did not cover the holiday insurance premium. This was explained in ABTA's handbook, to which customers were referred, but had not been seen by the teacher booking the holiday.

Decision: the public had been encouraged by ABTA to read the written 'ABTA promise' as creating a contractual obligation to reimburse all the expenses of the holiday. The court found that the claimant was entitled to full reimbursement.

6.4 A statement of intention

Advertising that an event such as an auction will take place is not an offer to sell. Potential buyers may not sue if the auction does not take place: *Harris v Nickerson 1873*

6.5 An invitation to treat

Where a party is initiating negotiations, he is said to have made an invitation to treat.

Definition

> An **invitation to treat** is an indication that someone is prepared to receive offers with the view to forming a binding contract. It is not an offer in itself.

There are four types of invitation to treat.

- Auction sales
- Advertisements
- Exhibition of goods for sale
- An invitation for tenders

Auction sales

An auctioneer's request for bids is not a definite offer to sell to the highest bidder. The bid itself is the offer, which the auctioneer is then free to accept or reject: *Payne v Cave 1789.* Acceptance is indicated by the fall of the auctioneer's hammer.

Advertisements

An advertisement of goods is an attempt to induce offers and is therefore classified as an invitation to treat.

Partridge v Crittenden 1968
The facts: Mr Partridge placed an advertisement in *Cage and Aviary Birds* magazine containing the words 'Bramblefinch cocks, bramblefinch hens, 25s

each'. The RSPCA brought a prosecution for offering for sale a protected species in contravention of the Protection of Birds Act 1953. The justices convicted Partridge. He appealed to the Court of Appeal.

Decision: the conviction was quashed. The prosecution could not rely on the offence of 'offering for sale', as the advertisement constituted an invitation to treat. He was therefore not making an offer.

The circulation of a price list is also an invitation to treat: *Grainger v Gough 1896.* It cannot be an offer because 'if it were so, the merchant might find himself involved in any number of contractual obligations to supply wine of a particular description which he would be quite unable to carry out, his stock of wine of that description being necessarily limited.'

Activity 1 **(10 minutes)**

In *Carlill v Carbolic Smokeball Co 1893*, the company published an advertisement for its patent medicine in which it undertook to pay £100 to anyone who, having used the medicine, became ill with influenza within a limited period thereafter.

At what time was the contract between Mrs Carlill and the company made?

A When she read the advertisement
B When she bought the patent medicine
C When she used the medicine and caught influenza
D When she notified the manufacturer of her claim

Exhibition of goods for sale

Displaying goods in a shop constitutes inviting customers to make offers to purchase, or an invitation to treat.

Fisher v Bell 1961
The facts: a shopkeeper was prosecuted for offering for sale an offensive weapon by exhibiting a flick knife in his shop window.

Decision: according to the ordinary law of contract, the display of an article with a price on it in a shop window is merely an invitation to treat.

Pharmaceutical Society of Great Britain v Boots Cash Chemists (Southern) 1952
The facts: certain drugs containing poisons could only be sold 'under the supervision of a registered pharmacist'. The claimant claimed this rule had been broken by Boots who put supplies of these drugs on open shelves in a self-service shop. Boots contended that there was no sale until the customer brought the goods to the cash desk and offered to buy them. A registered pharmacist was stationed at this point.

Decision: The court found for the defendant and commented that if it were true that a customer accepted an offer to sell by removing goods from the shelf he could not then change his mind and put them back because to do so would constitute breach of contract.

Invitation for tenders

A tender is an estimate submitted in response to a prior request. When a person tenders for a contract he is making an offer to the person who has advertised a contract as being available.

> **Activity 2** **(10 minutes)**
>
> Bianca goes into a shop and sees a price label on a CD for £15. She takes the CD to the checkout, but the till operator tells her that the label is misprinted and should read £20. Bianca maintains that she only has to pay £15. How would you describe the price on the price label in terms of contract law?

7 ACCEPTANCE

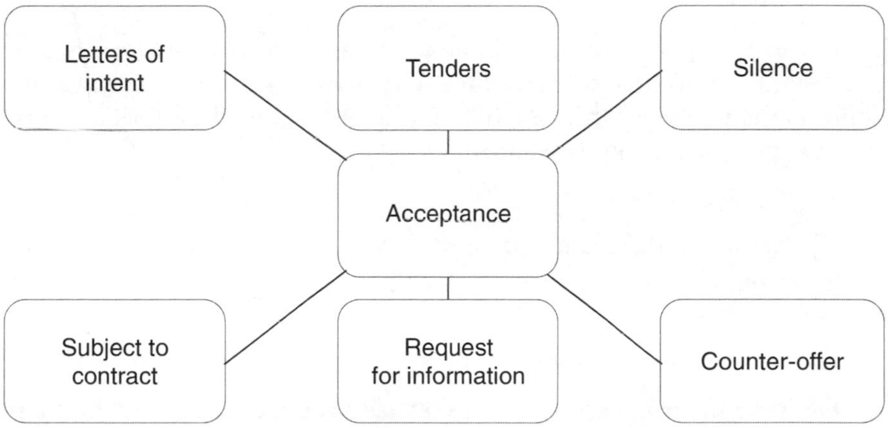

Acceptance can be defined as an unqualified agreement to the terms of the offer.

Acceptance may be by express words or by action (as in *Carlill's* case). It may also be inferred from conduct.

> *Brogden v Metropolitan Railway Co 1877*
> *The facts*: having supplied coal for many years to the defendant, the claimant suggested there should be a written agreement. The claimant continued to supply coal under the terms of the draft agreement but no version was ever signed. The claimant later denied that there was any agreement between him and the defendant.
>
> *Decision*: the conduct of the parties indicated that they both agreed to the terms of the draft. The draft agreement became a binding contract as soon as the defendant ordered and the claimant supplied coal.

7.1 Silence as acceptance

There must be some act on the part of the offeree to indicate his acceptance.

> *Felthouse v Bindley 1862*
> *The facts*: the claimant wrote to his nephew offering to buy the nephew's horse for £30.15s, adding 'If I hear no more about him, I consider the horse mine at that price'. The nephew intended to accept his uncle's offer but did not reply.

He instructed the defendant, an auctioneer, not to sell the horse. Owing to a misunderstanding the horse was sold at auction to someone else. The uncle sued the auctioneer in conversion (a tort alleging wrongful disposal of another's property).

Decision: the action failed. There could be no acceptance by silence in these circumstances. The claimant had no title to the horse and could not sue in conversion.

7.2 Unsolicited goods

Goods which are sent or services which are rendered to a person who did not request them are not 'accepted' merely because he does not return them to the sender. His silence is not acceptance of them, even if the sender includes a statement that he is deemed to have agreed to buy and/or pay unless he rejects them: Unsolicited Goods and Services Act 1971.

7.3 Counter-offer

As has been said, acceptance must be unqualified agreement to the terms of the offer. **Acceptance which purports to introduce any new terms is a counter-offer**. If a counter-offer is made, the original offeror may accept it, but if he rejects it his original offer is no longer available for acceptance.

Hyde v Wrench 1840
The facts: the defendant offered to sell property to the claimant for £1,000. Two days later, the claimant made a counter-offer of £950 which the defendant rejected. The claimant then informed the defendant he accepted the original offer of £1,000.

Decision: the original offer of £1,000 had been terminated by the counter-offer of £950.

A counter-offer may be accepted by the original offeror; this will have the effect of creating a binding contract.

Butler Machine Tool Co v Ex-cell-O Corp (England) 1979
The facts: the claimant offered to sell tools to the defendant. Their quotation included details of their standard terms and conditions of sale. The defendant 'accepted' the offer, enclosing their own standard terms, which differed from those of the claimant. The claimant acknowledged acceptance by returning a tear-off slip from the order form.

Decision: the defendant's order was really a counter-offer. The claimant had accepted this by returning the tear-off slip.

Activity 3 **(10 minutes)**

Mike offered to sell Barry his car for £5,000. Barry agreed but said he would pay by five instalments of £1,000. Mike then sold the car to Catherine. Barry plans to sue Mike for breach of contract. Will he succeed?

7.4 Request for information

It is possible, however, to respond to an offer by making a **request for information**.

> *Stevenson v McLean 1880*
> *The facts*: the defendant offered to sell iron at '40s per ton, open till Monday'. The claimant replied asking about delivery times, and then sent a letter accepting the offer. This crossed in the post with a letter from the defendant which revoked the offer. The defendant sold the iron to a third party.
>
> *Decision*: there was a contract since the claimant had merely enquired as to a variation of terms. The offer was still open when it was accepted by the claimant.

7.5 Acceptance 'subject to contract'

Acceptance 'subject to contract' means that the offeree is agreeable to the terms of the offer but proposes that the parties should negotiate a formal contract. Agreements for the sale of land in England are usually made 'subject to contract'. This gives the buyer protection, as he has time to investigate title and carry out a survey.

Acceptance 'subject to contract' must be distinguished from outright and immediate acceptance.

> *Branca v Cobarro 1947*
> *The facts*: a vendor agreed to sell a mushroom farm under a signed contract which was declared to be 'a provisional agreement until a fully legalised agreement, drawn up by a solicitor and embodying all the conditions herewith stated, is signed'.
>
> *Decision*: by the use of the word 'provisional', the parties had intended their agreement to be binding from the outset.

7.6 Letters of intent

Definition

> A **letter of intent** is a means by which one party gives a strong indication to another that he is likely to place a contract with him.

Usually, a letter of intent is worded so as not to create any legal obligation. However in some cases it may be phrased so that it includes an invitation to commence preliminary work. In such circumstances, it creates an obligation to pay for that work.

> *British Steel Corpn v Cleveland Bridge and Engineering Co Ltd 1984*
> *The facts*: the defendants approached the claimants with a view to engaging them to supply nodes for a complex steel lattice-work frame. They sent the claimants a letter of intent, stating their intention to place an order on the defendants' standard terms. The claimants stated that they were unwilling to contract on such terms, but started work, and eventually completed and delivered all the nodes. They sued for the value of the nodes and the defendants counter-claimed for damages for late delivery.

Decision: there was no contract, and so there could be no question of damages for late delivery. However, since the claimants had undertaken work at the request of the defendants and the defendants had accepted this work, the claimants were entitled to payment on a *quantum meruit* basis. (*Quantum meruit* is a reasonable remuneration for services rendered.)

7.7 Acceptance of a tender

A person who makes a tender is making an offer to the person who advertised the contract as being available. There are two distinct types of tender.

(a) A 'tender' to perform one task, such as building a new hospital, is an offer which can be accepted.

(b) A 'tender' to supply or perform a series of things, such as the supply of vegetables daily to a restaurant, is not accepted until an order is placed. It is a standing offer. Each order placed by the offeree is an individual act of acceptance creating a separate contract.

Until orders are placed there is no contract and the tenderer can terminate his standing offer.

Great Northern Railways v Witham 1873

The facts: the defendant tendered successfully for the supply of stores to the claimant over a period of one year. In his tender he undertook 'to supply ... such quantities as the company may order from time to time'. After making some deliveries he refused to fulfil an order which the claimant had given.

Decision: he was in breach of contract in refusing to fulfil the order given but might revoke his tender and need not then fulfil any future orders within the remainder of the 12 month period.

An invitation for tenders does not amount to an offer to contract with the person quoting the lowest/best price, except where the person inviting tenders makes it clear that he is in fact making an offer, for example by the use of words such as 'we confirm that if the offer made by you is the best offer received by us, we bind ourselves to accept such offer provided that such offer complies with the terms of this telex': *Harvela Investments Ltd v Royal Trust Co of Canada Ltd 1986*

8 COMMUNICATION OF ACCEPTANCE

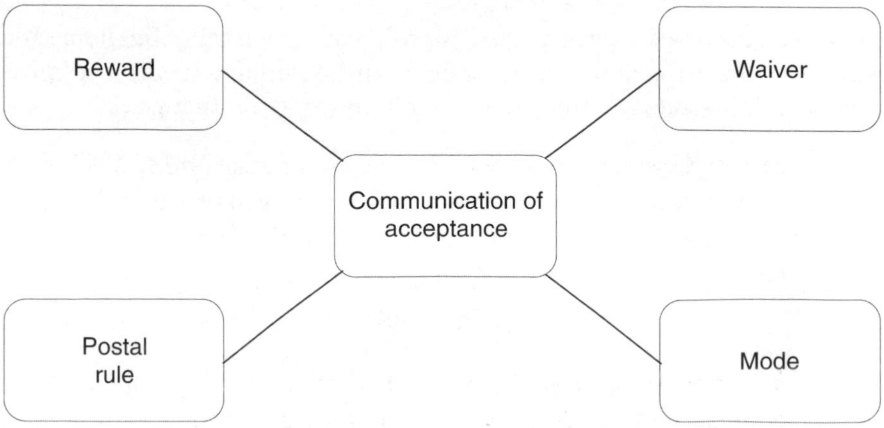

The general rule is that acceptance must be **communicated** to the offeror and is **not effective until this has been done.**

8.1 Waiver of communication

The offeror may, by his offer, dispense with the need for communication of acceptance. In *Carlill v Carbolic Smoke Ball Co 1893,* it was held that it was sufficient for the claimant to act on the offer without previously notifying her acceptance of it. This was an example of a **unilateral contract**, where the offer takes the form of a promise to pay money in return for an act.

8.2 Prescribed mode of communication

The offeror may call for acceptance by specified means. Unless he stipulates that this is the only method of acceptance which suffices, then acceptance by some other means equally expeditious would constitute a valid acceptance: *Tinn v Hoffmann 1873.* A telegram or even a verbal message could be sufficient acceptance of an offer inviting acceptance 'by return of post'. This would probably apply now also to acceptance by fax machine or e-mail.

> *Yates Building Co v R J Pulleyn & Sons (York) 1975*
> *The facts*: the offer called for acceptance by registered or recorded delivery letter. The offeree sent an ordinary letter which arrived without delay.
>
> *Decision*: the offeror had suffered no disadvantage and had not stipulated that acceptance must be made in this way only. The acceptance was valid.

8.3 The postal rule

This is quite complex, and you should read the facts of the relevant cases carefully, to ensure that you understand them.

(a) The offeror may expressly or by implication indicate that he expects acceptance by means of a letter sent through the post. The **postal rule** states that, where the use of the post is within the contemplation of both the parties, the acceptance is complete and effective as soon as a letter is **posted.**

> *Adams v Lindsell 1818*
> *The facts*: the defendants made an offer by letter to the claimant on 2 September 1817 requiring an answer 'in course of post'. The letter of offer was delayed and reached the claimants on 5 September; they immediately posted a letter of acceptance, which reached the defendants on 9 September. The defendants could have expected a reply by 7 September, and they assumed that the absence of a reply within the expected period indicated non-acceptance and sold the goods to another buyer on 8 September.
>
> *Decision*: the acceptance was made 'in course of post' and was effective when posted. The contract was made on 5 September, when the acceptance was posted.

(b) The intention to use the post for communication of acceptance may be deduced from the circumstances without express statement to that effect.

> *Household Fire and Carriage Accident Insurance Co v Grant 1879*
> *The facts*: the defendant handed a letter of application for shares to the claimant company's agent in Swansea with the intention that it should be

posted to the company in London. The company posted an acceptance (letter of allotment) which was lost in the post, and never arrived. The defendant was called upon to pay the amount outstanding on his shares.

Decision: the defendant had to pay. The contract between the company and him had been formed when the letter of allotment was posted, regardless of the fact that it was lost in the post.

(c) Under the postal rule, the offeror may be unaware that a contract has been made by acceptance of his offer. If that possibility is clearly inconsistent with the nature of the transaction, the postal rule is excluded and the letter of acceptance takes effect only when received.

Holwell Securities v Hughes 1974
The facts: Hughes granted to the claimant an option to purchase land to be exercised 'by notice in writing'. A letter giving notice of the exercise of the option was lost in the post.

Decision: the words 'notice in writing' must mean notice actually received by the vendor; hence notice had not been given to accept the offer.

(d) Acceptance of an offer may only be made by a person authorised to do so. This will usually be the offeree or his authorised agents.

Powell v Lee 1908
The facts: the claimant successfully applied for a post as a headmaster. Without authorisation, the claimant was informed of the appointment by one of the managers. Later, it was decided to give the post to someone else. The claimant sued for breach of contract.

Decision: he failed in his action for breach of contract. Since communication of acceptance was unauthorised, there was no valid agreement and hence no contract.

Activity 4 **(10 minutes)**

Jarvis wrote to Cocker on 1 April offering to sell him his mountain bike for £2,000, and asking Cocker to reply by post. Cocker received the letter on 2 April and the same day posted a letter of acceptance. On 3 April, Jarvis telephoned Cocker to say he was increasing the price to £2,500, but Cocker is insisting on buying at £2,000. What is the legal position?

8.4 Cross-offers

If two offers, identical in terms, cross in the post, there is no contract: *Tinn v Hoffmann 1873*.

8.5 Reward cases

The question arises as to whether contractual obligations arise if a party, in ignorance of an offer, performs an act which fulfils the terms of the offer. If A offers a reward to anyone who finds and returns his lost property and B, in ignorance of the offer, does in fact return it to him, is B entitled to the promised reward? In fact there is no contract by which A is obliged to pay the reward to B.

R v Clarke 1927
The facts: a reward of £1,000 was offered for information leading to the arrest and conviction of a murderer. C, an accomplice, gave the necessary information. He claimed the reward, admitting that he had acted only to save his own skin.

Decision: his claim failed. Although he had seen the offer, it was not present in his mind when he acted.

However, acceptance may still be valid even if the offer was not the sole reason for the action.

Williams v Carwardine 1833
The facts: a reward was offered to bring criminals to book. The claimant, an accomplice, supplied the information, with knowledge of the reward but moved primarily by remorse.

Decision: as the information was given with knowledge, the acceptance was related to the offer despite the fact that remorse was the prime motive.

9 TERMINATION OF OFFER

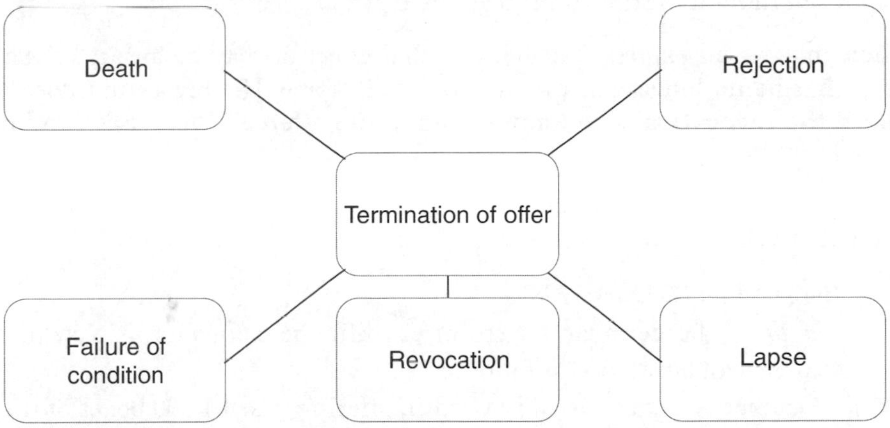

An offer is **terminated** in any of the following circumstances.

- Rejection
- Lapse of time
- Revocation by the offeror
- Failure of a condition to which the offer was subject
- Death of one of the parties

9.1 Rejection

Outright rejection terminates an offer. A counter-offer also terminates the original offer: *Hyde v Wrench 1840*

9.2 Lapse of time

An offer may be expressed to last for a **specified time.** If there is no express time limit set, it expires after a **reasonable time.** What is reasonable depends on the circumstances of the case.

Ramsgate Victoria Hotel Co v Montefiore 1866
The facts: the defendant applied to the company in June for shares and paid a deposit to the company's bank. At the end of November the company sent him an acceptance by issue of a letter of allotment and requested payment of the balance due. The defendant contended that his offer had expired and could no longer be accepted.

Decision: the offer was for a reasonable time only, so the offer had lapsed.

9.3 Revocation by the offeror

The offeror may revoke his offer at any time before acceptance: *Payne v Cave 1789*.

If he undertakes that his offer shall remain open for acceptance for a specified time he may nonetheless revoke it within that time, unless by a separate contract he has bound himself to keep it open for the whole of the specified time.

Routledge v Grant 1828
The facts: the defendant offered to buy the claimant's house for a fixed sum, requiring acceptance within six weeks. Within the six weeks specified, he withdrew his offer.

Decision: the defendant could revoke his offer at any time before acceptance, even though the time limit had not expired.

Revocation may be an express statement to that effect or may be an act of the offeror indicating that he no longer regards the offer as in force. His revocation does not take effect **until the revocation is communicated to the offeree**. This raises two important points.

While posting a letter is a sufficient act of acceptance, it is not a sufficient act of revocation of offer.

Byrne v Van Tienhoven 1880
The facts: the defendants were in Cardiff; the claimants in New York. The sequence of events was as follows:

1 October	Letter posted in Cardiff, offering to sell 1,000 boxes of tinplates.
8 October	Letter of revocation of offer posted in Cardiff.
11 October	Letter of offer received in New York and telegram of acceptance sent.
15 October	Letter confirming acceptance posted in New York.
20 October	Letter of revocation received in New York. The offeree had meanwhile resold the contract goods.

Decision: the letter of revocation could not take effect until received (20 October). Simply posting a letter does not revoke the offer until it is received.

While acceptance must be communicated by the offeree, revocation of offer may be communicated by any third party who is a sufficiently reliable informant.

Dickinson v Dodds 1876
The facts: the defendant, on 10 June, wrote to the claimant to offer property for sale at £800, adding 'this offer to be left open until Friday 12 June, 9.00 am'. On 11 June the defendant sold the property to another buyer. The intermediary between Dickinson and Dodds informed Dickinson that the

defendant had sold to someone else. On Friday 12 June, before 9.00 am, the claimant handed to the defendant a formal letter of acceptance.

Decision: the defendant was free to revoke his offer and had done so by sale to a third party; the claimant could not accept the offer after he had learnt from a reliable informant of the revocation of the offer to him.

Where an offer is meant to be accepted by conduct (a **unilateral** contract), it has been held that it cannot be revoked once the offeree has begun to try and perform whatever act is necessary.

Errington v Errington (1953)
The facts: a father bought a house for his son and daughter-in-law to live in. He paid the deposit, and the son and daughter-in-law were to make the mortgage repayments. The father told them that the house would be theirs when the mortgage was paid off. The son subsequently left his wife, who continued to live in the house.

Decision: The Court of Appeal ruled that the father could not eject the daughter-in-law from the property. Lord Denning said 'The father's promise was a unilateral contract – a promise of the house in return for their act of paying the instalments. It could not be revoked by him once the couple entered on the performance of the act …'.

9.4 Failure of a condition

An offer may be conditional. If the condition is not satisfied, the offer is not capable of acceptance.

Financings Ltd v Stimson 1962
The facts: the defendant wished to purchase a car, and on 16 March signed a hire-purchase form. The form, issued by the claimants, stated that the agreement would be binding only upon signature by them. On 20 March the defendant, not satisfied with the car, returned it to the motor dealer. On 24 March the car was stolen from the premises of the dealer, and was recovered badly damaged. On 25 March the claimants signed the form. They sued the defendant for breach of contract.

Decision: the defendant was not bound to take the car. His signing of the agreement was actually an offer to contract with the claimant. There was an implied condition in this offer that the car would be in substantially the same condition when the offer was accepted as when it was made.

9.5 Termination by death

The death of the **offeree** terminates the offer.

The **offeror's** death terminates the offer unless the offeree accepts it in ignorance of the offeror's death, and the offer is not of a personal nature.

Bradbury v Morgan 1862
The facts: X offered to guarantee payment by Y in respect of goods to be supplied by the claimant on credit to Y. X died and the claimant, in ignorance of his death, continued to supply goods to Y. The claimant then sued X's executors on the guarantee.

Decision: X's offer was a continuing commercial offer which the claimant had accepted by supply of goods after X's death. The guarantee stood.

10 AGREEMENT WITHOUT OFFER AND ACCEPTANCE

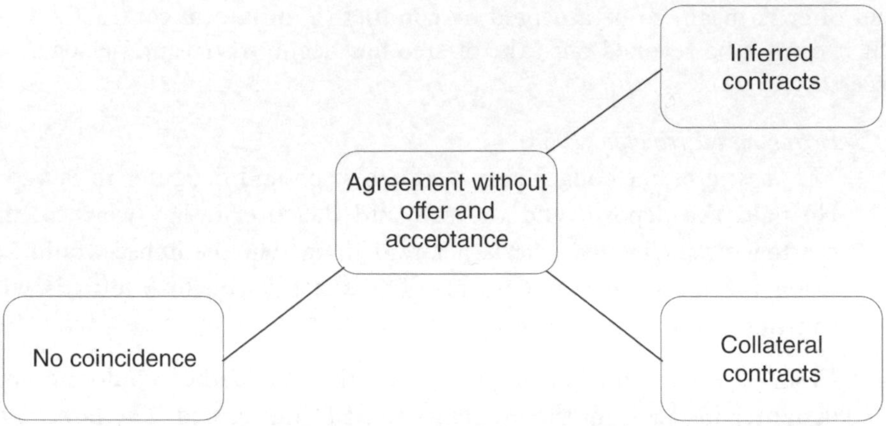

The rules applied by the courts to establish the existence of a contract are based on the assumption that there is agreement between the parties. In certain cases they may go beyond what can be inferred from the words and actions of the parties and construct a contract.

10.1 Inferred contracts

Clarke v Dunraven 1897
The facts: the owners of two yachts entered them for a regatta. Each undertook in a letter to the Club Secretary to obey the Club's rules, which included an obligation to pay 'all damages' caused by fouling. While they were manoeuvring before the start, the defendant's yacht fouled the claimant's yacht, which sank. The claimant sued for all damages. The defendant argued that his liability was under the Merchant Shipping Act 1862 and therefore limited to £8 per ton.

Decision: a contract had been created between the parties when they entered their yachts for the regatta, at which point they had accepted the Club's rules as being binding upon each other. The defendant was liable for all damages.

10.2 Collateral contracts

Definition

> A **collateral contract** is a contract the consideration for which is the making of some other contract.

If there are two separate contracts by offer and acceptance between on the one hand A and B and on the other hand A and C, on terms which involve some concerted action between B and C, there may be a contract between B and C. In contracting with A, both

B and C look forward to the possible relationship between them (B and C) which will result, and are deemed to offer and accept the terms of the relationship.

> *Shanklin Pier Ltd v Detel Products 1951*
> *The facts*: the defendants gave assurances to the claimants that their paint would be satisfactory and durable. The claimants in their contract with X and Co for the repainting of the pier, specified that X and Co should use this paint. The paint proved very unsatisfactory and the remedial work cost £4,127. The claimants sued the defendants for breach of contract. The defendants argued that there was no contract between the claimants and themselves.
>
> *Decision:* the contract between the claimants and X and Co requiring the use of the defendants' paint (to be purchased and supplied by X and Co) was the consideration for a contract between the claimants and the defendant, by which the latter guaranteed that their paint was of the quality described.

10.3 No coincidence of offer and acceptance

An interesting Court of Appeal case looks as if it might have re-opened a debate on whether there must be a matching offer and acceptance.

> *G Percy Trentham Ltd v Archital Luxfer Ltd 1993*
> *The facts*: the claimants were main contractors on a building contract. They entered into negotiations with the defendant for supply and installation of doors and windows. When the work was completed and paid for, they tried to recover a contribution towards a penalty which they had to pay under the main contract. The defendants denied that any binding contract had ever been formed. Although there had been exchanges of letters and telephone calls, there was no matching offer and acceptance and no clear agreement as to whose standard terms governed the contract.
>
> *Decision*: there was a valid and binding contract. This was a case of acceptance by conduct evidenced by the defendant's carrying out of the work in acceptance of the claimants' offer. The fact that performance had taken place was of significance.

Note that the issue here was simply whether a contract had come into existence and not the time at which it arose or the terms on which it arose. These are added complications which future cases might address.

Chapter roundup

- The three essential components of a contract are offer and acceptance, consideration and the intention of the parties to create legal relations
- A void contract is one which has no legal effect at any time: neither party can obtain rights or obligations under it
- A voidable contract is one which is valid unless and until it is avoided
- An unenforceable contract is one which is valid but which cannot be enforced by either of the parties should something go wrong
- Certain types of contract must be made by deed (for example the conveyance of land) in writing (for example consumer credit contracts) or evidenced in writing (for example guarantees)
- The first essential element of a binding contract is agreement. This is usually evidenced by offer and acceptance.
- An offer is a definite promise to be bound on specific terms, and must be distinguished from the mere supply of information and from an invitation to treat.
- Acceptance must be unqualified agreement to all the terms of the offer. It may be by express words or inferred from conduct. Inaction does not imply acceptance.
- A counter-offer is a rejection of the original offer.
- Acceptance is not effective until communicated to the offeror, with two exceptions.
  - The offeror may waive the need for communication of acceptance by making an offer to the entire world.
  - He may indicate that he expects acceptance through the post.
- In the latter case, the 'postal rule' applies: acceptance is complete and effective as soon as notice of it is posted.
- An offer is terminated, and no longer open for acceptance, in the following circumstances.
  - Rejection by the offeree
  - Lapse of time
  - Revocation by the offeror
  - Failure of a condition to which the offer was subject
  - Death of one of the parties.
- In certain circumstances, the courts may construct a contract where the formalities of offer and acceptance have not taken place.
- A **collateral contract** is a contract for which the consideration is the making of some other contract.

Quick quiz

1 What is a standard form contract?

2 What are the three essentials of a valid contract?

3 Define void, voidable and unenforceable contracts.

4 Give two examples of contracts which must be in writing.

NOTES

5 What case illustrates the principle that an offer may be made to the world at large?

6 What is an invitation to treat?

7 What happens when an offeree accepts an offer but applies different terms to it?

8 What does the postal rule say?

9 Can a third party communicate revocation of an offer?

10 What is a collateral contract?

Answers to quick quiz

1 Contract produced by large companies setting at compulsory terms. (see para 2.2)

2 Intention to create legal relations

- Offer and acceptance
- Consideration (para 3.1)

3 (a) A **void** contract is **not a contract** at all. The parties are not bound by it and if they transfer property under it they can sometimes (unless it is also an illegal contract) recover their goods even from a third party.

For example, A sells goods to B, who sells them on to C. B then fails to pay A for the goods and disappears without trace. If A can demonstrate that he was genuinely mistaken as to the identity of B and would not have dealt with him had he known who B really was, then A can recover the goods which were subject to the original contract from C. This is because the law takes the view in such a situation that the original contract between A and B was no contract at all and of no effect.

Therefore C, who was an innocent third party acting in good faith, has to return the goods to A and either bear the loss or find and sue B.

(b) A **voidable** contract is a **contract which one party may avoid**, that is terminate at his option. The contract is treated as valid unless and until it is avoided. Property transferred before avoidance is usually irrecoverable from a third party.

For example A sells goods to B on 1st June. On 8th June B sells them onto C. On 10th June, it is discovered that B had made a misrepresentation in the original contract between A and B and A seeks to recover the goods. Given these dates, A cannot do so, as the goods have been sold on to C *before* A tries to avoid the original contract, and at the time that B sells them he (B) still has good title.

If on the other hand, B did not sell the goods on to C until 12th June, which is after A seeks to avoid the original contract with B, that original contract has already been avoided, and B would not be able to pass good title on to C.

(c) An **unenforceable** contract is a **valid contract** and property transferred under it cannot be recovered even from the other party to the contract. If either party refuses to perform the contract, the other party cannot compel him to do so. A contract is usually

BPP PUBLISHING

unenforceable when the required evidence of its terms, for example, written evidence of a contract relating to land, is not available. Unenforceable contracts are only problematic if a dispute over the contract arises. (para 3.3)

4 Transfer of shares
Exchange of contracts on land (para 4.2)

5 Carlill v Carbolic Smokeball Co. 1893. (para 6.2)

6 An indication that someone is prepared to receive offers. (para 6.5)

7 A new offer is created which can be either accepted or rejected. (para 7.3)

8 The acceptance is effective as seen as it is posted, as long as the post is the expected means of communication. (para 8.3)

9 Yes, as long as he is reliable. (para 9.3)

10 A contract for which the consideration is the making of another contract. (para 10.2)

Answers to activities

1 When she used the medicine and caught influenza. This was acceptance of the offer which, because it was to the entire world, had dispensed with the need for communication of acceptance. The answer is C.

2 A price label is an invitation to treat (*Fisher v Bell 1961*) ie an invitation to the customer to make an offer which the shop can either accept or reject.

3 No. By introducing the payment terms, Barry has rejected Mike's original offer and made a counter-offer to buy the car for £5,000 but pay over five months. Mike is free to accept or reject this, and by selling to Catherine, rejects Barry's offer.

4 Cocker can enforce the contract. The post is seen as the means of acceptance and, following the postal rule, Cocker has accepted. There is a contract.

Assignment 1 **(30 minutes)**

Acceptance

'An acceptance in the law of contract involves an unconditional assent to the terms of the offer.'

Discuss.

Chapter 4 :
CONSIDERATION

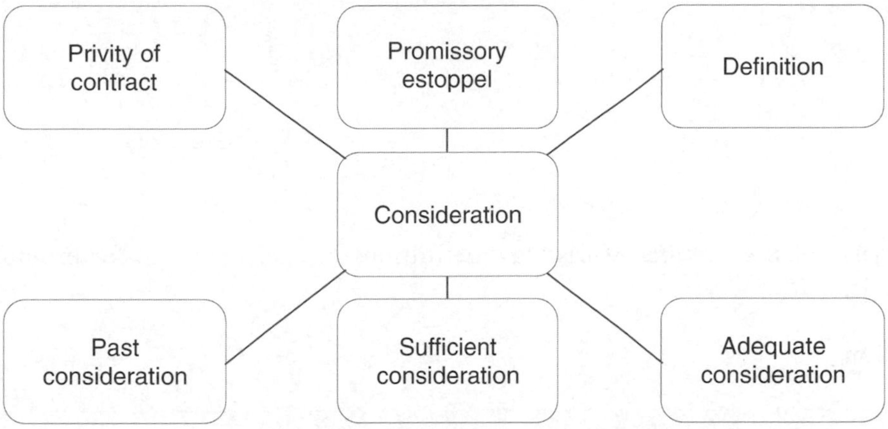

Introduction

Consideration is one of the three essential elements of a binding contract. The principle is that the parties to a contract must each provide something, whether money, the provision of a service or some other form of contribution to the contract. A contractual promise is one which is not purely gratuitous. If a window cleaner telephones you and promises as a special promotion to clean your windows tomorrow for free, but then fails to turn up, you cannot sue him for breach of contract. This is because there is no contract, because you have provided no consideration.

However, a contract made by deed, covered in the previous chapter, does not require consideration in order to be binding. For example, if you make a deed of covenant in favour of a charity, the charity does not have to supply anything in return for the contract to be binding. Gifts can be made by deed with no consideration from the recipient, and still be legally binding.

Your objectives

In this chapter you will learn about the following.

(a) The nature of consideration

(b) The rules governing past consideration

(c) The rules governing adequacy of consideration

(d) The rules governing sufficiency of consideration

(e) The rules governing the doctrine of promissory estoppel

(f) The rule of privity of contract

1 THE NATURE OF CONSIDERATION

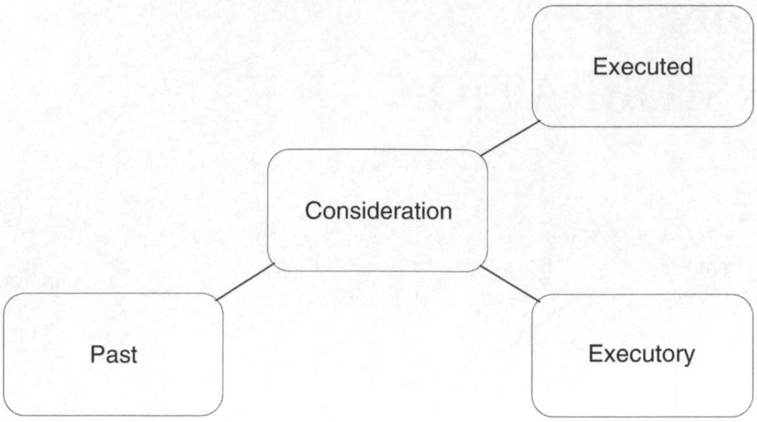

There have been a number of case law definitions of consideration, for example from *Currie v Misa 1875*

Definition

> 'A valuable **consideration** in the sense of the law may consist either in some right, interest, profit or benefit accruing to one party, or some forbearance, detriment, loss or responsibility given, suffered or undertaken by the other.'

Using the language of purchase and sale, it could be said that one party must know that he has bought the other party's promises either by performing some **act** of his own or by offering a **promise** of his own. Consideration has also been described as 'the price of the other person's promise'.

2 EXECUTORY, EXECUTED AND PAST CONSIDERATION

It is sometimes said that valid consideration may be **executed** or **executory**, but it **cannot be past**. These terms are explained below.

2.1 Executed consideration

Definition

> **Executed consideration** is a performed, or executed, act in return for a promise.

If, for example, A offers a reward for the return of lost property, his promise becomes binding when B performs the act of returning A's property to him. The claimant's act in Carlill's case in response to the smoke ball company's promise of reward was thus executed consideration.

2.2 Executory consideration

Definition

> **Executory consideration** is a promise given for a promise, not a performed act.

If, for example, a customer orders goods which a shopkeeper undertakes to obtain from the manufacturer, the shopkeeper promises to supply the goods and the customer promises to accept and pay for them. It would be breach of contract if either withdrew without the consent of the other.

2.3 Past consideration

Both executed and executory consideration are provided at the time when the promise is given.

Definition

> Anything which has already been done before a promise in return is given is **past consideration** which, as a general rule, is not sufficient to make the promise binding.

Re McArdle 1951

The facts: under the terms of a will, children were entitled to a house after their mother's death. In the mother's lifetime one of the sons and his wife lived in the house with the mother. The wife made improvements to the house. The children later agreed in writing to repay to the wife the sum of £488 'in consideration of your carrying out certain alterations and improvements' to the property. At the mother's death they refused to do so.

Decision: the work on the house had been completed before the documents were signed. At the time of the promise the improvements were past consideration.

If there is an existing contract and one party makes a further promise, no contract will arise.

Roscorla v Thomas 1842

The facts: the claimant agreed to buy a horse from the defendant at a given price. When negotiations were over and the contract was formed, the defendant told the claimant that the horse was 'sound and free from vice'. The horse turned out to be vicious and the claimant brought an action on the warranty.

Decision: the express promise was made after the sale was over and was unsupported by fresh consideration.

2.4 Exceptions to the doctrine of past consideration

In three cases past consideration for a promise can make the promise binding.

(a) Past consideration is sufficient to create liability on a **bill of exchange** (such as a cheque) under s 27 Bills of Exchange Act 1882.

(b) After six (or in some cases twelve) years the right to sue for recovery of a debt becomes statute barred by the **Limitation Act 1980**. If, after that period, the debtor makes written acknowledgement of the creditor's claim, the claim is again enforceable at law. The debt, although past consideration, suffices.

(c) When a request is made for a service this **request may imply a promise** to pay for it. If, after the service has been rendered, the person who made the request promises a specific reward, this is treated as fixing the amount to be paid under the previous implied promise.

Lampleigh v Braithwait 1615
The facts: the defendant had killed a man and had asked the claimant to obtain for him a royal pardon. The claimant did so, 'riding and journeying to and from London and Newmarket' at his own expense. The defendant then promised to pay him £100. He failed to pay it and was sued.

Decision: the defendant's request was regarded as containing an implied promise to pay, and the subsequent promise merely fixed the amount.

The third exception above has been somewhat revised by the courts, so that both parties must have assumed throughout their negotiations that the services were ultimately to be paid for.

Re Casey's Patents 1892
The facts: A and B, joint owners of patent rights, asked their employee, C, as an extra task to find licensees to work the patents. After C had done so, A and B agreed to reward him for his past services with one third of the patent rights. A died and his executors denied that the promise made was binding.

Decision: the promise to C was binding since it fixed the 'reasonable remuneration' which A and B by implication promised to pay before the service was given.

Activity 1 **(10 minutes)**

Which of the following is valid consideration?

(a) An action six months ago for which the person who carried it out is now demanding payment.

(b) A promise to pay for goods in six months time.

(c) A request to someone to clean your windows.

3 CONSIDERATION MUST MOVE FROM THE PROMISEE

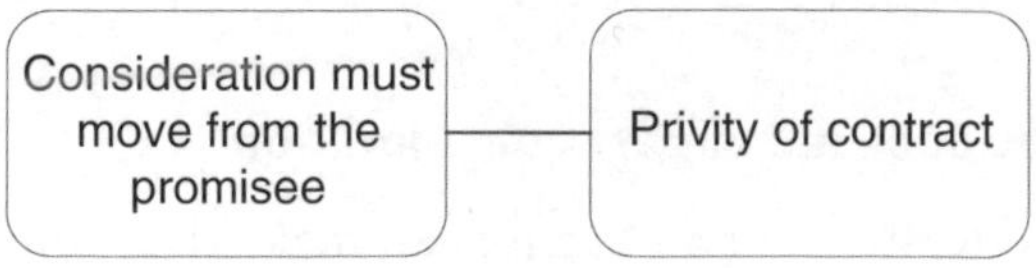

3.1 The rule of privity of contract

This is a critical rule in contract law, and reflects the fact that consideration is essential. If you don't provide consideration, you cannot sue on the contract.

This maxim means that **only the person who has paid the price of a contract can sue on it.** If, for example, A promises B that (for a consideration provided by B) A will confer a benefit on C, then C cannot as a general rule enforce A's promise.

> *Tweddle v Atkinson 1861*
> *The facts*: the claimant married the daughter of G. On the occasion of the marriage, the claimant's father and G exchanged promises that they would each pay a sum of money to the claimant. The agreement between the two fathers expressly provided that the claimant should have enforceable rights against them. G died without making the promised payment and the claimant sued G's executor for the specified amount.
>
> *Decision*: the claimant had provided no consideration for G's promise. In spite of the express terms of the agreement he had no enforceable rights under it and was not therefore "privy to the contract".

In *Tweddle's* case each father as promisee gave consideration by his promise to the other, but the claimant was to be the beneficiary of each promise. Each father could have sued the other but the claimant could not sue.

The rule that consideration must move from the promisee overlaps with the rule that only a party to a contract can enforce it. Together these rules are known as the principles of **privity of contract**. This principle is discussed later in this chapter.

4 ADEQUACY OF CONSIDERATION

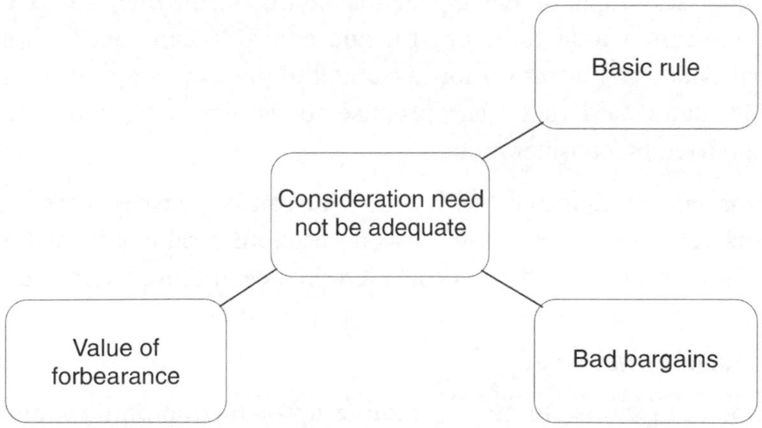

The law says that consideration need not be adequate. This means that the consideration need not be of equal value to the parties to the contract, but it must be of some value to the parties involved. This does not have to be financial or monetary value, although obviously in many contracts it often is. In a basic contract for the sale of goods, one party will provide money as his consideration, and the other party will provide the goods.

4.1 Illustration of the rule

Chappell & Co v Nestle Co Ltd

The facts: The defendants made a special offer, whereby if people collected three wrappers from Nestle bars of chocolate and then sent them in with a small sum of money, they could get a copy of a record called 'Rockin' Shoes'. The case arose because the claimants owned the copyright to the music and the two parties were trying to calculate the amount of royalties payable to Chappell, on the basis of the value of the records. The argument hinged on whether the wrappers, which were merely thrown away on receipt by Nestle, constituted part of the consideration and therefore should be included in the royalty calculation.

Decision: The defendants had required that wrappers were sent in as part of the special offer, for obvious commercial reasons. It was held that the wrappers were part of the consideration as they had commercial value in the eyes of Nestle, one of the parties to the contract.

4.2 No protection against a bad bargain

The courts have always made it clear that parties to a contract are expected to look after themselves, and the courts will not protect them if all they have done is made a 'bad bargain' and accepted inadequate consideration. Therefore, if someone sells their car, worth £10,000, for £2,000, they cannot expect the courts to step in, unless there has been some element of fraud or misrepresentation, which are discussed later in the book.

The courts will not seek to weigh up the comparative values of the promises.

Thomas v Thomas 1842

The facts: by his will the claimant's husband expressed the wish that his widow should have the use of his house during her life. The defendants allowed the widow to occupy the house (a) in accordance with her husband's wishes and (b) in return for her undertaking to pay a rent of £1 per annum. They later said that their promise to let her occupy the house was not supported by consideration.

Decision: compliance with the husband's wishes was not valuable consideration (because there was no economic value attached to it), but the nominal rent was sufficient consideration, even though inadequate as a rent.

4.3 The value of forbearance

Forbearance, or the promise to give something up or to stop doing something, can be adequate consideration, if it has some value or amounts to giving up something of value. For example, a contract in which one party promises to give up smoking would probably have adequate consideration.

However, although consideration need not be adequate it must be *sufficient*, which is discussed in the following section.

NOTES

5 SUFFICIENCY OF CONSIDERATION

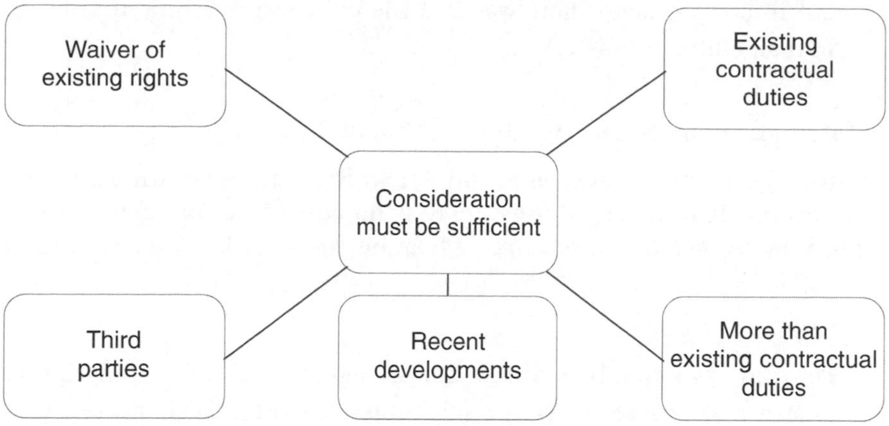

The term *sufficiency of consideration* means that the consideration must be something more than the party involved was already intended to do. It must be deemed actually to be consideration. For example the performance of an existing legal duty cannot be regarded as consideration, as the person involved would be going to do it anyway.

5.1 Performance of existing contractual duties

Performance of an **existing obligation** imposed by statute is **no consideration** for a promise of reward.

> *Collins v Godefroy 1831*
> *The facts*: the claimant had been subpoenaed (ie summoned to court) to give evidence on behalf of the defendant in another case. He alleged that the defendant had promised to pay him six guineas for appearing.
>
> *Decision*: there was no consideration for this promise, as the claimant was obliged to appear by law.

But if some extra service is given that is sufficient consideration.

> *Glasbrook Bros v Glamorgan CC 1925*
> *The facts*: at a time of industrial unrest, colliery owners, rejecting the view of the police that a mobile force was enough, asked and agreed to pay for a special guard on the mine. Later they repudiated liability saying that the police had done no more than perform their public duty of maintaining order.
>
> *Decision*: the extra services given, beyond what the police in their discretion deemed necessary, were consideration for the promise to pay. If the judgement of the police authorities had been that a special guard was necessary, they would not have been entitled to charge for it.

Where one party's actions lead to the need for heightened police presence, and the police deem this presence necessary, they may also be entitled to payment.

> *Harris v Sheffield United F.C. Ltd 1988*
> *The facts*: the defendants argued that they did not have to pay for a large police presence at their home matches.

Decision: they had voluntarily decided to hold matches on Saturday afternoons when large attendances were likely, increasing the risk of disorder. (An important factor here was that the police were required to be inside the football club's premises.)

5.2 Performance of more than existing contractual duties

If there is already a contract between A and B, and B promises additional reward to A if he (A) will perform his **existing duties**, there is **no consideration** from A to make that promise binding. A assumes no extra obligation and B obtains no extra rights or benefits.

Stilk v Myrick 1809
The facts: two members of the crew of a ship deserted in a foreign port. The master was unable to recruit substitutes and promised the rest of the crew that they should share the wages of the deserters if they would complete the voyage home short-handed. The shipowners however repudiated the promise.

Decision: in performing their existing contractual duties the crew gave no consideration for the promise of extra pay and the promise was not binding. The lack of two crew members did not mean that the remaining crew were doing more than their existing duty.

If a claimant does **more** than perform an existing contractual duty, this **may amount to consideration.**

Hartley v Ponsonby 1857
The facts: 17 men out of a crew of 36 deserted. The remainder were promised an extra £40 each to work the ship to Bombay. The claimant, one of the remaining crew-members, sued to recover this amount.

Decision: the large number of desertions made the voyage hazardous, and this had the effect of discharging the original contract. The claimant had a new contract, under which his promise to complete the voyage formed consideration for the promise to pay an additional £40.

5.3 Recent developments

The courts appear to be taking a slightly different line in recent years on the payment of additional consideration.

Williams v Roffey Bros & Nicholls (Contractors) Ltd 1990
The facts: the claimants agreed to do carpentry work for the defendants, who were engaged as contractors to refurbish a block of flats, at a fixed price of £20,000. The work ran late and so the defendants, concerned that the job might not be finished on time and that they would have to pay under a penalty clause in the main contract, agreed to pay the claimants an extra £10,300 to ensure the work was completed on time. They later refused to pay the extra amount.

Decision: the fact that there was no apparent consideration for the promise to pay the extra was not held to be important, and in the court's view both parties derived benefit from the promise. The telling point was that the defendants' promise had not been extracted by duress or fraud: it was therefore binding.

Re Selectmove 1994
The facts: a company which was the subject of a winding-up order offered to settle its outstanding debts by instalment. An Inland Revenue inspector agreed to this proposal. The company tried to enforce it.

Decision: despite the verdict in *Williams v Roffey Bros & Nicholls*, the court followed *Foakes v Beer* (see below) in holding that an agreement to pay in instalments is unenforceable.

5.4 Performance of existing contractual duty to a third party

If A promises B a reward if B will perform his existing contract with C, there is consideration for A's promise since he has obtained a benefit to which he previously had no right, and B assumes new obligations.

Shadwell v Shadwell 1860
The facts: the claimant, a barrister, was engaged to marry E (an engagement to marry was at this time a binding contract). His uncle promised the claimant that if he married E (as he did), the uncle would during their joint lives pay £150 p.a. until such time as the nephew was earning 600 guineas p.a. at the bar (which never transpired). The uncle died after eighteen years owing six annual payments. The claimant claimed the arrears from his uncle's executors, who denied that there was consideration for the promise.

Decision: the nephew had provided consideration as he was initially under a duty only to his fiancée, but by entering into the agreement he had put himself under obligation to the uncle too.

Activity 2 **(15 minutes)**

Which of the following is true of consideration?

(a) It must be of adequate and sufficient value.
(b) It must move from the promisee.
(c) It must never be past.
(d) It must be given in every binding agreement.
(e) It may be performance of an existing obligation.

5.5 Waiver of existing rights

Particular complications arise over sufficiency of consideration for promises to **waive existing rights**, especially regarding rights to common law debts.

If X owes Y £100 but Y agrees to accept a lesser sum, say £80, in full settlement of Y's claim, that is a promise by Y to waive his entitlement to the balance of £20. The promise, like any other, should be supported by consideration.

Foakes v Beer 1884
The facts: the defendant had obtained judgement against the claimant for the sum of £2,091. Judgement debts bear interest from the date of the judgement.

By a written agreement the defendant agreed to accept payment by instalments of the sum of £2,091, no mention being made of the interest. Once the claimant had paid the amount of the debt in full, the defendant claimed interest, claiming that the agreement was not supported by consideration.

Decision: she was entitled to the debt with interest. No consideration had been given by the claimant for waiver of any part of her rights against him.

5.6 Exceptions to the rule

There are, however, exceptions to the rule that the debtor (denoted by 'X' in the following paragraphs) must give consideration if the waiver is to be binding. These exceptions concern variation of the original contract terms.

(a) If X offers and Y accepts anything to which Y is not already entitled, the extra thing will be sufficient consideration for the waiver. This may be for example

- (i) goods instead of cash: *Anon 1495*; or
- (ii) payment before the date payment is due: *Pinnel's case 1602.*

(b) If X arranges with a number of creditors that they will each accept part payment in full settlement, that is a bargain between the creditors. X has given no consideration but he can hold the creditors individually to the agreed terms: *Wood v Robarts 1818.*

(c) If a third party (Z) offers part payment and Y agrees to release X from Y's claim to the balance, Y has received consideration from Z against whom he had no previous claim: *Welby v Drake 1825.*

(d) The principle of **promissory estoppel** may prevent Y from retracting his promise with retrospective effect.

> **Activity 3** **(10 minutes)**
>
> Hugo agreed to drive his friend Laurence (a nervous passenger) to Cardiff. He said that if Laurence paid him £25, he would not exceed the speed limit on the motorway. Is this promise enforceable?

6 PROMISSORY ESTOPPEL

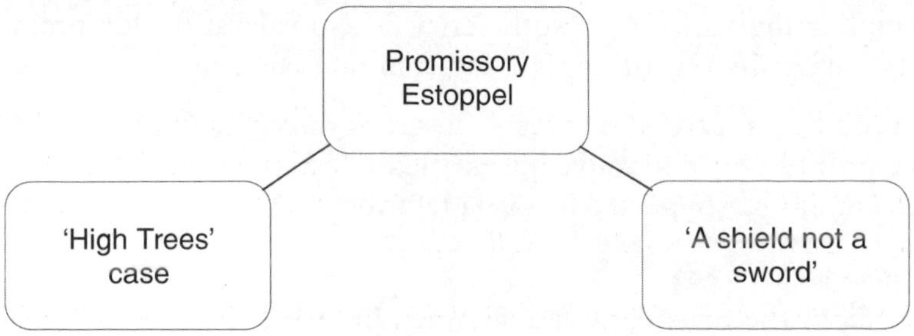

The equitable concept of **promissory estoppel** operates to prevent a person rescinding (ie going back on) his promise to accept a lesser amount. He cannot retract his waiver with retrospective effect, though it may permit him to insist on full rights in the future.

6.1 The 'High Trees' case

Central London Property Trust v High Trees House 1947
The facts: in September 1939, the claimants let a block of flats to the defendants at an annual rent of £2,500 p.a. It was difficult to let the individual flats in wartime, so in January 1940, the claimants agreed in writing to accept a reduced rent of £1,250 p.a. No time limit was set on the arrangement but it was clearly related to wartime conditions. The reduced rent was paid from 1940 to 1945 and the defendants sublet flats during the period on the basis of their expected liability to pay rent under the head lease at £1,250 only. In 1945 the flats were fully let. The claimants demanded a full rent of £2,500 p.a., both retrospectively and for the future. They tested this claim by suing for rent at the full rate for the last two quarters of 1945.

Decision: the agreement of January 1940 was a temporary expedient only and had ceased to operate early in 1945. The claim was upheld. However, had the claimants sued for arrears for the period 1940-1945, the 1940 agreement would have served to defeat the claim.

Definition

Estoppel operates when a person, by his words or conduct, leads another to believe that a certain state of affairs exists. If the other person, relying on that belief, alters his position to his detriment, the first person is **estopped** (prevented) from claiming later that a different state of affairs existed.

6.2 A 'shield not a sword'

In the *High Trees* case, if the defendants had sued on the promise, they would have failed for want of consideration. The principle is '**a shield not a sword**', ie it is a defence, which does not create new rights.

Combe v Combe 1951
The facts: a wife obtained a divorce. Her ex-husband promised that he would make maintenance payments of £100 per annum. The wife did not apply to the court for an order for maintenance, but this forbearance was not at the husband's request. No maintenance was paid and the wife sued on the promise. In the High Court the wife obtained judgement on the basis of the principle of promissory estoppel. The ex-husband appealed.

Decision: The Court of Appeal said that promissory estoppel 'does not create new causes of action where none existed before. It only prevents a party from insisting on his strict legal rights when it would be unjust to allow him to enforce them'. The wife's claim failed.

From this it can be seen that promissory estoppel applies only to a voluntary waiver of existing rights.

D and C Builders v Rees 1966

The facts: the defendants owed £482 to the claimants. The claimants, who were in acute financial difficulties, reluctantly agreed to accept £300 in full settlement. They later claimed the balance.

Decision: the debt must be paid in full. Promissory estoppel only applies to a promise voluntarily given. The defendants had been aware of and had exploited the claimants' difficulties. In this important case it was also held that payment by cheque (instead of in cash) is normal and gives no extra advantage which could be treated as consideration for the waiver under the rule in *Pinnel's case.*

6.3 Summary

Promissory estoppel is one of the most complex legal doctrines you will encounter in this book. In summary, three elements are required if promissory estoppel is to apply:

(a) a waiver of rights by one of the parties to the contract
(b) the other party must rely on that waiver to some extent
(c) some special or unusual circumstances must apply

These three components can be clearly illustrated by the *High Trees* case, as follows.

(a) Central London Property trust waived their right to the full rent while subletting was difficult

(b) High Trees relied on that waiver by in turn reducing the rents charged to their tenants

(c) the situation arose because of the war: an unusual set of circumstances

7 PRIVITY OF CONTRACT

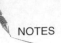

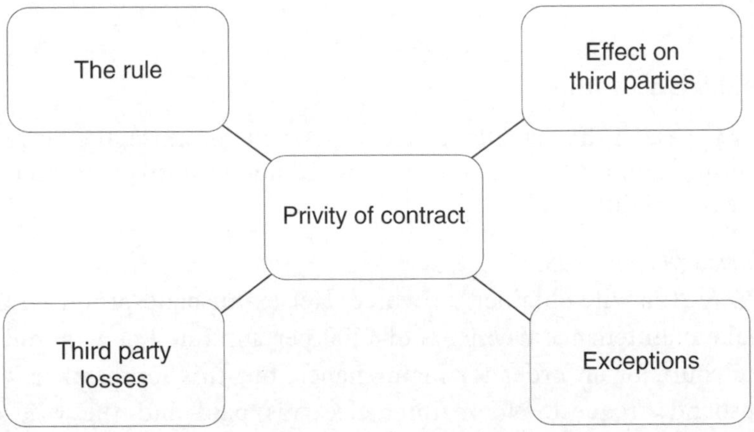

No-one may be entitled to or bound by the terms of a contract to which he is not an original party. A person is regarded as a party to the contract if he provides consideration.

7.1 The rule

As a general rule, only a person who is a party to a contract has enforceable rights or obligations under it. The following is the leading case in this area:

Dunlop v Selfridge 1915
The facts: the claimant, a tyre manufacturer, supplied tyres to X, a distributor, on terms that X would not re-sell the tyres at less than the prescribed retail price. If X sold the tyres wholesale to trade customers, X must impose a similar condition on those buyers to observe minimum retail prices (such clauses were legal at the time though prohibited since 1964 by the Resale Prices Act). X resold tyres on these conditions to the defendant. Under the terms of the contract between X and Selfridge, Selfridge was to pay to the claimant a sum of £5 per tyre if it sold tyres to customers below the minimum retail price. They sold tyres to two customers at less than the minimum price. The claimant sued to recover £5 per tyre as liquidated damages.

Decision: the claimant could not recover damages under a contract (between X and Selfridge) to which it was not a party.

Definition

> **Privity of contract** is the relation between the two parties to a contract. Third parties who are not privy to the contract generally have no right of action. This is true even if they receive benefits under it.

7.2 Effect on third parties

In these circumstances the party to the contract who imposes the condition or obtains a promise of a benefit for a third party can usually enforce it, but damages cannot be recovered on the third party's behalf unless the contracting party is suing an agent or trustee. Only nominal damages can be given if the contract was only for a third party's benefit. Other remedies may be sought however.

Beswick v Beswick 1968
The facts: X transferred his business to the defendant, his nephew, in consideration for a pension of £6.10s per week and, after his death, a weekly annuity to X's widow. Only one such annuity payment was made. The widow brought an action against the nephew, asking for an order of specific performance. She sued both as administratrix of her husband's estate and in her personal capacity as recipient.

Decision: as her husband's representative, the widow was successful in enforcing the contract for a third party's (her own) benefit. In her personal capacity she could derive no right of action.

7.3 Exception to the third party rule

Where the contract is one which provides something for the enjoyment of both the contracting party and third parties, such as a family holiday, the contracting party may be entitled to recover damages for his loss of the benefit: *Jackson v Horizon Holidays Ltd 1975*. If the contract is broken and the claimant seeks damages on the other parties' behalf he can also recover for the loss suffered by those other people: *Woodar Investment Development Ltd v Wimpey Construction (UK) Ltd 1980*.

7.4 Exceptions to the rule of privity of contract

There are a number of real or apparent exceptions to the general rule of privity of contract.

(a) *Implied trusts*

Equity may hold that an implied trust has been created.

Gregory and Parker v Williams 1817
The facts: P owed money to G and W. He agreed with W to transfer his property to W if W would pay his (P's) debt to G. The property was transferred, but W refused to pay G. G could not sue on the contract between P and W.

Decision: P could be regarded as a trustee for G, and G would therefore bring an action jointly with P.

(b) *Statutory exceptions*

(i) There are statutory exceptions which permit a person injured in a road accident to claim against the **motorist's insurers** (Road Traffic Act 1972) and which permit husband or wife to **insure his or her own life** for the benefit of the other under a trust which the beneficiary can enforce (Married Woman's Property Act 1882). A recent Law Commission Report (1996) has proposed that third parties should be able to enforce contracts entered into for their benefit (for example a person who has a present bought for them which turns out to be faulty).

(ii) The Landlord and Tenant (Covenants) Act 1996 abolishes privity of contract in relation to **leases** entered into after 1 January 1996. This means that the original lessee no longer takes responsibility for obligations under the lease when an assignee fails to comply.

(c) *Agency*

(i) In normal circumstances the **agent** discloses to a third party with whom he contracts that he is acting for a principal whose identity is also disclosed. The agent has no liability under the contract and no right to enforce it.

(ii) If a person enters into a contract apparently on his own account but in fact as agent on behalf of a principal, the doctrine of the **undisclosed principal** determines the position of the parties. An undisclosed principal may adopt a contract made for him by an agent. Until such time as the principal takes this action, the agent himself may sue the third party.

(d) *Covenants*

A restrictive covenant may run with land.

Tulk v Moxhay 1848
The facts: the claimant owned several plots of land in Leicester Square. He sold one to X, who agreed not to build on it, but to preserve it in its existing condition. It was sold on, eventually being purchased by the defendant, who, although he was aware of the restriction, proposed to build on it. The claimant sought an injunction.

Decision: the injunction was granted.

(e) *Assignment*

(i) A party to a contract can **assign** or transfer to another person **the rights** contained in the contract. He cannot assign the burden of his contractual **obligations**.

(ii) A legal assignment must be absolute, it must be in writing, and notice must be given to the other party: s 136 Law of Property Act 1925. It is **not possible** to assign:

(1) a **right of action**, which is a claim for unliquidated damages for breach of contract;

(2) **rights which are personal** to the original parties to the contract.

Kemp v Baerselman 1906
The facts: the defendant contracted to supply to the claimant, a cake manufacturer, all the eggs which the latter might require over a period of a year. During the year the manufacturer sold his business to a much larger concern (the National Bakery Company) and purported as part of the sale to assign the benefit of the egg supply agreement.

Decision: the assignment was invalid since the assignee's requirements were much larger and the supplier's right to supply all the assignor's requirements became valueless.

Activity 4 **(10 minutes)**

Julia arranges a party for her daughter Tamsin's 21st birthday, and books the band 'Mardi Gras'. On the day, the band fail to turn up and Tamsin is distraught. Who can sue them for breach of contract?

7.5 Loss arising for a third party

If it is foreseeable that damage caused by a breach of contract would cause a loss to a third party, the courts may find that damages can be claimed on behalf of that third party.

Linden Gardens trust Ltd v Lenesta Sludge Disposals Ltd 1994
The facts: the claimant and defendant entered into a contract for work to be carried out on a property which was soon to be sold to a third party. The work was defective, and the new owners (under the doctrine of privity) had no rights against the defendants because the contract had not been assigned to them.

Decision: the House of Lords held that under these circumstances the claimant should be able to claim full damages on behalf of the third party.

Although a party to a contract cannot escape from his contractual obligations by assignment, he may **delegate** performance to another person. But he remains liable if his substitute's performance is a breach of contract.

Chapter roundup

- 'A valuable consideration in the sense of the law may consist either in some right, interest, profit or benefit accruing to one party, or some forbearance, detriment, loss or responsibility given, suffered or undertaken by the other.' in Currie v Misa 1875.
- Consideration may be executed (an act in return for a promise) or executory (a promise in return for a promise). It may not be past, unless one of three recognised exceptions applies.
- Consideration need not be adequate, but it must be sufficient. This means that what is tendered as consideration must be capable in law of being regarded as consideration, but need not necessarily be equal in value to the consideration received in return (for example a peppercorn rent).
- The principle of promissory estoppel was developed in Central London Property Trust v High Trees House 1947.
- As a general rule, only a person who is a party to a contract has enforceable rights or obligations under it. This is the doctrine of privity of contract, as demonstrated in Dunlop v Selfridge 1915.

Quick quiz

1. What is executed consideration?
2. What is past consideration?
3. Give three situations where past consideration may make a promise binding.
4. Give the name of a case which illustrates the rule that consideration must move from the promisee.
5. What point of law is illustrated by Chappell & Co v Nestle Co 1960?
6. Summarise the facts of Stilk v Myrick 1809 and Hartley v Ponsonby 1857, showing the distinction between them.
7. List two situations in which a debtor need not give consideration for a creditor who promises to accept a lesser sum in full settlement of a debt to be bound by his promise.
8. What is the doctrine of promissory estoppel?
9. What is privity of contract?

Answers to quick quiz

1. An act which has been performed (executed) in return for a promise. (see para 2.1)
2. Anything which has been done before a promise is made to do something in return. (para 2.3)
3. Bills of exchange
   Elapse of time
   Request for services (para 2.4)
4. *Tweddle v Atkinson, 1861* (para 3.1)

5 Consideration need not be adequate. (para 4.1)

6 In Stilk v Myrick, 2 of the crew deserted, and the fact that the rest of the crew sailed the ship home was not sufficient consideration. In Hartley v Ponsonby, half of the crew deserted. The sailing home of the ship by the remainder **was** sufficient consideration for the wages promised. (5.2)

7 Part payment by a third party.

The offer of something different, eg goods instead of cash. (para 5.6)

8 It prevents someone going back on a promise to accept less consideration in certain circumstances. (para 6.1)

9 The rule that only the parties to a contract (ie those who provide consideration) may sue on it. (para 7.1)

Answers to activities

1 (b) and (c). (a) is not as consideration is past. (b) is executory consideration and (c) gives rise to an implied promise to pay, as in *Lampleigh v Braithwait 1615.*

2 (b) only. Consideration need only be sufficient, it need not be adequate (a). It can be past in limited circumstances (c). It need not be given in a contract by deed (d). Performance of an existing obligation cannot support a new contract (e) because there is no extra obligation.

3 No, as by keeping within the speed limit, Hugo is doing no more than his existing legal duty. He is not doing anything 'extra'.

4 Only Julia, as she was privy to the contract, while Tamsin is not.

Assignment 2 **(1 hour)**

Answer *both* parts of the following question, illustrating your answer from decided cases.

(a) 'Consideration in the English law of contract must be real, but need not be adequate.'

Discuss.

(b) Snowden organises a rock concert in a local field, complying with all relevant legal requirements. He is informed by the police that there will be a charge for the supervision of the crowds of people likely to be attracted to the event.

He goes ahead with the concert but, on the day of the event, the weather is exceptionally cold and only a small crowd attend. The police are now claiming their money for attending the concert, but Snowden is reluctant to pay because he says the police have only performed a public duty for which they are not entitled to payment.

Advise Snowden.

Chapter 5 :

INTENTION TO CREATE LEGAL RELATIONS AND THE CAPACITY TO CONTRACT

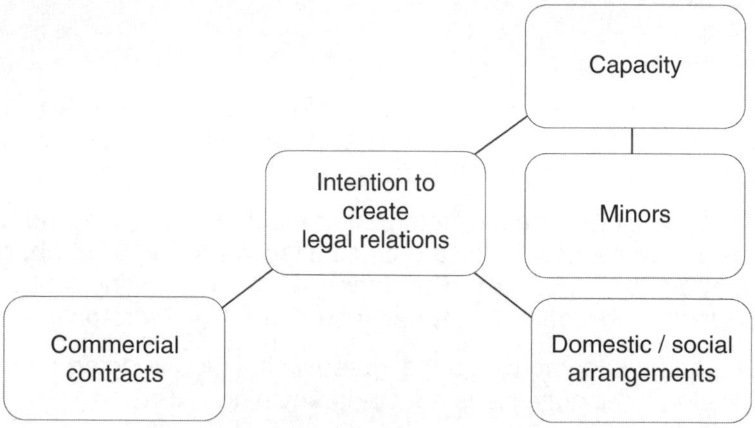

Introduction

An agreement is not a binding contract unless the parties intend to create legal relations. 'Legal relations' can be defined as the willingness to be bound by the terms of the contract. Where there is no express statement as to whether or not legal relations are intended (as may be said to be true of the majority of contracts), the courts apply one of two presumptions:

(a) Social, domestic and family arrangements are *not* usually intended by the parties involved to be binding;

(b) Commercial agreements *are* usually intended to be legally binding.

Your objectives

In this chapter you will learn about the following.

(a) The rules governing when spouses enter a contract with each other

(b) The rules governing commercial agreements

(c) The potential problems when minors enter a contract

NOTES

1 DOMESTIC ARRANGEMENTS

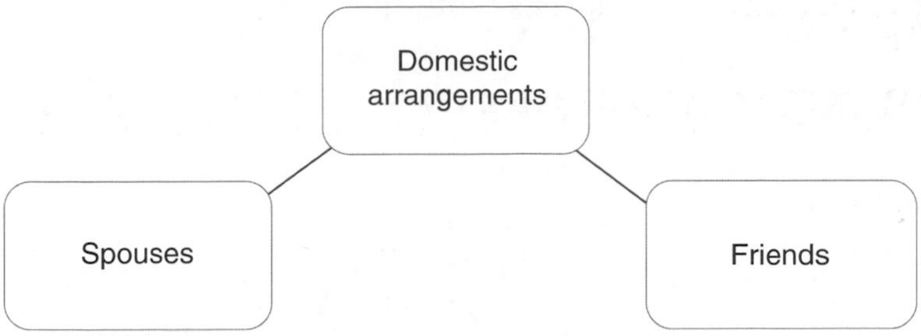

In most agreements no intention is expressly stated. If it is a domestic agreement between husband and wife, relatives or friends it is presumed that there is no intention to create legal relations unless the circumstances point to the opposite conclusion.

1.1 Spouses

However, where agreements between husband and wife or other relatives relate to property matters the courts are very ready to impute an intention to create legal relations.

Balfour v Balfour 1919
The husband was employed in Ceylon. He and his wife returned to the UK on leave but it was agreed that for health reasons she would not return to Ceylon with him. He promised to pay her £30 a month as maintenance. Later the marriage ended in divorce and the wife sued for the monthly allowance which the husband no longer paid.

Held: an informal agreement of indefinite duration made between husband and wife (whose marriage had not then broken up) was not intended to be legally binding.

Merritt v Merritt 1970
The husband had left the matrimonial home, which was owned in the joint name of husband and wife, to live with another woman. The spouses met and held a discussion in the husband's car in the course of which he agreed to pay her £40 a month out of which she agreed to keep up the mortgage payments on the house. The wife refused to leave the car until the husband signed a note of these agreed terms and an undertaking to transfer the house into her sole name when the mortgage had been paid off. The wife paid off the mortgage but the husband refused to transfer the house to her.

Held: in the circumstances, an intention to create legal relations was to be inferred and the wife could sue for breach of contract.

1.2 Other domestic arrangements

Domestic arrangements extend to those between people who are not related but who have a close relationship of some form. The nature of the agreement itself may lead to the conclusion that legal relations were intended.

Simpkins v Pays 1955
The defendant, her granddaughter and the claimant, a paying boarder, took part together in a weekly competition organised by a Sunday newspaper. The arrangements were informal and the entries were made in the grandmother's name. One week they won £750 but the paying boarder was denied a third share by the other two.

Held: there was a 'mutuality in the arrangements between the parties', amounting to a joint enterprise. As such it was not a 'friendly adventure' as the defendant claimed, but a contract.

2 COMMERCIAL AGREEMENTS

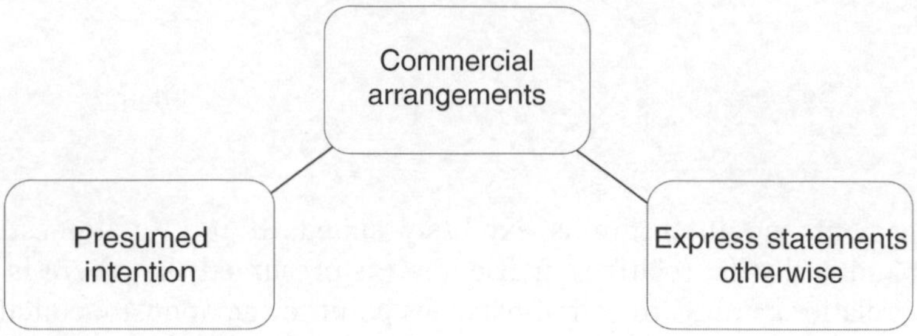

When businessmen enter into commercial agreements it is presumed that there is an intention to enter into legal relations unless this is expressly disclaimed or the circumstances displace that presumption. Any express statement by the parties of their intention not to make a binding contract is conclusive.

2.1 Rose and Frank v J R Crompton & Bros 1923

A commercial agreement by which the defendants (a British manufacturer) appointed the claimants to be their distributor in the USA expressly stated that it was 'not subject to legal jurisdiction' in either country. The defendants terminated the agreement without giving notice as required, and refused to deliver goods ordered by the claimants, although they had accepted these orders when placed.

Held: the general agreement was not legally binding, but the orders for goods were separate and binding contracts. The claim for damages for breach of the agreement failed, but the claim for damages for non-delivery of goods ordered succeeded.

2.2 Edwards v Skyways Ltd 1964

In negotiations over the terms for making an employee redundant, the employer undertook to make an ex gratia payment to him.

Held: although the defendants argued that the use of the phrase ex gratia showed no intention to create legal relations, this was a commercial arrangement and the burden of refuting the presumption of legal relations had not been discharged by them.

Procedural agreements between employers and trade unions for the settlement of disputes are not by their nature intended to give rise to legal relations in spite of their elaborate and very legal contents: s 179 Trade Union and Labour Relations (Consolidation) Act 1992.

Activity 1 **(10 minutes)**

A widow tells her adult son that he can stay at her house temporarily so long as he does his share of domestic chores. Consider whether there is likely to be a contract under which accommodation is supplied in return for housework. Give reasons for your answer.

3 CONTRACTUAL CAPACITY

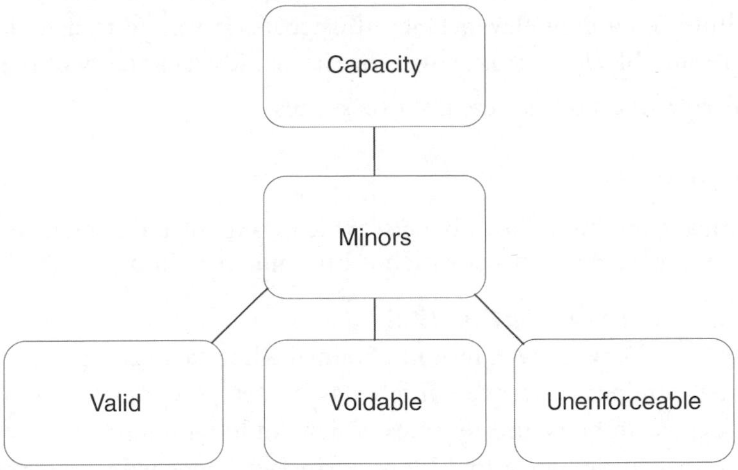

Capacity refers to the fact that the law regards some groups as being unable to enter into binding contractual arrangements, because they might not be in a position to fully understand the agreement they have entered into.

3.1 Minors

The legal capacity of minors (persons under the age of 18) is determined by the Minors' Contracts Act 1987. A contract between a minor and another party may be one of three types.

(a) A **valid** contract is binding in the usual way.

(b) A **voidable** contract is binding unless and until the minor rescinds the contract.

(c) An **unenforceable** contract is unenforceable against the minor unless he ratifies (adopts) it - but the other party is bound.

3.2 Valid contracts of a minor

Two sorts of contract are valid and binding on a minor: a contract for the supply of goods or services which are **necessaries**, and a **service contract** for the minor's benefit.

3.3 Necessaries

If goods or services which are necessaries are delivered to a minor under a contract made by him, he is bound to pay a reasonable price for them: s 3 Sale of Goods Act 1979. Necessaries are defined in s 3 Sale of Goods Act 1979 as goods or services **suitable** to the condition in life of the minor and to his **needs** at the time of sale and delivery.

(a) **Suitability** is measured by the living standards of the minor. Things may be necessaries even though they are luxurious in quality, if that is what the minor ordinarily uses. Food, clothing, professional advice and even a gold watch have been held to be necessaries.

(b) The second test is whether the minor requires the goods for the personal **needs** of himself (or his wife or child). Goods required for use in a trade are not necessaries, nor are goods of any kind if the minor is already well supplied with them.

Nash v Inman 1908

The facts: N was a Savile Row tailor who sued I on bills totalling £145 for clothes, including eleven fancy waistcoats. It was conceded that the clothes were suitable, but it was shown that he already had plenty of them.

Decision: the clothes were not necessaries.

3.4 Service contracts

A **service contract** for the minor's benefit which contains an element of education or training is the other type of contract which is binding on a minor.

Doyle v White City Stadium 1935

The facts: D, who was a minor, obtained a licence to compete as a professional boxer. Under his licence (which was treated as a contract of apprenticeship) he agreed to be bound by rules which could withhold his prize money if he was disqualified for a foul blow (as in fact happened). He asserted that the licence was a void contract since it was not for his benefit..

Decision: the licence enabled him to pursue a lucrative occupation. Despite the penal clause, it was beneficial as a whole.

3.5 Voidable contracts of a minor

A minor may enter into a contract by which he acquires an interest of a continuing nature. Such contracts are **voidable** by the minor during his minority and within a reasonable time after attaining his majority. If no such steps are taken, the contract is binding. Examples of voidable contracts are:

(a) Contracts concerning **land** - for example, leases.
(b) Purchases of **shares** in a company.
(c) **Partnership** agreements.

A contract of this type does not require any kind of ratification by the minor on his majority. It remains binding unless he **repudiates** it within a reasonable time.

Edwards v Carter 1893

The facts: A marriage settlement was made under which the father of the husband to be agreed to pay £1,500 per annum to the trustees. The husband to be, who was a minor at the time of the settlement, executed a deed under which all property which he might receive under his father's will would also be vested in the trustees. He attained his majority one month later, and three and a half years later his father died. A year after this, he repudiated the agreement.

Decision: the repudiation was too late and was ineffective.

The effect of repudiation is to relieve the minor of any contractual obligations arising after the repudiation. The key to liability or recovery of sums paid may well depend upon whether the minor received **consideration.**

Steinberg v Scala (Leeds) 1923

The facts: The claimant bought shares in the defendant company but repudiated the contract after paying some of the money. The company agreed to remove her name from the register of members but refused to refund her money.

Decision: the claimant had benefited from membership rights as consideration, and was not entitled to a refund.

3.6 Unenforceable contracts of a minor

All other contracts entered into by a minor are described as **unenforceable** - the minor is not bound (though he may ratify it) but the other party is bound.

Where a contract is voidable and is repudiated by the minor, or where it is unenforceable and is not ratified by the minor, any **guarantee** of the contract given by a capable (ie adult) person is still valid. In addition, a minor may be required to return property which he acquired under a repudiated or unenforceable contract.

A minor is generally liable for his **torts** (ie wrongful acts causing loss or damage to others). He will not, however, be liable if he commits a tort in procuring a contract which is not binding on him. If he were liable, the other party would effectively be able to enforce such a contract.

> *R Leslie Ltd v Sheill 1914*
> *The facts*: An infant obtained a loan of £400 by means of a fraudulent misstatement of his age.
>
> *Decision:* he could not be compelled to repay it, as this would constitute enforcement of the contract.

Activity 2 **(10 minutes)**

Would these contracts made by Arthur, aged 16, be valid and enforceable?

(a) A two month holiday staying in a 5 star hotel in Barbados.

(b) The purchase of shares in Amazon.com.

(c) The purchase of a pair of football boots which are compulsory for school.

(d) A partnership agreement with Tom, also aged 16, to establish a motor mechanic business.

Chapter roundup

- An agreement is not binding unless the parties intend to be bound by it.
- Legal relations are not normally intended in domestic situations (although there are exceptions to this).
- Legal relations are presumed to be intended in commercial agreements, unless clearly indicated otherwise.
- The only contracts entered into by a minor which are valid are those for necessary goods or services, and those for services for the minor's benefit.
- Some minors' contracts are voidable, so they are valid unless and until they are avoided.
- All others are unenforceable in that the minor is not bound, but the other party is
- Minors are generally liable for their own torts.

Quick quiz

1 Contrast *Balfour v Balfour* with *Merritt v Merritt* and explain why they had different outcomes

2 What general rule applies in commercial agreements?

3 What are the three categories of contracts entered into by a minor?

4 What sort of goods would be described as 'necessaries'?

5 What is the legal effect of a guarantee given by an adult person for the debts of a minor?

Answers to quick quiz

1 In Balfour v Balfour, the couple were still married at the time of the agreement, so it was not legally binding. In Merritt v Merritt, the couple were legally separating, so the agreement was legally binding. (see para 1.1)

2 They are presumed to be legally binding. (para 2.1)

3 Valid contracts
Voidable contracts
Unenforceable contracts (see para 3.1)

4 They must be suitable to his condition in life and needs at the time of sale and delivery. (see para 3.3)

5 It is valid. (para 3.6)

Answers to activities

1 No there is unlikely to be a contract, as in this domestic situation legal relations are unlikely to be intended.

2 (a) would only be valid if necessary: unlikely.
(b) is voidable.
(c) is valid and enforceable.
(d) is voidable.

Assignment 3 **(45 minutes)**

Explain whether the intention to create legal relations is an essential element in a binding contract.

Guidance notes

1 Social, domestic and family arrangements are assumed not to be legally binding unless the contrary is clearly shown.

2 Commercial agreements are assumed to be legally binding unless the contrary is clearly shown.

Chapter 6 :
TERMS AND EXCLUSION CLAUSES

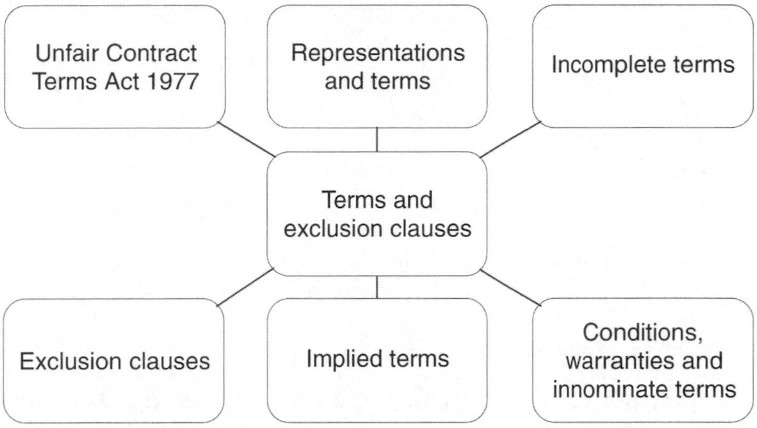

Introduction

As a general principle the parties may by their offer and acceptance include in their contract whatever terms they like, but certain legal rules apply and the law may modify these express terms in various ways.

(a) The terms must be sufficiently complete and precise to produce an agreement which can be binding. If they are vague there may be no contract.

(b) Statements made in the pre-contract negotiations may become *terms* of the contract or remain as *representations* to which different rules attach.

(c) The terms of the contract are usually classified as *conditions* or as *warranties* according to their importance.

(d) In addition to the express terms of the agreement, additional terms may be implied by law.

(e) Terms which exclude or restrict liability for breach of contract (exemption or exclusion clauses) are restricted in their effect or overridden by common law and statutory rules.

Your objectives

In this chapter you will learn about the following.

(a) The effects of incompleteness in the terms of a contract

(b) The distinction between representations and contract terms

(c) The concepts of condition, warranty and innominate term

(d) How terms may be implied into a contract

(e) The limitations on the effectiveness of exclusion clauses

(f) How exclusion clauses may fail to be effectively incorporated into a contract

(g) How exclusion clauses are interpreted

(h) The main provisions of the Unfair Contract Terms Act 1977

1 INCOMPLETE CONTRACTS

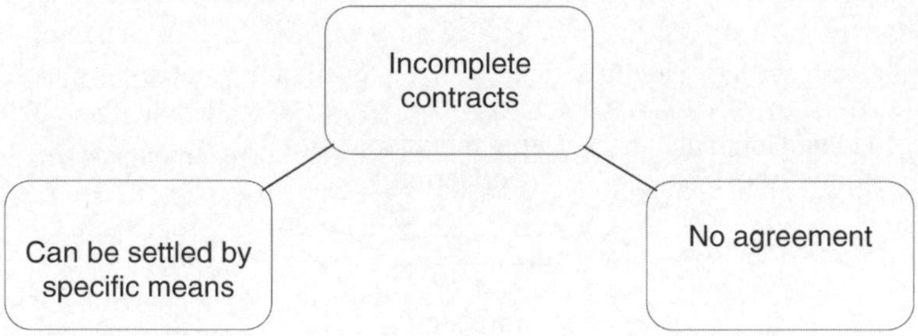

A legally binding agreement must be complete in its term otherwise there is no contract since the parties are still at the stage of negotiating the necessary terms.

> *Scammell v Ouston 1941*
>
> An agreement for the purchase of a van provided that the unpaid balance of the price should be paid over two years 'on hire purchase terms'.
>
> *Held:* there was no agreement since it was uncertain what terms of payment were intended. Hire purchase terms vary as to intervals between payments, interest charges to be added, and so on.

It is always possible for the parties to leave an essential term to be settled by specified means outside the contract. For example, it may be agreed to sell at the ruling open market price (if there is a market) on the day of delivery, or to invite an arbitrator to determine a fair price. The price may even be determined by the course of dealing between the parties: *Hillas & Co Ltd v Arcos Ltd 1932.*

If the parties use meaningless but non-essential words, for example by use of standard printed conditions some of which are inappropriate, such phrases may be disregarded: *Nicolene v Simmonds 1953.*

If however the parties expressly agree to defer some essential term for later negotiation there is no binding agreement. This is described as 'an agreement to agree' which is void, as the parties may subsequently fail to agree.

Activity 1 **(10 minutes)**

A contract contains a term which states that the price shall be £50,000 unless the parties agree otherwise within seven days of the contract's being signed.

Does this invalidate the contract? Give reasons for your answer.

2 REPRESENTATIONS AND CONTRACT TERMS

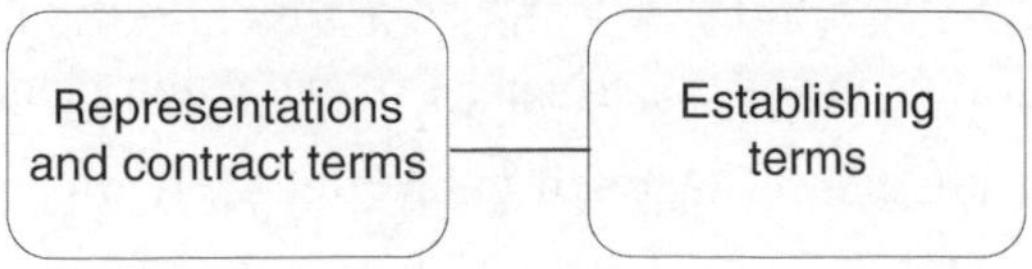

NOTES

If something said in pre-contract negotiations proves to be untrue, the party misled can only claim for breach of contract if the statement became a term of the contract. Otherwise his remedy is for misrepresentation only (explained in the next chapter).

2.1 Establishing contract terms

Even if the statement is not repeated or referred to in making the contract it may be treated as a contract term. But such factors as a significant interval of time between statement and contract, or the use of a written contract making no reference to the statement suggest that it is not a term of the contract. If, however, the party who makes the statement speaks with special knowledge of the subject it is more likely to be treated as a contract term.

> *Bannerman v White 1861*
> In negotiations for the sale of hops the buyer emphasised that it was essential to him that the hops should not have been treated with sulphur. The seller replied explicitly that no sulphur had been used. It was later discovered that a small proportion of the hops (bought in by the seller from another grower) had been treated with sulphur. The buyer refused to pay the price.
>
> *Held:* the representation as to the absence of sulphur was intended to be a term of the contract.
>
> *Oscar Chess v Williams 1959*
> A private motorist negotiated the sale of an old car to motor dealers in part exchange for a new car. The seller stated (as the registration book showed) that his car was a 1948 model and the dealer valued it at £280. In fact it was a 1939 model worth only £175 (the registration book had been altered by a previous owner).
>
> *Held:* the statement was a mere representation. The seller was not an expert and the buyer had better means of discovering the truth.

3 CONDITIONS AND WARRANTIES

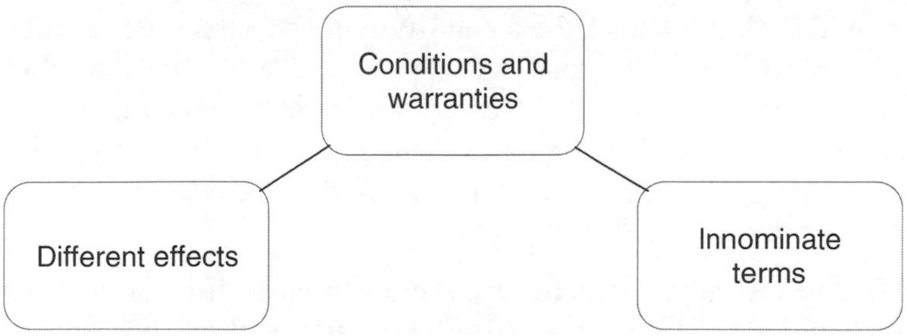

The terms of the contract are usually classified by their relative importance as conditions or warranties.

Definition

> Condition: a term which is vital to the contract, going to the root of the contract.
>
> Warranty: a less important term. It does not go to the root of the contract, but is subsidiary to the main purpose of the agreement.

3.1 Different effects of conditions and warranties

Non-observance of a condition will affect the main purpose of the agreement. Breach of a condition entitles the party not in breach to treat the contract as discharged. Breach of a warranty only entitles the injured party to claim damages.

The following two cases are very useful in highlighting the difference.

> *Poussard v Spiers 1876*
> Madame Poussard agreed to sing in an opera throughout a series of performances. Owing to illness she was unable to appear on the opening night or on the next few days. The producer engaged a substitute who insisted that she should be engaged for the whole run. When Mme Poussard had recovered, the producer declined to accept her services for the remaining performances.
>
> *Held:* failure to sing on the opening night was a breach of condition which entitled the producer to treat the contract for the remaining performances as discharged. Singing on the opening night could be regarded as fundamental to the contract.
>
> *Bettini v Gye 1876*
> An opera singer was engaged for a series of performances under a contract by which he had to be in London for rehearsals six days before the opening performance. Owing to illness he did not arrive until the third day before the opening. The defendant refused to accept his services, treating the contract as discharged.
>
> *Held:* the rehearsal clause was subsidiary to the main purpose of the contract. The contract did not fail because the singer missed some of the rehearsals. Breach of the clause must be treated as breach of warranty, so the producer was bound to accept the singer's services. He had no right to treat the contract as discharged and must compensate the claimant, though he could claim damages (if he could prove any loss) for failure to arrive in time for six days' rehearsals.
>
> *Schuler v Wickham Machine Tool Sales 1973*
> The claimants entered into a four-year contract with the defendants giving them the sole right to sell panel presses in England. A clause of the contract provided that it should be a condition of the agreement that the defendants' representative should visit six named firms each week to solicit orders. The defendants' representative failed on a few occasions to do so and the claimants claimed to be entitled to repudiate the agreement on the basis that a single failure was a breach of condition giving them an absolute right to treat the contract as at an end.
>
> *Held:* such minor breaches by the defendants did not entitle the claimants to repudiate. The House of Lords construed the clause on the basis that it was so unreasonable that the parties could not have intended it as a condition (giving the claimants a right of repudiation) but rather as a warranty. Thus the claimants were themselves in breach of contract leaving the defendants with a claim for damages against them.

Determining whether a contractual term is a condition or a warranty is clearly very important. Classification depends on the following issues.

(a) Statute often identifies implied terms specifically as conditions or warranties. Such identification must be followed by the courts. An example is the Sale of Goods Act 1979, which is covered later in this book.

NOTES

(b) Case law may also define particular clauses as conditions, for example a clause as to the date of 'expected readiness' of a ship let to a charterer: *The Mihalis Angelos 1971*.

(c) Where statute or case law does not shed any light, the court will consider the intention of the parties *at the time the contract was made* as to whether a broken term was to be a condition or a warranty.

3.2 Innominate terms

Where the term broken was not clearly intended to be a condition, and neither statute nor case law define it as such, it cannot necessarily be assumed that the term is a warranty. Instead, the contract must be interpreted; only if it is clear that in no circumstances did the parties intend the contract to be terminated by breach of that particular term can it be classed as a warranty. Such intention may be express or be implied from surrounding circumstances. Where it is not clear what the effect of breach of the term was intended to be, it will be classified by the court as innominate, intermediate or indeterminate (the three are synonymous).

The consequence of a term being classified as innominate is that the court must decide what is the actual effect of its breach. If the nature and effect of the breach is such as to deprive the injured party of substantially the whole benefit which it was intended he should obtain under the contract, then it will be treated as a breached condition, so that the injured party may terminate the contract and claim damages.

Hong Kong Fir Shipping Co Ltd v Kawasaki Kisa Kaisha Ltd 1962
The defendants chartered a ship from the claimants for a period of 24 months. A term in the contract stated that the claimants would provide a ship which was 'in every way fitted for ordinary cargo service'. They were in breach of this term since the ship required a competent engine room crew which they did not provide. Because of the engine's age and the crew's lack of competence the ship's first voyage was delayed for five weeks and further repairs were required at the end of it, resulting in the loss of a further 15 weeks. The defendants purported to terminate the contract so the claimants sued for beach of contract on the grounds that the defendant had no right to terminate; the defendants claimed that the claimants were in breach of a contractual condition.

Held: the term was innominate and could not automatically be construed as either a condition or a warranty. The obligation of 'seaworthiness' embodied in many charter party agreements was too complex to be fitted into one of the two categories. The term would be construed in the light of the actual consequences of the actual breach. The ship was still available for 17 out of 24 months. The consequences of the breach were not so serious that the defendants could be justified in terminating the contract as a result. The defendants were in breach of contract for terminating it when they did.

BPP PUBLISHING

Activity 2 **(10 minutes)**

A company contracts for the purchase of 200 mobile telephones 'immediately suitable for use in the UK'. Assume that this term is innominate. How would the court classify it if:

(a) the telephones supplied required tuning to particular frequencies, a task taking two minutes for each one?

(b) use of the telephones supplied was illegal in the UK, and they could not be modified to make their use legal?

How did you arrive at that conclusion?

4 IMPLIED TERMS

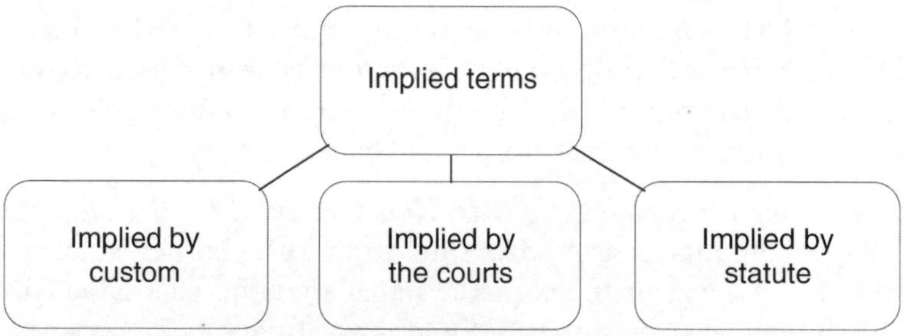

Additional terms of a contract may be implied by law.

4.1 Contractual terms implied by custom

The parties may be considered to enter into a contract subject to a custom or practice of their trade. For example, when a farm is let to a tenant it may be an implied term that local farming custom on husbandry and tenant rights shall apply: Hutton v Warren 1836. But any express term overrides a term which might be implied by custom.

Les Affreteurs v Walford 1919
A charter of a ship provided expressly for a 3% commission payment to be made on signing the charter. There was a trade custom that it should only be paid at a later stage. The ship was requisitioned by the French government before the charterparty began, and so no hire was earned.

Held: an express term prevails over a term otherwise implied by custom. The commission was payable on hire.

4.2 Contractual terms implied by statute

Terms may be implied by statute. In some cases the statute permits the parties to contract out of the statutory terms (thus the terms of partnership implied by the Partnership Act 1890 may be excluded). In other cases the statutory terms are obligatory. The protection given by the Sale of Goods Act 1979 (of which more shortly) to a consumer who buys goods from a trader cannot be taken away from him.

4.3 Contractual terms implied by the courts

Terms may be implied if the court concludes that the parties intended these terms to apply and did not mention them because they were taken for granted or because they were inadvertently omitted. The court may then supply a further term to prevent the failure of the agreement and to implement the manifest intention of the parties. The contract is given 'business efficacy'. In such cases the 'officious bystander' test is applied; if an officious bystander had intervened to remind the parties that in formulating their contract they had failed to mention a particular point they would have replied 'of course ... we did not trouble to say that; it is too clear'.

> *The Moorcock 1889*
> The owners of a wharf agreed that a ship should be moored alongside to unload its cargo. It was well known to both wharfingers and shipowners that at low tide the ship would ground on the mud at the bottom. At low tide the ship rested on a ridge concealed beneath the mud and suffered damage.
>
> *Held:* it was an implied term, though not expressed, that the ground alongside the wharf (which did not belong to the wharfingers) was safe at low tide since both parties knew that the ship must rest on it.

Terms will not be implied to contradict the express terms of the contract (see Les Affreteurs case above) nor to provide for events which the parties did not contemplate in their negotiations.

Activity 3 **(10 minutes)**

A qualified accountant undertakes to prepare a client's tax return. The accountant then finds that the tax return form has been redesigned, and that his computer system cannot cope with the new design. Consider whether he could claim that there was no term in the contract stating that he should be able to prepare a return in the new form, and that he is therefore not obliged to do so.

5 EXCLUSION CLAUSES

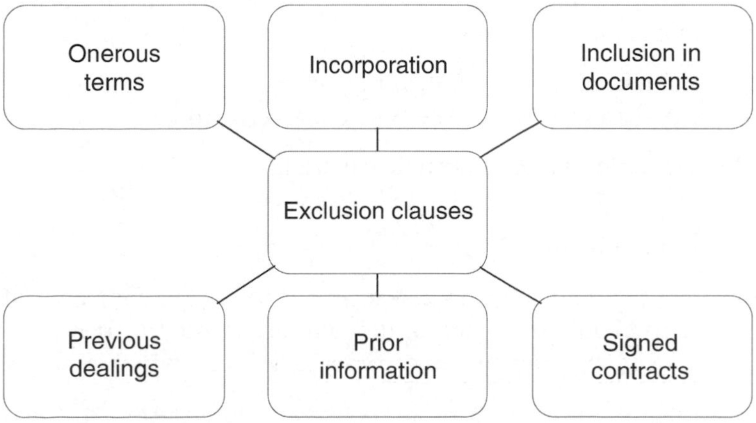

An exclusion (or exemption) clause is a clause which seeks to release one of the parties from liability should something go wrong with the contract.

If the parties negotiate their contract from positions of more or less equal bargaining strength and expertise, neither the courts nor Parliament have usually interfered. But there has been strong criticism of the use of exclusion clauses in contracts made between manufacturers or sellers of goods or services and private citizens as consumers.

In such cases there may be great inequality. The seller puts forward standard conditions of sale which the buyer may not understand and must accept if he wishes to buy. In those conditions the seller may try to exclude or limit his liability for failure to perform as promised for breach of contract or negligence, or he may try to offer a 'guarantee' which in fact reduces the buyer's rights.

5.1 Requirements of an exclusion clause

The main limitations on exclusion clauses are now contained in the Unfair Contract Terms Act 1977 which applies to clauses excluding or restricting liability in contract or tort.

An exclusion clause which is not void by statute may still be ineffectual. The courts have generally sought to protect the consumer from the harsher effects of exclusion clauses in two ways.

(a) An exclusion clause must be properly incorporated into a contract before it has any legal effect.

(b) Exclusion clauses are interpreted strictly; this may prevent the application of the clause.

5.2 The incorporation of exclusion clauses

Uncertainty often arises over which terms have actually been incorporated into a contract. It is not enough for one party to claim that he possesses a set of draft terms; it must be shown that any such terms were incorporated into the agreement between the parties when the agreement was formed. These rules apply to any contract and not just to exclusion clauses, although it is convenient to discuss them here, as many do concern exclusion clauses.

(a) The document containing notice of the exclusion clause must be an integral part of the contract.

(b) If the document is an integral part of the contract, a term may not usually be disputed if it is included in a document which a party has signed.

(c) The term cannot be part of the contract unless put forward before the contract is made.

(d) It is not a binding term unless the person whose rights it restricts was made sufficiently aware of it at the time of agreeing to it.

(e) Onerous terms must be sufficiently highlighted.

5.3 Contractual documents

The courts will not treat an exclusion clause as a term of the contract unless the party affected by it was sufficiently informed of it when he accepted it. It must be shown that this document is an integral part of the contract and is one which could be expected to contain terms.

Chapelton v Barry UDC 1940
There was a pile of deck chairs and a notice stating 'Hire of chairs 2d (1p) per session of 3 hours'. The claimant took two chairs, paid for them and

received two tickets which he put in his pocket. One of the chairs collapsed and he was injured. The defendant council relied on a notice on the back of the tickets by which it disclaimed liability for injury.

Held: the notice advertising chairs for hire gave no warning of limiting conditions and it was not reasonable to communicate them on a receipt. The disclaimer of liability was not binding on the claimant.

Thompson v LMS Railway 1930
An elderly lady who could not read asked her niece to buy her a railway excursion ticket on which was printed 'Excursion: for conditions see back'. On the back it was stated that the ticket was issued subject to conditions contained in the company's timetables. These conditions excluded liability for injury.

Held: the conditions had been adequately communicated and therefore had been accepted.

In the Chapelton case, the ticket was a mere receipt; in the Thompson case, it should have been obvious to a reasonable person that the ticket had contractual effect, as tickets of that kind generally contain contract terms.

5.4 Signed contracts

If a person signs a document containing a clause restricting his rights he is held to have agreed to the restriction even if he had not read the document. But this is not so if the party who puts forward the document for signature gives a misleading explanation of its legal effect.

L'Estrange v Graucob 1934
A sold to B, a shopkeeper, a slot machine under conditions which excluded B's normal rights under the Sale of Goods Act 1893. B signed the document without reading the relevant condition.

Held: the conditions were binding on B since she had signed them. It was not material that A had given her no information of their terms nor called her attention to them. (Under the law as it now stands, some rights under the Sale of Goods Act 1979, which replaced the 1893 Act, may not be excluded.)

Curtis v Chemical Cleaning Co 1951
X took her wedding dress to be cleaned. She was asked to sign a receipt on which there were conditions by which the cleaners disclaimed liability for damage however it might arise. Before signing X enquired what was the effect of the document and was told that it restricted the cleaner's liability in certain ways and in particular placed on X the risk of damage to beads and sequins on the dress. The dress was badly stained in the course of cleaning.

Held: the cleaners could not rely on their disclaimer since they had misled X as to the effect of the document which she signed. She was entitled to assume that she was running the risk of damage to beads and sequins only.

Activity 4 **(15 minutes)**

A contract between P and Q includes a clause excluding P's liability in certain circumstances. When Q enquires as to the meaning of this clause, P replies that he does not wish to provide an oral interpretation, but that Q must read the clause for herself. Q reads the clause and signs the contract. P later seeks to rely on the exclusion clause, and Q claims that P should have interpreted the clause for her. The clause itself is not misleadingly phrased. Consider whether Q is likely to be able to prevent P from relying on the clause.

5.5 Prior information on terms

Many contracts are entered into without the parties signing a document. In such cases, exclusion clauses may be stated on notices or tickets. However, since the terms of the contract are fixed at the moment of acceptance of the offer, an exclusion clause cannot be introduced thereafter (except by mutual consent). Each party must be aware of an exclusion clause at the time of entering into the agreement if it is to be binding.

> *Olley v Marlborough Court 1949*
> A husband and wife arrived at a hotel and paid for a room in advance. On reaching their bedroom they saw a notice on the wall by which the hotel disclaimed liability for loss of valuables unless handed to the management for safe-keeping. The wife locked the room and handed the key in at the reception desk. A thief obtained the key and stole the wife's furs from the bedroom.
>
> *Held:* the hotel could not rely on the notice disclaiming liability since the contract had been made previously (when the room was booked and paid for) and the disclaimer was too late.

Complications can arise when it is difficult to determine at exactly what point in time the contract is formed so as to determine whether or not a term is validly included.

> *Thornton v Shoe Lane Parking Ltd 1971*
> X saw a sign saying 'Parking' outside the defendant's car park. He drove up to the unattended machine and was automatically given a ticket. He had seen a sign disclaiming liability for damage to cars before obtaining the ticket and when he received the ticket he saw that it contained words which he did not read. In fact these made the contract subject to conditions which, if he had looked hard enough in the car park, also excluded liability for injury. When he returned to collect his car (which had been stacked in a special machine) there was an accident in which he was badly injured.
>
> *Held:* the contract was formed before he got the ticket (the offer was the 'Parking' sign; acceptance was parking his car so as to receive a ticket) so reference on the ticket to conditions was too late for the conditions to be included as contractual terms. (Note that since UCTA 1977 the personal injury clause would be void anyway.)

5.6 Previous dealings

An exception to the rule that there must be prior notice of the clause is where the parties have had consistent dealings with each other in the past, and the documents used then contained similar clauses: *J Spurling Ltd v Bradshaw 1956.*

If the parties have had previous dealings (not on a consistent basis) then the person to be bound by the exclusion clause may be sufficiently aware of it (as a proposed condition) at the time of making the latest contract. For this purpose it is necessary to show in a consumer contract that he actually knew of the condition; it is not sufficient that he might have become aware of it.

> *Hollier v Rambler Motors 1972*
> On three or four occasions over a period of five years H had had repairs done at a garage. On each occasion he had signed a form by which the garage disclaimed liability for damage caused by fire to customers' cars. On the latest occasion, however, he did not sign the form. The car was damaged by fire caused by negligence of garage employees. The garage contended that the disclaimer had by course of dealing become an established term of any contract made between them and H.
>
> *Held:* the garage was liable. There was no evidence to show that H knew of and agreed to the condition as a continuing term of his contracts with the garage.

But in a commercial contract it is sufficient to show that, by a previous course of dealings, the other party has constructive if not actual notice of the term: *British Crane Hire Corporation Ltd v Ipswich Plant Hire 1974.*

Activity 5 **(10 minutes)**

Customers of a self service shop take goods from the shelves and then walk down a corridor to a till. A conspicuous notice is hung across this corridor incorporating an exclusion clause into contracts for the purchase of goods from the shop. Could a customer claim that the exclusion clause was invalid because he had selected goods before seeing the notice?

Why is this so?

5.7 Onerous terms

Where a term is particularly unusual and onerous it should be highlighted so that the attention of the other party is drawn to it when the contract is being formed. Failure to do so may mean that it does not become incorporated into the contract.

> *Interfoto Picture Library Ltd v Stiletto Visual Programmes Ltd 1988*
> Forty-seven photographic transparencies were delivered to the defendant together with a delivery note with conditions on the back. Included in small type was a clause stating that for every day late each transparency was held a 'holding fee' of £5 plus VAT would be charged. They were returned 14 days late. The claimants sued for the full amount of £3,782.50.
>
> *Held:* the term was onerous and had not been sufficiently brought to the attention of the defendant. The court reduced the fee to 50p per transparency per day (one tenth of the contractual figure) to reflect more fairly the loss caused to the claimants by the delay.

NOTES

6 THE INTERPRETATION OF EXCLUSION CLAUSES

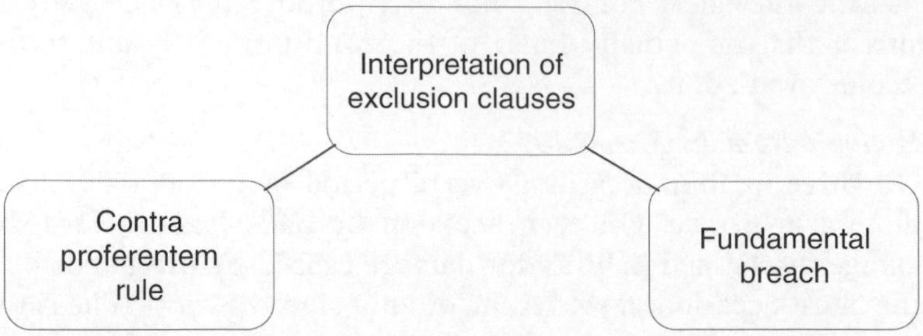

In deciding what an exclusion clause means, the courts interpret any ambiguity against the person at fault who relies on the exclusion. This is known as the *contra proferentem* rule (against the person relying on it).

6.1 The contra proferentem rule

Liability can only be excluded or restricted by clear words. In particular, if the clause gives exclusion in unspecific terms it is unlikely to be interpreted as covering negligence on the part of the person relying on it unless that is the only reasonable interpretation.

> *Hollier v Rambler Motors 1972*
> The facts are as given in section 5.6. The garage disputed liability for fire damage to the claimant's car on the basis of a contractual term which stated that the company was not liable for damage caused by fire to customers' cars on the premises.
>
> *Held:* as shown above, the term was not incorporated into the contract; as a matter of interpretation the disclaimer of liability could be interpreted to apply (a) only to accidental fire damage or (b) to fire damage caused in any way including negligence. It should therefore be interpreted against the garage in the narrower sense of (a) so that it did not give exemption from fire damage due to negligence.
>
> *Alderslade v Hendon Laundry 1945*
> The conditions of contracts made by a laundry with its customers excluded liability for loss of or damage to customers' clothing in the possession of the laundry. By its negligence the laundry lost A's handkerchief.
>
> *Held:* the exclusion clause would have no meaning unless it covered loss due to negligence. It did therefore cover loss by negligence.

When construing an exclusion clause the court will also consider the main purpose rule. By this, the court presumes that the clause was not intended to defeat the main purpose of the contract.

6.2 Fundamental breach

There used to be some doubt on how far an exclusion clause could exclude liability in a case where the breach of contract was a failure to perform the contract altogether (a fundamental breach). In the case given below the House of Lords overruled some earlier decisions of the Court of Appeal and so the legal position is now reasonably clear.

> *Photo Productions v Securicor Transport 1980*
> Securicor agreed to guard the claimants' factory under a contract by which Securicor were excluded from liability for damage caused by any of their employees. One of the Securicor guards deliberately started a small fire

which got out of hand and destroyed the factory and contents, worth about £615,000. It was contended (on the authority of earlier decisions of the Court of Appeal) that Securicor had entirely failed to perform their contract since they had not guarded the factory and so they could not rely on any exclusion clause in the contract.

Held: there is no principle that total failure to perform a contract deprives the party at fault of any exclusion from liability provided by the contract. It is a question of interpretation of the exclusion clause whether it is widely enough expressed to cover total failure to perform. In this case the exclusion clause was wide enough to cover the damage which had happened. (As the fire occurred before the UCTA came into force in 1977 the Act could not apply here. But if it had done it would have been necessary to consider whether the exclusion clause was reasonable.)

Activity 6 **(10 minutes)**

A road haulage company's standard conditions exclude liability for delays caused by factors beyond the company's control. Would this exclusion be interpreted to cover a delay due to a driver choosing to use minor roads because he found motorway driving boring, given that it is the company's policy never to interfere with drivers' choices of routes? Why?

7 THE UNFAIR CONTRACT TERMS ACT 1977 (UCTA)

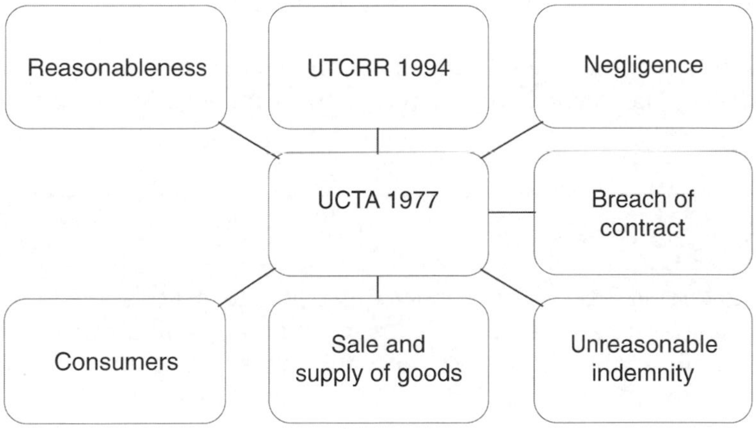

Before we consider the specific term of UCTA, it is necessary to describe how its scope is restricted.

(a) In general the Act only applies to clauses inserted into agreements by commercial concerns or businesses. In principle private persons may restrict liability as much as they wish.

(b) The Act does not apply to certain contracts, for example contracts relating to the creation or transfer of interests in land, contracts relating to company formation or securities transactions and insurance contracts.

The Act uses two techniques for controlling exclusion clauses: some types of clauses are void, whereas others are subject to a test of reasonableness. The main provisions of the Act are as follows.

NOTES

7.1 Avoidance of liability for negligence (s 2)

A person acting in the course of a business cannot, by reference to any contract term, restrict his liability for death or personal injury resulting from negligence. In the case of other loss or damage, a person cannot restrict his liability for negligence unless the term is reasonable. 'Negligence' covers breach of contractual obligations of skill and care, the common law duty of skill and care and the common duty of occupiers of premises under the Occupiers' Liability Acts 1957 and 1984.

7.2 Avoidance of liability for breach of contract (s 3)

The person who imposes the standard term, or who deals with the consumer, cannot *unless the term is reasonable*:

(a) restrict liability for his own breach or fundamental breach; or

(b) claim to be entitled to render substantially different performance or no performance at all.

7.3 Unreasonable indemnity clauses (s 4)

A clause whereby one party undertakes to indemnify the other for liability incurred in the other's performance of the contract is void if the party giving the indemnity is a consumer, unless it is reasonable.

7.4 Sale and supply of goods (ss 6-7)

A consumer contract for the sale of goods, hire purchase, supply of work or materials or exchange of goods cannot exclude or restrict liability for breach of the conditions relating to description, quality, fitness for the purpose for which sold and sample implied by the Sale of Goods Act 1979 and the Supply of Goods and Services Act 1982. In a non-consumer contract these implied conditions may be excluded if the exclusion clause is *reasonable*. The implied condition as to title cannot be excluded in any contract.

Activity 7 **(10 minutes)**

A contract for the sale of a washing machine to a consumer contains the following clause: 'The seller undertakes to repair any defects arising within the first 12 months free of charge, and the buyer shall accordingly not be permitted to return the machine if it does not work at the time of sale'. A consumer would normally have a statutory right to return the machine if it did not work at the time of sale. Consider whether this right has effectively been excluded by the clause.

7.5 The statutory definition of consumer (s 12)

A person deals as a consumer if:

(a) he neither makes the contract in the course of a business, nor holds himself out as doing so; and

(b) the other party does make the contract in the course of a business; and

(c) the goods are of a type ordinarily supplied for private use or consumption.

Where a business engages in an activity which is merely incidental to the business, the activity will not be in the course of the business unless it is an integral part of it and it will not be an integral part of it unless it is carried on with a degree of regularity.

> *R & B Customs Brokers Ltd v United Dominions Trust Ltd 1988*
> The claimants, a company owned by Mr and Mrs Bell and operating as a shipping broker, bought a second-hand Colt Shogun. The car was to be used partly for business and partly for private use.
>
> *Held:* this was a consumer sale, since the company was not in the business of buying cars.

7.6 The statutory test of reasonableness (s 11)

The term must be fair and reasonable having regard to all the circumstances which were, or which ought to have been, known to the parties when the contract was made. The burden of proving reasonableness lies on the person seeking to rely on the clause. Statutory guidelines have been included in the Act to assist in the determination of reasonableness although the court has discretion to take account of all factors. For example, for the purposes of ss 6 and 7, the court will consider the following.

(a) The relative strength of the parties' bargaining positions and in particular whether the customer could have satisfied his requirements from another source.

(b) Whether any inducement (such as a reduced price) was offered to the customer to persuade him to accept a limitation of his rights and whether any other person would have made a similar contract with him without that limitation.

(c) Whether the customer knew or ought to have known of the existence and extent of the exclusion clause (having regard, where appropriate, to trade custom or previous dealings between the parties).

(d) If failure to comply with a condition (for example, failure to give notice of a defect within a short period) excludes or restricts the customer's rights, whether it was reasonable to expect when the contract was made that compliance with the condition would be practicable.

(e) Whether the goods were made, processed or adapted to the special order of the customer.

Activity 8 **(10 minutes)**

A contract under which a consumer buys a 20 volume encyclopaedia contains a clause excluding liability for defects not notified within a week of delivery. Two weeks after delivery, the buyer finds that several pages which should have been printed are blank. Will the seller be able to rely on the exclusion clause?

What is the reason for your answer?

7.7 The Unfair Terms in Consumer Contracts Regulations 1994 (UTCCR)

These regulations, which came into effect on 1 July 1995, implement a European Community directive on unfair contract terms. UCTA 1977 continues to apply.

NOTES

Companies supplying goods and services to consumers and non-consumers will have to have regard to both laws, as no consolidation has yet taken place. There are now three layers of relevant legislation.

(a) The common law, which applies to all contracts, regardless of whether or not one party is a consumer

(b) UCTA 1977, which applies to all contracts and which has specific provisions for consumer contracts

(c) The Regulations, which only apply to consumer contracts and to terms which have not been individually negotiated

The regulations apply to contracts for the supply of goods or services.

(a) They apply to terms in consumer contracts. A consumer is defined as 'a natural person who, in making a contract to which these regulations apply, is acting for purposes which are outside his business'.

(b) They apply to contractual terms which have not been individually negotiated, that is they have been drafted in advance and the consumer has not been able to influence their substance.

(c) There are a number of exceptions, including contracts relating to family law or to the incorporation or organisation of companies and partnerships and employment contracts.

A key aspect of the regulations is the definition of an unfair term. This is:

> 'any term which contrary to the requirement of good faith causes a significant imbalance in the parties' rights and obligations under the contract to the detriment of the consumer.'

In making an assessment of good faith, the courts will have regard to the following. (The first three of these are very similar to UCTA terms on reasonableness.)

(a) The strength of the bargaining positions of the parties

(b) Whether the consumer had an inducement to agree to the term

(c) Whether the goods or services were sold or supplied to the special order of the consumer

(d) The extent to which the seller or supplier has dealt fairly and equitably with the consumer

The effect of the regulations is to render certain terms in consumer contracts unfair, for example:

(a) excluding or limiting liability of the seller when the consumer dies or is injured, where this results from an act or omission of the seller (UCTA 1977 covers only negligent acts or omissions);

(b) excluding or limiting liability where there is partial or incomplete performance of a contract by the seller (as in UCTA 1977); and

(c) making a contract binding on the consumer where the seller can still avoid performing the contract.

Terms should be written in plain, intelligible language; where they are unclear, they will be construed against the seller.

Two forms of redress are available. The second is an interesting one.

(a) A consumer who has concluded a contract containing an unfair term can ask the court to find that the unfair term should not be binding. The remainder of the contract will remain valid if it can continue in existence without the unfair term.

(b) A complaint, for example by an individual, a consumer group or a trading standards department can be made to the Director General of Fair Trading who is empowered to seek injunctions against unfair terms. He can bring an action against sellers and suppliers, manufacturers, franchisors and trade associations.

Chapter roundup

- If a purported contract omits an essential term, and gives no means for settling that term, there is no contract.
- Statements made in the course of negotiations may not become terms of a contract at all. They may only amount to representations.
- A condition is a term which is vital to a contract, and its breach allows the party not in breach to treat the contract as discharged. Breach of a warranty, on the other hand, only entitles the injured party to damages.
- Innominate terms can only be classified as conditions or warranties once the effects of their breach can be assessed.
- Some terms may be implied by law whereas others are so obvious that they are implied under the 'officious bystander' test.
- Exclusion clauses are not automatically illegal, but some such clauses are ruled out to prevent abuses of economic power by one party.
- Exclusion clauses must be properly incorporated into a contract at or before the time of acceptance, and must not be presented in a misleading manner.
- Exclusion clauses are interpreted strictly, against the person seeking to rely on them.
- The Unfair Contract Terms Act 1977 makes certain exclusion clauses void, and others void unless they are reasonable.
- The UTCCR 1994 defines what is meant by an unfair term.

Quick quiz

1. What is the difference between a representation and a contract term?
2. What is the difference between a condition and a warranty?
3. Explain the significance of an innominate term.
4. In what circumstances may additional terms, not expressed in the contract, nonetheless be implied as part of it?
5. When will a court treat an exclusion clause as void because the affected party was not properly informed?
6. What effect does the fact that parties have had previous dealings have on an exclusion clause?
7. If there is ambiguity in an exclusion clause, how does the court interpret the clause?
8. When may liability for negligence never be excluded?
9. What tests are applied to determine the reasonableness of an exclusion clause?
10. How does UCTA 1977 define a consumer?

Answers to quick quiz

1. A representation is something said before the contract. A term is something incorporated within the contract. (see para 2.1)
2. Condition: central to the contract so a breach causes the contract to fail

   Warranty: less important, so a breach does not cause the contract to fail (para 3.1)
3. It can be interpreted as either a condition or a warranty, depending on the effects of the breach. (para 3.2)
4. By custom
By statute
By the courts (para 4.1-4.3)
5. Where it was not properly incorporated in the contractual documents. (para 5.3)
6. If the previous dealings were consistent, the exclusion clause may be upheld. (para 5.6)
7. Against the person trying to enforce the exclusion clause. (para 6.1)
8. In cases of death or personal injury. (para 7.1)
9. Relative strength of bargaining positions
Inducements offered
Knowledge of the exclusion clause
Failure to observe a condition
Special treatment of the goods (para 7.6)
10. The consumer

    - is not acting in the course of a business
    - the other party is acting in the course of a business
    - the goods would normally be supplied for private use (para 7.5)

Answers to activities

1 No: if there is no agreement, a definite price (£50,000) is automatically fixed.

2 (a) A warranty
(b) A condition

In the latter situation the buyer is being deprived of the whole benefit of the contract.

3 No: it is an implied term that a qualified accountant can prepare a tax return in any form required by the Inland Revenue.

4 No: Q has not been misled.

5 No: the exclusion clause was notified before the contract was made at the till.

6 No: the company could choose to control its drivers' choices of routes.

7 No: a consumer contract cannot exclude the statutory term that goods are fit for their purpose.

8 No: it is not reasonable to expect a consumer to find all printing defects in a 20 volume work within the first two weeks of use.

Assignment 4 **(60 minutes)**

Brian was driving his car through Birmingham looking for a convenient car park. He noticed two car parks adjacent to each other where the car parking charges were identical. Whilst deciding which one to use he saw a notice displaying 'closed circuit television in operation' in the car park owned by 'Secure Car Parks Ltd'. He decided that he would park his car in that car park because of the additional security measures.

As he drove in, and before he had taken a ticket from the machine, he also saw another notice: 'Cars parked at owners' risk'. No responsibility whatsoever is accepted for any cars damaged or stolen, howsoever caused'.

When he returned to his car some three hours later he was annoyed to find that a car window had been smashed and his radio and cassettes had been stolen.

He immediately contacted the attendant to explain what had happened but the rather unhelpful attendant simply pointed to the notice by the entrance. Brian, admitting knowledge of the notice excluding liability, asked the attendant if he could look at a video recording from the cameras in the hope that he could identify the culprit. The attendant said that it was not possible to play a recording because the cameras had not worked for three months since they were struck by lightning.

Brian was astounded by this revelation and threatened legal action against the car park owners.

Advise Brian on any possible action(s) he may have and any defences that Secure Car Parks Ltd may have.

BPP PUBLISHING

Chapter 7 :
SPECIALIST TERMS IN CONTRACTS

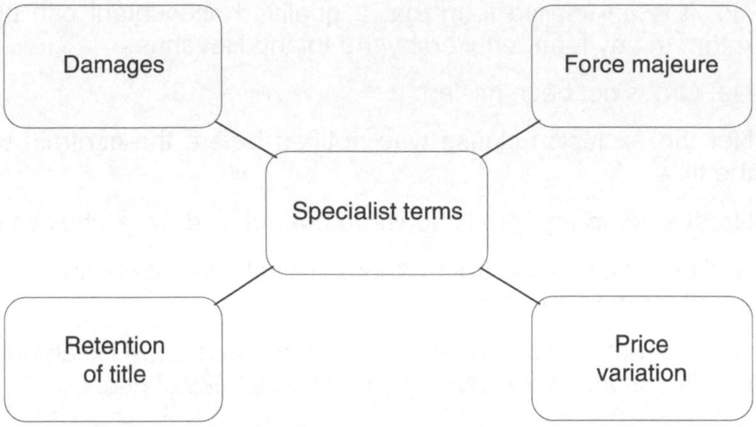

Introduction

There are many specialist terms which are used in contract law, and the ones with which your syllabus is concerned tend to relate to specific business situations.

You need to be able to recognise them if used in assignments, and also appreciate their importance.

Your objectives

In this chapter you will learn about the following.

(a) The principle of *force majeure*

(b) The principles of price variation

(c) The doctrine of retention of title

(d) What is meant by liquidated damages

1 FORCE MAJEURE

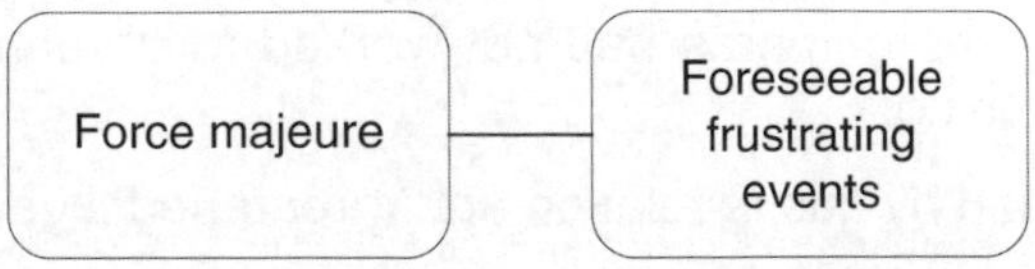

Force majeure clauses are also sometimes referred to as hardship clauses.

1.1 Definition

Force majeure clauses are inserted into contracts, sometimes as a matter of routine, when the parties can foresee that difficulties are likely to arise but the parties cannot foresee their precise nature or extent.

This is especially common in the engineering or building trades.

The subject matter of force majeure clauses can range from the effect of an engineering component being unavailable, so that a contract cannot be completed in its current form, to such 'acts of God' as a ship sinking with all of the contract's necessary supplies on it.

Force majeure clauses are closely linked with the doctrine of frustration, which will be covered later in this book.

2 PRICE VARIATION CLAUSES

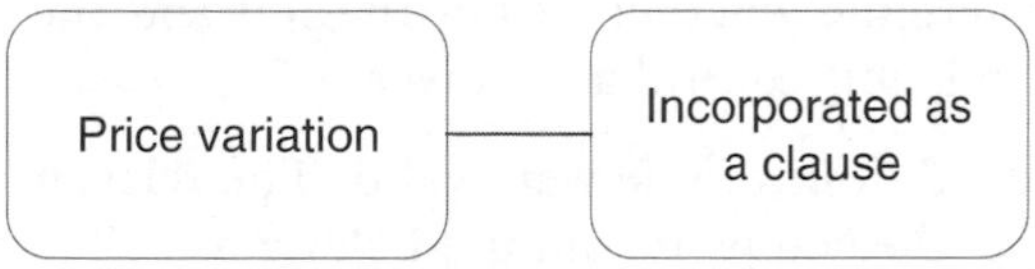

As you have already seen, once a contract has been established, any change to the contract can only be achieved if both of the parties provide some form of fresh consideration, effectively therefore making an additional contract on top of the one which already exists.

Therefore it is difficult for one party to amend the price of the goods subject to the contract once it is in existence.

However, some contracts may include in them a clause stating that the price may be varied, and if this were in itself a contractual term, it would be valid. This type of clause is especially likely where thc subject of the contract is some commodity whose price fluctuates, such as sugar, or where the contract is not likely to be fulfilled for some time.

A practical example is seen in the cases where people made hotel and other bookings to celebrate the Millennium a long time in advance (in many cases years in advance) but the price was not finally fixed until much closer to the event. The purchasers involved would have had an opt-out clause to enable them not to buy, but if they did proceed with the contract they would be bound by the contractual price.

3 RETENTION OF TITLE CLAUSES

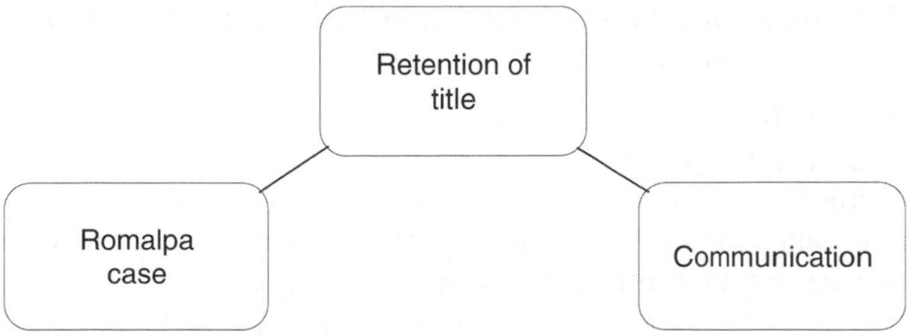

The terms of a retention of title clause provide that where goods are sold, the seller can retain title to the goods (in other words still be the legal owner of them) until he is paid for them by the purchaser. The seller retains legal title even where possession of the goods passes to the seller. The advantage of this is that if the purchaser becomes insolvent, or for some other reason does not pay, the seller can recover the goods.

The goods, once recovered, may not be in as good condition as they were at the time of sale, and hence not worth as much, but it does give the seller some protection against losing all the value of his goods.

3.1 The Romalpa case

Retention of title clauses are often called Romalpa clauses after the first big case on the issue.

> *Aluminium Industrie Vaassen BV v Romalpa Ltd 1976*
> Romalpa purchased aluminium foil on terms that the stock of foil (and any proceeds of sale) should be the property of the Dutch supplier until the company had paid to the supplier all that it owed. Romalpa got into financial difficulties and a receiver was appointed. The receiver found that the company still held aluminium foil and proceeds of selling other stocks of foil, and had not paid its debt to the supplier. The receiver applied to the court to determine whether or not the foil and the cash were assets of the company under his control as receiver.
>
> *Held:* the conditions of sale were valid. The relevant assets, although in the possession of the company, did not belong to it. The receiver could not deal with these assets since his authority under the floating charge was restricted to assets of the company.

3.2 Further issues

The extent to which a Romalpa clause protects an unpaid seller depends to a great extent on the wording of the actual clause. A retention of title clause may be effective even though goods are resold or incorporated into the buyer's products so as to lose their identity if it expressly states that they can be used in these ways before title has passed: *Clough Mill Ltd v Martin 1985.*

Unless the clause expressly retains title even after resale or incorporation, the supplier is not entitled to a proportionate part of the sale proceeds of the manufactured product: *Borden (UK) Ltd v Scottish Timber Products Ltd 1979.* Where there is no express provision, resale or incorporation is conversion of the supplier's property but a third party will still get good title.

If the buyer resells the goods when there is an express provision allowing resale before title passes, the proceeds of sale are held by the buyer as trustee for the supplier.

One critical point about retention of title clauses is their communication. As with other contractual terms, they must be adequately communicated to the other party to the contract *before* the contract is entered into. A party who is expected to be bound by a retention of title clause must be aware of it prior to entering the contract, otherwise he cannot be expected to be bound by it.

Many companies include their retention of title clauses on their invoices. This is too late, as an invoice is not a pre-contractual document, and the contract has already been made by the time the invoice is sent to the purchaser. In order to be legally valid, a retention of title clause should be on a document such as an order form, or in a statement of terms sent out before the contract is agreed.

4 LIQUIDATED DAMAGES CLAUSES

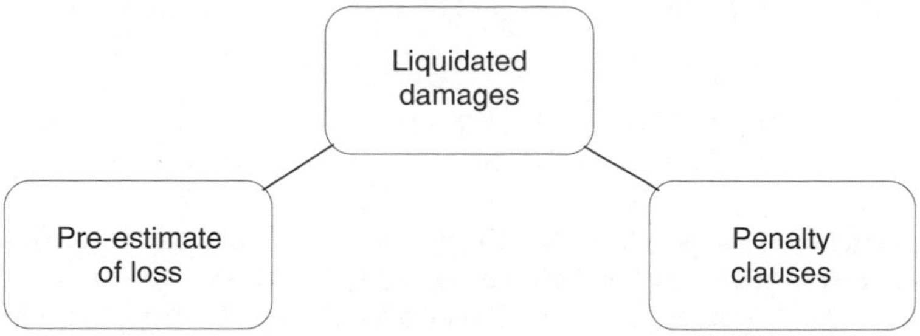

To avoid calculations or disputes later over any amount payable, the parties may include in their contract a formula - **liquidated damages** for determining the damages payable for breach.

4.1 A genuine pre-estimate of loss

In construction contracts it is usual to provide that if the building contractor is in breach of contract by late completion a deduction is to be made from the contract price The formula will be enforced by the courts if it is '**a genuine pre-estimate of loss**'.

> *Dunlop Pneumatic Tyre Co Ltd v New Garage & Motor Co Ltd 1915*
> *The facts*: the contract imposed a minimum retail price. The contract provided that £5 per tyre should be paid if they were resold at less than the prescribed retail price. The defendant did sell at a lower price and argued that £5 per tyre was a 'penalty' and not a genuine pre-estimate of loss.
>
> *Held:* in this case the formula was an honest attempt to agree on liquidated damages and would be upheld.

Compare this with:

> *Ford Motor Co (England) Ltd v Armstrong 1915*
> *The facts*: the defendant had undertaken not to sell the claimant's cars below list price, not to sell Ford cars to other dealers and not to exhibit any Ford cars without permission. A £250 penalty was payable for each breach.
>
> *Held*: since the same sum was payable for different kinds of loss it was not a genuine pre-estimate of loss and was in the nature of a penalty.

4.2 Penalty clauses

Penalty clauses may look similar to liquidated damages clauses, but are designed to intimidate , rather than just to make good a loss.

A contractual term designed as a **penalty clause** to discourage breach is **void** and not enforceable. Relief from penalty clauses is an example of the influence of equity in the law of contract.

> *Bridge v Campbell Discount Co 1962*
> *The facts*: a clause in a hire purchase contract required the debtor to pay on termination, a sum which amounted to two thirds of the HP price and additionally to return the goods.
>
> *Held*: this was a penalty clause and void since the creditor would receive on termination more than 100% of the value of the goods.

Note that queries as to the validity of a clause being a liquidated damages clause or a penalty presuppose that the contract was actually breached. If the contract is still current then the question will not arise.

Activity 1 **(10 minutes)**

Jeremy entered a contract with Big Builders plc to design a new energy efficient style of house, using solar panels. Big Builders had no firm orders for this new style of house and no decision had yet been taken as to whether the project would proceed. The contract said that if Jeremy failed to produce the new design by 1 September, he would be liable to compensate Big Builders the sum of £50,000 as liquidated damages. Jeremy did not produce the design by 1 September. Will Big Builders plc be successful in claiming the money from him?

Chapter roundup

- A force majeure clause can try to pre-empt the effect of a problem cropping up in the contract.
- Force majeure clauses are common in the building and engineering industries.
- Price variation clauses may be valid where the contract provides for it.
- Retention of title means that the seller of goods can retain ownership of them until they have been paid for by the purchaser.
- Liquidated damages are calculated by reference to a pre-agreed formula included in the contract.

Quick quiz

1. What is meant by force majeure?
2. Are price variation clauses valid?
3. What happened in the Romalpa case?
4. What is a penalty clause?

Answers to quick quiz

1. Clauses which are included in contracts when difficulties are foreseen. (see para 1.1)
2. Yes, if the clause allowing variation is a part of the contract itself. (para 2)
3. A company had bought foil but not yet paid for it. When it went into receivership, the supplier of the foil was able to recover it. (para 3.1)
4. A clause which imposes a far greater penalty than the actual loss suffered in a breach. It is designed to intimidate. (para 4.2)

Answers to activities

1 No. This is clearly a penalty clause designed to intimidate Jeremy into carrying out the contract, and it is not any kind of estimate of a loss suffered by Big Builders. They will not be able to enforce the payment.

Assignment

We have not included an assignment specifically on the content of this chapter. This is because these terms are more likely to be assessed in the context of wider aspects of contract law, rather than in isolation. They are tested in assignments elsewhere in this course book.

Chapter 8 :
VITIATING FACTORS IN CONTRACTS

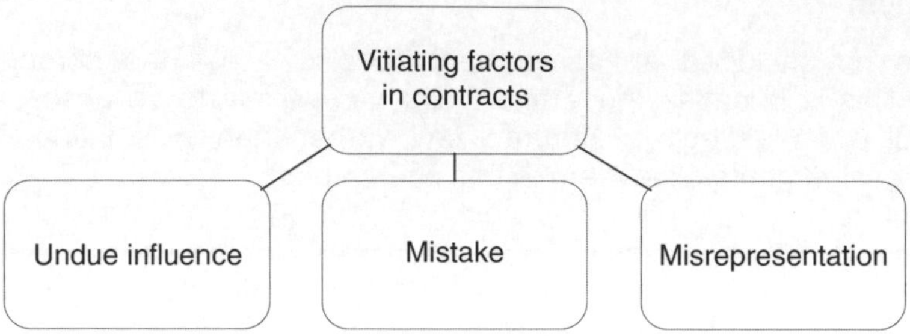

Introduction

Even if the essential elements can be shown, a contract may not necessarily be valid. The validity of a contract may also be affected by any of the following factors.

(a) As we have already seen, the parties may in general enter into a contract on whatever terms they choose. But a contract can only be enforced if it is sufficiently complete in its terms. Some terms which the parties do not express may be implied and some terms which the parties do express are overridden.

(b) We have also seen how some contracts must be made in a particular form.

(c) Some persons have only restricted capacity to enter into contracts and are not bound by agreements made outside those limits.

(d) A misrepresentation or mistake made by one party to the contract may affect the validity of the contract.

(e) A person induced to enter into a contract by duress or undue influence is entitled to avoid the contract at common law.

(f) The courts will not enforce a contract which is deemed to be illegal or contrary to public policy.

Your objectives

In this chapter you will learn about the following.

(a) The nature of a representation, and what may constitute a misrepresentation

(b) The types of misrepresentation, and the available remedies

(c) The types of operative mistake and their effect on a purported contract

(d) The remedies in cases of mistake

(e) How undue influence may arise, and the remedies available

NOTES

1 VITIATED CONTRACTS

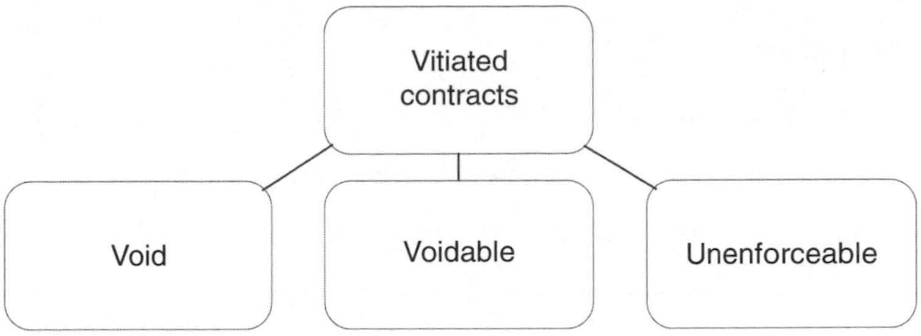

You have already seen that a contract which does not satisfy the relevant tests may be either void, voidable or unenforceable.

Definitions

> Void contract: a contract which has no legal effect.
>
> Voidable contract: a contract which is capable of being rendered void at the option of one of the parties, but is valid until the option is exercised.
>
> Unenforceable contract: a contract which is not actionable in a court.

A *void* contract is not a contract at all. The parties are not bound by it and if they transfer property under it they can sometimes (unless it is also an illegal contract) recover their goods even from a third party.

A *voidable* contract is a contract which one party may avoid, that is terminate at his option. Property transferred before avoidance is usually irrecoverable from a third party.

An *unenforceable* contract is a valid contract and property transferred under it cannot be recovered even from the other party to the contract. But if either party refuses to perform or to complete his part of the performance of the contract, the other party cannot compel him to do so. A contract is usually unenforceable when the required evidence of its terms, for example, written evidence of a contract relating to land, is not available.

2 MISREPRESENTATION

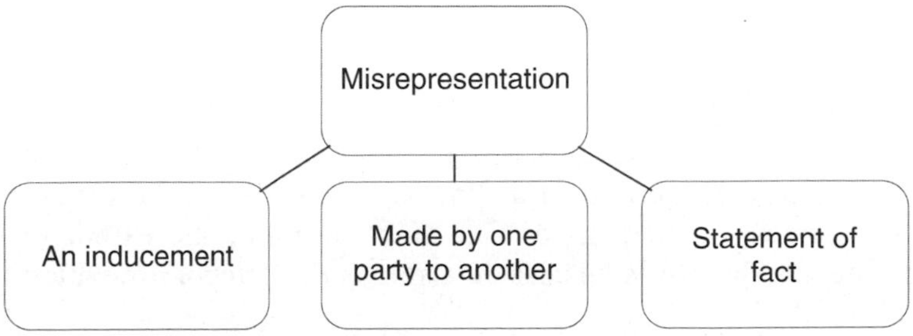

A statement made in the course of negotiations may become a term of the contract. If it is a term of the contract and proves to be untrue, the party who has been misinformed may claim damages for breach of contract. If, however, the statement does not become a term of the contract and it is untrue, the party misled may be able to treat it as a misrepresentation and rescind (cancel) the contract, or in some cases, recover damages. The contract is voidable for misrepresentation.

Definition

> A misrepresentation is:
>
> - a statement of fact which is untrue;
> - made by one party to the other before the contract is made;
> - an inducement to the party misled actually to enter into the contract.

3 REPRESENTATION

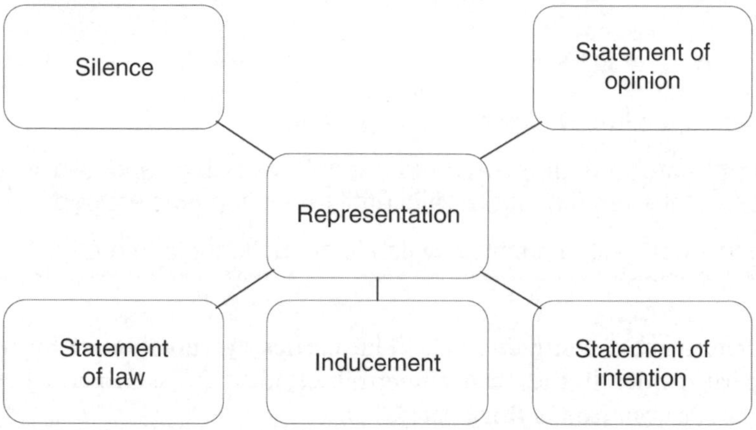

In order to analyse whether a statement may be a misrepresentation, it is first of all necessary to decide whether it could have been a representation at all.

(a) A statement of fact is a representation.

(b) A statement of law, intention, opinion or mere sales talk is not a representation.

(c) Silence is not usually a representation.

Therefore, if these three are not representations, they cannot by definition become misrepresentations.

3.1 Statement of opinion

A statement of opinion or intention is a statement that the opinion or intention exists, but not that it is a correct opinion or an intention which will be realised. In deciding whether a statement is a statement of fact or of opinion, the extent of the speaker's knowledge as much as the words he uses determines the category to which the statement belongs.

> *Bisset v Wilkinson 1927*
> A vendor of land which both parties knew had not previously been grazed by sheep stated that it would support about 2,000 sheep. This proved to be untrue.
>
> *Held:* in the circumstances this was an honest statement of opinion as to the capacity of the farm, not a statement of fact.

NOTES

Smith v Land and House Property Corporation 1884
A vendor of property described it as 'let to F (a most desirable tenant) at a rent of £400 per annum for 271□2 years thus offering a first class investment'. In fact F had only paid part of the rent due in the previous six months by instalments after the due date and he had failed altogether to pay the most recent quarter's rent.

Held: the description of F as a 'desirable tenant' was not a mere opinion but an implied assertion that nothing had occurred which could make F an undesirable tenant. As a statement of fact this was untrue.

3.2 Statement of intention

A statement of intention, or a statement as to future conduct, is not actionable. An affirmation of the truth of a fact (a representation) is different from a promise to do something in the future. If a person enters into a contract or takes steps relying on a representation, the fact that the representation is false entitles him to remedies at law. However, if he sues on a statement of intention – a promise – he must show that that promise forms part of a valid contract if he is to gain any remedy.

Maddison v Alderson 1883.
The claimant had been the defendant's housekeeper for ten years. She had received no wages in this period. She announced that she wished to leave and get married. She alleged that the defendant had promised that, if she stayed with him, he would leave her in his will a life interest in his farm. She agreed to remain with him until he died. He left a will which included this promise, but because it had not been witnessed it was void. She claimed that the promise to make a will in her favour was a representation.

Held: 'the doctrine of estoppel by representation is applicable only to representations as to some state of facts alleged to be at the time actually in existence, and not to promises de futuro which, if binding at all, must be binding as contracts'

3.3 Statement of the law

A statement of the law is not a representation and hence no remedy is available if it is untrue. However, most representations on law are statements of the speaker's opinion of what the law is; if he does not in fact hold this opinion then there is a misrepresentation of his state of mind and hence a remedy may be available.

Activity 1 **(10 minutes)**

P sells a car to Q. Which of the following statements by P to Q could be misrepresentations?

(a) 'The car can do 120 mph.'

(b) 'I have enjoyed driving the car.'

(c) 'You should get the brakes checked before you agree to buy the car.'

3.4 Silence

As a general rule neither party is under any duty to disclose what he knows. If he keeps silent that is not a representation, so silence cannot be a misrepresentation. But there is a duty to disclose information in the following cases.

(a) What is said must be complete enough to avoid giving a misleading impression. A half truth can be false.

R v Kylsant 1931
When inviting the public to subscribe for its shares, a company stated that it had paid a regular dividend throughout the years of the depression. This clearly implied that the company had made a profit during those years. This was not the case since the dividends had been paid out of the accumulated profits of the pre-depression years.

Held: the silence as to the source of the dividends was a misrepresentation since it distorted the true statement that dividends had been paid.

(b) There is a duty to correct an earlier statement which was true when made but which may become untrue before the contract is completed.

With v O'Flanagan 1936
A contract was made for the sale of a medical practice. In the intervening period before completion, the profits fell substantially. The failure of the seller to tell the buyer of this was a misrepresentation, and the contract could be avoided.

(c) In contracts of 'utmost good faith' (*uberrimae fidei*) there is a duty to disclose the material facts which one knows. Contracts of insurance fall into this category.

The person to whom a representation is made is entitled to rely on it without investigation, even if he is invited to make enquiries.

Redgrave v Hurd 1881
R told H that the income of his business was £300 per annum and produced to H papers which disclosed an income of £200 per annum. H queried the figure of £300 and R produced additional papers which R stated showed how the additional £100 per annum was obtained. H did not examine these papers which in fact showed only a very small amount of additional income. H entered into the contract but later discovered the true facts and he refused to complete the contract.

Held: H relied on R's statement and not on his own investigation. H had no duty to investigate the accuracy of R's statement and might rescind the contract.

3.5 Statement made by one party to another

Although in general a misrepresentation must have been made by the misrepresentor to the misrepresentee, there are two exceptions to the rule.

(a) A misrepresentation can be made to the public in general, as where an advertisement contains a misleading representation.

(b) The misrepresentation need not be made directly on a one-to-one basis. It is sufficient that the misrepresentor knows that the misrepresentation would be passed on to the relevant person.

Pilmore v Hood 1873
H fraudulently misrepresented the turnover of his pub so as to sell it to X. X had insufficient funds and so repeated the representations, with H's knowledge, to P. On the basis of this P purchased the pub.

Held: H was liable for fraudulent misrepresentation even though he had not himself misrepresented the facts to P.

3.6 Inducement to enter into the contract

If the claimant was not aware of the misrepresentation, his action will fail.

Horsfall v Thomas 1862
H made a gun to be sold to T and, in making it, concealed a defect in the breech by inserting a metal plug. T bought the gun without inspecting it. The gun exploded and T claimed that he had been misled into purchasing it by a misrepresentation (the metal plug) that it was sound.

Held: T had not inspected the gun at the time of purchase. Therefore the metal plug could not have been a misleading inducement because he was unaware of it, and did not rely on it when he entered into the contract.

Since to be actionable a representation must have induced the person to enter into the contract, it follows that he must have known of its existence, allowed it to affect his judgement and been unaware of its untruth.

> **Activity 2** **(10 minutes)**
>
> R sells some farmland to S. Before the contract is made, R states that the land is good for grazing. In fact it is good for grazing sheep, but not cattle. R also suggests that S might like to get an independent opinion on the quality of the land. Has R made a misrepresentation to S?

4 TYPES OF MISREPRESENTATION

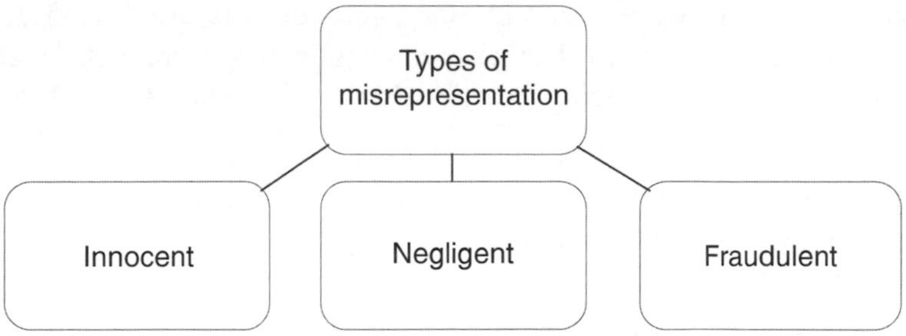

Misrepresentation is classified (for the purpose of determining what remedies are available) as:

(a) *fraudulent misrepresentation:* a statement made with knowledge that it is untrue, or without believing it to be true, or recklessly careless whether it be true or false;

(b) *negligent misrepresentation:* a statement made in the belief that it is true but without reasonable grounds for that belief;

(c) *innocent misrepresentation:* a statement made in the belief that it is true and with reasonable grounds for that belief.

4.1 Fraudulent misrepresentation

There must be an absence of honest belief that the statement is true.

> *Derry v Peek 1889*
> D and other directors of a company published a prospectus inviting the public to apply for shares. The prospectus stated that the company (formed under a special Act of Parliament) had statutory powers to operate trams in Plymouth, drawn by horses or driven by steam power. The Act required that the company should obtain a licence from the Board of Trade for the operation of steam trams. The directors assumed that the licence would be granted whenever they might apply for it, but it was later refused.
>
> *Held:* the directors honestly believed that the statement made was true and so this was not a fraudulent misrepresentation. The false representation was not made knowingly, without belief in its truth or recklessly, and so the directors escaped liability.

4.2 Negligent misrepresentation

This is effectively a reckless statement. Historically, this has been an area of common law, but is now also covered by the statutory implications of The Misrepresentation Act 1967.

In 1963 the House of Lords reached an important decision by which it held that in certain instances an action in tort for negligent misstatement might be possible.

> *Hedley Byrne & Co Ltd v Heller & Partners Ltd 1963*
> The claimants were advertising agents acting for a new client E. If E defaulted on payment, the claimants would themselves be liable. They checked E's financial position by asking their bank to make enquiries of E's bank (the defendants). Relying on the replies they placed orders and suffered substantial losses when E went into liquidation.
>
> *Held:* the action failed because the defendants were able to rely on a disclaimer. However, had it not been for this, an action for negligence would have succeeded. Liability for negligent statements depends upon the existence of a 'special relationship'; the defendants knew what the information was to be used for.

At the same time as case law on negligent misrepresentation was developing as outlined above, the Law Reform Committee recommended that damages should be given for negligent misrepresentation.

Their recommendations resulted in the Misrepresentation Act 1967. Under s 2(1) of the Act, where a person has entered into a contract after a misrepresentation has been made to him by another party to the contract and has as a result suffered loss, then, if the person making the misrepresentation would be liable to damages if the misrepresentation had been made fraudulently, he will be liable to damages notwithstanding that the misrepresentation was not made fraudulently. He will escape liability if he can prove that he had reasonable grounds to believe, and did believe, up to the time the contract was made, that the facts represented were true.

This puts the burden of proof on the person making the representation. He will be deemed negligent and liable to pay damages unless he can disprove negligence. This suggests that it may be more advantageous for a claimant to bring a claim under the Act than at common law.

> *Howard Marine and Dredging Co Ltd v A Ogden & Sons (Excavations) Ltd 1978*
> The defendants required two barges for use in an excavation contract. During negotiations with the claimants, the claimant's marine manager stated that the payload of two suitable barges was 1,600 tonnes. This was based on figures given by Lloyds Register, which turned out to be in error. The payload was only 1,055 tonnes. The defendants stopped paying the hire charges and were sued. They counterclaimed for damages at common law and under the Misrepresentation Act 1967.
>
> *Held:* the court was unable to decide on whether there was a duty of care (in the common law action), but the claimants had not discharged the burden of proof under the Act, as shipping documents in their possession disclosed the real capacity.

4.3 Innocent misrepresentation

Following the creation of the two categories of negligent misrepresentation, an innocent misrepresentation is any misrepresentation made without fault. (Before this, an innocent misrepresentation was any non-fraudulent misrepresentation.)

5 REMEDIES FOR MISREPRESENTATION

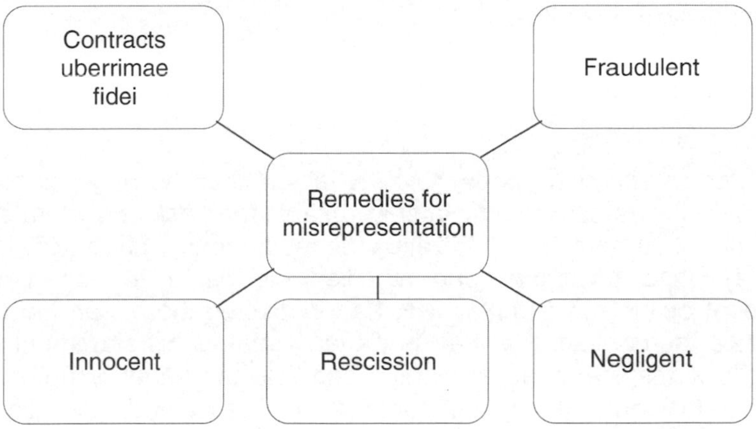

One of the main remedies for misrepresentation, regardless of the type, is rescission. This entails setting the contract aside as if it had never been made. The principle seeks to ensure that the parties are restored to their original position, as it was before the contract was made.

5.1 Fraudulent misrepresentation

In a case of fraudulent misrepresentation the party misled may, under common law, rescind the contract (since it is voidable), refuse to perform his part of it and/or recover damages for any loss by a common law action for deceit (which is a tort).

5.2 Negligent misrepresentation

In a case of negligent misrepresentation the party misled may, under equitable principles, rescind the contract and refuse to perform his part under it. In order to gain a remedy, the claimant must show that the misrepresentation was in breach of a duty of care which arose out of a special relationship.

> *Esso Petroleum Co Ltd v Mardon 1976*
> E negligently told M that a filling station, the tenancy for which they were negotiating, had an annual turnover of 200,000 gallons. This induced M to take the tenancy, but in fact the turnover never rose to more than 86,000 gallons.
>
> *Held:* E owed a special duty of care and was in breach. Damages were awarded to M.

5.3 Innocent misrepresentation

In a case of innocent misrepresentation the party misled may also, in equity, rescind the contract and refuse to perform his part of it. He is not ordinarily entitled to claim damages for any additional loss.

Under the Misrepresentation Act 1967 a victim of negligent misrepresentation can claim damages for any actual loss caused by the misrepresentation. It is then up to the party who made the statement to prove, if he can, that he had reasonable grounds for making it and that it was not in fact negligent. As noted above, this placing of the burden of proof on the maker of the statement makes an action under the Act easier for the victim to win than an action at common law.

Under s 2(2) of the Act the court may in the case of non-fraudulent (negligent or innocent) misrepresentation award damages instead of rescission. This may be a fairer solution in some cases. But damages may only be awarded instead of rescission if the right to rescind has not been lost.

Activity 3 **(10 minutes)**

X negotiates to sell some paper to Y. X tells Y that the paper is suitable for colour printing, whereas in fact it is only suitable for black and white printing. In making the statement to Y, X relies on statements made to him by the (reputable) paper merchant who supplied the paper to him, and on the independent opinion of a printer who had inspected the paper. However, two days before the contract is made (but after X makes his statement to Y), the printer tells X that he made a mistake and that the paper is not suitable for colour printing. Could X's misrepresentation to Y be treated as negligent?

5.4 Loss of the right to rescind

The principle of rescission is that the parties should be restored to their position as it was before the contract was made. The right to rescind is lost in any of the following circumstances.

(a) If the party misled affirms the contract (ie continues to act according to the contract) after discovering the true facts he may not afterwards rescind. For this purpose it is not necessary that he should expressly affirm the contract. Intention to affirm may be implied from conduct indicating that the party is treating the contract as still in operation. In a number of cases concerned with untrue prospectuses, subscribers have lost the right to rescind by continuing to exercise their rights as shareholders even though they did not realise that this would be the effect. Mere inaction over a period of time may also be treated as affirmation.

Long v Lloyd 1958
The claimant bought a lorry for £750 after the defendant had described it as being in first class condition. On the claimant's first business journey, the dynamo failed, an oil seal leaked, a wheel cracked and the vehicle returned only five miles to the gallon. The claimant told the defendant of the problems; the latter agreed to pay half the cost of the dynamo but denied knowledge of any other problems. On the next business journey the lorry broke down and was declared by an expert to be unroadworthy. The claimant sought to rescind the contract.

Held: acceptance of a financial contribution, together with the embarking upon the second journey, constituted affirmation of the contract.

(b) If the parties can no longer be restored to substantially the pre-contract position, the right to rescind is lost.

Clarke v Dickson 1858
The contract related to a business which at the time of the misrepresentation was carried on by a partnership. It was later reorganised as a company and the claimant's interest was with his consent converted into shares. He later sought to rescind.

Held: the conversion of the claimant's interest in the partnership into shares in the company was an irreversible change which precluded restoration to the original position. The right to rescind had been lost.

(c) If the rights of third parties, such as creditors of an insolvent company, would be prejudiced by rescission, it is too late to rescind.

(d) Lapse of time may bar rescission where the misrepresentation is innocent.

Leaf v International Galleries 1950
An innocent misrepresentation was not discovered for five years. The seller of a painting had said that it was a Constable. The court said rescission was not possible after the lapse of time. "Delay defeats equity".

Where misrepresentation is fraudulent, lapse of time does not, by itself, bar rescission because time only begins to run from the discovery of the truth.

5.5 Contracts uberrimae fidei

The general rule is that a party to a contract has no duty to disclose what he knows which may affect the willingness of the other party to enter into the contract, either spontaneously or in answer to questions. Three types of contract carry a duty of utmost good faith (*uberrimae fidei*), which means that failure to disclose material facts gives rise to a right for relief. The types are:

(a) contracts of insurance;

(b) contracts preliminary to family arrangements, such as land settlements; and

(c) contracts where there is a fiduciary relationship, such as exists between solicitor and client, or partner and partner.

Activity 4 **(10 minutes)**

Nigel enters a contract with Megapru plc to insure his car. He does not disclose to Megapru that he has tunnel vision in both eyes. What effect do you think that this would have on the contract of insurance?

6 MISTAKE

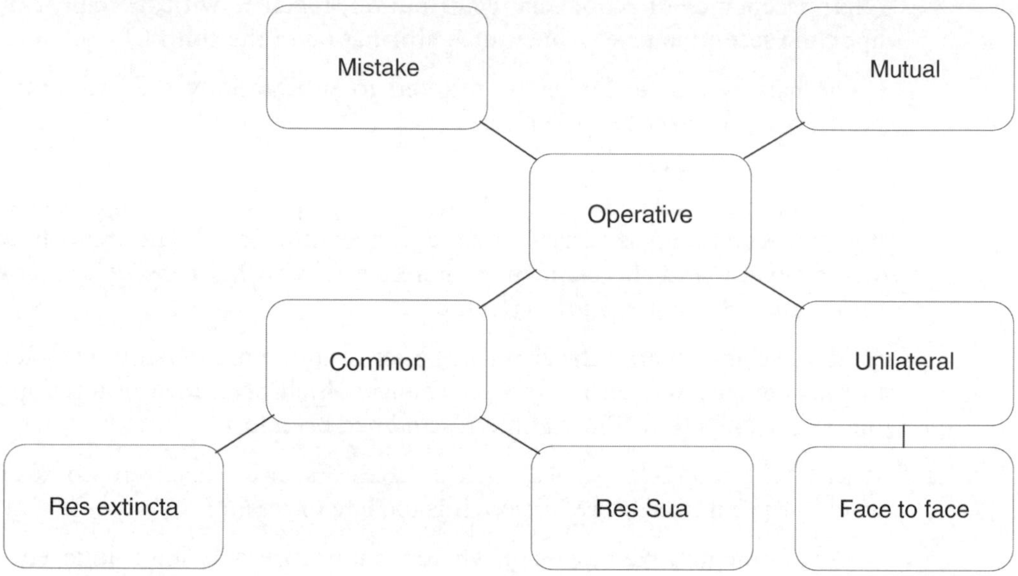

There are many types of mistake in contract law, and it is important that you understand each of them.

6.1 Operative mistake

Operative mistake is usually classified as follows.

(a) **Common mistake** - there is complete agreement between the parties but both are equally mistaken as to some fundamental point.

(b) **Mutual mistake** - each believes that the other agrees with him and does not realise that there is a misunderstanding.

(c) **Unilateral mistake** - one party is mistaken and the other (who may have induced the mistake) is aware of it.

The basic principles of operative mistake are rules of common law. A key point is that the mistake, to be recognised at law, must exist at the time that the contract is formed.

> *Amalgamated Investments and Property Co Ltd v John Walker & Sons Ltd 1976*
>
> *The facts:* The claimants were buying a property from the defendants. In response to pre-contract enquiries, the defendants replied on 14 August that the property was not designated as a building of special historical interest. Neither party was aware that the Department of the Environment was planning to list the building. On 25 September a contract was signed. On 26 September the defendants were informed that the building was to be listed; this took effect from 27 September. The result was that the building was

worth £210,000 instead of the contract price of £1.71 million. The claimants sought rescission of the contract on the grounds of common mistake.

Held: The critical date was the date of the contract. At that date there was no mistake.

6.2 Common mistake

(a) *Res extincta*

If the parties make a contract relating to subject matter which, unknown to them both, does not exist, or which has ceased to exist, there is no contract between them.

Couturier v Hastie 1852
The facts: A contract was made in London for the sale of a cargo of corn thought to have been shipped from Salonika. Unknown to the parties the cargo had already been sold by the master of the ship at Tunis since it had begun to rot. The London purchaser repudiated the contract and the agent who had sold the corn to him was sued.

Held: The claim against the agent failed. The corn was not in existence when the contract was made.

Galloway v Galloway 1914
The facts: A man and a woman entered into a separation agreement relating to their apparent status as husband and wife. Neither then knew that their marriage was null and void.

Held: The contract related to non-existent subject matter and was void.

(b) *Res sua*

The rule on non-existent subject matter (*res extincta*) has been extended to the infrequent cases where a person buys what already belongs to him (*res sua*).

Cochrane v Willis 1865
The facts: Under a family settlement A would inherit property on the death of his brother B. B had become bankrupt in Calcutta and, to save the property from sale to a third party, A agreed with B's trustee in bankruptcy in England, to purchase the property from B's bankrupt estate. Unknown to A and B's trustee, B had already died in Calcutta and so the property had passed to A by inheritance before he bought it.

Held: The contract was void and A was not liable to pay the agreed contract price.

Cooper v Phibbs 1867
The facts: Cooper had agreed to take a lease of a fishery from Phibbs, his uncle's daughter, who became apparent owner of it on her father's death. However, Cooper's uncle had been mistaken as to how the family land was held and the fishery, unbeknown to Cooper or Phibbs, belonged to Cooper already. Cooper brought an action to set aside the lease.

Held: This was an example of *res sua*.

An alternative approach to common mistake has been taken by the High Court of Australia.

> *McRae v Commonwealth Disposals Commission 1951*
> *The facts:* The defendants invited tenders 'for the purchase of an oil tanker lying on Jourmaund Reef, which is approximately 100 miles north of Samarai'. There was in fact no tanker near this latitude, and no such place as Jourmaund Reef. The claimants submitted a tender and, upon its acceptance, prepared a salvage expedition. They then discovered the mistake.
>
> *Held:* The Commission had implicitly warranted the existence of the contractual subject matter. Damages were awarded to the claimant.

The **leading case on both parties being equally mistaken** on some fundamental point left open the question as to whether common mistake could be extended any further.

> *Bell v Lever Bros 1932*
> *The facts:* L, the controlling shareholder of a Nigerian company, appointed B to be the managing director. Before five years had elapsed, B became redundant owing to a merger and L negotiated with B for the cancellation of his service agreement on payment to B of £30,000. Later L discovered that while serving as managing director, B had used inside information to trade in cocoa on his own account. This was serious misconduct for which B might have been summarily dismissed. B was said to have forgotten the significance of his past conduct in negotiating the cancellation of his service agreement and it was treated as a case of common mistake. L's claim to recover £30,000 from B was that the service agreement for which L had paid £30,000 was in fact valueless to B, since he could have been dismissed without compensation.
>
> *Decision:* L's claim may have been correct in its theoretical basis but there was not a sufficiently fundamental mistake as to the 'quality' of the subject matter.

Common mistake resulting in **a contract being void from the beginning** was upheld in the following case.

> *Associated Japanese Bank (International) v Credit du Nord SA 1988*
> *The facts:* A rogue entered into a sale and leaseback agreement with the claimant to fund the purchase of four machines. The defendant guaranteed the transaction as a leasing agreement. The claimant advanced £1m to the rogue, who made one quarterly repayment before being arrested for fraud, and adjudged bankrupt. The machines did not exist, and so the claimant sued to enforce the guarantee. The defendant claimed the contract was void for common or mutual mistake since the non-existence of the machines made the subject of the contract essentially different.
>
> *Held:* The non-existence of the machines in the principal contract (the lease) on which the secondary contract (the guarantee) relied was so fundamental as to render the subject-matter essentially different. Hence there was common mistake - the guarantee was void and could not be enforced.

6.3 Mutual mistake

If the parties are at cross-purposes without either realising it, the **terms of the contract** usually resolve the misunderstanding in favour of one or the other.

Tamplin v James 1880

The facts: J went to an auction to bid for a public house. J believed that the property for sale included a field which had been occupied by the publican. The sale particulars, which J did not inspect, made it clear that the field was not included. J was the successful bidder but when he realised his mistake refused to proceed with the purchase.

Held: J was bound to pay the price which he had bid for the property described in the particulars of sale. The contract was quite clear and his mistake did not invalidate it.

The parties may have failed to reach any agreement at all if the terms of the contract fail to identify the subject matter. Such a mistake renders the contract void.

Raffles v Wichelhaus 1864

The facts: A and B agreed in London on the sale from A to B of a cargo of cotton to arrive 'Ex *Peerless* from Bombay'. There were in fact two ships named *Peerless* with a cargo of cotton from Bombay; one sailed in October and the other in December. B intended the contract to refer to the October sailing and A to the December one.

Held: As a preliminary point B could show that there was an ambiguity and that he intended to refer to the October shipment. If the case had gone further the contract would have been void.

If each party is unaware that the other intends subject matter of a different quality he may perform his side of the contract according to his intention.

Smith v Hughes 1871

The facts: Oats were bought by sample. The buyer believed that they were old oats. The seller (who was unaware of the buyer's impression) was selling new oats which are less valuable. On discovering that they were new oats the buyer refused to complete the sale.

Held: The contract was for the sale of 'oats' and the buyer's mistake as to a quality did not render the contract void. The seller was entitled to deliver and to receive payment for his oats.

Scriven Bros v Hindley & Co 1913

The facts: At an auction a buyer bid for two lots believing both to be hemp. In fact one lot was a mixed batch of hemp and tow. It was not normal practice to sell hemp and tow together and the sale particulars were confusing.

Held: In the circumstances there was no agreement by which the buyer was bound to accept the mixed hemp and tow. The contract was therefore not binding.

6.4 Unilateral mistake

A **unilateral mistake** is usually the result of misrepresentation by one party. The party misled is entitled to rescind the contract for misrepresentation but it may then be too late to recover the goods. If, on the other hand, the contract is void for mistake at the outset, no title passes to the dishonest party and it may be possible for the party misled to recover his goods.

Most of the case law on this type of mistake is concerned with **mistake of identity**. A contract is only void for mistake by the seller about the buyer's identity if the seller intended to sell to someone different from the actual buyer.

The parties may negotiate the contract by correspondence without meeting face to face. If the buyer fraudulently adopts the identity of another person known to the seller the sale to the actual buyer is void.

> *Cundy v Lindsay 1878*
> *The facts:* Blenkarn wrote to C to order goods and signed the letter so that his name appeared to be 'Blenkiron & Co', a respectable firm known to C. The goods were consigned to Blenkiron & Co and Blenkarn re-sold the goods to L. C sued L for conversion to recover the value of the goods.
>
> *Held:* C intended to sell only to B & Co, and no title passed to Blenkarn. L was liable to C for the value of the goods.

But if the buyer fraudulently adopts the alias of a non-existent person who could not have been known to the seller, the contract is only voidable for misrepresentation.

> *King's Norton Metal Co v Edridge Merrett & Co 1897*
> *The facts:* The claimants received an order for goods from 'Hallam & Co', an alias assumed by a rogue called Wallis. The claimants had not heard of H & Co. On receiving the goods (consigned to H & Co), W re-sold them to the defendants and the claimants sued the defendants for the value of the goods.
>
> *Held:* The claimants intended to sell to the writer of the letter, who was W trading as H & Co. There was a mistake as to the quality of creditworthiness, not as to identity. W acquired title to the goods and the defendants in turn acquired title before the contract between the claimants and W was rescinded by the claimants. The defendants were not accountable for the value of the goods.

6.5 Unilateral mistake: face-to-face transactions

When the parties meet face to face it is generally inferred that the seller intends to sell to the person whom he meets.

> *Phillips v Brooks 1919*
> *The facts:* A rogue entered a jeweller's shop, selected various items and proposed to pay by cheque. The jeweller replied that delivery must be delayed until the cheque had been cleared. The rogue then said that he was Sir George Bullough and the jeweller checked that the real Sir G.B. lived at the address given by the rogue. The rogue then asked to take a ring away with him and the jeweller accepted his cheque and allowed him to have it. The rogue pledged the ring to a pawnbroker, who was sued by the jeweller.
>
> *Held:* The action must fail. The jeweller had intended to contract with the person in the shop. There was no mistake of identity which made the contract void but only a mistake as to the creditworthiness of the buyer. Good title had passed to the rogue until the contract was avoided.
>
> *Lewis v Averay 1971*
> *The facts:* Lewis agreed to sell his car to a rogue who gave the impression that he was the actor Richard Greene. The rogue paid with a bad cheque signed in

the name R A Green and was allowed to take the car and documents when he produced a pass for Pinewood Studios with an official stamp.

Held: Lewis had contracted to sell the car to a rogue. The contract might be voidable for fraud but it was not void for mistake. Perusal of a pass was insufficient to demonstrate that he only wished to contract with the actor.

6.6 Mistakes over documents - *non est factum*

The law recognises the problems of a blind or illiterate person who signs a document which he cannot read. If it is not what he supposes he may be able to repudiate it as not his deed (*non est factum*). The relief will not ordinarily be given to a person who merely failed to read what it was within his capacity to read and understand.

In the Saunders case described below the following conditions were laid down which must be satisfied in repudiating a signed document as *non est factum*:

(a) there must be a **fundamental difference** between the legal effect of the document signed and that which the person who signed it believed it to have; and

(b) the mistake must have been made **without carelessness** on the part of the person who signs.

Saunders v Anglia Building Society 1971 (also known as *Gallie v Lee*)
The facts: Mrs Gallie agreed to help her nephew, Parkin, to raise money on the security of her house provided that she might continue to live in it until her death. Parkin arranged that Lee, a solicitor's clerk, should prepare the mortgage. Lee produced a document which was in fact a transfer of the house on sale to Lee. However, Lee told Mrs Gallie that the document was a deed of gift to Parkin and she signed it at a time when her spectacles were broken and she could not read. Lee paid nothing to Mrs Gallie or to Parkin. Mrs Gallie sought to repudiate the document as *non est factum.*

Held: Mrs Gallie knew that she was transferring her house and her act in signing the document during a temporary inability to read amounted to carelessness. The claim to repudiate the transfer failed.

Foster v Mackinnon 1869
An elderly man of feeble sight was asked to sign a guarantee. He had done so before. The document put before him to sign was in fact a bill of exchange which he signed as acceptor. He repudiated it as *non est factum.*

Held: The document signed was so different from what it was believed to be that a defence of *non est factum* could be available.

Lloyds Bank plc v Waterhouse 1990
The facts: The bank obtained a guarantee from a father as security for a loan to his son to buy a farm. It also took a charge over the farm. The father did not read the guarantee because he was illiterate (which he did not tell the bank) but he did enquire of the bank about the guarantee's terms. As a result he believed that he was guaranteeing only the loan for the farm. In fact he signed a guarantee securing all the son's indebtedness to the bank. The son defaulted and the bank called on the father's guarantee for that amount of the son's debts which was not repaid following the farm's sale.

Held: The father had made adequate attempts to discover his liability by questioning the bank's employees. They had caused him to believe he was signing something other than he believed. This was a case of both *non est factum* and negligent misrepresentation.

7 EQUITABLE RELIEFS FOR MISTAKE

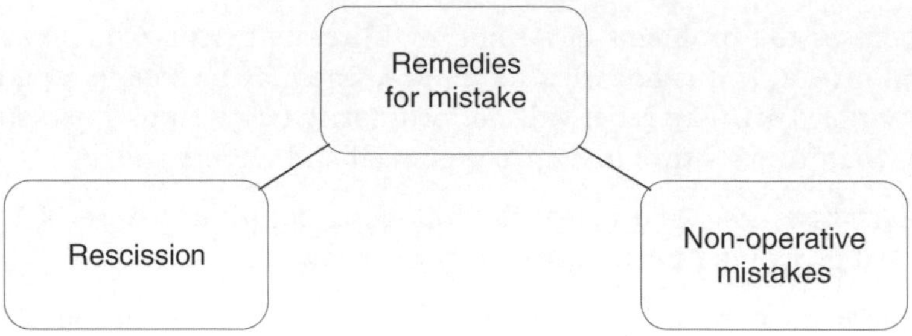

7.1 Rescission

As you have seen, this is an equitable remedy which is available when a contract is voidable. A different type of relief - **rectification** - may be claimed when the document does not correctly express the common intention of the parties.

Joscelyne v Nissen 1970
The facts: J lived in the same house with his married daughter N. J agreed to transfer his car hire business to N and N undertook as part of the bargain to pay all the household expenses including the electricity, gas and coal bills due in respect of the part of the house occupied by J. The bargain, not amounting at that stage to a contract, was then expressed in a written agreement which made no reference to N's liability to pay the household bills.

Held: J was entitled to have the written agreement rectified.

Definition

Rectification can be defined as an equitable remedy whereby a court may correct a written document, which, by mistake, does not represent the real intentions of the parties.

7.2 Non-operative mistakes

Unless it is unfair, a party who has made a non-operative mistake must abide by his contract.

Equity will sometimes impose a compromise on the parties:

Solle v Butcher 1950
The facts: Extensive improvements were made to what had been a rent-controlled flat. Both landlord and tenant believed that the flat had therefore ceased to be subject to rent control. It was let at a rent of £250 per

annum. It was discovered that the flat was still subject to rent control. The tenant sought to recover the excess rent and the landlord to rescind the lease.

Held: The tenant should have the choice between a surrender of the lease and accepting a new lease at a controlled rent increased to make allowance for the landlord's improvements.

If A was aware of B's mistake but did not bring it about by misrepresentation, the court may refuse an order for specific performance since A is seeking to take unfair advantage of a mistake of the other party.

Webster v Cecil 1861
The facts: A was negotiating the purchase of property from B. A knew that B had refused an offer of £2,000. B however, wrote a letter to A offering to sell the property for £1,250. The court concluded that A knew that B wished to offer it at a price of £2,250. A sued for specific performance of the contract to purchase the land.

Held: The order for specific performance would not be made (for the reasons indicated above).

8 UNDUE INFLUENCE

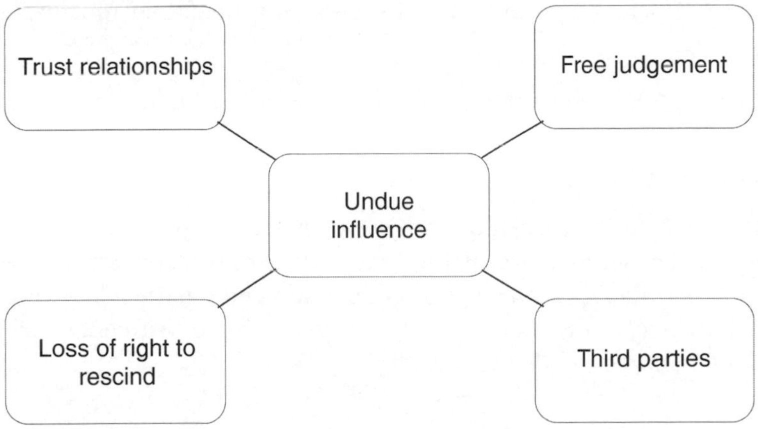

A contract is voidable if the party who made the contract or gift did so under the undue influence of another person. This is an equitable relief.

To succeed in a claim for undue influence, the following must be shown.

(a) A relationship of **trust and confidence** existed (in some cases this is assumed).

(b) The weaker party **did not exercise free judgement** in making the contract.

(c) The resulting contract is to the **manifest disadvantage** of the weaker party and the obvious benefit of the stronger.

(d) The weaker party has sought to **avoid** the contract as soon as the undue influence ceased to affect him or her.

8.1 Relationship of trust and confidence

When the parties stand in certain relationships the law assumes that one has undue influence over the other.

(a) Parent and child
(b) Solicitor and client
(c) Trustee and beneficiary under the trust
(d) Religious adviser and disciple
(e) Doctor and patient
(f) Guardian and ward

Note that the following relationships are not assumed to be ones in which undue influence is exerted - although this assumption may of course be rebutted.

(a) Bank and customer
(b) Husband and wife
(c) Employer and employee

The courts will look at all the facts in ascertaining whether in a particular case undue influence has in fact been exercised.

> *Hodgson v Marks 1970*
> *The facts:* An elderly lady transferred her house to her lodger and allowed him to manage her affairs. He later sold the house.
>
> *Held:* Undue influence was to be inferred from the relationship and the benefits obtained by the lodger.

> *Williams v Bayley 1866*
> *The facts:* A bank official told an elderly man that the bank might prosecute his son for forgery and to avoid such action the father mortgaged property to the bank.
>
> *Held:* There is no presumption of undue influence in the relation of the bank and customer but it could be proved to exist (as it did in this case) by the relevant facts.

It is perfectly possible for a relationship to exist where one person places trust and confidence in another without a resulting contract being voidable for undue influence. It is only where the stronger person steps outside **a fair and businesslike relationship** and obtains a benefit from the abuse of trust that undue influence arises: *National Westminster Bank v Morgan 1985*. (See below).

8.2 Free judgement

If it appears that there is undue influence, the party who is deemed to have the influence may resist the attempt to set aside the contract by showing that the weaker party did in fact exercise a free judgement in making the contract.

> *Lloyds Bank v Bundy 1975*
> *The facts:* On facts very like those of *Williams v Bayley* above a customer gave the bank a charge over his house.
>
> *Held:* Since the bank had not arranged for the customer to have independent advice the charge in favour of the bank would be set aside.

However, there may be undue influence even where the defendant tries to rebut the presumption by showing that the claimant has refused independent advice.

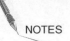

Goldsworthy v Brickell 1987

The facts: G, an 85 year old man entered into an agreement to give tenancy of a farm to B, who had been helping him run it. The terms were highly favourable to B, but G had rejected opportunities to consult a solicitor. G sought for the agreement to be rescinded.

Held: Although there had been no domination, the fact that the agreement's terms were clearly unfair and that G placed trust in B meant that the presumption could not be rebutted by showing that free exercise of judgement was allowed. G could rescind.

8.3 Manifest disadvantage

A transaction will not be set aside on the ground of undue influence unless it can be shown that the transaction is to the **manifest disadvantage** of the person subjected to undue influence.

National Westminster Bank v Morgan 1985

The facts: A wife (W) signed a re-mortgage of the family home (owned jointly with her husband H) in favour of the bank, to prevent the original mortgagee from continuing with proceedings to repossess the home. The bank manager told her in good faith, but incorrectly, that the mortgage only secured liabilities in respect of the home. In fact, it covered all H's debts to the bank. W signed the mortgage at home, in the presence of the manager, and without taking independent advice. H and W fell into arrears with the payments and soon afterwards H died. At the time of his death, nothing was owed to the bank in respect of H's business liabilities. The bank sought possession, but W contended that she had only signed the mortgage because of undue influence from the bank and, therefore, it should be set aside.

Held: The House of Lords, reversing the Court of Appeal's decision, held that the manager had not crossed the line between explaining an ordinary business transaction and entering into a relationship in which he had a dominant influence. Furthermore, the transaction was not unfair to W. Therefore, the bank was not under a duty to ensure that W took independent advice.

The case below identifies what is and is not manifest disadvantage.

Bank of Credit and Commerce International v Aboody 1988

The facts: Mrs A purchased the family home in 1949 and it was registered in her sole name. Mr A ran a business in which his wife took no interest but in 1959 she became a director of his company on the understanding that she would have to do nothing. Between 1976 and 1980 she signed three guarantees and three mortgages over her house. Mr A deliberately concealed matters from his wife. The company collapsed due to Mr A's fraud and the bank sought to enforce the guarantees against Mr and Mrs A.

Held: There had been actual undue influence over his wife by Mr A but Mrs A had suffered no manifest disadvantage since, at the time she signed the documents, her husband's business was comfortably supporting her and there was no indication that it would not continue to do so.

8.4 Undue influence and third parties

The scenario where a wife (or cohabitee) mortgages their share of the home to secure a partner's business liabilities is an example of contracting with a third party due to the undue influence of another dominant party. As a general rule such a transaction cannot be set aside but there are two exceptions:

(a) where the dominant party is the **agent** of the third party;

(b) where the third party **has notice** of the dominant party's undue influence and did not recommend that the complainant take legal advice.

The leading case is:

> *Barclays Bank v O'Brien 1993*
> *The facts:* Mrs O'Brien signed a document mortgaging her share of the matrimonial home to Barclays as a security for all her husband's business liabilities. The husband had falsely represented to her that the security was limited to £60,000 for 3 weeks. Barclays prepared the documents and Mrs O'Brien signed them without reading. The bank manager did not explain the documents or recommend that she take legal advice. When the husband's business failed the Bank enforced the mortgage for £154,000. In her defence Mrs O'Brien pleaded that the bank had notice of her husband's misrepresentation.
>
> *Held:* Her plea succeeded (except to the extent of £60,000).

8.5 Loss of right to rescind

The right to rescind the contract for undue influence is lost if there is delay in taking action.

> *Allcard v Skinner 1887*
> *The facts:* Under the influence of a clergyman, the claimant entered a Protestant convent in 1868 and, in compliance with a vow of poverty, transferred property worth about £7,000 to the Order by 1878. In 1879 she left the order and became a Roman Catholic. Six years later she demanded the return of £1,671, the unexpended balance of her gift, claiming undue influence.
>
> *Held:* This was a case of undue influence for which a right of rescission may be available, since, among other things, the rule of the order forbade its members from seeking the advice of outsiders.

The right to rescission is also lost if the party affirms the contract by performing obligations without protest, or if an innocent third party has acquired rights.

Chapter roundup

- A representation is a statement made in pre-contract negotiations, intended to induce the other party to enter into the agreement; it may or may not subsequently become a contract term.
- A contract entered into following a misrepresentation is voidable by the person to whom the misrepresentation was made. A misrepresentation is a statement of fact which is untrue, made by one party to the other in order to induce the latter to enter into the agreement, and a matter of some importance actually relied upon by the person misled.
- Fraudulent misrepresentation is a statement made knowing it to be untrue, not believing it to be true or recklessly, careless whether it be true or false. Remedies are rescission, refusal to perform and damages for loss in the tort of deceit.
- Negligent misrepresentation is a statement made in the belief that it is true but without reasonable grounds for that belief. Remedies are rescission, refusal to perform, damages for loss under the Misrepresentation Act 1967 and damages instead of rescission.
- Innocent misrepresentation, the residual category, is any statement made in the belief that it is true and with reasonable grounds for that belief. Remedies are rescission, refusal to perform and damages instead of rescission.
- The general rule is that a party to a contract is not discharged from his obligations because he is mistaken as to the terms of the contract or the relevant circumstances. There are a number of exceptional circumstances in which 'operative mistake' may render the contract void.
  - Common mistake occurs where the parties are both mistaken as to some fundamental point, for example the existence of the subject matter of the contract.
  - Mutual mistake occurs where the parties, without realising it, are at cross-purposes.
  - Unilateral mistake arises where one party is mistaken and the other is aware of it.
- Undue influence may arise where a relationship of trust and confidence exists and one party exerts influence on the other party to a contract to the disadvantage of the weaker party.

Quick quiz

1. What is a misrepresentation?
2. Can silence be a misrepresentation?
3. What are the two categories of negligent misrepresentation?
4. How may the representee affirm a contract following a misrepresentation?
5. List four situations in which the right to rescind is lost.

NOTES

6 What is *res sua*?

7 What is the effect of a mistake concerning the qualities of the subject matter of a contract?

8 What is *non est factum*?

9 Give three examples of relationships where a relationship of trust and confidence is assumed to exist.

10 What were the facts of *Allcard v Skinner 1887?*

Answers to quick quiz

1 A false statement of fact made by one party to the other, before the contract is made, inducing the party misled to enter the contract. (see para 2)

2 Not usually. But it is if it is a half-truth or the situation has changed or in a contract uberrimae fidei. (para 3.4)

3 Negligent (ie reckless) and innocent (ie without fault). (paras 4.2, 4.3)

4 By continuing to act under the contract after he is aware of the misrepresentation. (para 5.4)

5 Party misled affirms the contract
Pre-contractual position cannot be restored
Rights of third parties prejudiced
Lapse of time (para 5.4)

6 When a person unwittingly buys something which already belongs to him. (para 6.2)

7 The contract would remain valid. (para 6.3)

8 A legal plea that a document can be repudiated because it is not the deed of the person who signed it. (para 6.6)

9 Parent – child
Solicitor – client
Doctor – patient (para 8.1)

10 It was undue influence when a nun renounced all her worldly goods on entering a convent. She had been influenced by a clergyman. (para 8.5)

Answers to activities

1 (a) and (b). Both are statements of fact.

2 Yes. He was not sufficiently specific.

3 Yes. When the contract was made, X had lost his reasonable grounds for believing that his representation was true.

4 It would render it invalid, as Nigel has not acted *uberrimae fidei.*

BPP PUBLISHING

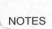

Assignment 5 **(40 minutes)**

James informed Graham that Alan, a mutual friend, had a 1993 Renault 19 motor car for sale, when in fact it was a 1991 model. Graham, anxious to acquire the car, telephoned Alan and agreed to buy the car unseen without any reference to its date of manufacture.

When Alan delivered the car, Graham realised his mistake and refused to accept the car. Alan is threatening to sue Graham for breach of contract, whereas Graham rejects this outright, arguing that it was simply a mistake which does not bind him.

Advise Alan and Graham on how mistake, in the law of contract, will affect their respective legal positions.

Chapter 9 :

DISCHARGE OF CONTRACT AND REMEDIES FOR BREACH

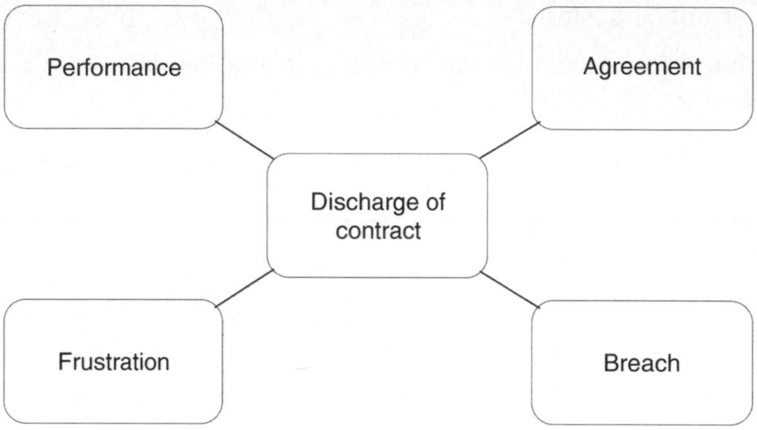

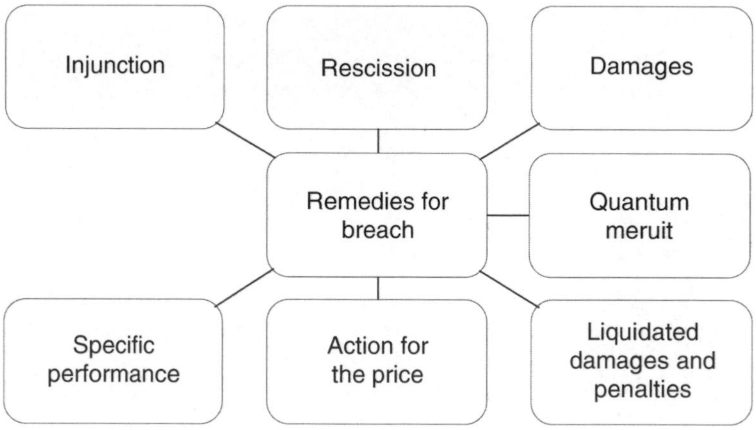

Introduction

A party who is subject to the obligations of a contract may be discharged from those obligations in one of four ways. The agreement is then at an end. The four ways are performance, agreement, breach and frustration. After a discussion of these, we look at remedies for breach of contract

A party has a number of remedies when the other party is in breach of contract. Damages are a form of compensation for loss caused by the breach. An action for the price may be commenced where the breach is failure to pay. A *quantum meruit* is payment to the claimant for the value of what he has done. Specific performance, an equitable remedy, is a court order to the defendant to perform the contract. An injunction is a court order for the other party to observe negative restrictions.

Damages and action for the price are common law remedies and are most frequently sought when a remedy is needed for breach of contract, since they arise as of right. A *quantum meruit* claim enables the injured party to claim for the value of the work done.

Your objectives

In this chapter you will learn about the following

(a) The necessary elements for a contract to be discharged by performance

(b) How a contract may be discharged by an agreement which is binding on the parties

(c) The types of repudiatory breach of contract, and how anticipatory breach may arise

(d) The effects of termination and affirmation

(e) The circumstances in which frustration arises and when it cannot be pleaded

(f) The position of the parties following frustration

(g) Which losses may give rise to damages, and how damages are computed

(h) Liquidated damages and penalty clauses

(i) The limitations on action for the price

(j) The uses of quantum meruit, specific performance, injunction and rescission as remedies

(k) How actions for breach of contract may be limited by the passage of time

1 DISCHARGE BY PERFORMANCE

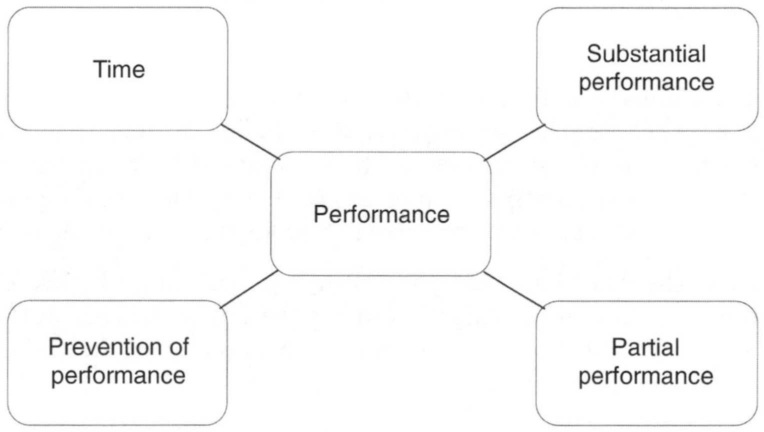

This is the normal method of discharge. Each party fulfils or performs his contractual obligations and the agreement is then ended. As a general rule contractual obligations are discharged only by complete and exact performance. Partial performance does not usually suffice, nor does incorrect performance.

> *Cutter v Powell 1795*
> The defendant employed C as second mate of a ship sailing from Jamaica to Liverpool at a wage for the complete voyage of 30 guineas [£31.50]. The voyage began on 2 August, and C died at sea on 20 September, when the ship was still 19 days from Liverpool. C's widow sued for a proportionate part of the agreed sum.
>
> *Held:* C was entitled to nothing unless he completed the voyage.

Bolton v Mahadeva 1972
The claimant agreed to install a central heating system in the defendant's home for £800. The work was defective: the system did not heat adequately and it gave off fumes. The defendant refused to pay for it.

Held: the claimant could recover nothing.

In each of these cases the defendant might appear to have profited to an undue degree, since he obtained part of what the claimant contracted to deliver without himself having to pay anything. Although these cases can be justified on their facts, the courts have developed a number of exceptions to the rule to ensure that the interests of both parties are protected.

1.1 Substantial performance

The doctrine of substantial performance may be applied, especially in contracts for building work and the like. If the building contractor has completed the essential work and in doing so has completed a very large part of it, he may claim the contract price less a deduction for the minor work outstanding. This may also be regarded as a deduction of damages for breach of warranty when the contract price is paid.

Hoenig v Isaacs 1952
The defendant employed the claimant to decorate and furnish his flat at a total price of £750. There were defects in the furniture which could be put right at a cost of £56. The defendant argued that the claimant was only entitled to reasonable remuneration.

Held: the defendant must pay the balance owing of the total price of £750 less an allowance of £56, as the claimant had substantially completed the contract.

Sumpter v Hedges 1898
The claimant undertook to erect buildings on the land of the defendant for a price of £565. He partially erected the buildings, then abandoned the work when it was only completed to the value of £333. The defendant completed the work using materials left on his land. The claimant sued for the value of his materials used by the defendant and for the value of his work.

Held: the defendant must pay for the materials since he had elected to use them but he had no obligation to pay the unpaid balance of the charges for work done by the claimant before abandoning it. It was not a case of substantial performance of the contract.

1.2 Partial performance

The promisee may accept partial performance and must then pay for it. For example, A orders a dozen bottles of beer from B; B delivers ten which is all he has in stock. A may reject the ten bottles but if he accepts them he must pay for ten bottles at the appropriate rate. The principle here is that although the promisor has only partially fulfilled his contractual obligations, it may sometimes be possible to infer the existence of a fresh agreement by which it is agreed that payment will be made for work already done or goods already supplied. Mere performance by the promisor is not enough; it must be open to the promisee either to accept or reject the benefit of the contract. Thus in Bolton v Mahadeva, above, this could not apply once the heating system had been installed.

1.3 Prevention of performance

The promisee may prevent performance. In that case the offer (tender) of performance is sufficient discharge. For example, if the buyer will not accept delivery of the contract goods and the seller sues for breach of contract, the seller need only show that he tendered performance by offering to deliver.

If one party is prevented by the other from performing the contract completely he may sue for damages for breach of contract, or alternatively bring a quantum meruit action to claim for the amount of work done.

> *Planché v Colburn 1831*
> *The facts*: the claimant had agreed to write a book on costumes and armour for the defendants' 'Juvenile Library' series. He was to receive £100 on completion. He did some research and wrote part of the book. The defendants then abandoned the series.
>
> *Held*: the claimant was entitled to 50 guineas as reasonable remuneration on a *quantum meruit* basis.

Activity 1 **(5 minutes)**

Why could the doctrine of partial performance not be applied in Cutter v Powell?

1.4 Time of performance

If one party fails to perform at the agreed time he may perform the contract later – the contract continues in force, unless prompt performance is an essential condition ('time is of the essence'). In that case the injured party may refuse late performance and treat the contract as discharged by breach. Where time is not of the essence the injured party may claim damages for any loss or expense caused by the delay but must accept late performance.

If the parties expressly agree that time is of the essence and so prompt performance is to be a condition, that is conclusive and late performance does not discharge obligations.

Severable contracts

The contract may provide for performance by instalments with separate payment for each of them (a divisible or severable contract).

> *Taylor v Laird 1856*
> The claimant agreed to captain a ship up the River Niger at a rate of £50 per month. He abandoned the job before it was completed. He claimed his pay for the months completed.
>
> *Held:* he was entitled to £50 for each complete month. Effectively this was a contract that provided for performance and payment in monthly instalments.

NOTES

2 DISCHARGE BY AGREEMENT

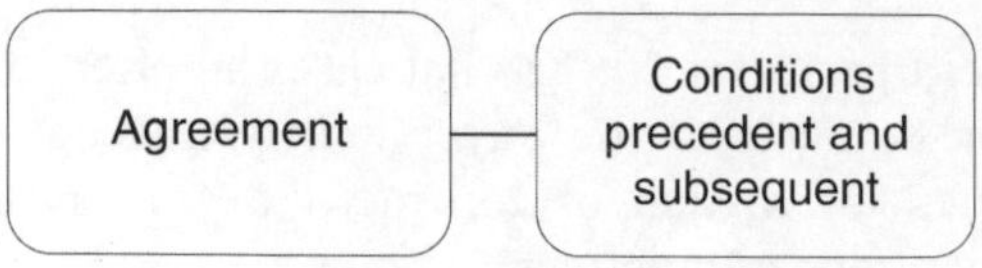

The parties may agree to cancel the contract before it has been completely performed on both sides. But the agreement to cancel is itself a new contract for which consideration must be given (unless it is a contract for release by deed).

If there are unperformed obligations of the original contract on both sides (that is, it is an executory contract), each party provides consideration for his own release by agreeing to release the other (bilateral discharge). Each party surrenders something of value.

But if one party has completely performed his obligations, his agreement to release the other from his obligations (unilateral discharge) requires consideration, such as payment of a cancellation fee. This is called accord and satisfaction.

If the parties enter into a new contract to replace the unperformed contract, the new contract provides any necessary consideration. This is called novation of the old contract.

2.1 Conditions precedent and subsequent

A contract may include provision for its own discharge by imposing a **condition precedent**, which prevents the contract from coming into operation unless the condition is satisfied. Alternatively, it may impose a **condition subsequent** by which the contract is discharged on the later happening of an event. Effectively these are contracts whereby discharge may arise through agreement.

> *Aberfoyle Plantations Ltd v Cheng 1960*
> *The facts*: the parties agreed in 1955 to sell and buy a plantation which included 182 acres in respect of which the leases had expired in 1950. The vendor had tried without success in the intervening years to obtain a renewal of the leases. The agreement provided that 'the purchase is conditional on the vendor obtaining a renewal' of the leases. If he was 'unable to fulfil this condition, this agreement shall become null and void'. The vendor failed to obtain the renewal.
>
> *Held*: the purchaser could recover the deposit he had paid, as the renewal of the leases was a condition precedent.
>
> *Head v Tattersall 1871*
> *The facts*: the claimant bought a horse guaranteed 'to have been hunted with the Bicester hounds', on the understanding that it could be returned within a time limit if it did not answer the description. The horse was injured and the claimant discovered that it had never hunted with the Bicester hounds. The claimant returned it and sued for the return of the price.
>
> *Held*: a contract had come into existence, but the option to return the horse was a condition subsequent. The claimant was entitled to cancel the contract, return the horse and recover the price.

3 BREACH OF CONTRACT

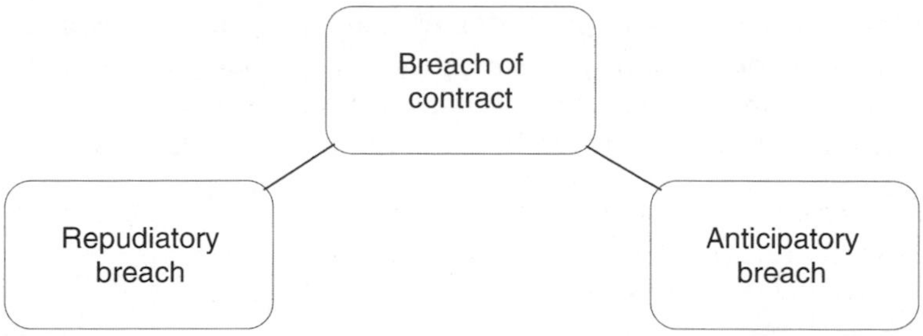

A party is said to be in breach of contract where, without lawful excuse, he does not perform his contractual obligations precisely. This may be because he refuses to perform them, he fails to perform them, he incapacitates himself from performing them or he performs them defectively.

Breach of contract gives rise to a secondary obligation to pay the other party damages but, unless breach is treated as repudiation, the primary obligation to perform the contract's terms remains.

A person has a lawful excuse not to perform primary contractual obligations (that is, what he promised to do under his side of the bargain) in the following situations.

(a) Where performance is impossible.
(b) Where he has tendered performance but this has been rejected.
(c) Where the other party has made it impossible for him to perform.
(d) Where the contract has been discharged through frustration.

3.1 Repudiatory breach

A repudiatory breach is a serious actual breach of contract. It does not automatically discharge the contract. The injured party has a choice.

(a) He can elect to treat the contract as repudiated by the other, recover damages and treat himself as being discharged from his primary obligations under the contract. This is termination of the contract for repudiatory breach, or

(b) he can elect to affirm the contract.

Types of repudiatory breach

Repudiatory breach giving rise to a right either to terminate or to affirm arises in the following circumstances.

(a) *Refusal to perform (renunciation)*. One party renounces his contractual obligations by showing that he has no intention to perform them nor to be otherwise bound by the contract. Such refusal may be express or implied.

(b) *Failure to perform an entire obligation*. An entire obligation is one where complete and precise performance of it is a precondition of the other party's performance. As noted earlier, partial performance alone is not usually sufficient. Thus a contractual condition is often an entire obligation, so failure to perform the acts required by a condition can amount to a repudiatory breach.

(c) *Incapacitation*. Where a party, by his own act or default, prevents himself from performing his contractual obligations he is treated as if he refused to perform them. For instance, where A sells a thing to C even though he promised to sell it to B he is in repudiatory breach of his contract with B.

Genuine mistakes, even to one party's detriment will not necessarily repudiate a contract. This was the decision in *Vaswani Motors (Sales and Services) Ltd 1996*. A seller of a motor vehicle, acting in good faith, mistakenly demanded a higher price than that specified in the contract. However, the buyer could not evade his responsibilities under the contract, since he could have offered to pay the original price.

Activity 2 **(10 minutes)**

J contracts to sell a painting to K, and K contracts to sell it to L. However, when the time comes for the contract between J and K to be completed, K refuses to pay for the painting so J will not let him have it. Which two types of repudiatory breach arise in relation to the two contracts?

Termination for repudiatory breach

As noted above, the innocent party in a case of repudiatory breach may elect to accept the contract as terminated or discharged by breach, thereby discharging himself from any further obligation to perform. Alternatively, he may affirm the contract. If he decides to terminate for repudiatory breach the innocent party must notify the other of his decision. This may be by way of refusal to accept defects in performance, to accept further performance or to perform his own obligations. The effects of such termination are as follows for the innocent party.

(a) He is not bound by his future or continuing contractual obligations, and cannot be sued on them.

(b) He need not accept nor pay for further performance.

(c) He can refuse to pay for partial or defective performance already received.

(d) He can reclaim money paid to a defaulter if he rejects defective performance.

(e) He is not discharged from the contractual obligations which were due at the time of termination.

The innocent party can also claim damages from the defaulter for:

(a) losses sustained by him in respect of unperformed contractual obligations due at the time of default (the defaulter is in theory still bound); and

(b) losses sustained by him in relation to contractual obligations which were due in the future.

Finally an innocent party who began to perform his contractual obligations but who was prevented from completing them by the defaulter can claim reasonable remuneration on a quantum meruit basis.

Affirmation after repudiatory breach

If a person is aware of the other party's repudiatory breach and of his right to terminate the contract as a result but still decides to treat the contract as being in existence he is said to have affirmed the contract. Such a decision should be a conscious or active one; it

NOTES

is not deemed to have been made purely by virtue of the fact that a person retains defective goods while he or she decides what to do.

The effect of affirmation is that the contract remains fully in force, so each party is bound to perform existing and future obligations and may sue to enforce them. If the election is unconditional – 'I shall keep the goods despite their defects' – it may not be revoked. If it is conditional – 'I will keep the defective goods provided they are mended free of charge' – and the condition is not satisfied, the contract may then be terminated.

Activity 3 **(10 minutes)**

G and H make a contract under which H is to redecorate G's lounge. After stripping the old wallpaper, H declares (without any reason) that he will not do any more work. G then notifies H that he is terminating the contract for repudiatory breach. G has already paid H £50, but refuses to pay any more. H claims a further £200 for the work done. Advise G as to the legal position.

3.2 Anticipatory breach

A party may break a condition of the contract merely by declaring in advance that he will not perform it when the time for performance arrives, or by some other action which makes future performance impossible. The other party may treat this as *anticipatory breach* and can choose between treating the contract as discharged forthwith and allowing it to continue until there is an actual breach.

The risk is that, in the latter case, the party guilty of anticipatory breach may subsequently change his mind and perform the contract after all. If the contract is allowed to continue in this way the parties may be discharged from their obligations without liability by some other cause which occurs later.

> *Hochster v De La Tour 1853*
> T engaged H as a courier to accompany him on a European tour commencing on 1 June. On 11 May T wrote to H to say that he no longer required his services. On 22 May H commenced legal proceedings for anticipatory breach of contract. T objected that there was no actionable breach until 1 June.
>
> *Held:* H was entitled to sue as soon as the anticipatory breach occurred on 11 May.
>
> *Avery v Bowden 1855*
> There was a contract to charter a ship to load grain at Odessa within a period of 45 days. The ship arrived at Odessa and the charterer told the master that he did not propose to load a cargo. The master remained at Odessa hoping the charterer would change his mind-that is, he did not there and then treat the contract as discharged by the charterer's anticipatory breach. Before the 45 days for loading cargo had expired the outbreak of the Crimean war discharged the contract by frustration.
>
> *Held:* the shipowner, through the master, had waived his right to sue for anticipatory breach (with a claim for damages). The contract continued and had been discharged later by frustration (the outbreak of war) without liability for either party.

If the innocent party elects to treat the contract as still in force despite the other party's anticipatory breach, the former may continue with his preparations for performance and recover the agreed price for his services. But any claim for damages will be assessed on the basis of what the claimant has really lost.

> *The Mihalis Angelos 1971*
> There was a charter of a ship to be 'ready to load at Haiphong' (in Vietnam) on 1 July 1965. The charterers had the option to cancel if the ship was not ready to load by 20 July. On 17 July the charterers repudiated the contract believing (wrongly) that they were entitled to do so. The shipowners accepted the repudiation and claimed damages. On 17 July the ship was still in Hong Kong and could not have reached Haiphong by 20 July.
>
> *Held:* the shipowners were entitled only to nominal damages since they would have been unable to perform the contract and the charterers could have cancelled it without liability on 20 July.

Activity 4 **(10 minutes)**

X contracts to sell a computer to Y. Ten days before the date for delivery and payment, Y tells X that he does not intend to go ahead with the purchase. Does X need to deliver the computer immediately in order to secure his legal position against Y?

4 DISCHARGE BY FRUSTRATION

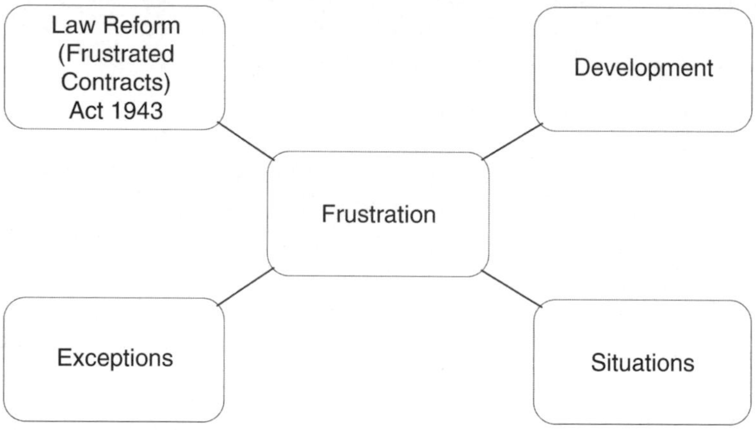

If it is impossible to perform the contract when it is made, there is usually no contract at all: it is void and each party is released from performing any obligation after the frustrating event. In addition, the parties are free to negotiate 'escape clauses' or force majeure clauses covering impossibility which arises after the contract has been made. If they fail to do so, they are, as a general rule, in breach of contract if they find themselves unable to do what they have agreed to do.

> *Paradine v Jane 1647*
> A tenant who was being sued for rent pleaded that he had been dispossessed of the land for the previous three years by the King's enemies.
>
> *Held:* his plea failed. 'Where a party by his own contract creates a duty or charge upon himself, he is bound to make it good, notwithstanding any

NOTES

accident by inevitable necessity, because he might have provided against it by his contract.'

4.1 Development of the doctrine of frustration

The basic rule, outlined above, was to the effect that impossibility in carrying out a contract, which was not in itself anticipated by a contractual term, would cause the contract to be in breach. For example in *Cutter v Powell* which you saw in the context of discharge by performance, no part of the contract was regarded as having been carried out. This rather harsh interpretation of the law led to some arguably very unfair decisions, as a result of which the doctrine of frustration has evolved.

This says that where the performance of a contract becomes impossible because of the occurrence of an event which was not anticipated by the parties, it may be regarded as frustrated and will be discharged. This is not the same as saying that the contract is to be regarded as void *ab initio* (ie from the outset) but rather that it would be discharged automatically for the future.

The doctrine applies in a number of situations:

(a) Destruction of the subject matter. This case was the origin of the doctrine of frustration.

Taylor v Caldwell 1863
A hall was let for a series of concerts on specified dates. Before the date of the first concert the hall was destroyed by fire. The concert organiser sued the owner of the hall for damages for failure to let him have the use of the hall as agreed.

Held: destruction of the subject matter rendered the contract impossible to perform and discharged the contract.

(b) Personal incapacity to perform a contract of personal service. Other instances of frustration in this category are where the person dies, is called up for military service or is interned in wartime.

Condor v Barron Knights 1966
C, aged 16, contracted to perform as drummer in a pop group. His duties, when the group had work, were to play on every night of the week. He fell ill and his doctor advised that he should restrict his performances to four nights a week. The group terminated his contract.

Held: a contract of personal service is based on the assumption that the employee's health will permit him to perform his duties. If that is not so the contract is discharged by frustration.

F C Shepherd & Co Ltd v Jerrom 1986
J entered into a contract of apprenticeship with S & Co. Subsequently he was sentenced to a period of borstal training following a conviction for conspiring to assault and to cause affray. He served 39 weeks. The employers told J's father that they were not prepared to take J back.

Held: the contract has been discharged by frustration.

(c) Government intervention or supervening illegality

Re Shipton, Anderson & Co etc 1915
The contract was for the sale of wheat stored in a Liverpool warehouse. It was requisitioned by the government under emergency wartime powers.

Held: it was no longer lawful for the seller to deliver the wheat. The contract had been discharged by frustration.

(d) Non-occurrence of an event if it is the sole purpose of the contract. Two contrasting examples of this application of the doctrine are provided by the so-called 'coronation cases'.

Krell v Henry 1903
A room overlooking the route of the coronation procession of Edward VII was let for the day of the coronation for the purpose of viewing the procession. The coronation was postponed owing to the illness of the King. The owner of the room sued for the agreed fee, which was payable on the day of the coronation.

Held: the contract was made for the sole purpose of viewing the procession. As that event did not occur the contract was frustrated.

Herne Bay Steamship Co v Hutton 1903
A steamboat was hired for two days to carry passengers round the naval review at Spithead and for a day's cruise round the fleet. The review had been arranged as part of the coronation celebrations. The review was cancelled owing to the King's illness but the steamboat could have taken passengers for a trip round the assembled fleet, which remained at Spithead.

Held: the royal review of the fleet was not the sole occasion of the contract and the contract was not discharged. The owner of the steamboat was entitled to the agreed hire charge less what he had earned from the normal use of the vessel over the two day period.

(e) Interruption which prevents performance of the contract in the form intended by the parties

In some cases, the parties may make express provision for certain contingencies. However if the effect of the contingency is to frustrate the essential object of the contract, the contract will nevertheless be discharged.

Jackson v Union Marine Insurance Co 1874
The parties contracted in November 1871 for a charter of a ship to proceed immediately from Liverpool to Newport, 'damages and accidents of navigation excepted', to load cargo for San Francisco. Having sailed on 2 January, the ship went ashore off the coast of Wales on 3 January and could not be refloated for a month. Thereafter she needed repairs in Liverpool to make her fit for the voyage; these were still in progress in August. Meanwhile the charterers hired another vessel. The claimant claimed on his policy of insurance.

Held: the interruption had put an end to the contract in the commercial sense. It was no longer possible to perform the contract intended. The contract was discharged by frustration. The claimant had no claim against the charterer and could claim from the defendants.

Gamerco SA v ICM/Fair Warning (Agency) Ltd 1995
Gamerco SA, pop concert promoters, agreed to promote a concert to be held by the defendant group at a stadium in Spain. However, the stadium was found by engineers to be unsafe and the authorities banned its use and revoked the claimants' permit to hold the concert. No alternative site was available and the concert was cancelled.

Held: The contract was frustrated because the stadium was unsafe, a circumstance beyond the control of Gamerco SA.

Activity 5 **(10 minutes)**

A small company of coal merchants has contracts to supply householders. The main lorry driver of the company dies suddenly, and the remaining staff cannot manage to deal with all the orders placed. A householder whose order is not fulfilled sues for breach of contract. Consider whether or not the company can plead discharge by frustration.

4.2 When the doctrine does not apply

A contract is not discharged by frustration in the following circumstances.

(a) If an alternative mode of performance is still possible.

Tsakiroglou & Co v Noblee and Thorl GmbH 1962
There was a contract for the sale of 300 tons of Sudan groundnuts to be delivered to Hamburg. The normal and intended method of shipment from Port Sudan (on the Red Sea coast) was by a ship routed through the Suez Canal to Hamburg. Before shipment the Suez Canal was closed; the sellers refused to ship the cargo arguing that it was an implied term that shipment should be via Suez or, alternatively, that shipment via the Cape of Good Hope would make the contract 'commercially and fundamentally' different, so that it was discharged by frustration.

Held: both arguments failed. There was no evidence to support the implied term argument nor was the use of a different (and more expensive) route an alteration of the fundamental nature of the contract sufficient to discharge it by frustration.

(b) If performance suddenly becomes more expensive.

Davis Contractors v Fareham UDC 1956
DC agreed to build 78 houses at a price of £94,000 in eight months. Labour shortages caused the work to take 22 months and cost £115,000. DC wished to claim frustration so that they could then claim for their work on a quantum meruit basis.

Held: hardship, material loss or inconvenience did not amount to frustration; the obligation must change such that the thing undertaken would, if performed, be a different thing from that contracted for.

(c) If one party has accepted the risk that he will be unable to perform.

Budgett & Co v Binnington & Co 1891
A bill of lading provided that if the consignee could not unload his cargo within ten days, demurrage (compensation) would be payable. A strike prevented the unloading during the ten days.

Held: the consignee had accepted the risk and must pay the demurrage as agreed.

(d) If one party has induced frustration by his own choice between alternatives.

Maritime National Fish v Ocean Trawlers 1935
There was a contract for the hire of a trawler for use in otter trawling. The hirers had four other trawlers of their own. They applied to the Canadian government for the necessary licences for five trawlers but were granted only three licences. They nominated three of their own trawlers for the

licences and argued that the contract for the hire of a fifth trawler had been frustrated since it could not lawfully be used.

Held: the impossibility of performing the hire contract was the result of a choice made by the hirers: the trawler on hire could have been nominated for one of the three licences. This was not a case for discharge by frustration.

4.3 The Law Reform (Frustrated Contracts) Act 1943

Where a contract is frustrated, the common law provides that the loss shall lie where it falls; money paid before frustration cannot be recovered and money payable at the time of frustration remains payable, unless there is a complete failure of consideration. The consequences of this can be harsh.

Chandler v Webster 1904
The defendant agreed to let the claimant have a room for £141.15s [£141.75] for the purpose of viewing the coronation procession of Edward VII. The contract provided that the money was payable immediately. The coronation was postponed owing to the illness of the King. The claimant sued for the return of his £100 and the defendant counterclaimed for the unpaid amount of £41.15s.

Held: the obligation to pay rent had fallen due before the frustrating event. The claimant's action failed and the defendant's claim was upheld.

This case can be contrasted with *Krell v Henry 1903*, where the contract stipulated that payment was due on the day of the procession. The common law provides that the loss shall lie where it falls; money paid before frustration cannot be recovered and money payable at the time of frustration remains payable. Only in 1942 was the doctrine modified, so that, where there is a complete failure of consideration, the contract can be held void ab initio: *Fibrosa v Fairbairn 1942.*

4.4 Effects of the Act

In most cases the rights and liabilities of parties to a contract discharged by frustration are now regulated by the Law Reform (Frustrated Contracts) Act 1943 as follows.

(a) Any money paid under the contract by one party to the other is (subject to rule (b) below) to be repaid. Any sums due for payment under the contract then or later cease to be payable.

(b) A party who is liable under rule (a) to repay money received (or whose entitlement to payments already accrued is due for payment at the time of frustration is cancelled), may at the discretion of the court be allowed to set off (or to recover) out of those sums the whole or part of his expenses incurred in performing the contract up to the time when it is discharged by frustration. But he cannot recover from the other party his expenses insofar as they exceed sums paid or due to be paid to him at the time of discharge.

(c) If either party has obtained a valuable benefit (other than payment of money) under the contract before it is discharged, the court may in its discretion order him to pay to the other party all or part of that value. If, for example, one party has delivered to the other some of the goods to be supplied under the contract, the latter may be ordered to pay the amount of their value to him.

Activity 6 **(15 minutes)**

A contract between F and G is frustrated, and the Law Reform (Frustrated Contracts) Act 1943 applies. At the time of frustration, G has paid F £600 and F has incurred expenses of £270. G has not so far received any valuable benefit. Had the contract not been frustrated, F would have incurred further expenses of £430 and G would have paid F a further £500, giving F a profit of £400. If the court exercises its discretion in favour of F, what final settlement between F and G will be made?

We now move on to remedies for breach of contract.

5 DAMAGES

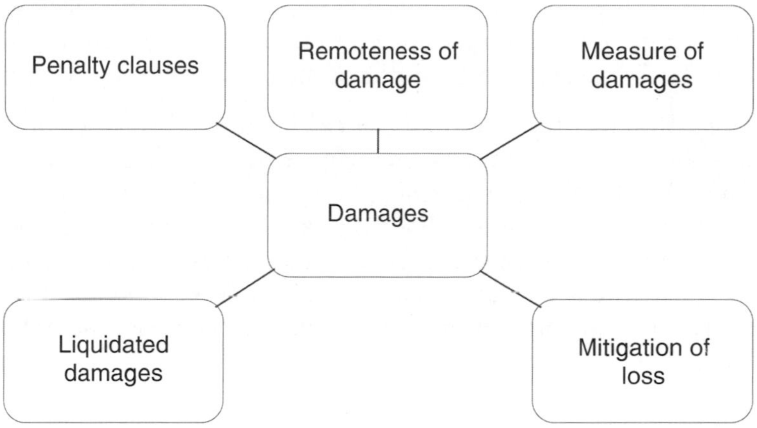

Definition

Damages: the sum claimed or awarded in a civil action in compensation for the loss or injury suffered by the claimant.

Damages are a common law remedy and are primarily intended to restore the party who has suffered loss to the same position he would have been in if the contract had been performed. They are *not* meant to be a punishment, which is a criminal, not a civil, measure. In addition, they should not allow the party to whom they are awarded to profit, nor to achieve a better result: the law will not make up for a bad bargain.

In a claim for damages the first issue is *remoteness of damage:* how far down the sequence of cause and effect should the consequences of breach be traced before they become so indirect that they should be ignored? Secondly, the court must decide how much money (the *measure of damages*) to award in respect of the breach and its relevant consequences.

5.1 Remoteness of damage

Under the rule in *Hadley v Baxendale* (below) damages may only be awarded in respect of loss as follows.

(a) (i) The loss must arise naturally, according to the usual course of things, from the breach; or

(ii) the loss must arise in a manner which the parties, in making the contract, may reasonably be supposed to have contemplated as the probable result of the breach of it.

(b) A loss outside the natural course of events will only be compensated if the exceptional circumstances which cause the loss are within the defendant's knowledge, actual or constructive, when he made the contract.

Hadley v Baxendale 1854
H owned a mill at Gloucester which came to a standstill because the main driving shaft had broken. H made a contract with B, a carrier, for the transport of the broken shaft to the makers at Greenwich to serve as a pattern for making a new shaft. Delivery was to be made at Greenwich the following day. Owing to neglect by B delivery was delayed and the mill was out of action for a longer period than would have resulted if there had been no delay. B did not know that the mill would be idle during this interval. He was merely aware that he had to transport a broken mill shaft from H's mill. H claimed for loss of profits of the mill during the period of delay.

Held: although the failure of the carrier to perform the contract promptly was the direct cause of the stoppage of the mill for an unnecessarily long time, the claim must fail, since B did not know that the mill would be idle until the new shaft was delivered (part (b) of the rule did not apply) and it was not a natural consequence of delay in transport of a broken shaft that the mill would be out of action meanwhile (part (a) of the rule did not apply). The importance of the shaft was not obvious; the miller might have had a spare.

Victoria Laundry (Windsor) v Newman Industries 1949
N contracted to sell a large boiler to V 'for immediate use' in V's business of launderers and dyers. Owing to an accident in dismantling the boiler at its previous site delivery was delayed by a period of four months. V claimed damages for (i) normal loss of profits (£16 per week) for the period of delay and (ii) loss of abnormal profits (£262 per week) from losing 'highly lucrative' dyeing contracts to be undertaken if the boiler had been delivered on time.

Held: damages for loss of normal profits were recoverable since in the circumstances failure to deliver major industrial equipment ordered for immediate use would be expected to prevent operation of the plant: it was a natural consequence covered by the first head of the rule. The claim for loss of special profits fell under the second head of the rule; it failed because N had no knowledge of the dyeing contracts and the abnormal profits which they would yield.

The Victoria Laundry judgement was confirmed by the House of Lords in the Heron case (below).

The Heron II 1969
There was a contract for the shipment of a bulk cargo of sugar from the Black Sea to Basra in Iraq. K, the shipowner, was aware that C were sugar merchants but he did not know that C intended to sell the cargo as soon as it reached Basra. The ship arrived nine days late and in that time the price of sugar on the market in Basra had fallen. C claimed damages for the loss due to the fall in market value of the cargo over the period of delay.

Held: the claim succeeded. It is common knowledge that market values of commodities fluctuate so that delay might cause loss. It was sufficiently obvious that a bulk cargo of sugar owned by merchants was destined for sale to which the market value would be relevant.

> **Activity 7** **(10 minutes)**
>
> Draft a clause which could have been included in the contract in Hadley v Baxendale 1854 in order to enable Hadley to recover damages for loss of profits during any delay.

5.2 The measure of damages

As a general rule the amount awarded as damages is the amount needed to put the claimant in the position he would have achieved if the contract had been performed. If, for example, there is failure to deliver goods at a contract price of £100 per ton and at the due time for delivery similar goods are obtainable at £110 per ton, damages are calculated at the rate of £100 per ton (s 51 (3) Sale of Goods Act 1979).

More complicated questions of assessing damages can arise. The general principle is to compensate for actual financial loss.

Thompson Ltd v Robinson (Gunmakers) Ltd 1955
The defendants contracted to buy a Vanguard car from the claimants. They refused to take delivery and the claimants sued for loss of profit on the transaction. There was at the time a considerable excess of supply of such cars over demand for them and the claimants were unable to sell the car.

Held: the market price rule, which the defendants argued should be applied, was inappropriate in the current market. The seller had lost a sale and was entitled to the profit which would have resulted from the purchase.

Charter v Sullivan 1957
The facts were the same as in the previous case, except that the sellers were able to sell every car obtained from the manufacturers.

Held: only nominal damages were payable.

5.3 Non-financial loss

At one time damages could not be recovered for any non-financial loss arising from breach of contract. In some recent cases, however, damages have been recovered for mental distress where that is the main result of the breach. It is uncertain how far the courts will develop this concept.

5.4 Mitigation of loss

In assessing the amount of damages it is assumed that the claimant will take any reasonable steps to reduce or mitigate his loss.

Payzu v Saunders 1919
There was a contract for the supply of goods to be delivered and paid for by instalments. The purchaser failed to pay for the first instalment when due, one month after delivery. The seller declined to make further deliveries unless the buyer paid cash in advance. The buyer refused to accept delivery

on those terms. The price of the goods rose and he sued for breach of contract.

Held: the seller was in breach of contract, as he had no right to repudiate the original contract. But the buyer should have mitigated his loss by accepting the seller's offer of delivery against cash payment. Damages were limited to the amount of the buyer's assumed loss if he had paid in advance, which was interest over the period of pre-payment. 'In commercial contracts, it is generally reasonable to accept an offer from the party in default.'

The injured party is not, however, required to take discreditable or risky measures to reduce his loss since these are not 'reasonable': Pilkington v Wood 1953. Moreover in a case of anticipatory breach, if the injured party elects to treat the contract as still in being he may continue with his own performance of it, even though in doing so he increases the loss for which, when actual breach occurs, he will recover damages.

5.5 Liquidated damages and penalty clauses

To avoid complicated calculations of loss or disputes over the amount the parties may include in their contract a formula (liquidated damages) for determining the damages payable for breach. In construction contracts, for example, it is usual to provide that if the building contractor is in breach of contract by late completion a deduction is to be made from the contract price (1% per week subject to a maximum of 10% in all is a typical example). The formula will be enforced by the courts if it is 'a genuine pre-estimate of loss' (without enquiring whether the actual loss is greater or smaller).

Dunlop Pneumatic Tyre Co Ltd v New Garage & Motor Co 1915
The contract for sale of tyres to a garage imposed a minimum retail price (resale price maintenance was then legal). The contract provided that £5 per tyre should be paid by the buyer if he re-sold at less than the prescribed retail price or in four other possible cases of breach of contract. He did sell at a lower price and argued that £5 per tyre was a penalty and not a genuine pre-estimate of loss.

Held: as a general rule when a fixed amount is to be paid as damages for breaches of different kinds, some more serious in their consequences than others, that is not a genuine pre-estimate of loss and so it is void as a penalty. But the general rule is merely a presumption which does not always determine the result. In this case the formula was an honest attempt to agree on liquidated damages and would be upheld, even though the consequences of the breach were such as to make precise pre-estimation almost impossible.

A contractual term designed as a penalty clause to discourage breach is void and not enforceable. The court will disregard it and require the injured party to prove the amount of his loss.

Activity 8 **(10 minutes)**

Under a contract between C and D, D must pay C damages of £100 if a particular type of breach occurs. This amount is a reasonable estimate of the loss which C would suffer. The breach occurs, and C's actual loss is £200. How much must D pay C?

6 ACTION FOR THE PRICE

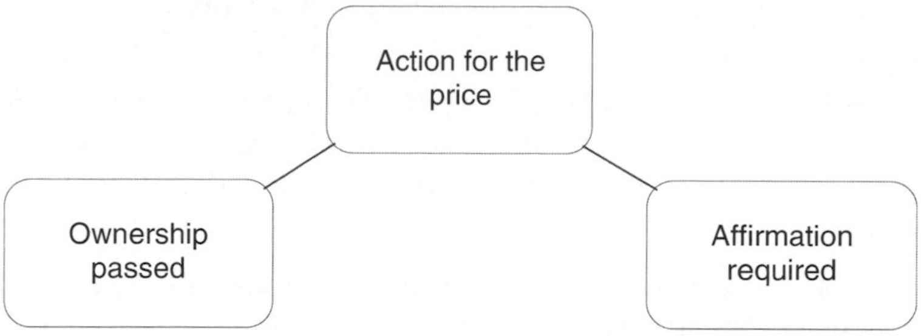

If the breach of contract arises out of one party's failure to pay the contractually agreed price due under the contract, the creditor should bring an action to recover that sum.

This is a fairly straightforward procedure but is subject to two specific limitations. The first is that an action for the price under a contract for the sale of goods may only be brought if property has passed to the buyer, unless the price has been agreed to be payable on a specific date (s 49 Sale of Goods Act 1979).

Secondly, whilst the injured party may recover an agreed sum due at the time of an anticipatory breach whether or not he continues the contract then, sums which become due *after* the anticipatory breach may not be recovered unless he affirms the contract: that is, he carries on with his side of the bargain. Even where he does affirm the contract, he will be unable to recover the price if:

(a) the other party withholds its co-operation so that he cannot continue with his side in order to make the price due; or

(b) the injured party had no other reason or 'legitimate interest' in continuing his obligations than to claim damages. Such a legitimate interest may be obligations which have arisen to third parties.

These points were decided in *White & Carter (Councils) v McGregor 1961*, where the party who affirmed the contract succeeded in an action for the price.

7 QUANTUM MERUIT

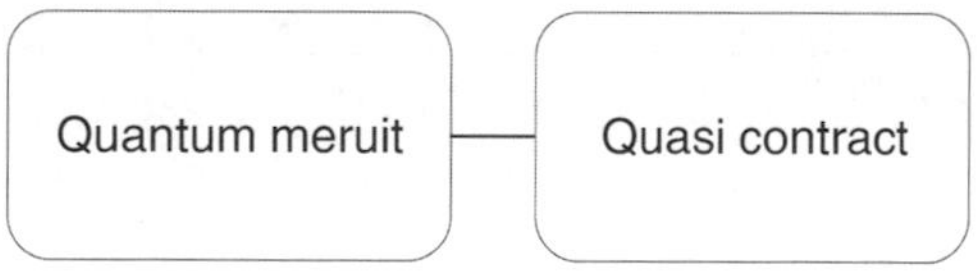

In particular situations, a claim may be made on a *quantum meruit* basis as an alternative to an action for damages for breach of contract. A quantum meruit claim is treated as a claim in quasi-contract. In some circumstances where there is no contract the law seeks to achieve a just result by treating the persons concerned as if (quasi means 'as if') they had entered into a contract on the appropriate terms.

The phrase *quantum meruit* literally means 'how much it is worth'. It is a measure of the value of contractual work which has been performed. The aim of such an award is to restore the claimant to the position he would have been in if the contract *had never been made*. It is a restitutory award. (By contrast, an award of damages aims to put the claimant in the position he would have been in *if the contract had been performed*. It is a compensatory award.)

Quantum meruit is likely to be sought where one party has already performed part of his obligations and the other party then repudiates the contract (repudiatory breach).

BPP PUBLISHING

Provided the injured party elects to treat the contract as terminated, he may claim a reasonable amount for the work done. In most cases, a quantum meruit claim is needed because the other party has unjustifiably prevented performance.

> *Planché v Colburn 1831*
> P agreed to write a book on costumes and armour for C's 'Juvenile Library' series. He was to receive £100 on completion. He did some research and wrote part of the book, but then C abandoned the series, preventing P's completion.
>
> *Held:* P could recover £50 as reasonable remuneration for the work done on a quantum meruit basis.

8 EQUITABLE REMEDIES

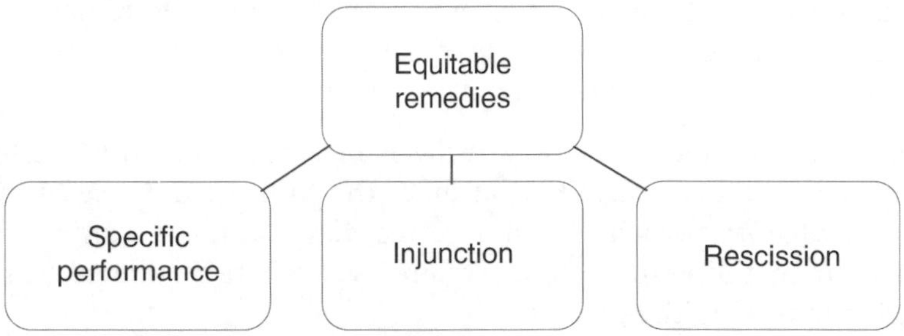

These are remedies which can be applied by the courts in cases where common law remedies are inadequate.

8.1 Specific performance

The court may in its discretion order the defendant to perform his part of the contract instead of letting him 'buy himself out of it' by paying damages for breach.

Specific performance will only be ordered in a case where the common law remedy of damages is inadequate.

For example, an order will be made for specific performance of a contract for the sale of land since the claimant may need the land for a particular purpose and would not be adequately compensated by damages for the loss of his bargain. He could not obtain another piece of land which is identical. For this reason specific performance of a contract for sale of goods is unlikely to be ordered unless the goods are unique and therefore no substitute could be obtained.

The order will not be made if it would require performance over a period of time and the court could not ensure that the defendant did comply fully with the order. Therefore specific performance is not ordered for contracts of employment or personal service nor usually for building contracts. By contrast, a contract for the sale of land requires only that the vendor should execute and deliver a transfer and other documents, so the order is readily enforceable.

Only contracts where consideration has passed may be remedied by an order for specific performance, since it is an equitable remedy and equity will not assist a volunteer; that is, it will not provide a remedy for someone who has given nothing.

Specific performance will be refused unless the claimant on his side has behaved fairly and the principle of mutuality is satisfied. This principle has two aspects, positive and negative.

(a) As the purchaser of land may obtain an order for specific performance the same remedy is available to the vendor, even though for him damages might be an adequate remedy.

(b) If the claimant could not be ordered to perform the contract, for example, if he is a minor, the defendant will not be ordered to do so.

Activity 9 **(5 minutes)**

Would specific performance of a contract for the sale of the Mona Lisa be likely to be ordered against the buyer?

8.2 Injunction

An injunction is (in this context) also a discretionary court order, requiring the defendant to observe a negative restriction of a contract. An injunction may be made even to enforce a contract of personal service for which specific performance would be refused.

> *Warner Bros v Nelson 1937*
>
> N (the film star Bette Davis) agreed to work for a year for WB (film producers) and not during the year not to work for any other film or stage producer nor 'to engage in any other occupation' without the consent of WB. N came to England during the year to work for a British film producer. WB sued for an injunction to restrain N from this work and N resisted arguing that if the restriction were enforced she must either work for WB (indirectly it would be an order for specific performance of a contract for personal service which should not be made) or abandon her livelihood.
>
> *Held:* the court would not make an injunction if it would have the result suggested by N. But WB merely asked for an injunction to restrain N from working for a British film producer. This was one part of the restriction accepted by N under her contract and it was fair to hold her to it to that extent. But the court would not have enforced the 'any other occupation' restraint. Moreover, an English court would only have made an injunction restraining N from breaking her contract by taking other work in England.

An injunction is an equitable remedy limited to enforcement of contract terms which are in substance negative restraints, that is they tell one of the parties what he cannot do.

8.3 Rescission

Strictly speaking the equitable right to rescind an agreement is not a remedy for breach of contract: it is a *right* which exists in certain circumstances, such as where a contract is voidable for misrepresentation, duress or undue influence.

Rescinding a contract means that it is cancelled or rejected and the parties are restored to their pre-contract condition, as if it had never been entered into. Refer back to the section on misrepresentation for more information.

Activity 10

J will need 3,000 litres of liquid fertiliser over the next 12 months. He therefore contracts with K to purchase at least 2,500 litres over that period, at an agreed price which is less than the normal price because of the quantity involved. J then negotiates to buy 1,000 litres from L, so that he would only require 2,000 litres from K. K finds out about this before J makes a contract with L. Would K be able to obtain an injunction to ensure that J buys at least 2,500 litres from him? Why?

9 LIMITATION TO ACTIONS FOR BREACH OF CONTRACT

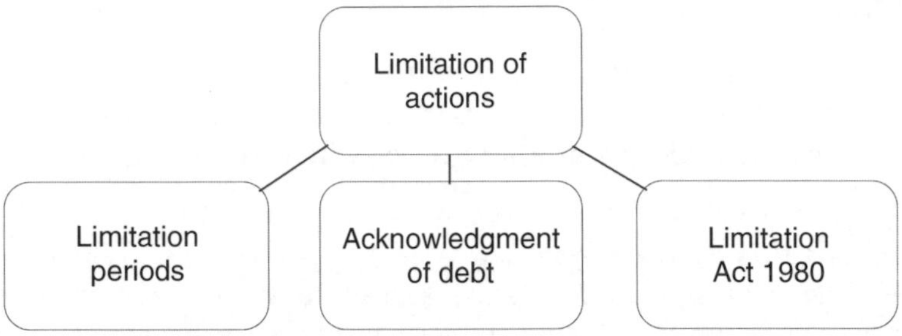

Where an action is to be brought for breach of contract, the injured party must do so:

- within six years of the breach in the case of a simple contract; or
- within 12 years of the breach in the case of a contract done by deed.

The periods are set by the Limitation Act 1980.

In two situations the six year period begins not at the date of the breach but later.

(a) If the claimant is a minor or under some other contractual disability (for example unsound mind) at the time of the breach of contract, the six year period begins to run only when his disability ceases or he dies, whichever is the earlier.

(b) If the defendant or his agent conceals the right of action by fraud (which here denotes any conduct judged to be unfair by equitable standards) or if the action is for relief from the results of a mistake, the six year period begins to run only when the claimant discovered or could by reasonable diligence have discovered the fraud, concealment or mistake.

Where the claim can only be for the equitable reliefs of specific performance or injunction, the Limitation Act 1980 does not apply. Instead, the claim may be limited by the equitable doctrine of delay or 'laches'. This considers whether an unreasonably long time has elapsed before the action is brought.

The limitation period may be extended if a debt, or any other certain monetary amount, is either acknowledged at any time or is paid in part before the original six (or 12) years has expired. Hence if a debt accrues on 1 January 1999, the original limitation period expires on 31 December 2004. But if part payment is received on 1 January 2003, the debt is reinstated and does not then become 'statute barred' until 31 December 2008. The following conditions apply.

(a) Acknowledgement. The claim must be acknowledged as existing, not just as possible, but it need not be quantified. The acknowledgement must be in writing, signed by the debtor and addressed to the creditor.

(b) Part payment. To be effective, the part payment must be identifiable with the particular debt, not just a payment on a running account.

Activity 11 **(10 minutes)**

R owes S £100. The debt is incurred on 1 July 1996, but S does not press R for payment and R forgets about the debt. On 1 July 2003, S reviews his records and discovers that the debt has never been paid. He writes to R asking for payment of 'the £500 you owe me'. R then remembers that in fact only £100 is owed, and he drafts a letter pointing out S's error. Should he send the letter?

Chapter roundup

- Complete and exact performance is generally required to discharge a contract by performance. In some cases, part payment may be recovered for incomplete performance.
- Contracts may be discharged by agreement, and each party normally gives consideration for being released from his obligations by releasing the other party.
- Repudiatory breach may be by refusal to perform, by failure to perform an entire obligation or by incapacitation. The party not in breach may treat the contract as repudiated, or may affirm the contract.
- In cases of anticipatory breach, the party not in breach may sue immediately or may wait to see whether the other party performs his obligations after all.
- A contract may be discharged by frustration when certain underlying conditions are no longer satisfied. However, changes not rendering performance impossible, or arising from one party's choices, do not discharge a contract by frustration.
- Losses will only be compensated by damages if they arise in the usual course of things or are within the reasonable contemplation of the parties. Damages are calculated so as to put the claimant in the position he would have been in if the contract had been performed. Liquidated damages will be enforced, but not penalty clauses.
- An action for the price is used when one party does not pay money due under the contract. Such an action is limited in its effects in cases of anticipatory breach.

Chapter roundup continued...

- In cases of partial performance, damages may be claimed on a *quantum meruit* basis. The aim of an award is to put the claimant in the position he would have been in if the contract had never been made, so the profit he would have made is lost.
- Specific performance forces one party to perform his obligations under the contract. It will only be awarded when its enforcement is practicable. Like injunction, it is an equitable remedy. An injunction will only be granted to enforce an essentially negative restriction in a contract.
- Actions for breach of contract must normally be brought within six years of the breach occurring, or 12 years for a contract made by deed.

Quick quiz

1 In what ways may a party to a contract be discharged from his obligations under it?

2 Is it a condition of a contract that it shall be performed at the appointed time?

3 In what circumstances may a party who has not completed the performance of his part of a contract be entitled to payment for what he has done?

4 When must the principle of 'accord and satisfaction' be applied?

5 What types of repudiatory breach are there?

6 What are the effects of an innocent party's termination of a contract for repudiatory breach? What happens if the innocent party decides to affirm such a contract?

7 What are the alternatives open to an innocent party if the other party declares in advance that he will not perform his obligations

8 Give three examples of circumstances by which a contract may be frustrated.

9 What are the rules on payments to be made when a contract is discharged by frustration?

10 State the two principles of the rule in Hadley v Baxendale.

11 What is the principle by which the court generally determines the amount payable as damages for breach of contract?

12 What is the duty to mitigate loss and on whom does it fall?

13 What is the difference between liquidated damages and a penalty for non-performance?

14 What is the purpose of a quantum meruit claim?

15 In what circumstances may the claimant obtain an order from the court requiring the defendant to perform his part of the contract?

16 What is meant by limitation? What are the limitation periods?

17 How may a limitation period be extended?

Answers to quick quiz

1 Performance
Agreement
Frustration
Breach (see introduction)

2 Only if it is agreed that time is of the essence. (para 1.4)

3 Substantial performance
Partial performance
Prevention of performance (paras 1.1-1.3)

4 Where one party has carried out his side of the contract and releases the other. (para 2)

5 Refusal to perform (renunciation)
Failure to perform an entire obligation
Incapacitation (para 3.1)

6 He is not bound and cannot be sued
He need not accept or pay for further performance
He can refuse to pay for partial or defective performance
He can reclaim money paid (para 3.1)

7 Treat the contract as discharged forthwith
Allow it to continue until the breach actually occurs (para 3.2)

8 Destruction of the subject matter
Personal incapacity
Government intervention (para 4.1)

9 Any money already paid is to be repaid
No further monies are payable (except expenses) (para 4.4)

10 Loss must arise naturally from the breach
Loss must have been in the contemplation of the parties (para 5.1)

11 The amount needed to put the claimant in the position he would have been in if the contract had been performed. (para 5.2)

12 The claimant has the duty to reduce the loss he has suffered. (para 5.4)

13 Liquidated damages are devised by a formula set out in the contract as an estimate of the loss.

A penalty clause is designed to discourage breach and is far bigger than the amount of any breach. (para 5.5)

14 To give someone the value of the work they have actually done. (para 7)

15 When the remedy of damages is not adequate. (para 8.1)

16 The fact that the injured party must claim for his loss within a certain time.

Simple contracts: 6 years
Contracts done by deed: 12 years (para 9)

17 By acknowledgement of the debt by the debtor to the creditor. (para 9)

Answers to activities

1 Partial performance can only be accepted by the promisee when he has a choice of acceptance or rejection. In Cutter v Powell, performance consisted of Cutter's services as second mate. Once he had provided those services, they could not be returned by the shipowners after his death.

2 K refuses to perform his contract with J, and K incapacitates himself in relation to his contract with L.

3 G has terminated the contract for repudiatory breach and has given H notice of this. As the innocent party, G may refuse to pay for the defective performance already received and may reclaim the £50 already paid to H.

4 No: X may allow the contract to continue and see whether there is actual breach on the completion date.

5 The company could not plead frustration on the basis of personal incapacity because it would have been possible to hire another lorry driver. Unlike a singer, a lorry driver is not an artist hired for his unique talents.

6 F will repay £(600 – 270) = £330 to G.

7 'If the broken shaft is not delivered to Greenwich on the next day after collection from Hadley, then Baxendale shall pay Hadley the sum of £10 for each day's delay, being the lost profits from the mill's being out of action.'

8 £100.

9 Yes, because it would be enforced against the seller.

10 K would not be able to obtain an injunction because an injunction will only be granted to enforce a negative restraint.

11 No: if he does so, he will have acknowledged the debt in writing and it will cease to be statute barred.

Assignment 6 **(60 minutes)**

Iggins Ltd, a sports promotion company, organised an international billiards competition to be staged in Birmingham. Thirty two of the leading players in the world were contracted to attend the two week event.

Four of the players, Brown, Green, White and Black were unable to participate for the following reasons.

Brown who intended to arrive the day before his first round match, was not allowed to leave his country because his passport had expired.

Green had severely gashed his hand and arm when attempting to remove a small branch caught up in the rotor blades of his lawn mower.

White had unfortunately contracted a viral infection and was unable to travel.

Black had learned that some of the other competitors had negotiated appearance money in excess of the sum he had agreed with Iggins Ltd. As a result of a failure to renegotiate better terms, Black informed Iggins Ltd that he would not be attending.

Due to the non-appearance of the above mentioned players, Iggins Ltd decided to cancel the competition on the day the event was scheduled to commence. They believed that the logistical implications of having only twenty eight players created organisational problems that could not be remedied and that attendance would be reduced because of the absence of four leading players.

The remaining players are threatening to sue Iggins Ltd as they have travelled to Birmingham and are willing to play.

Explain the legal position of Iggins Ltd, Brown, Green, White, Black and the remaining twenty eight players.

PART B

CONSUMER PROTECTION LEGISLATION

Chapter 10 :
THE SALE OF GOODS ACT

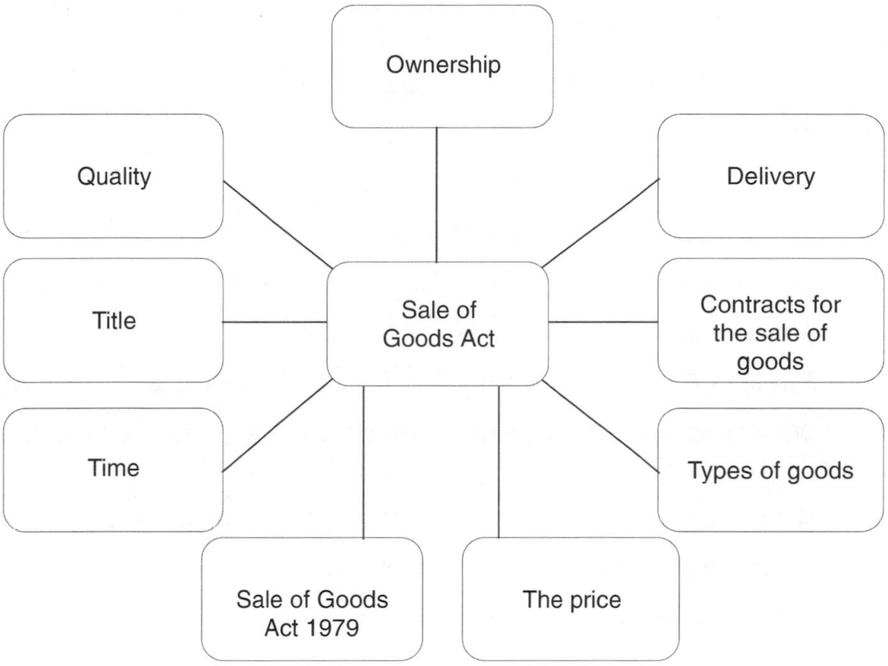

Introduction

The Sale of Goods Act 1979 and various other pieces of sale of goods legislation feature in two parts of the Unit 6 syllabus.

- In Part 1, Principles of Law, the purely contractual aspects of sale of goods are covered, as a specialist form of contract. There are specific rules governing for example the transfer of property in a contract for the sale of goods, as well as delivery of the goods and remedies available in a case of breach of contract.
- Part 2, Consumer Protection Legislation, includes the detailed provisions of the Sale of Goods Act 1979 which cover the rights of the buyer (usually a consumer) in a contract for the sale of goods. There are several sections of the Act each of which provides protection for the purchaser in certain situations.

Contracts for the sale of goods are also subject to the Unfair Contract Terms Act 1977 which you have already seen in the context of exclusion clauses and contractual terms generally.

You will also meet the Supply of Goods and Services Act 1982, which largely extends the terms of the Sale of Goods Act 1979 to contracts where a service is being purchased. Examples include a contract for the repair of shoes or a contract to purchase the services of a plumber.

You will find in this and subsequent chapters that the basic legal principles you have covered until now will be extended and applied to specific situations.

As with any other contract, a contract for the sale of goods may be breached. In addition to the usual common law remedies (damages and action for the price) the parties have rights peculiar to this type of contract. The remedies which are against goods are described as 'real remedies', all others are called 'personal remedies'.

Statutory references in this chapter are to the Sale of Goods Act 1979 unless otherwise noted.

Your objectives

In this chapter you will learn about the following.

(a) What constitutes a sale of goods

(b) Existing, future, specific and ascertained goods

(c) How the price for goods may be fixed

(d) What terms are implied by the Sale of Goods Act 1979 (as amended)

(e) When time is of the essence

(f) The significance of the seller's title and the consequences of defective title

(g) What is meant by the description of goods, and the implied conditions in a sale by sample

(h) What is meant by satisfactory quality and by fitness for purpose

(i) When property and risk pass to the buyer

(j) The rule *nemo dat quod non habet* and the exceptions to it

(k) The rules on delivery

(l) The limits on the buyer's right to reject the goods

(m) What remedies the parties may have against each other

(n) The effect of the Supply of Goods and Services Act 1982

1 DEFINITION OF A CONTRACT FOR THE 'SALE OF GOODS'

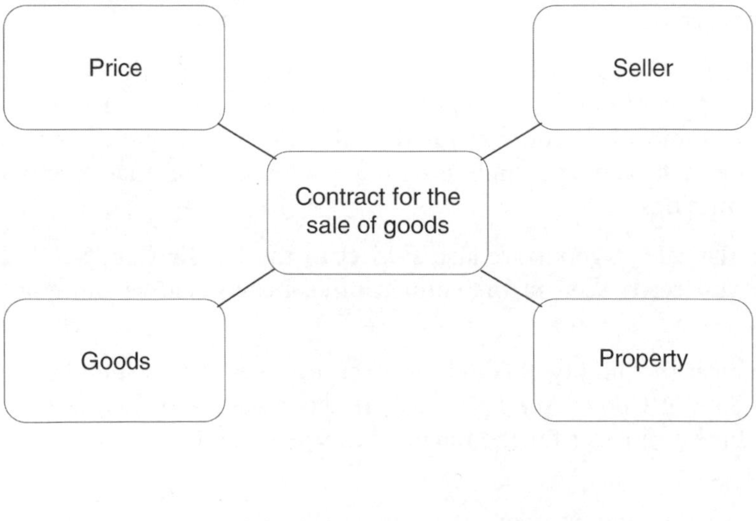

NOTES

Definition

> A contract for the sale of goods is 'a contract by which the seller transfers, or agrees to transfer, the property in goods to a buyer for a money consideration, called the price' s 2 (1).

Sale includes both an immediate sale, such as purchase of goods in a shop, and an agreement by which the seller is to transfer ownership (in this context called 'property') in goods to the buyer at a future date.

2 TYPES OF GOODS

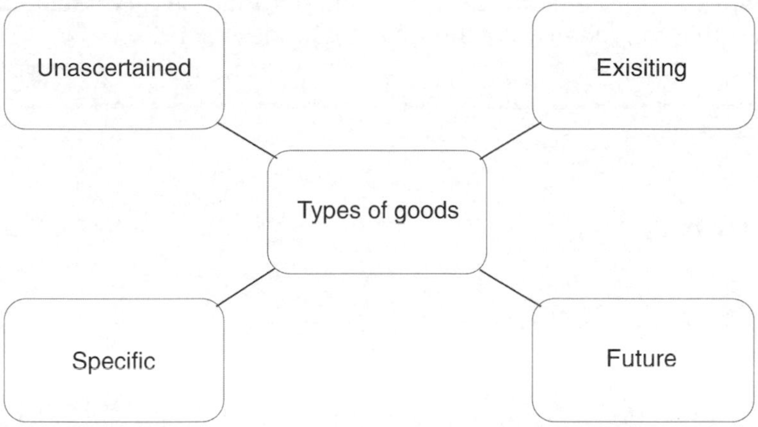

The rules on sale of goods make the following distinctions.

(a) Existing goods are those which exist and are owned by the seller at the time when the contract is made. Future goods are those which do not exist or which the seller does not yet own when he contracts to sell them. The main point of this distinction is that property (the ownership of the goods) cannot usually pass from seller to buyer unless, or until, the goods exist as specific or ascertained goods.

(b) Specific goods are those which are identified as the goods to be sold at the time when the contract is made, such as 'my Ford Focus, registration no W123 ABC'. Goods which are not specific are unascertained and become ascertained goods when they are subsequently identified as the goods to be sold under the contract.

2.1 Goods which have perished

In a contract for sale of specific goods there are rules laid down regarding the contract's status if the goods are perishable.

(a) If, unknown to the seller, the goods have perished at the time when the contract is made, the contract is void: s 6.

(b) If the goods perish after the contract is made, without fault of either party and before the risk (ie the responsibility for loss or damage) passes to the buyer, the contract is avoided: s 7.

In addition to simple destruction, goods may 'perish' when they deteriorate to such an extent as to lose their commercial identity. The case law is concerned mainly with rotting of produce; it is a question of degree as to when they perish.

H R & S Sainsbury v Street 1972
S agreed to sell a 275 ton crop of barley to be grown on his farm to H. Due to general adverse conditions, his crop failed and only 140 tons were yielded. These he sold at a higher price to a third party.

Held: although 135 tons of produce had perished so that the contract in that respect was frustrated, S should have offered the remainder to the claimant. Hence the contract as a whole had not been avoided.

Activity 1 **(10 minutes)**

A agrees to sell a car to B on hire purchase. B must pay regular hire charges for two years, and at the end of that period B will have an option to buy the car on payment of a further sum. Consider whether there is a contract for the sale of goods within the meaning of the Sale of Goods Act 1979.

3 THE PRICE

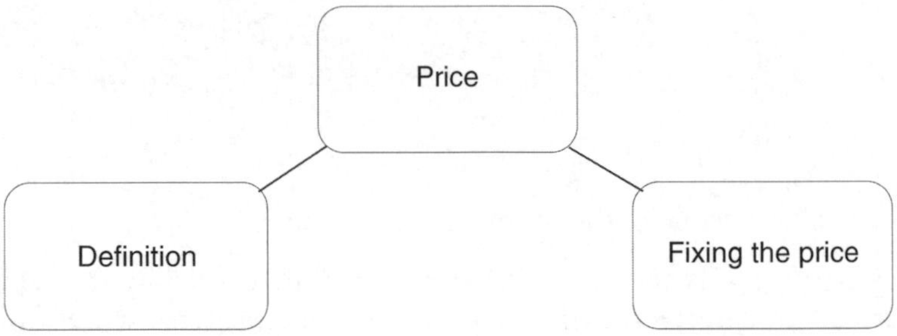

The definition states that there should be 'a money consideration, called the price'. This means that an exchange (barter) for other goods does not give rise to a sale of goods. The implication of that is that the parties in such a contract would not be subject to the Sale of Goods Act. However, provided some money changes hands, as with a trade-in arrangement for a car, there is a contract for the sale of goods even though goods are also given. But there can be complications regarding 'money consideration'.

3.1 Defining price

Esso v Commissioners of Customs & Excise 1976
With every four gallons of petrol purchased from its filling stations, Esso promised to give away a free coin depicting a member of England's 1966 World Cup squad. Customs & Excise argued that this constituted a sale of goods and that therefore Esso had to pay purchase tax (now abolished) on all the World Cup coins it bought and gave away.

Held: there was a valid contract in respect of the World Cup coins, in that Esso had offered to give them away and any customer who purchased four gallons of petrol thereby accepted that offer and could enforce the contract. However, it was accepted that it was not a contract of sale, since the customer gave not a money consideration in return but a separate contract (for the purchase of petrol). There were two contracts, the one for the coins being a collateral contract to the one for the sale of petrol. The collateral contract was not one for the sale of goods.

Activity 2 **(10 minutes)**

If, in the case of Esso v Commissioners of Customs & Excise 1976, Esso had not offered a free coin with every four gallons of petrol but had instead offered 'four gallons of petrol and one World Cup coin for £2', would there have been a collateral contract for the coins?

3.2 Fixing the price

The price may be fixed by the contract or in a manner set out in the contract, such as the ruling market price on the day of delivery, or by the course of dealing between the parties. If there is no agreed price, a reasonable price must be paid: s 8.

Foley v Classique Coaches 1934
A bus company agreed to purchase its petrol from F 'at a price to be agreed in writing from time to time'; any dispute between the parties was to be submitted to arbitration. For three years the bus company purchased its petrol from F at the current price but there was no formal agreement on price. Thc bus company then repudiated the agreement arguing that it was incomplete since it was an agreement to agree on the price.

Held: in view of the course of dealing between the parties and the arbitration clause there was an agreement that a reasonable price (at any given time) should be paid. The agreement was therefore enforceable.

4 TERMS IMPLIED BY THE SALE OF GOODS ACT 1979

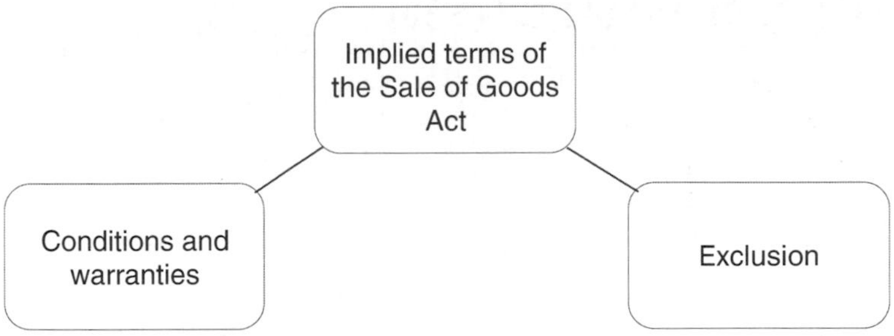

One of the main functions of the Sale of Goods Act 1979 is to codify the terms implied into contracts of sale. These have largely evolved from case law. Much depends on whether an implied term is a condition or a warranty, and on whether one party to the contract is dealing as a consumer.

4.1 Conditions and warranties

The Sale of Goods Act 1979 states that conditions and warranties are both terms of the contract, unlike a representation, which is a statement of fact made by one party which induces the other party to enter into the contract. A condition is a central or important term of the contract. It is so essential to the contract that its non-fulfilment 'may give rise to a right to treat the contract as repudiated': s 11(3). A warranty is 'an agreement with reference to goods which are the subject of a contract of sale, but collateral to the main purpose of such contract, the breach of which gives rise to a claim for damages but not a right to reject the goods and treat the contract as repudiated': s 61. This reflects the definitions of conditions and warranties which you have already seen.

A sale of goods may be subject to statutory rules on:

(a) the effect of delay in performance (s 10);
(b) title, or the seller's right to sell the goods (s 12);
(c) the description of the goods (s 13);
(d) sale by sample (s 15);
(e) the quality of the goods (s 14);
(f) the fitness of the goods for the purpose for which they are supplied (s 14).

4.2 Exclusion of implied terms

In addition, the Unfair Contract Terms Act 1977 prohibits or restricts the possibility of modifying these statutory rules (other than those on time) by the use of exclusion clauses as follows.

(a) It is not possible to exclude or restrict:

  (i) the statutory terms on the seller's title (s 12) in any circumstances;

  (ii) the statutory terms relating to contract description or sample, quality or fitness for a purpose (ss 13-15) when the buyer is dealing as a consumer; that is when he is not buying in the course of a business but the seller is selling in the course of a business: ss 6 and 12 UCTA 1977.

(b) In a contract under which the buyer is not dealing as a consumer, that is when seller and buyer are both engaging in the transaction in the course of business, the terms of ss 13-15 may be excluded or restricted, but only if the exclusion or restriction satisfies the statutory requirement of reasonableness.

5 TIME OF PERFORMANCE (S 10)

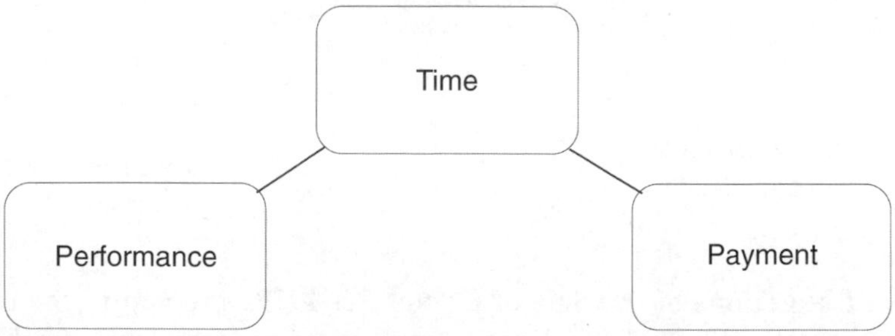

5.1 Time of performance of the contract

Whether time of *performance* is of the essence depends on the terms of the contract. If it is, then breach of it is breach of a condition, which entitles the injured party to treat the contract as discharged. In commercial contracts for the supply of goods for business use, it will readily be assumed that time is of the essence even where there is no express term to that effect. Often one party is given a period of time within which to perform his obligation, say for delivery of goods. That party is not in breach until the whole period has elapsed without performance.

The contract may stipulate that the party should use his 'best endeavours' to perform his side by a certain time. If he fails to make that date, he must perform his obligations within a reasonable time. (Under s 29, similar reasonableness is required if no date is set by the contract.) In any case, time of performance stipulates a 'reasonable hour' for obligations to be performed: this is a question of fact. Hence it is not reasonable to offer delivery of perishable goods to a factory on the Friday evening before a two week shutdown of which the seller is aware.

5.2 Time of payment under the terms of the contract

Time for *payment* is not of the essence unless a different intention appears from the contract.

For example A, a manufacturer, orders components from B and B fails to deliver by the agreed date. A can treat the contract as discharged and refuse to accept late delivery by B. But if B delivers a first instalment on time and A pays the price a week after the agreed date, B could not (under a continuing contract) refuse to make further deliveries, and treat the contract as discharged. If, however, A failed to pay altogether, that is not a delay in payment but rather a breach of an essential condition that the price is payable in exchange for the goods (unless otherwise agreed).

6 SELLER'S TITLE (S 12)

It is an implied *condition* that the seller has, or will have at the time when property (ie ownership) in the goods is to be transferred, a right to sell the goods: s 12(1). This is probably one of the single most important sections of the Sale of Goods Act.

In the ordinary way the seller satisfies this condition if he has title to the goods at the moment when property is to pass to the buyer. (In this statutory code 'title' and 'property' are both used in different contexts to mean the same thing, ownership.) But the condition is broken if the seller, although he owns the goods, can be stopped by a third party from selling them: the right to transfer ownership is essential.

6.1 Illustration

> *Niblett v Confectioners Materials 1921*
> A seller sold condensed milk in tins labelled with the name 'Nissly'. When the goods arrived in the UK the well known company Nestlé took legal action to have them detained as infringing the Nestlé trademark. The buyers were obliged to remove the labels from the tins in order to have them released from the customs warehouse in which they were held at the instance of Nestlé.

> *Held:* as Nestlé could have obtained an injunction to prevent the sale of the goods, the seller was in breach of the implied condition that he had a 'right to sell'.

If the seller delivers goods to the buyer without having the right to sell, there is a total failure of consideration, and the buyer does not obtain the ownership of the goods which is the essential basis of the contract. If the buyer has then to give up the goods to the real owner he may recover the entire price from the seller, without any allowance for the use of the goods meanwhile.

> *Rowland v Divall 1923*
> D bought a car from a third party and then sold it on to R a dealer. It subsequently transpired that the car had been stolen from its original owner, before it was sold to D. The car was then returned to its original owner, and R sued D for the recovery of the price he had paid to the latter.
>
> It was held that D had been in breach of what is now S12 Sale of Goods Act 1979, as he did not have title to the car at the time he sold it to R. D had to repay the entire price, with no deduction for the period of use.

6.2 Implied warranty of quiet possession

The seller also gives implied *warranties* that the buyer shall have quiet possession of the goods and that the goods are free of any encumbrance or challenge by a third party (unless disclosed to the buyer when the contract is made): s 12(2).

> *Microbeads A.C. v Vinhurst Road Markings 1975*
> A road marking machine was sold by the defendant to the claimant. Unbeknown to either of them, a third party was at that point applying for a patent on the machine. This meant that use of the machine by the purchaser was an infringement of that patent, and the owner of the patent was able to demand royalties from the purchaser.
>
> It was held that this constituted a breach by the seller of the implied warranty of quiet possession in S12, and the purchaser was able to claim damages.

6.3 Exclusion of s 12

Although the seller cannot contract out of these terms by stipulating that they shall not apply, he can achieve a rather similar result by undertaking to transfer only such title as he (or some third party from whom he acquired the goods) may have (or have had). This stipulation puts the buyer on notice that the seller is uncertain of title. Furthermore, the seller must disclose to the buyer any charges or encumbrances of which the seller knows. But if the buyer is prepared to buy the goods on that basis he gets what he bargained for, and there is no breach of contract if the seller's title is imperfect.

Activity 3 **(10 minutes)**

A and B are in dispute over which of them owns some corn which is in A's possession. A sells the corn to C (who is unaware of the dispute) for £1,000. The dispute is then resolved in favour of B, who obtains possession of the corn from C. By that time its value has fallen to £800. Advise C as to his legal position.

7 DESCRIPTION OF THE GOODS (S 13)

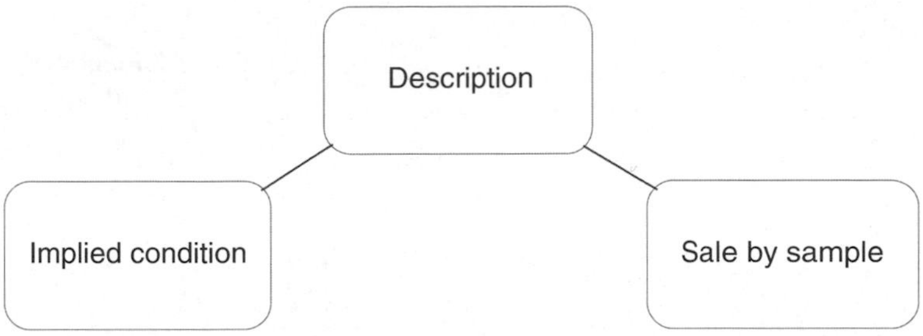

In a contract for sale of goods by description, a condition is implied that the goods will correspond to the description. If a description is applied to the goods by the contract, it is a sale by description even though the buyer may have inspected the goods.

7.1 Illustration

Beale v Taylor 1967
The defendant advertised a Triumph as a 'Herald convertible, white, 1961'. The claimant came to inspect the car and subsequently bought it. After buying the car he found that only the back half corresponded with the description. It had been welded to a front half which was part of an earlier Herald 948 model. The defendant relied on the buyer's inspection and argued that it was not a sale by description.

Held: the advertisement described the car as a 1961 Herald, and this formed part of the contract description. It was a sale by description in spite of the buyer's pre-contract inspection.

7.2 Sale by sample

Where the sale is by sample as well as by description, the bulk must correspond to the sample and the description.

Compliance with the description must be complete and exact.

Arcos v E and A Ronaasen and Son 1933
The contract was for half-inch wooden staves. Some of the staves delivered by the seller were thicker than the measurements described.

Held: The buyer was entitled to reject the consignment.

'Description' is widely interpreted to include ingredients, age, date of shipment, packing, quantity, and so on.

Re Moore & Co and Landauer & Co 1921
The buyers agreed to buy 3,000 tins of Australian canned fruit packed in cases of 30 tins. The correct total quantity was delivered, but it was found that half the goods were packed in cases of 24 tins.

Held: although there was no difference in value there had been a breach of s 13 and the buyers were entitled to reject.

In this case it did not matter that there was no effect on the value of the goods.

If the seller uses a false description he may also commit an offence punishable under the Trade Descriptions Act 1968.

8 SALE BY SAMPLE (S 15)

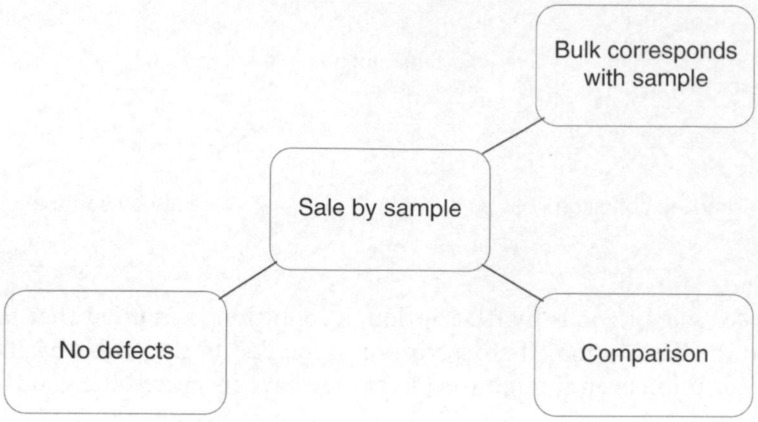

In a sale by sample there are implied *conditions* that:

(a) the bulk corresponds in quality with the sample;

(b) the buyer shall have a reasonable opportunity of comparing the bulk with the sample; and

(c) the goods are free of any defect rendering them unsatisfactory which would not be apparent on a reasonable examination of the sample.

> **Activity 4** **(10 minutes)**
>
> There is a contract for the sale of '200 cases of 1958 Bordeaux wine'. If the seller were to supply wine made in 1959, is it likely that he could force the buyer to proceed with the purchase? Give reasons for your answer.

9 SATISFACTORY QUALITY (S 14 (2))

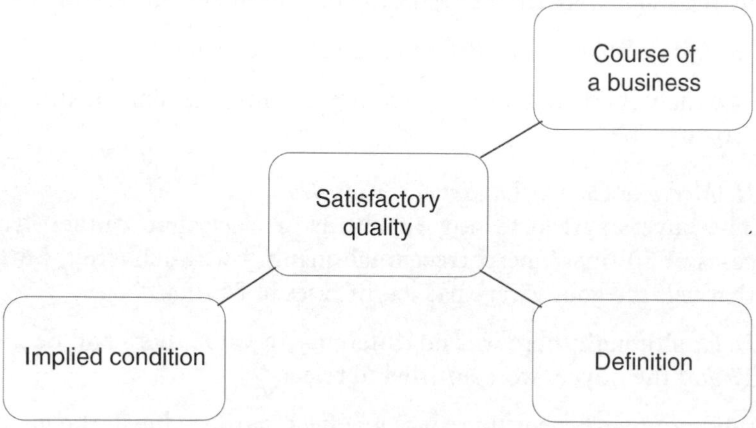

There is an implied condition that goods supplied under a contract are of satisfactory quality. This *condition* applies only to goods sold 'in the course of a business'; the seller must be carrying on a business or profession and make the sale in connection with that activity. Goods sold privately by a seller who is not selling in the course of a business therefore fall outside the scope of this section. It does not apply, for example, to goods bought at jumble sales or car boot sales.

The condition applies to all 'goods supplied under the contract': not only to the goods themselves therefore but also to the packaging in which they are sold and also to any instructions provided for the use of the goods.

The condition that the goods supplied under the contract are of satisfactory quality is excluded if the buyer's attention is drawn to defects before the contract is made or the buyer examines the goods before the contract is made, and that examination ought to reveal the defects.

9.1 Definition of satisfactory quality

Satisfactory quality is met if the goods 'meet the standard that a reasonable person would regard as satisfactory, taking account of any description of the goods, the price (if relevant) and all other relevant circumstances'. The Act lists some of the attributes which are to be taken into account in deciding whether the goods are of satisfactory quality, including fitness for the purpose, appearance and finish, freedom from minor defects, safety and durability.

The Act (s 14(2B)) identified factors which may in appropriate cases be aspects of the quality of goods.

(a) Fitness for **all** the purposes for which goods of the kind in question are commonly supplied. If the goods are fit for one purpose, but not others, that is not acceptable.

(b) Appearance and finish. Until recently, goods with superficial damage but which operated properly could be of satisfactory quality. This aspect is likely to affect such matters as sales of new motor cars, an area in which there was much dissatisfaction with the old law.

(c) Freedom from minor defects. A series of minor defects could, under existing case law, render goods of unsatisfactory quality. Under statute, the goods must be free of minor defects.

(d) Safety. This is a new aspect, as there is no clear case law on this.

(e) Durability. Goods will have to remain of satisfactory quality for a period which could be expected by a reasonable person.

Activity 5 **(10 minutes)**

P sells an expensive new pen to Q. Q finds that it can only be made to write with difficulty. P claims that the pen is of satisfactory quality, because it can write and because its casing is perfect so that it can be used as a status symbol (as expensive pens sometimes are used). Consider whether P's claim is likely to be accepted by the courts.

NOTES

10 FITNESS FOR PURPOSE (S 14(3))

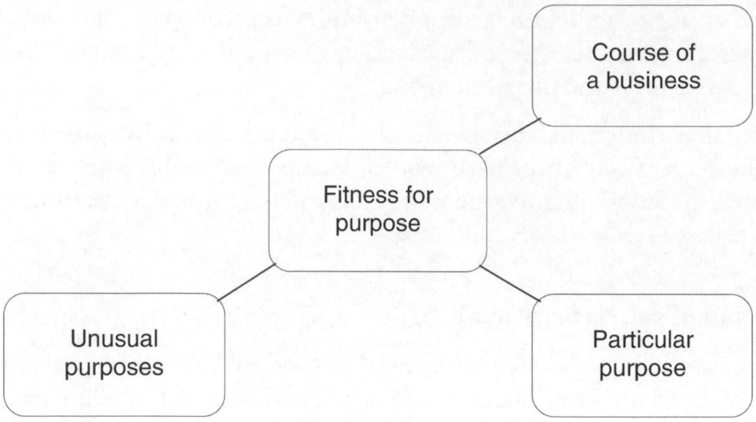

This condition applies only to goods sold 'in the course of business'.

Where the buyer expressly or by implication makes known to the seller any particular purpose for which the goods are bought, it is an implied condition that the goods supplied under the contract are reasonably fit for that purpose (whether or not that is the common purpose of such goods), unless the circumstances show that the buyer does not rely, or that it is unreasonable for him to rely, on the skill or judgement of the seller.

10.1 The particular purpose

A buyer may specify the 'particular purpose' quite broadly without listing all possible uses within that particular purpose. Thus where a substance is commonly used as fertiliser or as animal feedstuff it is sufficient to specify the latter without naming each kind of animal to which it might be fed.

> *Ashington Piggeries v Christopher Hill 1972*
> B gave S a recipe for mink food and requested that S should mix the food in accordance with the recipe and supply it to B. S told B that they had never supplied mink food before although they were manufacturers of animal foodstuffs. One of the ingredients was herring meal which had been stored in a chemical which created a poisonous substance damaging to all animals but particularly damaging to mink. As a result many of the mink died.
>
> *Held:* because the poison affected all animals the food was unfit for its disclosed purpose since B relied on S's skill and judgement to the extent that S was an animal food manufacturer and should not have supplied a generally harmful food. If the poison had only affected mink then B's skill and judgement demonstrated by its supply of a recipe would have made it unreasonable to rely on S's skill or judgement.

If the goods have only one obvious purpose, the buyer by implication makes known his purpose merely by asking for the goods.

> *Priest v Last 1903*
> A customer at a chemist's shop asked for a hot water bottle and was told, in answer to a question, that it would withstand hot water but should not be filled with boiling water. It burst after only five days in use.
>
> *Held:* if there is only one purpose, that particular purpose is disclosed by buying the goods. Because it was not an effective hot water bottle, there was a breach of s 14(3). (This was followed by Frost v Aylesbury Dairy Co 1905:

NOTES

in the purchase of milk supplied to a domestic address the buyer discloses his purpose, which is human consumption.)

10.2 Unusual purposes

There are two further variations on the interpretation of 'particular purpose'. Where goods are required for a particular purpose which is not obvious to the seller or where they are required for a particular purpose known to the seller but there is some peculiarity about that purpose, the buyer must make clear to the seller the particular purpose or the peculiarity involved.

Manchester Liners v Rea 1922
The defendant supplied coal for a particular ship. The coal was unsuitable for that ship but would have been suitable for other ships.

Held: coal merchants knew well enough that ships differed in their types and requirements. If a merchant undertook to supply coal for a particular ship, he must supply coal suitable for that ship.

Griffiths v Peter Conway Ltd 1939
The claimant contracted dermatitis from a Harris Tweed coat purchased from the defendants. She had an unusually sensitive skin and the coat would not have harmed a normal person.

Held: the claimant's sensitive skin rendered the required use so special that she had not made known the particular purpose for which the coat was to be used.

Activity 6 **(10 minutes)**

R buys a filing cabinet from S, who runs an office furniture shop. R tells S that he will use the cabinet to store land certificates issued by the Land Registry, and asks S whether the cabinet is of the right size for such certificates. S replies that he does not know how large land certificates are, but R goes ahead and buys the cabinet. If the cabinet proved to be too small, why could R not claim that S had breached the condition of reasonable fitness?

11 PASSING OF PROPERTY AND RISK

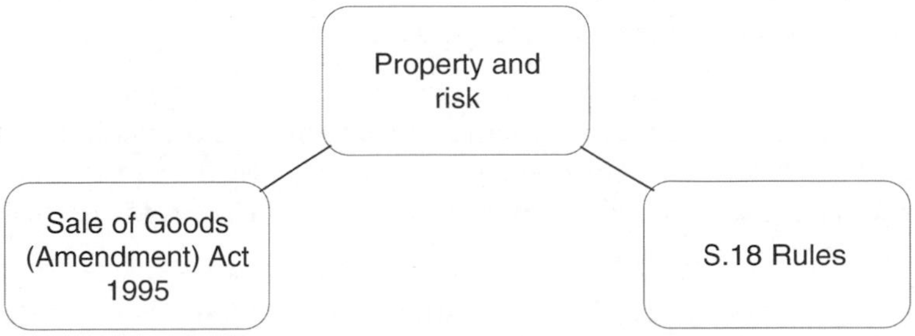

Remember that in this context 'property' is ownership and 'risk' is responsibility, should the goods suffer any loss or damage.

In determining when property in goods passes, the following general principles apply.

(a) No property can pass in goods which are unascertained and not yet identified as the goods to be sold under the contract: s 16.

(b) The property in specific or ascertained goods is transferred to the buyer at the time when the parties intend it to be transferred. Their intention may be deduced from the terms of the contract, the conduct of the parties and the circumstances of the case: s 17.

(c) Unless a different intention appears (and the parties can agree upon whatever terms they like) the rules of s 18 are applied to ascertain what their intention is on the passing of property to the buyer.

Many contracts for the supply of goods contain a clause stating that title to the goods remains with the seller until the contract price is paid. Such 'retention of title' or 'Romalpa' clauses are a common example of the s 17 rule that title to specific goods passes when the parties so intend.

11.1 Passing of property: the s 18 rules

Section 18 of the Sale of Goods Act lists a number of precise rules on the passing of property.

(a) *Rule 1.* If the contract is unconditional and the goods are specific or identified, property passes when the contract is made. It is immaterial that the seller has not yet delivered the goods or that the buyer has not yet paid the price. However, the seller may, and often does, stipulate that property shall not pass until the price is paid (a retention of title clause).

If the seller insists on retaining the goods or documents relating to them (such as the registration book of a car which has been sold) until the price is paid then it will readily be inferred that he intended (and the buyer agreed) that property would not pass on making the contract, but only on payment of the price.

(b) *Rule 2.* If, under a contract for sale of specific goods, the seller is bound to do something to put the goods into a deliverable state, property does not pass until the seller has done what is required of him and the buyer has notice of this.

Underwood v Burgh Castle Brick and Cement Syndicate 1922
The claimants entered into a contract for the sale of a condensing engine to be loaded onto a railway wagon. At the time of making the contract the engine, which weighed over 30 tons, was embedded in cement foundations at a factory. It was expected that it would take the sellers about two weeks to dismantle it. In loading it into the railway wagon the sellers broke part of the machine. The buyers refused to accept it.

Held: property had not passed when the contract was made, because the engine was not in such a condition that the defendants had to take delivery of it. At the time of the damage the engine was still in the sellers' ownership and so at their risk. The buyers were entitled to reject it in its damaged state and to refuse to pay the price.

(c) *Rule 3.* Where there is a contract for the sale of specific goods in a deliverable state but the seller is bound to weigh, measure or test them to fix the price, property passes when he has done so and the buyer has notice of this. The rule does not apply when it is the buyer who must take this action.

(d) *Rule 4.* When goods are delivered to the buyer on approval, that is on sale or return terms, the property passes to the buyer when:

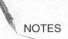

(i) he signifies to the seller that he approves, or indicates approval by dealing with them; or

(ii) he retains the goods beyond the time fixed for their return without giving notice of rejection or, if no time has been fixed, if he retains them beyond a reasonable time.

(e) *Rule 5*. When there is a contract for the sale of unascertained or future goods by description, and goods of that description and in a deliverable state are unconditionally appropriated to the contract by the seller with the assent of the buyer, or by the buyer with the assent of the seller, the property then passes to the buyer.

Such assent may be express or implied and given before or after the appropriation is made. For example, if the buyer orders goods to be supplied from the seller's stock he gives implied assent to the seller to make an appropriation from his stock.

To bring rule 5 into operation, something more definite is required than merely selecting or setting aside goods for delivery to the buyer. The act must be irrevocable, for example where the seller sets aside goods and also informs the buyer that they are ready for collection.

Delivery of goods to the buyer, or to a carrier for transmission to the buyer, without reserving to the seller a right of disposal, is an unconditional appropriation which brings rule 5 into operation. However, delivery to a carrier does not pass the property if identical goods destined to be sent to different buyers are mixed and need to be counted or sorted by the carrier.

Healey v Howlett & Sons 1917
The defendant ordered 20 boxes of mackerel from the claimant. 190 boxes were despatched, instructions being given to railway officials to set aside 20 for the defendant and the rest for two other buyers. The train was delayed before this was done and by the time the officials were ready to set them aside the fish had deteriorated badly.

Held: neither property nor risk had passed before the boxes were set aside.

Rule 5 only applies to appropriation of goods in a deliverable state.

Philip Head & Sons v Showfronts 1970
The parties entered into a contract for supply and laying of carpet at the buyer's premises. A roll of carpet was delivered but it was stolen before it could be laid.

Held: the carpet was deliverable to the buyer when laid and not before. It was the seller's property when stolen. The risk of loss remained with him.

Activity 7 **(10 minutes)**

On Monday, a contract is made for the sale of goods which are unascertained at that time. On Tuesday, the seller takes goods from stock and decides that these are the goods to be supplied to the buyer. However, the goods must first be packed. This is done on Wednesday and the buyer is notified on Thursday that this has been done and that the goods are ready for collection. Identify the day on which property in the goods passes to the buyer.

NOTES

11.2 Sale of Goods (Amendment) Act 1995

The Sale of Goods (Amendment) Act 1995 is now in force. It deals with the passing of ownership in goods which are unascertained in the sense that they have not been set aside for the buyer but are nevertheless to come from an ascertained source – 'I will buy 20 boxes of goods out of the stock of 60 boxes being transported to Doncaster by train.'

If there is no appropriation of a particular 20 boxes to the buyer, the ownership remains with the seller and if the seller goes insolvent, the goods are available for sale by the relevant insolvency practitioner. This is particularly unfortunate where the buyer has made a whole or partial pre-payment. The goods do not belong to him and he cannot recover the pre-payment but only some form of dividend in the insolvency which may be worthless.

This is a problem which those engaged in commerce have long recognised as an injustice. The Sale of Goods (Amendment) Act 1995 effects a change in the above situation where the buyer has made a whole or partial part payment. In such a case, he becomes a co-owner with others having a claim on the entire bulk. The bulk does not then pass into the control of an insolvency practitioner on the seller's insolvency. The right of the buyer to claim damages for injury to the goods is also enhanced by this provision.

12 NEMO DAT QUOD NON HABET

The general rule is that only the owner, or an agent acting with his authority, can transfer the title in goods to a buyer. This is expressed in the Latin maxim *nemo dat quod non habet*: no one can give what he does not have. To the general rule there are a number of exceptions to protect an honest buyer against loss.

12.1 Exceptions to the rule

(a) *Agency* (s 21). If an ordinary agent (that is, someone acting on behalf of someone else) sells goods without actual or apparent authority, there is usually no transfer of title to the buyer. But a mercantile agent, that is an agent whose business is selling goods for others, may have possession of goods (or documents of title to them) with the owner's consent. He can then sell them, in the ordinary course of his business, to a buyer who buys in good faith and without notice that the agent had no authority to sell (or was exceeding his authority). The buyer acquires title to the goods: s 21.

(b) *Estoppel*. If, by his conduct, the true owner leads the buyer to believe that the person who makes the sale owns the goods, the true owner is prevented (estopped) from denying the seller's authority to sell. Merely to put goods in the possession of another is not to represent that he is the owner.

(c) *Sale under voidable title* (s 23). A person may acquire goods under a contract which is voidable, say for misrepresentation. He then has title to the goods

BPP PUBLISHING

until the contract is avoided. If, before the sale to him is avoided, he re-sells to a person who buys in good faith and without notice of his defective title, that buyer obtains a good title to the goods. Normally the first contract of sale is not avoided until the person entitled to avoid it communicates his decision to the other party but if that party has disappeared other evidence of intention to avoid the first sale, such as reporting the matter to the police, will suffice: *Car & Universal Finance Co v Caldwell 1965.*

(d) *Re-sale by seller in possession* (s 24). If a seller, or a mercantile agent acting for him, continues in possession of the goods (or documents of title to them) after a sale, and he makes a delivery of them to a person who receives them in good faith and without notice of the previous sale, the transaction takes effect as if the seller were authorised for that purpose.

Suppose that A sells specific goods to B and B, to whom the ownership of the goods passes, immediately leaves them in A's possession until B can collect them. A by mistake then re-sells the goods and delivers them to C, who is unaware of the previous sale to B. C gets good title to the goods; B's only remedy is to sue A. But if A does not actually deliver the goods to C, B has the better right.

(e) *Re-sale by a buyer in possession* (s 25). The seller may permit the buyer to take possession of the goods before ownership has passed to the buyer, as when the seller makes delivery but retains title until the price is paid. If the buyer then makes a re-sale or other disposition in the normal course of business as mercantile agent, with actual delivery or transfer of the goods (or documents of title), to a person who takes them in good faith and without notice of the original seller's rights, title passes to that person as if the buyer had acted as a mercantile agent. This applies even if the buyer has a voidable title which is actually avoided (say by notifying police of the buyer's lack of title).

Newtons of Wembley v Williams 1965
X purchased a car and paid the price by cheque. The seller stipulated that title to the car should not pass until the cheque was cleared, but allowed X to take possession of the car. The cheque was dishonoured and the sellers informed the police and thereby avoided the sale to X in the only way available to them. But X sold the car for cash in an established secondhand car market to Y who took delivery forthwith.

Held: Y acquired good title since X was a buyer in possession with the seller's consent and the re-sale in the market was a disposition in the ordinary course of business of a mercantile agent. The loss must fall on the original seller if he could not recover from X.

To be a buyer in possession, the person must have obtained possession of the goods or documents of title to goods with the seller's consent. It is immaterial that the seller withdraws consent after the buyer has obtained possession, and that the latter obtains possession after contracting to sell to the innocent purchaser. He is a buyer in possession provided he obtains possession before delivering possession to the innocent purchaser: *Cahn v Pockett's Bristol Channel Steam Packet Co 1899.*

However, s 25 does not allow good title to be given to an innocent purchaser from a buyer in possession if the latter had obtained possession from a 'seller' not entitled to sell, that is, a thief: *National Mutual General Insurance Association Ltd v Jones 1988.*

NOTES

(f) *The sale of a motor vehicle acquired under hire purchase*. By the Hire Purchase Act 1964 a private (but not a trade) purchaser of a motor vehicle sold by a hirer under a hire purchase agreement or a buyer under a conditional sale agreement obtains good title (even though the seller had none) if the purchaser takes the vehicle in good faith and without notice that it was only let on hire purchase. The innocent buyer's purchase may be an ordinary sale or a hire purchase or conditional sale agreement. If there are intermediaries who are not private purchasers, the protection is available only to the first private purchaser. For example, A, who has a car under a hire purchase agreement, purports to sell it to B, a car dealer, who sells it to C, a private purchaser. B does not obtain title but C does. This is so even if B is a car dealer buying a vehicle for private, not business, purposes: *Stevenson v Beverley-Bentinck 1976*.

Activity 8 **(10 minutes)**

R buys a car and pays with a fraudulent cheque. The seller is unable to communicate with him, but informs the police and the AA of the fraud. R resells the car to J. Does J get good title to the car?

(g) *Special powers of sale*. The court may order goods to be sold. Various persons, such as pawnbrokers, unpaid sellers, hotel keepers and bailees (such as dry cleaners) in possession of abandoned goods for which charges are owing, have specific powers of sale.

Activity 9 **(10 minutes)**

Peter sells a car bearing the distinctive registration number DAWN 10 to Dawn Smith, who tells her friend Dawn Jones that she has just bought this car. The car is still with Peter when Dawn Jones calls on him, and attempts to buy the same car. Peter confuses the two Dawns, accepts Dawn Jones's cash and allows her to take the car away. When Dawn Smith claims the car from her, Dawn Jones relies on Section 24 of the Sale of Goods Act 1979 to retain the car.

Consider whether the car belongs to Dawn Jones or Dawn Smith.

13 DELIVERY

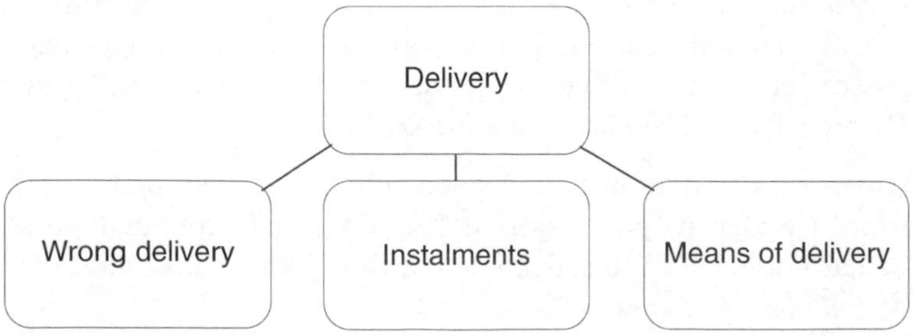

BPP PUBLISHING

Unless otherwise agreed, the seller is entitled to receive the price before delivering the goods to the buyer, but he must deliver them as soon as the price is paid: s 28. The parties may agree on whatever delivery arrangements may suit them. But unless otherwise agreed the following rules apply.

(a) *Method*. Delivery is the voluntary transfer of possession from one person to another (s 61). It may be by physical transfer of possession, or of the means of control (such as the key of a warehouse) or by arranging that a third party who has the goods acknowledges ('attorns') to the buyer that he holds them on his behalf, or by delivery of a document of title to the goods.

(b) *Place*. Delivery is to be made at the seller's place of business or, if he has none, at his residence, unless the goods are specific and, to the knowledge of both parties when the contract is made, the goods are at some other place. Delivery is, in those circumstances, to be at that other place.

(c) *Time*. If no time is agreed, delivery is to be made within a reasonable time and at a reasonable hour: s 29(5).

(d) *Expense*. The seller bears the expense of putting the goods into a deliverable state (for example by packing or bagging them).

13.1 Delivery by instalment

Unless otherwise agreed the buyer is not obliged to accept delivery by instalments: s 30(1). He may reject a delivery of part only of the goods.

If the contract does provide for delivery by instalments with separate payment for each instalment, the contract is severable or divisible. If one or more instalments under a severable contract are defective, this may amount to repudiation of the entire contract or it may merely give a right to claim compensation for the defective deliveries only. It depends on the ratio of defective to sound deliveries and the likelihood or otherwise that future instalments will also be defective.

13.2 Wrong delivery

If the seller delivers the wrong quantity the buyer may reject the whole quantity, but if he accepts what is delivered he must pay at the contract rate for the quantity accepted. When the seller delivers too much the buyer may also accept the correct quantity and reject the rest: s 30.

If the seller delivers the contract goods mixed with other goods the buyer may reject the whole or accept the contract goods and reject others: s 30.

Where the contract requires that the goods be moved in the course of delivery:

(a) delivery to a carrier for transmission to the buyer is deemed to be delivery to the buyer unless the contrary intention appears, as when the seller consigns the goods to himself or his agent at their destination: s 32;

(b) the seller must make a reasonable arrangement with the carrier and (if the goods are sent by sea) give the buyer notice in time to permit the buyer to arrange insurance: s 32;

(c) the buyer must bear the risk of any deterioration necessarily incidental to the course of transit: s 33.

14 ACCEPTANCE AND REJECTION

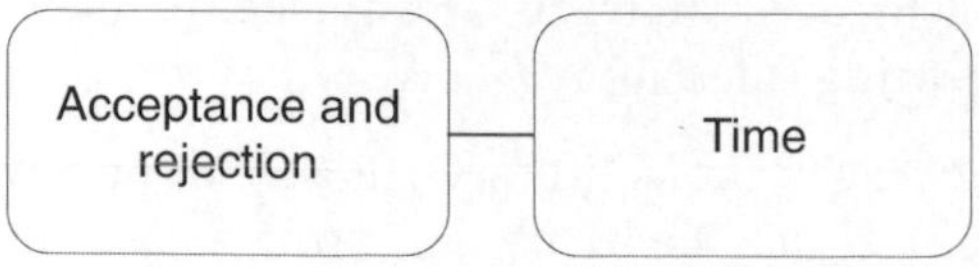

Acceptance of goods or part of them (unless the contract is severable), deprives the buyer of his right to treat the contract as discharged by breach of condition (for example, as to the quality of the goods) on the part of the seller. But he may claim damages.

14.1 Time of acceptance

The buyer is not deemed to have accepted the goods until he has had a reasonable opportunity of examining them for the purpose of ascertaining whether they are in conformity with the contract: s 34. The buyer is deemed to have accepted the goods in the following circumstances (s 35, as amended by Sale and Supply of Goods Act 1994).

(a) When he intimates to the seller that he has accepted them, provided that he has had a reasonable opportunity of ascertaining whether they are in conformity with the contract;

(b) When the goods have been delivered to the buyer and he does any act in relation to them which is inconsistent with the ownership of the seller, for example, using or reselling them;

(c) When after the lapse of a reasonable time he retains the goods without intimating to the seller that he has rejected them. In determining whether a reasonable time has elapsed, one factor is whether the buyer has been afforded a reasonable opportunity of examination, for example by use. For example, if A buys a car which is not of satisfactory quality but continues to drive it for 5,000 miles, he would probably at that point be unable to rescind the contract.

Where the seller has breached a condition the buyer may treat the contract as repudiated and hence reject the goods. The buyer does not have to return the goods to the seller – he merely has to inform the seller of his rejection: s 36.

The buyer loses his right to reject goods if:

(a) he waives the breached condition;

(b) he elects to treat the breach of condition as a breach of warranty;

(c) he has accepted the goods (in a contract which is not severable); or

(d) he is unable to return the goods because, for example, he has sold them on to a buyer who keeps them.

Activity 10 **(10 minutes)**

The parties to a contract for the sale of non-perishable goods agree that the goods shall be delivered to the buyer's premises 'during normal business hours'. The seller then states that the only time of day that the goods can be delivered is 10 pm and that the goods must be accepted or rejected immediately on delivery. At that time a caretaker will be present to receive the goods, but he is not competent to inspect them. In what ways has the seller failed to meet his legal obligations?

NOTES

15 THE PARTIES' REMEDIES

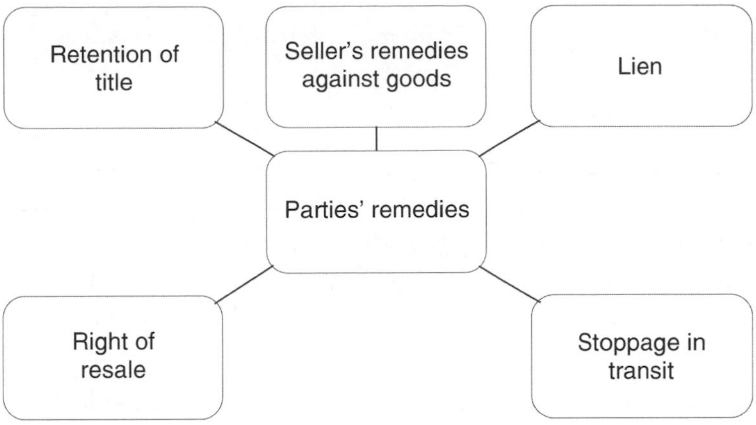

As with any other contract, one for sale of goods may be breached. Aside from the usual common law remedies (damages, action for the price, and so on) the parties have rights peculiar to this type of contract. They are categorised as:

(a) the seller's remedies against the goods;
(b) the seller's remedies against the buyer;
(c) the buyer's remedies against the seller.

The remedies which are against goods are described as ' real remedies' (*action in rem*); all others are called ' personal remedies' (*action in personam*).

15.1 The seller's remedies against the goods

Ownership of goods often passes to the buyer before they are delivered to the buyer in exchange for the price. If the buyer then defaults, for example by failing to pay the price when due, the seller is given rights against the goods in his possession or under his control although those goods are now owned by the buyer. It is usually more satisfactory to him to retain the goods than merely to sue a buyer, who may well be insolvent, for breach of contract.

These rights are given only to an 'unpaid seller' (s 38). He is unpaid if either:

(a) the whole of the price has not been paid or tendered to him; or
(b) he has received a bill of exchange and the bill has been dishonoured.

An unpaid seller of goods which are now the property of the buyer has the following statutory rights in respect of the goods (s 39):

(a) a lien on the goods so long as they are in his possession;

(b) a right of stoppage in transit if the buyer is insolvent and the goods are in the hands of a carrier;

(c) a right of resale in certain circumstances.

15.2 Lien

Definition

> Lien: the seller's right to retain the goods in his possession until the price is paid or tendered (s 41).

BPP PUBLISHING

The unpaid seller's right of lien applies:

(a) where the goods are sold without any stipulation as to credit;

(b) where they have been sold on credit terms but the credit period has expired; or

(c) where the buyer becomes insolvent.

Even if part of the goods have been delivered to the buyer, the unpaid seller has a lien on the rest unless part delivery indicates his agreement to give up his lien altogether: s 42.

The unpaid seller loses his lien when he delivers the goods to a carrier or warehouseman for transmission to the buyer (unless the seller reserves a right of disposal), or when the buyer or his agent lawfully obtains possession of the goods, or when the seller waives his lien: s 43.

Lien merely gives a right to retain possession until the price is paid. It does not rescind the contract, deprive the buyer of his ownership nor entitle the seller to re-sell the goods.

15.3 Stoppage in transit

The right of stoppage in transit (s 44-45) exists when the buyer becomes insolvent. He is insolvent if he has ceased to pay his debts in the ordinary course of business or cannot pay his debts as they fall due: it is not necessary to wait until he becomes bankrupt.

While goods are in transit, neither seller nor buyer has possession of the goods since they are in the possession of a carrier. The unpaid seller may stop the goods in transit by issuing an order to the carrier. The goods cease to be in transit and the seller's right of stoppage ends:

(a) on delivery to the buyer or his agent (whether at the appointed destination or before);

(b) if the carrier acknowledges to the buyer or his agent that the goods (arrived at their original destination) are now held on behalf of the buyer. It is immaterial that the buyer may have indicated to the carrier that the goods are to be taken on to a further destination; or

(c) if the carrier wrongfully refuses to make delivery to the buyer or his agent.

But if the buyer refuses to accept the goods which remain in the possession of the carrier, they are still in transit.

Activity 11 **(10 minutes)**

A seller of goods consigns them to a carrier for transmission to the buyer, thereby ending his lien. Why is the seller's lien not automatically replaced by a right of stoppage in transit at that point?

15.4 Right of resale

As between the unpaid seller and the buyer of the goods, the seller has a right of resale:

(a) if the goods are of a perishable nature;

(b) if the seller gives notice to the buyer of his intention to re-sell and the buyer fails within a reasonable time to pay or tender the price; or

(c) If the seller reserves a right of resale under the contract.

If the seller does not, by resale, recover the full amount of his loss he may sue the buyer for damages for breach of contract: s 48. On a sale in these circumstances the second buyer gets good title to the goods.

15.5 Retention of title clauses

These should be familiar from an earlier chapter.

Many commercial contracts now contain a retention of title clause, often known as a Romalpa clause after the case discussed below. Under such a clause, possession may pass to the buyer but ownership does not pass until the price is paid.

> *Aluminium Industrie Vaassen BV v Romalpa Ltd 1976*
> Romalpa purchased aluminium foil on terms that the stock of foil (and any proceeds of sale) should be the property of the Dutch supplier until the company had paid to the supplier all that it owed. Romalpa got into financial difficulties and a receiver was appointed. The receiver found that the company still held aluminium foil and proceeds of selling other stocks of foil, and had not paid its debt to the supplier. The receiver applied to the court to determine whether or not the foil and the cash were assets of the company under his control as receiver.
>
> *Held:* the conditions of sale were valid. The relevant assets, although in the possession of the company, did not belong to it. The receiver could not deal with these assets since his authority under the floating charge was restricted to assets of the company.

The extent to which a Romalpa clause protects an unpaid seller depends to a great extent on the wording of the actual clause. A retention of title clause may be effective even though goods are resold or incorporated into the buyer's products so as to lose their identity if it expressly states that they can be used in these ways before title has passed: *Clough Mill Ltd v Martin 1985.*

Unless the clause expressly retains title even after resale or incorporation, the supplier is not entitled to a proportionate part of the sale proceeds of the manufactured product: *Borden (UK) Ltd v Scottish Timber Products Ltd 1979*. Where there is no express provision, resale or incorporation is conversion of the supplier's property but a third party will still get good title.

If the buyer resells the goods when there is an express provision allowing resale before title passes, the proceeds of sale are held by the buyer as trustee for the supplier.

A reservation of title clause can cover, besides the price of the goods specifically subject of the particular contract of sale, other debts due to the seller under unrelated contracts.

> *Armour and Carron Co Ltd v Thyssen Edelstahlwerke AG 1990*
> The defendants transferred possession in steel strip to a buyer under a contract of sale. The buyer agreed that it would not acquire the property (ownership) until all amounts due to the defendant had been paid. The claimants were appointed receivers of the assets of the buyer; the steel strip had not been paid for. The buyer argued that the clause was an attempt to create a security over moveable property and that it was therefore void.
>
> *Held:* it was not possible to create a security over goods which you did not own. Under Sale of Goods Act s 19(1) 'where there is a contract for the sale of specific goods ... the seller may ... reserve the right to disposal of the goods until certain conditions are fulfilled'. The defendant had reserved this right until fulfilment of the condition that all the buyer's debts had been

paid, including those due under other contracts. They therefore remained owners of the steel strip.

16 THE SELLER'S REMEDIES AGAINST THE BUYER

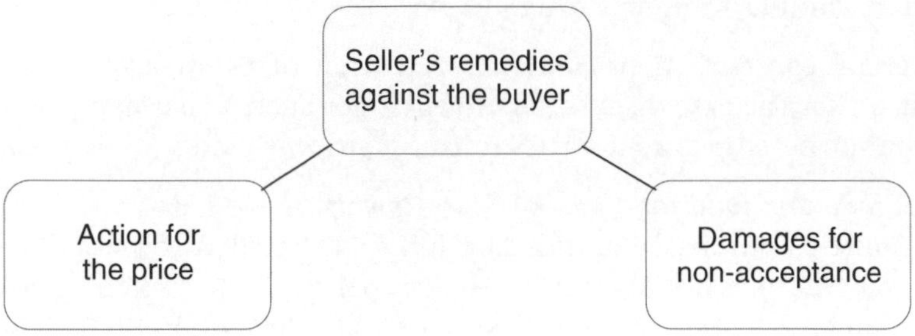

The seller has two possible remedies against the buyer personally.

(a) He may bring an *action for the price* if:

- (i) the ownership of the goods has passed to the buyer and he wrongfully neglects or refuses to pay the price according to the terms of the contract; or
- (ii) the price is payable on a certain day (regardless of delivery) and the buyer wrongfully neglects or refuses to pay it.

(b) The seller may sue for damages for non-acceptance if the buyer wrongfully refuses or neglects to accept and pay for the goods. In this case the claim may include any expense incurred by the seller (for example in storing the goods) caused by the buyer's failure to take delivery after being requested to do so.

When the seller claims damages, the first head of the rule in *Hadley v Baxendale* applies. If there is an available market for this type of goods, the measure of damages is usually the difference between the contract price and the market price on the day when the goods should have been accepted.

Activity 12 **(10 minutes)**

Some nuts and bolts are sold to Z Ltd subject to a retention of title clause, the full text of which is as follows.

'Property in the goods shall not pass to the buyer until the buyer has paid for the goods in full'.

Before paying for the nuts and bolts, Z Ltd incorporates them into electric motors which are sold. If Z Ltd fails to pay for the nuts and bolts, what remedy might the supplier seek?

17 THE BUYER'S REMEDIES AGAINST THE SELLER

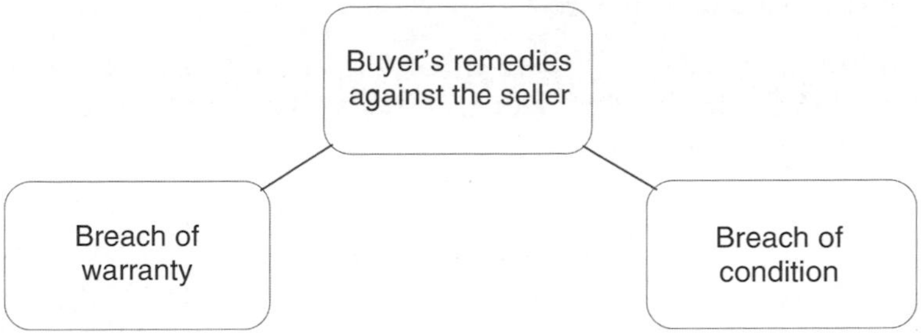

17.1 Breach of condition

If the seller is in *breach of a condition* of the contract, the buyer may reject the goods unless he has lost his right to do so by accepting the goods or part of them. In addition he may claim damages.

If the buyer has paid the price and the consideration has failed entirely, for example if the seller has no title or delivers goods which the buyer is entitled to reject, the buyer may sue to recover the price: s 54.

17.2 Breach of warranty

If there is a *breach of warranty* by the seller, or if the buyer is obliged (or prefers) to deal with a breach of a condition by a claim for damages, the buyer may either reduce the amount paid to the seller by an allowance for the breach or sue for damages. The amount of damages is determined on principles similar to those of the seller's claim against the buyer.

It is open to the buyer to base his claim on any circumstances within the general scope of these rules.

> *Mason v Burningham 1949*
> The claimant had been sold a typewriter which turned out to be stolen property. She had to return it to the owner. In addition to the price paid she claimed damages for breach of implied warranty of quiet enjoyment including her expenditure in having the typewriter overhauled.
>
> *Held:* damages should be awarded as claimed.

A buyer may also claim damages for non-delivery, calculated on the same principles as described earlier when a seller claims damages. This claim may be made if the seller either fails to deliver altogether or delivers goods which the buyer is entitled to, and does, reject.

The buyer's claim for damages for loss of profit or liability for damages arising on that contract is not affected by a resale by him, unless it can be shown that the parties to the original sale contemplated that there would be a resale.

> *Williams v Agius 1914*
> There was a contract for the sale of coal at 16s 3d [81p] per ton. The buyers resold at 19s 6d [97p] per ton. The market price at the date for delivery was 23s 6d [£1.17]. per ton. The sellers failed to deliver. The sellers contended that the buyer's actual loss was the difference between the contract price (16s.3d) and the resale price (19s.6d) per ton only.

Held: the buyers should be awarded damages of 7s 3d [36p] per ton, the full difference between the market price and the contract price; the resale contract should be ignored.

In an action for breach of contract to deliver specific or ascertained goods, the court may order specific performance or delivery of the goods. But it will only do so if damages would be an inadequate remedy: s 51.

Activity 13 **(10 minutes)**

Why, in a case such as Williams v Agius 1914, might the buyer/reseller's loss (for which he would need to be compensated) be the difference between the full market price (23s 6d per ton in that case) and the originally agreed price (16s.3d per ton)?

18 THE SUPPLY OF GOODS AND SERVICES ACT 1982

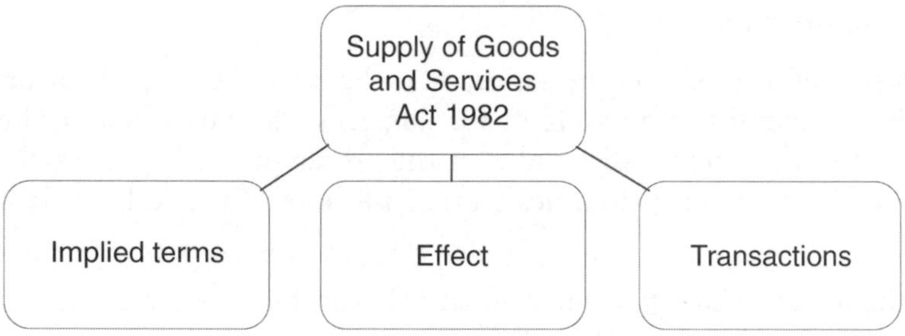

The Supply of Goods and Services Act 1982 (SGSA 1982) applies to certain contracts which do not fall within the definition of a sale of goods even though they do involve a transfer of ownership.

18.1 Transactions covered

(a) *contracts of exchange or barter:* these are not contracts of sale of goods because there is no money consideration involved;

(b) *contracts of repair:* although some goods are supplied (for example spare parts) the substance of the contract is the provision of services (see below);

(c) *contracts of hire:* these are not contracts for the sale of goods because they contain no provision for ownership to pass to the hirer;

(d) *collateral contracts to the sale of goods:* for example, where a person buys a car and receives a free set of seat covers as part of a special deal, the purchase of the car is governed by the Sale of Goods Act 1979 but the seat covers, for which consideration was given by buying the car, are part of a collateral contract governed by the Supply of Goods and Services Act 1982.

The Act specifically does not cover contracts of apprenticeship or employment (s 12).

If the main purpose of a contract is, for example, the provision of skilled labour, whilst an ancillary object is the transfer of ownership of goods (such as a spare part for a washing machine), the contract is one governed by the 1982 Act.

18.2 Effect of the Act

The general effect of the Act is to provide safeguards similar to those provided by the Sale of Goods Act in respect of contracts for sale of goods. Where the supply of goods is a part of the transaction, ss 2-5 of the 1982 Act imply certain terms relating to the goods. The terms implied relate to the goods supplied and are similar to those of the Sale of Goods Act 1979, dealing with strict liability regarding:

(a) title, freedom from encumbrances and quiet possession (s 2);
(b) description (s 3);
(c) satisfactory quality and fitness for purpose (s 4);
(d) sample (s 5).

Under the Unfair Contract Terms Act 1977, clauses purporting to exclude or restrict liability under these headings are subject to the same rules as similar exclusion clauses in sale of goods contracts.

18.3 Implied terms

Where the contract is wholly or substantially for the provision of services, the 1982 Act implies a number of further terms.

(a) Where the supplier of the service is acting in the course of a business, there are implied terms that he will carry out the service with reasonable care and skill (s 13) and within a reasonable time (s 14).

(b) Where the consideration is not determined by the contract, there is an implied term that the party contracting with the supplier will pay a reasonable charge (s 15).

These terms are implied whether there is a supply of goods or not. But they are not conditions of strict liability, and may be excluded so long as such exclusion complies with the reasonableness requirement of the Unfair Contract Terms Act 1977: s 16 SGSA 1982.

Activity 14 **(10 minutes)**

Robinson v Graves 1935 concerned a contract to paint a portrait. Marcel (Furriers) Ltd v Tapper 1953 concerned a contract for the supply of a mink jacket of a special style made to the customer's requirements. In both cases materials were worked on by skilled persons, but in one case it was held that there was a sale of goods and in the other case it was held that there was a supply of services. In which case do you think it was held that there was a sale of goods?

Chapter roundup

- Contracts for the sale of goods are subject to the Sale of Goods Act 1979 as amended by the Sale and Supply of Goods Act 1994. In considering such contracts, we must distinguish between existing and future goods, and between specific and unascertained goods.
- If the price for goods is not determined by the contract then a reasonable price must be paid.
- The Sale of Goods Act 1979 implies several terms into contracts for the sale of goods, and the Unfair Contract Terms Act 1977 limits the extent to which these implied terms may be overridden.
- If time is not of the essence, it may be made so. Performance must be tendered at a reasonable time.
- There is an implied condition that the seller of goods has a right to sell, but the seller may put the buyer on notice that his title may be defective.
- In a sale by description, the goods must match the description given. In a sale by sample, the bulk must correspond to the sample.
- Goods are of satisfactory quality if they meet the standard that a reasonable person would regard as satisfactory.
- If the seller of goods knows the purpose for which the goods are being bought, it is normally an implied condition that the goods are reasonably fit for that purpose.
- The property in goods passes when the parties intend that it shall pass. Where such intention is not otherwise made clear, the rules of s 18 Sale of Goods Act 1979 apply to fix the time. Goods are generally at the buyer's risk from the time that property passes.
- A person not owning goods cannot in general transfer title to a buyer. However, there are several exceptions to protect an innocent buyer.
- Goods must be delivered as agreed, but there are rules which apply in the absence of agreement.
- A buyer must be given an opportunity to inspect and if necessary reject goods, but once he has accepted the goods, either explicitly or by conduct, he cannot later reject them.
- An unpaid seller of goods may be able to retrieve the goods even if title has passed to the buyer. He may also attempt to protect his position by retaining title until he has been paid. Failing such remedies, the seller may sue the buyer. If the seller breaches a condition of the contract, the buyer may reject the goods. The buyer may also sue the seller for breaches of conditions or warranties.
- The Sale of Goods Act 1979 applies only to sales of goods. The Supply of Goods and Services Act 1982 makes similar provisions for contracts outside the scope of the 1979 Act.

Quick quiz

1 What terms are covered by statutory conditions implied (as part of the contract) by the Sale of Goods Act 1979?

2 What is the implied condition as to the seller's right to sell the goods?

3 What is a sale of goods by description and what is implied in such a sale?

4 What is satisfactory quality?

5 When are defects of quality not a breach of the condition of satisfactory quality?

6 Give three exceptions to the rule *nemo dat quod non habet.*

7 What is a severable contract?

8 When is a buyer deemed to have accepted goods?

9 What are the seller's remedies if he is not paid?

10 What is a retention of title clause?

11 What are the buyer's remedies for breach of contract?

12 What terms are implied into a contract which is wholly or substantially for the provision of services?

Answers to quick quiz

1 Delay
Title
Description of goods
Sale by sample
Quantity of goods
Fitness for purpose of the goods (see para 4.1)

2 That the seller has the right to sell the goods, ie he can pass good title. (para 6)

3 Implied condition that goods will correspond to the description of them, where they are sold by description. (para 7)

4 Goods 'meet the standard a reasonable person would regard as satisfactory'. (para 9.1)

5 When goods are used not for the particular purpose sold, or for an unusual purpose. (para 10.1)

6 Agency
Sale under voidable title
Resale by seller in possession (see para 12.1)

7 A contract where delivery is made by instalments. (para 3.1)

8 Once he has had a reasonable opportunity of examining them. (para 14.1)

9 Lien
Stoppage in transit
Right of resale
Retention of title (paras 15.2-15.5)

10 A clause stating that possession of goods does not pass to the buyer until he has paid for them. (para 15.5)

11 Recovery of the price
Rejection of the goods
Damages for non-delivery
Specific performance (para 17.1, 17.2)

12 Implied term that the provider of the service will carry it out with reasonable care and skill and on time.

Implied term that a reasonable charge will be paid. (para 18.3)

Answers to activities

1 This is not a contract for the sale of goods because there is no agreement to transfer ownership of the car until B exercises the option to buy.

2 No: there would have been a single contract to sell petrol and coins for cash.

3 C may recover the entire price (£1,000) from the seller, A, because C did not receive ownership of the corn and the depreciation in value is irrelevant.

4 No: although 1959 is very close to 1958, the exact year is crucial for wine.

5 P's argument would fail because, although the pen can be made to write with difficulty, this is not the standard of quality expected from an expensive pen.

6 S made it clear that he did not have the skill or judgement on which R sought to rely.

7 Property passes on Thursday under Rule 2 of s 18 Sale of Goods Act 1979.

8 No: This is a case of sale under voidable title and the seller has rescinded the contract by taking all reasonable steps.

9 The car belongs to Dawn Smith because Dawn Jones has attempted to purchase the car while having notice of the previous sale and acting in bad faith. Section 24 does not apply.

10 Ten pm is not during normal business hours, and the seller has not given the buyer a reasonable opportunity to inspect the goods.

11 The buyer may not become insolvent, or the carrier may be the buyer's agent.

12 The seller may bring an action for the price. The retention of title clause does not mention incorporation into Z Ltd's products, so it cannot be relied upon in this case.

13 The buyer/reseller might have to buy coal from other suppliers at the market price (23s 6d per ton) in order to fulfil the contract for resale. The loss on that transaction of 23s 6d – 19s.6d = 4s. per ton would have to be added to the lost profit of 3s 3d per ton.

14 Marcel (Furriers) Ltd v Tapper 1953.

NOTES

Assignment 7 **(60 minutes)**

(a) Jay purchased a car from Rob. Unknown to Jay, Rob had stolen the car from Don. Some three months after the purchase by Jay, police officers confiscated the car in question.

Both Jay and Don believe they are entitled to the car.

Advise them of their respective legal positions.

Sarah and her friend Pally were anxious to purchase two motor cars to enable them to travel independently to their respective places of work.

(b) Sarah had enough money saved to purchase a two year old second hand car for £8,000 that had travelled 16,000 miles. Pally, on the other hand, only had sufficient money to purchase a ten year old car for £1,200 that had travelled 160,000 miles.

Some three months after purchase Sarah was advised by a friend, a qualified mechanic, that the engine had seized and the car was no longer roadworthy.

The following month, some four months after purchase, Pally could not start her car following extreme overnight weather conditions. The same mechanic who assisted Sarah informed Pally that the problem was terminal and that the car was no longer roadworthy. Pally was really upset, having spent all her savings and being assured by the garage who sold her the car that the '*car would be roadworthy for 6 months*'.

Advise Sarah and Pally of their respective legal positions.

Chapter 11 :
CONSUMER PROTECTION

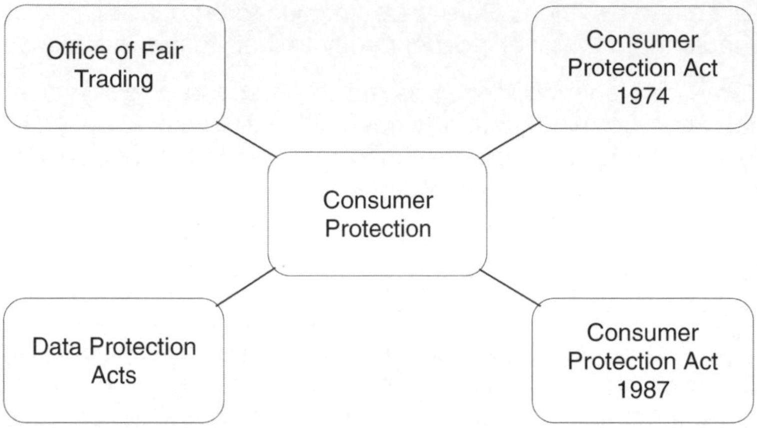

Introduction

In the last twenty years or so, different governments have tried to improve protection for the consumer, reflecting the increasingly consumer-oriented nature of society. There are three main pieces of legislation with which you should be familiar: the Consumer Protection Act 1987, the Consumer Credit Act 1974 and the Data Protection Acts 1994 and 1998.

Your objectives

In this chapter you will learn about the following.

(a) The rights of a consumer given by the Consumer Protection Act 1974

(b) The scope of actions for product liability under Part 1 of the Consumer Protection Act 1987

(c) The impact of the Data Protection Acts and the extent to which they can protect the consumer and other individuals

(d) The role of the main regulatory agency concerned with consumer protection, namely the Office of Fair Trading.

NOTES

1 THE CONSUMER CREDIT ACT 1974

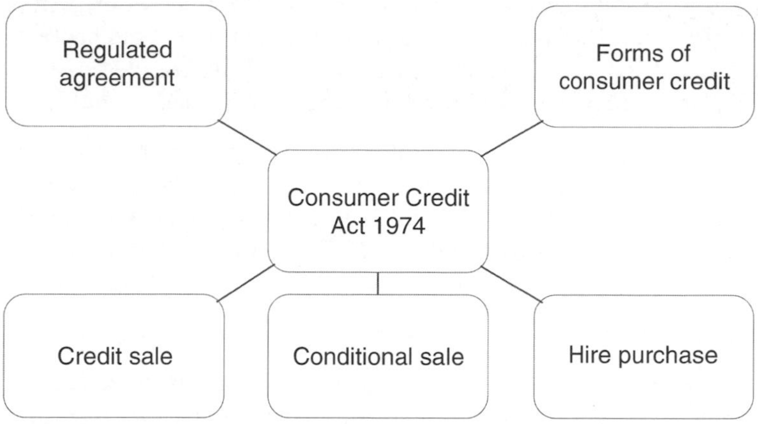

The Consumer Credit Act 1974 was passed to protect consumers by introducing a new concept, that of 'truth in lending'. The Act applies to any defined lending transactions to individuals, not to companies, and its main provisions govern lending up to and including £15,000. As an example of its scope, all lending institutions regulated by the Act must inform borrowers of all charges connected with regulated lending, and the rate of interest must be calculated and quoted in a similar way. These are the twin phenomena of the Total Charge for Credit and the Annual Percentage Rate.

Typical problems encountered before the Act were inaccurate advertising, canvassing and the charging of extortionate rates of interest by lenders. The Act is a complex piece of legislation and seeks to regulate transactions (those which are not exempt, such as mortgages of land) including hire purchase agreements, conditional sale transactions, credit sales and personal loans.

Statutory references in this section are to the Consumer Credit Act 1974 unless otherwise noted.

1.1 Forms of consumer credit

Consumer credit takes a variety of forms. The simplest form is a loan to a customer which he may use to purchase whatever goods or services he requires. But the creditor often prefers to supply goods himself to the consumer on hire purchase terms so that the goods remain the creditor's property until the consumer has paid the price including credit charges, and can be recovered if the debtor defaults. It is a common business practice for a trader to sell his goods to a finance company so that the latter, in providing credit to a customer of the trader, can do so under a hire purchase or related transaction. There are also other special forms of credit transaction such as those involving bank credit cards, shop budget accounts, loans by pawnbrokers on the security of chattels deposited with them, and so on.

1.2 Hire purchase

There are two elements in a hire purchase transaction.

(a) Goods are bailed (or delivered) to the possession of the hirer, for his use, by the creditor who has purchased the goods from the dealer.

(b) The hirer has an option to purchase the goods when he has completed payment of a number of instalments which represent the cash price plus a charge for credit.

The legal effect of a hire purchase agreement is that the hirer is not a buyer in possession of goods, the property in which has not yet passed to him. He has an option to buy the goods but he is not bound to exercise that option. He does not yet own the goods nor can he pass ownership to another person by an unauthorised sale. This protects the owner of the goods from losing title to them: the hirer is not legally competent to deprive him of it (with an exception under the Hire Purchase Act 1964 limited to motor vehicles).

The same conditions and warranties (in substance) are implied by law in a hire purchase agreement as in a sale of goods: Supply of Goods (Implied Terms) Act 1973. There are the same restrictions on contracting out of these terms by the use of exclusion clauses as apply to agreements for the sale of goods: s 6 Unfair Contract Terms Act 1977.

1.3 Conditional sale

The conditional sale agreement was developed as a means of avoiding the controls applied to hire purchase agreements. But it no longer has this effect since the same rules apply to either type of agreement. The essential features of a conditional sale agreement are as follows.

(a) The buyer agrees to buy goods from the creditor, who purchased them from the dealer, and to pay the price by instalments.

(b) The buyer obtains immediate possession but the transfer of ownership is postponed until he has paid all the instalments.

(c) He is not a buyer or person who has agreed to buy goods for the purposes of Sale of Goods Act 1979 and so he cannot transfer ownership (which he has not yet obtained) to another person.

The Sale of Goods Act 1979 applies to such agreements.

1.4 Credit sale

A credit sale agreement is an agreement under which ownership as well as possession is transferred to the buyer by the creditor without delay, but the price is payable by instalments. The buyer is free to sell before the price has been paid. Such a sale is subject to regulation (to protect the buyer) under the Consumer Credit Act 1974.

Activity 1 **(5 minutes)**

In which one of a hire purchase agreement, a conditional sale agreement and a credit sale agreement can the consumer pay all the instalments required yet still not acquire ownership of the goods?

1.5 What is a regulated agreement?

The Consumer Credit Act 1974 (CCA) regulates the provision of credit. 'Credit' includes a cash loan and any other form of financial benefit including hire purchase, conditional sale and credit sale agreements.

Except in respect of extortionate credit bargains (which are discussed later in this chapter) the CCA only applies to regulated agreements. These are agreements meeting the following conditions set out in ss 8-9.

(a) *Individuals* (not companies) obtain credit. The use of the phrase consumer credit here is rather misleading since a sole trader or partnership obtaining credit for commercial purposes is protected by the 1974 Act.

(b) *Credit not exceeding £15,000* is provided. The amount of credit given is not the total price paid by the debtor, but rather that total less any initial payment paid when the agreement is made and any charges for credit. If, for example, the debtor is to pay £16,500 in total (of which £500 is paid on signing the agreement), and £1,000 in interest charges, the credit given is £15,000 (£16,500 less £500 less £1,000) and so the agreement is regulated by the 1974 Act.

(c) The agreement is not *exempt*. The CCA does not apply (s 16) to certain transactions, for example, building society loans for the purchase of land, running account credit which is settled in full (as with American Express cards), credit sale agreements for less than £50 or agreements where the creditor does not act in the course of a business.

2 THE CLASSIFICATION OF REGULATED AGREEMENTS

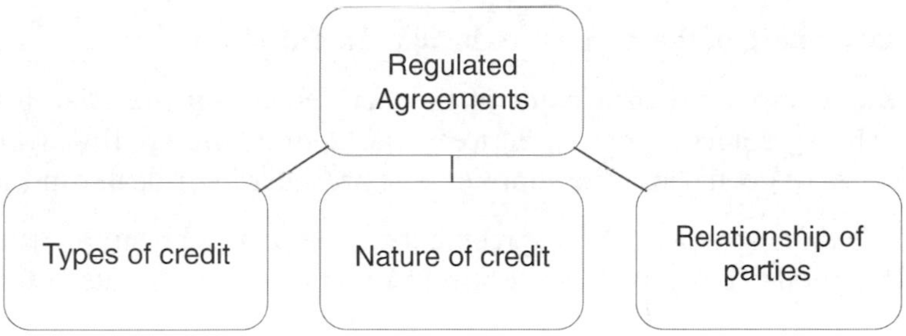

The 1974 Act uses an elaborate classification of consumer credit agreements to apply rules selectively to some types but not others. Small and non-commercial agreements, for example, are not subject to all the rules. What follows applies generally both to agreements for lending money and to agreements for the supply of goods under hire purchase and related types of agreement. References to 'debtor' and 'creditor' are to the hirer and the owner of goods let under a hire purchase agreement respectively. A regulated agreement is one covered by the Act.

To understand the Act we need to look at how regulated agreements are classified. This means analysing:

(a) the type of credit;
(b) the nature of the credit; and
(c) the relationship of the parties to the agreement.

2.1 The type of credit

There are two types of credit, identified by s 10 of the Act.

(a) In *running account credit*, also known as a revolving credit, the debtor does not have to apply for further amounts of credit after making the original credit agreement but automatically has the right to further credit, although there is usually a credit limit. Common examples are bank overdrafts and shop or credit card agreements.

(b) *Fixed sum credit* is a once-only credit, such as a single loan. If the creditor later agrees to make a further loan there are deemed to be two fixed-sum credits, since the debtor had no automatic right to receive further credit.

2.2 The nature of the credit

A distinction is made as to the nature of credit in s 11 between an agreement whereby the creditor exercises some control over the use of his finance and one where he has no such control.

(a) *Restricted use credit* (RUC) is seen in agreements whereby

- (i) the creditor pays the funds direct to a supplier;
- (ii) the debtor receives a credit token (such as a credit card which can only be used in a particular group of stores) which may only be used in transactions with those suppliers who have agreed to take it; or
- (iii) the creditor also acts as supplier.

(b) *Unrestricted use credit* (UUC) is the residual category where the creditor merely supplies funds and the debtor can use them in any way he sees fit.

2.3 The relationship of the parties to the agreement

Many of the more important provisions of the Act depend on the relationship between the parties to the agreement: that is, between the debtor, the creditor (the provider of finance and owner of goods) and the supplier (the provider of or dealer in the goods).

(a) In a *debtor-creditor* (D-C) agreement the persons who supply the finance and the goods respectively are entirely separate. Thus the use of an overdrawn current account at a bank to purchase a hi-fi from a shop is a debtor-creditor agreement.

(b) In a *debtor-creditor-supplier* (D-C-S) agreement, there are arrangements whereby the creditor and supplier of goods are linked: s 12. An arrangement whereby a car sales agency provides credit via its linked finance house is such an agreement; so too is a credit card transaction where, although creditor and supplier are different persons, a business arrangement exists between them that the supplier will accept the creditor's card produced by the buyer.

It is important to distinguish the two types of agreement above in order to see how rights are protected under the Act. In particular a creditor is jointly and severally liable with the supplier for misrepresentations made by the supplier (s 56) or for breach of contract by the supplier (s 75) in a D-C-S agreement.

A *linked transaction* is one which is subsidiary to but in some way connected with the main credit transaction: s 19. It is thus automatically terminated if the main transaction is cancelled.

NOTES

Activity 2 **(10 minutes)**

George borrows £5,000 from his bank as a loan of a fixed amount at 2% over base rate for an unspecified purpose. He uses the money to buy double glazing for his house.

(a) Is there a regulated credit agreement?

(b) Has RUC or UUC been provided?

(c) Is the bank liable for misrepresentations by the double glazing company?

3 THE PROTECTION OF DEBTORS

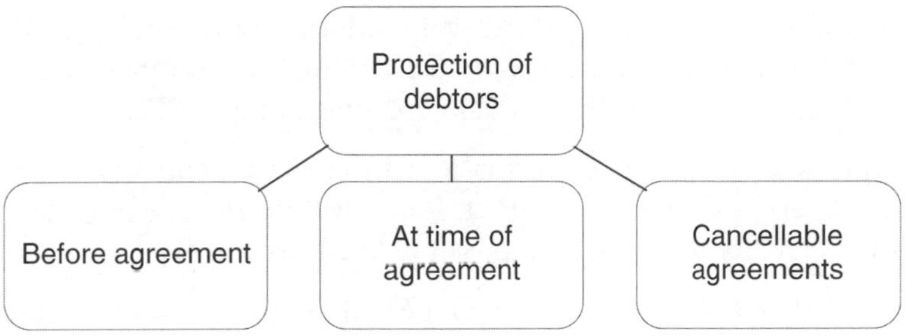

We have seen that the main object of the 1974 Act is the protection of individual debtors. The way in which it does this can be analysed into protection given *before* the agreement is made, *at the time* the agreement is made and *after* the agreement has been made.

3.1 Protection of the debtor before the agreement is made

It often happens that a 'negotiator' is involved in the 'antecedent negotiations' of a consumer credit agreement. This can happen in two ways.

(a) A person buying, say, a motor car and wishing to finance it by a hire purchase agreement will obtain the car from a dealer. The dealer will arrange the finance on behalf of the purchaser through a credit institution. In effect, the car dealer, acting as negotiator, is a credit broker.

(b) A person buys goods from a shop and pays by credit card.

In these cases s 56 provides of the Act that the 'negotiator' (the car dealer or the shop) is the agent of the creditor. This has two effects. The creditor is liable for any misrepresentations made by the negotiator as though he had made them himself, and any money paid by the debtor to the negotiator will be regarded as having been received by the creditor.

Two further rules protect the debtor who has not yet entered into a binding regulated agreement.

(a) A debtor is not bound by any prior agreement to enter into a regulated agreement, such as an option (s 59). Without this protection, the detailed rules covering regulated agreements could be circumvented by a prior promise to enter into obligations.

(b) The debtor may withdraw from the agreement at any time before all the formalities are completed by giving notice to the creditor, the negotiator or the creditor's agent (s 57). Thus he may withdraw up to the time when the agreement is fully executed.

3.2 Protection of the debtor at the time the agreement is made

To protect the debtor at the time the agreement is being made the Act lays down detailed requirements as to the formalities of execution and the provision of copies.

Formalities of execution

The agreement must be in writing and its form (printed) and content are prescribed by regulations to ensure that the debtor is made aware of his rights and obligations, particularly his rights of cancellation and termination. The terms of the agreement must be complete and legible and all necessary insertion of particulars in blank spaces must be made before the debtor signs the agreement. Signature must be made in the 'signature box'.

The debtor must be supplied with all 'relevant information' relating to the agreement, including the cash price, the deposit paid, the timing and number of instalments, the total charge for credit (TCC) and the annual percentage rate (APR).

Failure to comply with the required formalities in making a consumer credit agreement makes it an improperly executed agreement. It can still be enforced by the debtor but the creditor will find it either difficult or impossible to enforce. It is:

(a) *unenforceable* by the creditor (s 127) if it did not contain the basic terms when the debtor signed it or the requirements for copies (and notices for a cancellable agreement) were not met (see below);

(b) *difficult to enforce* in other circumstances: for example, court orders will be required and security and repossession will be more difficult to enforce (ss 65 and 113).

The provision of copies

When the agreement is sent or presented to the debtor for his signature, he must be provided with a copy (which he may keep) of the agreement and of any document (such as conditions of sale of goods) referred to in the agreement. If, unusually, the creditor signs at the same time, this will be the only copy the debtor receives. If, as is common practice, the agreement has to be signed by the creditor or some other person, such as a guarantor, after the debtor has signed, the debtor is entitled within seven days of the agreement becoming completely executed (being signed by all parties) to receive a *second copy* of the executed agreement and all documents referred to in it.

Activity 3 **(10 minutes)**

What types of insertions in blank spaces might an unscrupulous creditor try to make after a debtor has signed an agreement, were it not for the law against doing so?

3.3 Protection of the debtor after the agreement has been made: cancellable agreements

Even after the agreement has been made and the provisions as to formalities and copies have been met the debtor is protected to a limited extent by virtue of the fact that certain agreements are cancellable.

A cancellable agreement is one (other than most agreements for loans made in land transactions to which alternative safeguards apply) made in the following circumstances.

(a) There have been *oral representations*, for example statements concerning the terms of the loan or the quality of the goods, made in the presence of the debtor by or on behalf of the person with whom the debtor negotiates before the agreement is made.

(b) The agreement is signed by the debtor *elsewhere than at the place of business* of the creditor, supplier of the goods or other negotiator: s 67.

This rather involved definition is designed to protect the debtor who may have been persuaded to enter into the agreement by a sales representative or other agent, usually in the course of a visit to the debtor's house. In such cases the debtor has a limited opportunity to cancel the agreement even after he has signed it. But if the debtor goes to the creditor's office to sign the agreement that is treated as a deliberate act, no longer influenced by salesmanship, and the debtor has no right of cancellation.

Notice and cooling off

The debtor must be given written notice of his right to cancel a cancellable agreement. If he is entitled, as he usually is, to receive a second copy of the agreement when executed, it suffices to send him by post that copy which must include a statement of his rights. If, however, he is not entitled to a second copy of the agreement (because debtor and creditor sign together), he must be sent by post a separate notice of his right of cancellation within the same period of seven days after the agreement is made.

On receiving notice of his right of cancellation the debtor has a five day 'cooling off' period in which he may exercise it. If he decides to cancel he must give notice in writing to the appropriate person (designated in the notice of his cancellation rights). It takes effect as soon as it is posted.

If the procedures for notification of rights of cancellation are not observed, the creditor may not enforce the agreement against the debtor without obtaining the leave of the court.

The effect of cancellation

The effect of cancelling an agreement depends in part on the particular circumstances. In a D-C-S agreement for restricted use credit (such as a hire purchase agreement):

(a) the debtor is no longer bound to make payments under the agreement and may recover any payments made (or goods which he has supplied in part exchange: in some circumstances he may have their value instead);

(b) any goods supplied to the debtor may be collected from him at his address by the creditor; while waiting for recovery the debtor must for 21 days take reasonable care of the goods and he has a lien on them for any money or goods (see (a) above) to be returned to him.

Where there is simply a D-C agreement for unrestricted use credit (such as a cash loan), cancellation means that the debtor must repay that amount of the loan already received with interest. The agreement continues in force in relation to repayment of the debt and interest (including terms relating to timing and method), although if he repays the loan either within one month of cancellation or before the date of the first instalment due the debtor will not have to repay interest. Cancellation of an unrestricted use credit agreement has no effect on a linked transaction unless it is also a D-C-S agreement.

Activity 4 **(10 minutes)**

S signs a credit agreement on 4 May. The notice of her right of cancellation is posted to her on 7 May and she receives it on 9 May. She posts a notice of cancellation on 13 May and it is received on 16 May. Is her notice of cancellation effective?

4 TERMINATION OF CREDIT AGREEMENTS

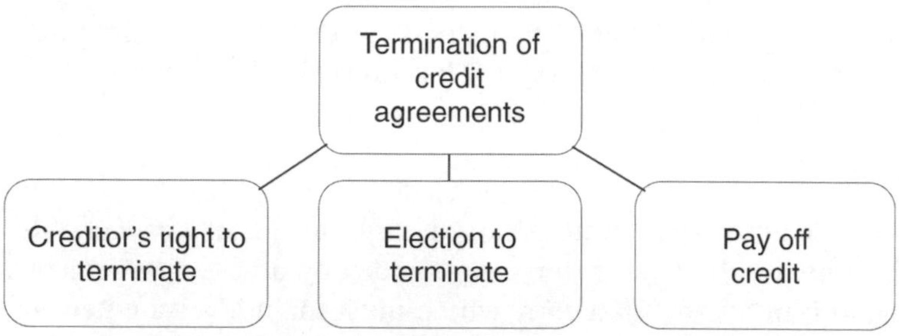

Once it has come into operation, an agreement may be terminated before it is fully performed.

4.1 Debtor's election to pay off credit

No provision in a consumer credit agreement may prevent the debtor from paying off the entire amount of credit early. He will obtain a rebate of the interest which he is required to pay under the agreement but which is not yet due. He may either give notice of his intention to repay or merely pay the balance less the rebate. In the latter case the notice immediately takes effect (although some future date may be specified on which it is to take effect).

4.2 Debtor's election to terminate

The debtor has a statutory right (which cannot be excluded by the agreement) to terminate a hire purchase or conditional sale agreement at any time if he pays an amount which raises his aggregate payments to half of the total price plus the whole of any installation charge: s 100.

Suppose, for example, that the total price is £100 and the installation charge £10. The debtor has paid instalments of £30 in all plus the installation charge, and owes an instalment of £10. The debtor may terminate the agreement and must raise the aggregate of his payment to £60 (half of £100 plus £10). As he has paid £40 already his liability on giving notice of termination is to pay a further £20. If he had paid instalments of £50 in aggregate plus the installation charge and owed £10 as an overdue instalment he would be liable to pay that £10 since (although he has already paid half the total price) it is a payment due at the time of termination.

If the debtor considers that the above formula produces an excessive amount, he may apply to the court to order a reduction. The debtor must of course permit the creditor to retake possession of the goods. If the debtor has not taken reasonable care of the goods while in his possession, the creditor is entitled (in addition to the sums payable as described above) to recover compensation for the damage to his goods caused by the debtor's failure to take care of them.

4.3 Creditor's right to terminate

By s 98 the creditor is allowed to terminate the agreement if the debtor is in breach of one of the contract's terms other than that relating to repayment. For example, he may terminate where the debtor made misrepresentations, where the debtor has become insolvent or where the goods are destroyed. The creditor usually then has the right to repossess the goods and the debtor must pay up to half of the price. Seven days' notice must be given.

If the creditor is entitled to terminate the agreement by reason of the debtor's failure to maintain the agreed payments, the creditor must first serve on the debtor a *default notice* which specifies the default alleged, requires it to be remedied (if remediable) or demands compensation (if irremediable) and specifies a period of not less than seven days in which action is to be taken as required. This gives the debtor time to apply to the court if he decides to do so: s 87.

Repossession of goods

If the debtor is in breach of a hire purchase or conditional sale agreement and he has paid at least one third of the total price for the goods (plus the whole of any installation charges) the goods are then 'protected goods' which the creditor may only repossess from the debtor after obtaining an order of the court: s 90.

If the creditor recovers possession of protected goods without a court order, the regulated agreement is terminated and the debtor is released from all liability under the agreement: he may even recover all sums he has paid under it: s 91.

Activity 5 **(10 minutes)**

D obtained credit of £3,000 under a hire purchase agreement, falsely representing that he is a homeowner. When the creditor discovers the facts, he decides to repossess the goods and terminate the agreement. At that time D has paid £1,300 and is not in arrears. How should the creditor proceed, and what is the most he can hope to obtain?

5 EXTORTIONATE CREDIT BARGAINS

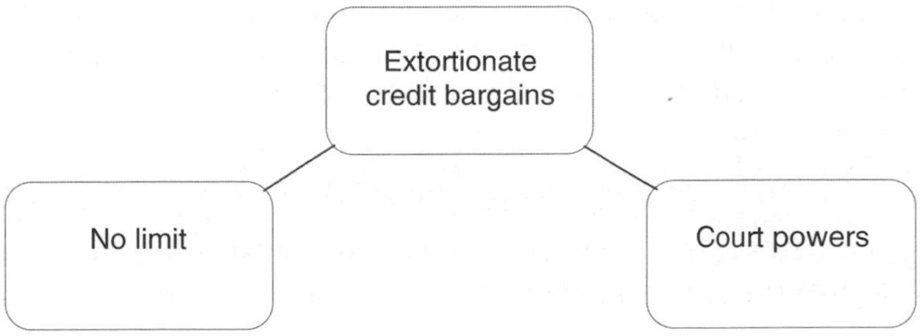

Unlike the rest of the 1974 Act there is no £15,000 limit on the application of the Act to an extortionate credit bargain: s 137.

This part of the CCA gives the court the power to re-open and make appropriate orders in relation to a credit agreement made on terms which the court finds 'grossly exorbitant' or 'contrary to ordinary principles of fair dealing'. It is intended to apply, for example, to moneylending at very high rates of interest. However, the rate of interest is not the only factor considered by the court: Ketley v Scott 1981. The courts also look at 'other relevant circumstances': s 138. These circumstances include the debtor's age and business experience, the degree of sales pressure and the extent of explanations. If it does decide to reopen an agreement the court has wide powers to relieve the debtor of having to make payments beyond what is 'fairly due and reasonable': s 139.

The extortionate credit bargains provision can be used in one of two ways: as a separate action in itself or as a defence to an action brought by the creditor to enforce the agreement.

6 THE CONSUMER PROTECTION ACT 1987 (PART 1)

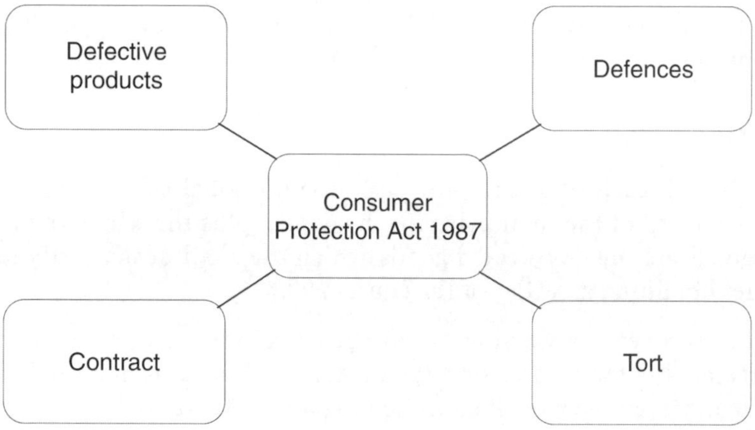

A person who suffers injury or loss in connection with defective or dangerous goods may have remedies in contract, in tort or under Part I of the Consumer Protection Act 1987.

6.1 Contract

If he is the purchaser he can probably recover damages from the vendor for breach of the statutory implied conditions of quality imposed by the Sale of Goods Act 1979. If he deals as consumer he cannot be deprived of these safeguards; in any other case an attempt to exclude or restrict them is void unless it satisfies a test of reasonableness: Unfair Contract Terms Act 1977.

6.2 Tort

If he suffers personal injury or damage to property by a defective product he may be able to recover damages for negligence from the manufacturer under the law of tort. Any attempt to exclude liability for personal injury or death due to negligence is void, and exemption from other liability is usually subject to a test of reasonableness: Unfair Contract Terms Act 1977.

To succeed in an action for negligence, the claimant must show three things.

(a) The existence of a duty of care by the defendant. A manufacturer's liability for physical damage or injury to users of his products has been well established since the case of Donoghue v Stevenson 1932. In this celebrated case, the House of Lords ruled that a person might owe a duty of care to another with whom he had no contractual relationship at all. The law of negligence applies in product liability cases such as Donoghue v Stevenson itself where physical injury or damage results from a failure to take proper precautions. However if the consumer/user has a reasonable opportunity of avoiding the injury by intermediate inspection or by routine precautions, there is no duty to a claimant who could have avoided it by these means.

(b) A breach of that duty by the defendant. When a duty of care exists, it must be of a 'reasonable' standard. This requires that the person concerned should do what a reasonable man 'guided upon those considerations which ordinarily regulate the conduct of human affairs' would do, and abstain from doing what a reasonable man would not.

(c) Injury or damage (or in some cases financial loss) suffered by the claimant as a foreseeable consequence of the breach. For a claim to succeed, the third element must be proved. In deciding whether a claim should be allowed, the court will consider whether the breach of duty of care gave rise to the harm (a question of fact) and whether the harm was too remote from the breach (a question of law).

Activity 6 **(10 minutes)**

M bought a new fridge. The fridge bore a conspicuous notice that the instruction booklet should be read in full before the fridge was used. The booklet stated that the fridge should be left for three hours before being turned on, so that the refrigerant could settle. M ignored the notice and the booklet and turned the fridge on immediately. There was a small explosion, damaging her kitchen. Advise M as to whether she would be able to sue the manufacturer for negligence?

6.3 Consumer Protection Act 1987

Part I of the Consumer Protection Act 1987 deals with liability for defective products. It covers strict liability for death, personal injury and damage to consumer property. It was brought into force in March 1988 to implement a European Community Directive. For the consumer the Act has the advantage that he does not have to prove negligence, nor that there was any privity of contract between him and the person he is suing. In other words the Act imposes strict civil liability, and this liability cannot be excluded by any disclaimer.

Claims for losses caused by defects in a product may be brought against any of the following.

(a) The manufacturer of the end-product;

(b) The manufacturer of a defective component (although he has a defence if he can show that he followed the instructions or specifications of the manufacturer of the end-product);

(c) An importer into the EC (the principle behind this is that anybody responsible who is outside the EC may be much more difficult to find);

(d) An 'own-brander';

(e) A supplier, who is usually a retailer.

Because of the potential liability of the parties above, it is usual for a supplier only to be liable if he will not disclose the identity of the importer or manufacturer.

The burden of proof is on the consumer to prove that:

(a) the product contained a defect;
(b) he suffered damage;
(c) the damage resulted from the defect; and
(d) the defendant was either the producer or some other person listed above.

'Defective' product

A product will be found to be unsafe where it is not as safe as it is reasonable to expect. This standard of relative safety requires a court to take into account all circumstances surrounding the product-the way it is advertised, the time at which it was supplied, its anticipated normal use, the provision of instructions for use, even its likely misuse-in establishing the standard required. The benefit to society and the cost of making the product safer can also be considered.

Scope of the Act

Consumers and other users (such as the donee of an electric iron received as a gift), but not business users, can claim compensation for death, personal injury or damage to other property (not to the product itself or for economic loss, that is loss caused by the product not working). There is unlimited liability but the following limitations apply.

(a) A claim must be brought within three years of the fault becoming apparent.

(b) No claim may be brought more than ten years after the original supply.

(c) Where the claim is for damage to property, it must not be business property which is damaged and the amount of the damage must be more than £275.

6.4 Defences

The defendant in a case under this Act has six possible defences.

(a) The product complied with mandatory statutory or EC standards;

(b) The product was not at any time supplied to another;

(c) The supply was otherwise than in the course of a business;

(d) The defect did not exist in the product when originally supplied;

(e) 'Development risk' – the state of knowledge at the time of manufacture and supply was such that no manufacturer could have been expected to detect the fault. The inclusion of this defence in the Act means that many victims of drugs which had damaging side-effects may be left without a remedy. The defence was kept so as not to discourage medical research;

(f) The defect was wholly attributable to the design of a subsequent product into which the product in question was incorporated.

Although liability under the Act to a person who has suffered damage cannot be excluded or limited by any contract term or by a notice, parties other than the person damaged who are in the chain of distribution are free to adjust the liabilities between themselves, subject to any common law or statutory controls, such as the Unfair Contract Terms 1977.

NOTES

Activity 7 **(10 minutes)**

A gas cooker is made by A Ltd. A Ltd uses gas valves made by B Ltd to A Ltd's specification. A Ltd sells the cooker to C (Retailers) Ltd, which sells it to D, a private individual. The cooker explodes because the gas valve, although correctly made to A Ltd's specification, had been fitted wrongly. C (Retailers) Ltd are unable to identify the manufacturer. Consider whether D may claim under Part 1 of the Consumer Protection Act 1987.

7 DATA PROTECTION ACTS 1984 AND 1998

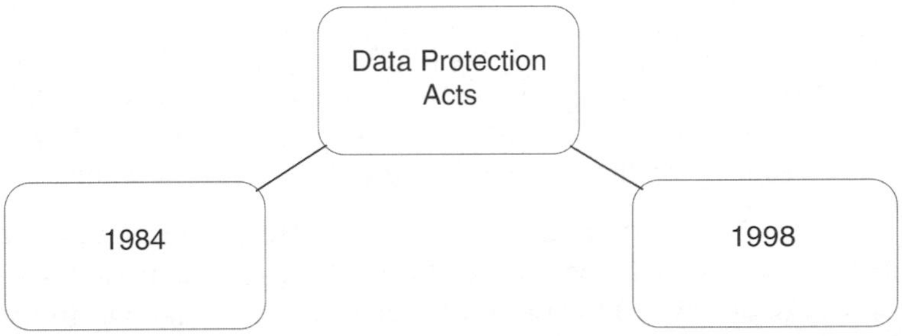

The **Data Protection Act** 1984 was the first piece of legislation to come into force that addressed growing popular fear that information about individuals which was stored on computer files and processed by computer could be **misused**. In particular, it was felt that an individual could easily be harmed by the existence of computerised data which was **inaccurate** or misleading.

The Act attempted to afford some measure of protection to **the individual** regarding data which is processed mechanically, that is by 'equipment operated automatically in response to the instructions given for that purpose'.

(a) **Personal data** is information about a living individual, including expressions of opinion about him or her.

(b) **Data users** are organisations or individuals who control the contents and use of files of personal data.

(c) A **data subject** is an individual who is the subject of personal data.

(d) A **computer bureau** processes personal data for data users, or allows data users to process personal data on its equipment.

7.1 The main features of the Data Protection Act

(a) With certain exceptions, all data users and all computer must **register** under the Act with the Data Protection Registrar. This currently costs £75 for three years.

(b) Data subjects are awarded certain legal rights, such as the right of access to information held about them.

(c) Data users and computer bureaux must adhere to data protection principles.

(d) The Act establishes certain civil proceedings and a number of criminal offences.

(e) The office of Data Protection Registrar was set up to establish a register of data users and computer bureaux and to consider complaints about the contravention of the principles or the Act's provisions.

7.2 Data Protection Act 1998

The terms of the Data Protection Act 1984 have now been extended by the **Data Protection Act 1998**, which implements the EU Data Protection Directive in the UK. The Act received Royal Assent in July 1998. It contains familiar elements from the current legislation, but there are additional requirements imposed by the EU Directive which have been reflected in the new law.

Some new data subject rights were created by the Act. It is now possible for a data subject to find out not only what data is being held, but what it is being held for. In the case of inaccurate data, an individual can apply to the courts for correction, blocking, erasure or destruction. The Act specifies the following.

(i) Express consent is needed when processing sensitive data such as ethnic origin or criminal convictions. Data subjects will have the right not to have certain decisions made about them which are based solely on automated processing, eg psychometric tests for recruitment decisions.

(ii) The new Act is extended to cover data held in any kind of 'relevant filing system' where 'specific information relating to a particular individual is readily accessible.' This may be taken to include manual filing methods, not just computer records.

(iii) The Data Protection Registrar is to be renamed the Data Protection Commissioner, whose powers will be strengthened.

(iv) The transfer of personal data outside the EU is restricted.

8 THE OFFICE OF FAIR TRADING

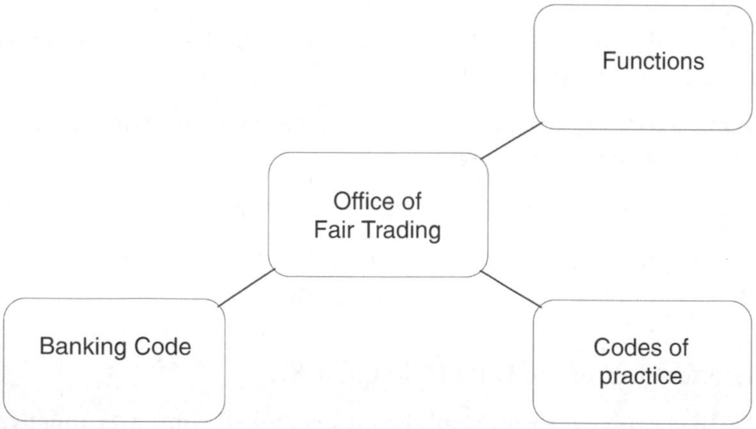

The legal powers of the Office of Fair Trading (OFT) derive from The Fair Trading Act 1973. The OFT promotes Codes of Practice.

Definition

> The Office of Fair Trading: a government department staffed by over 300 people and financed by the Department of Trade and Industry. It is headed by the Director General of Fair Trading (DGFT), supported by a Deputy Director General. It does not usually deal with complaints received directly from members of the general public, but acts on information from the following sources:
>
> (a) its own investigations;
> (b) information provided by local authority trading standards departments;
> (c) the courts (who inform the DGFT of material convictions);
> (d) news media.

8.1 Functions of the Office of Fair Trading

The functions of the OFT are as follows:

(a) various activities in relation to monopolies, mergers, restrictive practices and uncompetitive practices;

(b) review of the carrying on of the commercial supply to consumers of goods and services;

(c) collation of evidence of harmful practices that may adversely affect the interests of consumers;

(d) taking action against persons who persist in conduct detrimental to the consumer;

(e) encouraging relevant associations to prepare codes of practice (see below);

(f) supervision of consumer credit activity;

(g) supervision of the working and enforcement of the Estate Agents Act 1979;

(h) powers under the Control of Misleading Advertisements Regulations 1988.

The UK's approach is to encourage industries to regulate themselves.

8.2 Codes of practice

Definitions

> 1 Code of practice: lays out a set of procedures and policies that a firm will follow. For example: 'we will always give you two weeks notice of withdrawal of overdraft facilities'. Adherence to the code is sometimes necessary for membership of certain trade associations.
>
> 2 Ombudsman: used to describe the provision of a final independent appeal that a dissatisfied customer may make against what he or she believes to be unfair or incompetent treatment. (The term is Swedish and does not have a satisfactory English translation.) Some Ombudsmen are provided with government support. In the private sector, banks, building societies and insurance companies may support Ombudsmen on a voluntary basis.

Many codes of practice exist, including the Code of Banking Practice. Some provide for the existence of an Ombudsman. Codes of practice can be classified into four groups:

(a) codes carrying the DGFT's endorsement;
(b) enforceable codes;
(c) statutory codes;
(d) other codes of practice with limited status.

These are described briefly below.

Codes of practice carrying the DGFT's endorsement

The DGFT is responsible under the FTA for promoting codes of practice amongst traders. After negotiations between the DGFT and the relevant trade association a list of rules of conduct is drawn up, in order:

(a) to promote a high standard of trade practice; and
(b) to protect the consumer's interests.

Activity 8 **(60 minutes)**

Carry out an investigation to find out what codes of practice exist to fulfil the functions identified above. You could work in groups, with each group looking at a different trade or industry.

The weakness inherent in any system of voluntary codes is that they do not bind traders who are not members of an appropriate association. Even disciplinary action by a trade association may be of questionable value since there is the obvious question of bias towards its members. However, the existence of codes can help the consumer to derive reasonable expectations as to acceptable levels of service and facilities.

Enforceable codes of practice

Definition

Enforceable code of practice: a code of practice that is enforceable by means of sanctions falling short of legal proceedings. It will set down codes of conduct that can be enforced against people engaged in a certain trade or business, even though they are not members of the relevant trade body.

EXAMPLE: BRITISH CODE OF ADVERTISING PRACTICE

The British Code of Advertising Practice is an enforceable code of practice. It was developed and promoted by the Advertising Standards Authority (ASA), an independent body. Under the code, advertisements must be 'legal, decent, honest and truthful'. It contains provisions relating to specific products, for example tobacco and mail order advertisements. Complaints are invited from members of the public, and the ASA will carry out investigations and publish the results, issuing warnings to offenders where appropriate.

NOTES

Activity 9 **(10 minutes)**

What do you think is meant by 'legal, decent, honest and truthful'? Do you think all advertisements satisfy this requirement? What are the difficulties in enforcing this?

Statutory codes of practice

Codes that are drawn up with the involvement of government departments and the approval of the relevant minister may be given full or partial legal status. Such codes are increasingly common if people feel that other types of code of practice are ineffective. Examples includes the Highway Code (which may be relied upon in legal proceedings to establish liability), the Sex Discrimination Code of Practice (which may be taken into account by Industrial Tribunals) and the Code of Practice on Picketing in the case of strikes.

Other codes of practice

Because of the aura of respectability imparted to a trade that has an association and a code of practice, many commercial areas have acquired codes of practice that have no legal status at all and afford neither legal nor practical assistance.

The Banking Code

An example of a code of practice is the Banking Code, which became effective from March 1992 and which was last revised in 1997. It was prepared by the British Bankers' Association, the Building Societies Association and the Association for Payment Clearing Services. It is a voluntary code and sets out the standards of good banking practice to be observed by UK banks and building societies in their dealings with personal customers. These are the key commitments to personal customers (note - not business customers):

(a) to act fairly and reasonably in all dealings with customers;

(b) to ensure that all services and products comply with the Code, even if they have their own terms and conditions;

(c) to give information on services and products in plain language, and offer help if there is any aspect which customers do not understand;

(d) to help customers to choose a service or product to fit their needs;

(e) to help customers understand the financial implications of a mortgage, other borrowing, savings and investment products, and card products;

(f) to help customers to understand how their accounts work;

(g) to have safe, secure and reliable banking and payment systems';

(h) to ensure that the procedures followed by staff reflect the commitments set out in the Code;

(i) to correct errors and handle complaints speedily;

(j) to consider cases of financial difficulty and mortgage arrears sympathetically and positively;

(k) to ensure that all services and products comply with relevant laws and regulations.

FOR DISCUSSION

Do you think the Banking Code is too general? Why is it general? As a customer of a bank or building society, what would you like to see included in the Banking Code?

Chapter roundup

- Consumer credit arises in simple loans and overdrafts, in credit card transactions, in revolving credit arrangements and in hire purchase, conditional sale and credit sale agreements.
- Agreements regulated under the Consumer Credit Act 1974 are non-exempt agreements to provide credit of up to £15,000 to individuals.
- Credit may be running account or fixed sum, and it may be restricted use or unrestricted use.
- Agreements may be debtor-creditor agreements or debtor-creditor-supplier agreements, and there may be linked transactions.
- A debtor is protected before an agreement is made in that a negotiator may be treated as the creditor's agent, agreements to enter into regulated agreements are not binding and the debtor may withdraw at any time before completion of the formalities.
- The formalities of execution protect the debtor at the time of making an agreement.
- Some agreements are cancellable by the debtor even after they have been made. The debtor may recover payments made, but must give up goods supplied.
- An agreement may be terminated by the debtor's election to pay off credit, by the debtor's election to terminate or (in certain circumstances) by the creditor.
- The courts can make orders in respect of extortionate credit bargains.

Quick quiz

1. What is (a) a hire purchase agreement and (b) a conditional sale?
2. To what transactions does the Consumer Credit Act 1974 apply?
3. What is the difference between a debtor-creditor and a debtor-creditor-supplier consumer credit agreement?
4. What form must a regulated agreement take?
5. When must a debtor be given a copy of the agreement?
6. What is a cancellable regulated agreement?

7 How long after signing the agreement may a debtor in a cancellable agreement cancel?

8 What is a default notice?

9 What are protected goods?

10 How may the court regulate extortionate credit bargains?

Answers to quick quiz

1 HP – option to purchase on making the final payment

Conditional sale – ownership transfers on making the last payment (see para 1.2, 1.3)

2 Cash loans
Hire purchase
Conditional sale
Credit sale (para 1.5)

3 Debtor-creditor: suppliers of finance and goods are completely separate

Debtor-creditor-supplier: creditor and supplier of goods are linked (eg finance house owned by the same group) (para 2.3)

4 In writing
Complete
Legible
Blank spaces filled in
Signatures in the right place
All information included (para 3.2)

5 When the agreement is sent or given to the debtor for signature. (para 3.2)

6 An agreement where there have been oral representations or it is signed other than at the creditor's place of business. (para 3.3)

7 5 days (para 3.3)

8 Notice issued by the creditor to the debtor when the latter has failed to maintain the agreed payments. (para 4.3)

9 Goods in an HP or conditional sale where more than one third of the total price has been paid. (para 4.3)

10 However it thinks fit. (para 5)

Answers to activities

1 A hire purchase agreement.

2 (a) Yes
(b) UUC
(c) No

3 The rate of interest and the levels of penalties for defaults are two obvious examples.

4 Yes: 13 May is within five days of 9 May.

5 He should seek a court order. He may obtain the goods plus a further £200 (£3,000/2 – £1,300).

6 M would probably fail in bringing an action in negligence against the manufacturer because it is she who has failed to take reasonable precautions.

7 D would be able to sue C (Retailers) Ltd because they as the supplier have failed to identify the manufacturer (A Ltd).

8 There are codes of practice for many different trades and industries, including the motor trade, shoes, funeral services, dry cleaning, and estate and travel agents. There are about 20 in all. These codes are purely voluntary in that they are not enforced by the courts, but the OFT monitors their operation and the trade associations themselves try to ensure that the standards are adhered to by their members. Common features in these codes would be an agreement not to limit legal liability except in special, stated circumstances (and obviously within the limits of the Unfair Contract Terms Act 1977), a set standard of care, a disciplinary procedure for members and agreed procedures for the settlement of disputes, such as arbitration.

9 Adverts are not always legal, decent, honest and truthful. There are many complaints made each year about advertisements that have given offence. Recently, there have been a number of complaints made about Bennetton adverts that showed graphic scenes of war, people dying of aids and new-born babies. Some people found them offensive. A newspaper advertisement showing three political party leaders hanging from a noose was also the subject of complaints. The problem with enforcement is that people have different interpretations of what is 'legal, decent, honest and truthful'.

Assignment 8 **(60 minutes)**

Price Cutters Ltd is a company whose business is that of retailing electrical goods. A customer of theirs, Ashok, recently bought an electric fire as a present for his sister Indira. When the fire was first used it burst into flames causing both Ashok and Indira to sustain burns to their faces and arms. Fortunately the fire was extinguished without the need to call out the fire services but some damage was caused to the living room where the electric fire was situated.

As soon as Price Cutters Ltd were advised of the situation they immediately contacted purchasers of the electric fire to recall them, and also withdrew from sale any further such electric fires. It has transpired that the electric fires were purchased from an overseas manufacturer.

This matter caused some concern to the board of directors and they are worried about possible liability. As company secretary of Price Cutters Ltd you have been requested to prepare a report to the board explaining whether the company is liable both to Ashok and Indira for their personal injuries and damage to their property.

PART C

EMPLOYMENT PROTECTION LEGISLATION

Chapter 12 :

EMPLOYMENT PROTECTION LEGISLATION

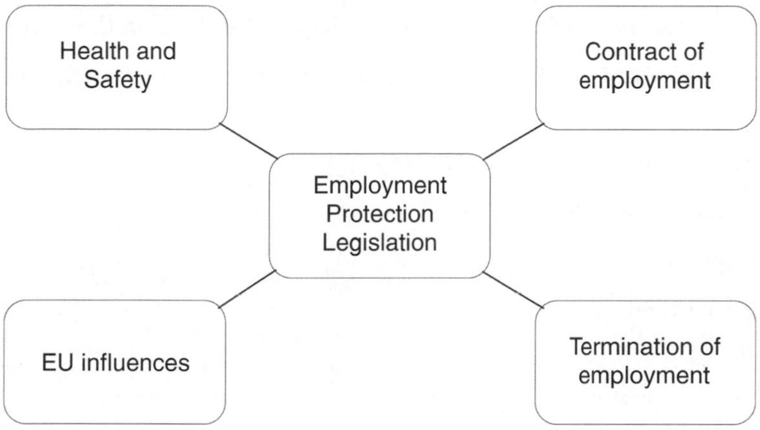

Introduction

In this chapter, we consider employment protection: legislation which confers protection and benefits on employees under a contract of service. Employment protection is basically related to job security: it provides for minimum periods of notice, remedies for unfair dismissal, compensation for redundancy and so on. The main legislation in this area, currently, is the Employment Rights Act 1996, although it is an area which is often subject to new legislation and change.

Your objectives

In this chapter you will learn about the following.

(a) The nature and requirements of a contract of employment

(b) Legislation and codes of practice relating to discipline, dismissal and redundancy

(c) European influences on UK legislation and practice

(d) Health and Safety at Work legislation

1 THE CONTRACT OF EMPLOYMENT

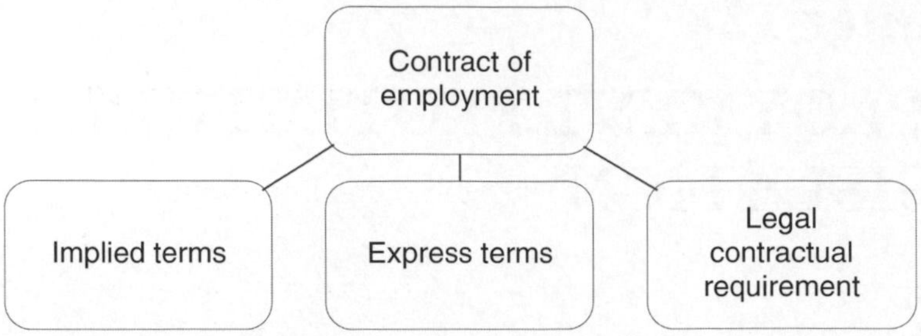

Remember, a contract is an agreement which is legally binding on the parties to it.

In order to be considered valid, a contract requires the elements which you have already seen:

(a) The intention to create legal relations.

(b) Offer and acceptance.

(c) Capacity.

(d) Consideration.

Activity 1 **(15 minutes)**

As with any form of contract, an agreement for employment requires the essential elements of a binding contract. How would each of the points discussed in (a) to (d) above be manifested in an employment contract? Give an example of how the absence of each of these points might invalidate the employment contract.

1.1 The contract of employment

If you think about it, all the elements of a valid contract can be achieved without putting anything in writing.

A contract of employment may be written, oral or a mixture of both. At the one extreme (usually in regard to senior personnel) it may be a document drawn up by solicitors and signed by both parties, with specific agreed terms on confidentiality/secrecy, restraint of trade and so on. At the other extreme, it may consist of a handshake and a 'See you on Monday'. Generally, employees would sign a standard form of contract, or exchange letters with the employer, or simply agreed to terms discussed in a job interview.

Each of these scenarios (subject to the requirements outlined below with regard to written particulars) will result in a value contract of employment as long as there has been basic agreement (offer and acceptance) on essential terms such as hours and wages.

Definitions

> The terms of a contract are the matters which have been agreed on by the parties: the 'content' of the contract.
>
> Express terms are those specifically stated and agreed upon.
>
> Implied terms are those which are not actually stated, but still impose obligations on the parties, because of other legal requirements (such as the duty to provide a safe working environment) and reasonable assumptions (eg that an employee will obey a lawful and reasonable order within the scope of his/her employment).

Express terms of the contract of employment

In general a contract of employment need not be made in writing, but within two months of the beginning of the employment the employer must give to an employee a written statement of prescribed particulars of his or her employment (Employment Rights Act 1996). This requirement applies to all employees except merchant seamen, employees engaged in work wholly or mainly outside the UK and persons who already have a written contract of employment which gives all the necessary details.

The statement should identify the following.

(a) The names of *employer* and *employee*.

(b) The *date* on which employment began (important if it becomes necessary to decide what period of notice should be given).

(c) Whether any service with a previous employer forms part of the employee's *continuous period of employment* (important if the employee wished to claim for redundancy or unfair dismissal).

(d) *Pay* - scale or rate and intervals at which paid.

(e) *Hours of work* (including any specified 'normal working hours')

(f) Any *holiday* and holiday pay entitlement (including any right to accrued holiday pay on termination of employment).

(g) *Sick leave* and *sick pay* entitlement (if any).

(h) *Pensions* and pension schemes (unless statutory).

(i) Length of *notice* of termination to be given on either side (or the expiry date if employed for a fixed term).

(j) The *title* of the job which the employee is employed to do.

(k) Details of *disciplinary and grievance procedures* – unless these are provided to the employee in a separate booklet.

The purpose of these rules is to ensure that the employee has precise information of the terms on which he or she is employed. Some employers invite the employee to countersign and return a second copy of the particulars as evidence that he or she has received them. But the statement is not the contract itself – it is merely written evidence. If the particulars contain an error, the true agreed terms prevail.

Activity 2 **(60 minutes)**

Get hold of a standard employment contract or statement of written particulars: you may have one from your employer, or you may have to ask round. (Mass employers like McDonalds might be a ready source.) Does it contain helpful information? What else would you want to know before committing yourself to the organisation?

Implied terms of the contract of employment

It may have occurred to you, looking at the requirements for written particulars, that there are other aspects of employment that are not covered, but that you might wish to have some clear guarantees about. What is the organisation's position on maternity leave, say, or sexual harassment, or taking time off to attend union meetings?

Various pieces of legislation imply terms into contracts of employment. (We will see how, specifically, in the following chapters.) They include legislation on employment protection (Employment Rights Act 1996), health and safety (Health and Safety at Work Act 1974), equal opportunity (Sex Discrimination Acts 1975 and 1986, Race Relations Act 1996) and so on.

In addition, there are some obligations which are assumed to be part of a contract of employment.

(i) The employer has the following obligations.

- (1) *Trust:* to behave in a proper and responsible way.
- (2) *Care:* to provide safe conditions and methods, and compensation for any negligence.
- (3) *Provision of work:* the general obligation to ensure work, especially for those such as salesmen on commission or specialists for whom idleness might mean loss of skills; to allow the opportunity to earn overtime and to work out notice periods.

(ii) The employee also has obligations.

- (1) *Fidelity:* to give faithful service and show concern for the organisation's interests.
- (2) *Obedience:* to obey any lawful order within the scope of his/her employment, and without undue risk to him/herself.
- (3) *Care:* to carry out the work reasonably and responsibly.

FOR DISCUSSION

As an employer, how would you wish to define the duties of trust and care towards your employees? What would it mean in practice? What would you see as the limits of your responsibility?

The formation of a contract signals the beginning of an employment relationship. (It may have occurred to you that the implied terms are a bit like marriage vows!) That relationship is finite: it comes to an end. This is obviously so of fixed-term contracts, where a person is employed for a certain period of time or the duration of a specific project. But even indefinite contracts, where a person is employed on an open-ended basis, come to an end sooner or later. We will now consider how.

1.2 How does the contract end?

Contracts of employment can be 'terminated' in the following ways.

(a) *By performance*

The employee does what he or she was hired to do, and the employer gives the agreed consideration: the contract is fulfilled. This is common in fixed contracts and contracts for specific services. It may also be said to apply in the case of retirement.

(b) *By mutual agreement*

Both parties can agree to terminate the contract at any time, say in the event of 'irreconcilable differences.'

(c) *By notice*

One party can terminate the contract, but must give adequate notice or warning to the other. This happens in the case of:

(i) resignation by the employee;
(ii) dismissal of the employee; and
(iii) redundancy.

(d) *Breach of contract*

If one party 'breaks' or fails to fulfil the terms of the contract, the other party has the option of considering the contract terminated. (In addition, he or she may seek legal remedies to compensate for, or minimise the effects of, the breach.) Failure by the employer to pay the agreed wage, or dishonest conduct by the employee, would be in breach of the employment contract.

(e) *Frustration*

A contract is 'frustrated' when it is prevented from being fulfilled – for example, because of the death, illness or imprisonment of one of the parties.

Activity 3 **(30 minutes)**

(a) Alan countersigns his employment contract and written statement with Sheerbrow Ltd but after two weeks is told that the holiday entitlement of four weeks per annum as stated in the particulars should have read three weeks, as was originally agreed. What can he do?

(b) Anita was engaged for a two-year period as sub-editor of a newspaper. Six months later, however, the publishers sold the newspaper and ceased to publish it. What has happened to Anita's contract?

(c) Ambrose attended a selection interview for a job due to begin on September 1. The interviewer said he was impressed with Ambrose's CV; he felt that Ambrose was an ideal candidate, and he would get back to him as soon as possible after the selection process was finished. Owing to confusion in the personnel department, no-one subsequently contacted Ambrose. Ambrose turned up to work on September 1, and (owing to further confusion in the personnel department) put in a day's work before it was realised that he was not, in fact, the successful candidate! The company told Ambrose to leave, and refused to pay him for the day's work. What can Ambrose do?

2 DISMISSAL

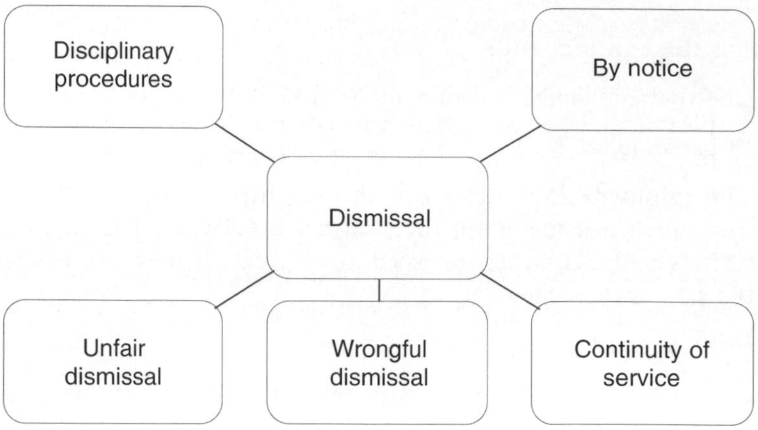

Definition

> Dismissal is the termination of an employee's contract by his/her employer.
>
> Constructive dismissal is termination by the employee, where he/she is entitled to assume that the employer has in effect terminated the contract, by: 'Conduct [on the part of the employer] which is a significant breach of the contract of employment or which shows that the employer no longer intends to be bound by one or more of the essential terms of the contract ... . The conduct must be sufficiently serious to entitle him to leave at once.' (Quotation from Western Excavating v Sharp 1978, a legal case)

2.1 Dismissal by notice

If an employer terminates the contract of employment by giving notice:

(a) the period of notice given must not be less than the statutory minimum – whatever the contract may specify (although it may specify a longer notice period); and

(b) notice may be given without a specific reason being stated, unless the contract requires otherwise.

Either party may waive their right to notice, or accept payment in lieu of notice. If an employee asks, he/she is entitled to a written statement of the reasons for their dismissal within 14 days.

Employee's length of service	*Minimum notice to be given by the employer*
1 month–2 years	1 week
2–12 years	1 week for each year of 'continuous employment'
12 years and over	12 weeks

2.2 Continuity of service

Many of the rights given to employees under the Employment Rights Act 1996, in areas such as redundancy and unfair dismissal, are only available if an employee has a specified period of continuous employment.

In calculating length of service (for all purposes including notice, redundancy pay and compensation for unfair dismissal) the following rules apply.

(a) A 'week' is a week during which the employee is employed for at least eight hours or in which his or her employment is subject to a contract which involves employment for eight hours or more. Employees attain continuous employment after two years. (A recent European Union directive gave equal rights to part-time workers, in this respect, as those given to full-time workers.)

(b) A period of absence (through sickness, injury, secondment or pregnancy) can be included in calculating length of service. Other absences (including strikes) do not break continuity of service, but are not counted in length of service.

(c) When an 'undertaking' – a business in the UK or a part of it – is transferred, the employees in the business are automatically transferred (on the same terms and with unbroken continuity of service) to the employment of the new owner.

2.3 Wrongful dismissal

A claim for *wrongful dismissal* is open to employees at common law, if they can show they were dismissed without notice or without a reasonable cause. The employee must show that he or she was dismissed in breach of contract (for example, with less than the required notice) and that he or she thereby suffered loss. He/she may then be able to claim damages compensating for the amount lost: accrued wages, payment for an entitlement to notice, or the balance of wages due under a fixed-term contract. In practice, such claims are less common now that unfair dismissal provisions offer wider remedies, but the common law remedy is still useful for those who cannot claim unfair dismissal (for example, because they have not been continuously employed for long enough to qualify).

Wrongful dismissal is compensated under common law – but only to the amount lost by the employee. Employment protection legislation aimed to widen the scope of protection and to increase the range of remedies available. The concept of 'unfair dismissal' is an extremely important element of this legislation.

2.4 Unfair dismissal

Certain categories of employee are excluded from the statutory unfair dismissal code, under the Employment Rights Act 1996, including:

(a) persons ordinarily employed outside Great Britain; and

(b) employees employed under a contract for a fixed term of one year or more;

(c) employees dismissed while taking unofficial strike or other industrial actions.

Subject to these exclusions, every employee who:

- is under the normal retiring age applicable to his job, or under 65; and
- has been continuously employed for two years (whether full-time or part-time).
- has the statutory right not to be unfairly dismissed.

So what is a 'fair' dismissal or an 'unfair' dismissal?

Dismissal is fair and justified	Dismissal is unfair
(a) Redundancy (provided that the selection for redundancy was fair).	(a) Redundancy where the selection is unfair.
(b) Legal impediment – the employee could not continue to work in his/her present position without breaking a legal duty or restriction. (This is fair only if the employee was offered suitable alternative employment.)	(b) Trade Union Membership (actual or proposed) and activities.
(c) Lack of capability or qualifications to perform the work (provided that adequate training and warnings had been given).	(c) Pregnancy, unless by reason of it the employee becomes incapable of doing her work adequately.
(d) Misconduct (provided that warnings suitable to the offence have been given – so the disciplinary procedures of the organisation are vitally important).	(d) A spent conviction under the Rehabilitation of Offenders Act 1974.
(e) Some other 'substantial' reason: for example, the employee marries a competitor, or refuses to accept a reorganisation made in the interests of the business and with the agreement of other employees.	(e) Dismissal on transfer of the undertaking (unless there are ETO – 'economic, technical or organisational' – reasons justifying it).
	(f) The employee took steps to avert danger to health and safety at work.
	(g) The employee tried to enforce employment rights eg written particulars of their employment.

To claim compensation for unfair dismissal, three issues have to be considered.

(a) The employee must show that he or she is a qualifying employee and that he or she has in fact been dismissed.

(b) Then the employer must show:

  (i) what was the only or principal reason for dismissal; and

  (ii) that it was one of the justifiable reasons listed above, or was otherwise a 'substantial reason of a kind such as to justify the dismissal of an employee' in this position.

(c) Application has to be made within three months of dismissal.

Activity 4 **(30 minutes)**

All other criteria being met, would the following cases be fair or unfair?

(a) Bernie is a van-driver for a carrier firm. After a number of driving infringements in his own car and in his own time – ie not on the job – Bernie has lost his driving licence. The carrier firm dismisses him.

(b) Berenice is a shop manageress, but after an period when it has been observed that she leaves the shop dirty and untidy, fails to maintain cash registers and does not put stock away, the chain of shops dismisses her.

(c) Bernadette worked in telecommunications. The global economy and internet usage requires increased staffing at night, and the company proposes a change in its shift-working, which is accepted by the trade union following a vote. Bernadette refuses to work night shifts. She is dismissed.

(d) Benedict has noticed that he is not getting an itemised pay statement, and believes that he is entitled to one by law. The personnel department is evasive. Benedict consults the union representatives, who press the question. The personnel department stalls. Benedict starts putting up posters and holding meetings. He is told to stop 'being a trouble maker'. He refuses, and continues lobbying his colleagues. He is dismissed for persistent trouble-making.

In order to avoid unnecessary ambiguities about fairness – not to mention interpersonal unpleasantness – the personnel function needs to ensure that:

(a) standards of performance and conduct are set, clearly defined and communicated to all employees;

(b) warning is given to employees where a gap is perceived between standard and performance;

(c) a clearly defined and reasonable period for improvement is allowed – with help and advice where necessary – and clear improvement targets;

(d) disciplinary procedures and the ultimate consequences of continued lack of improvement are made clear.

The safeguards just listed are often part of the disciplinary procedures of the organisation. The Advisory, Conciliation and Arbitration Service (ACAS) has laid down guidelines for disciplinary procedures. We will look at them briefly here.

2.5 Disciplinary procedures

Definition

Discipline can be considered as: 'a condition in an enterprise in which there is orderliness in which the members of the enterprise behave sensibly and conduct themselves according to the standards of acceptable behaviour as related to the goals of the organisation'.

NOTES

'Negative' discipline is the threat of sanctions designed to make employees choose to behave in a desirable way, although this need not be a wholly negative matter. Disciplinary action may be punitive (punishing an offence), deterrent (warning people not to behave in that way) or reformative (calling attention to the nature of the offence so that it will not happen again).

Any disciplinary action must be undertaken with sensitivity and sound judgement: its purpose is not punishment, or retribution, but improvement of the future behaviour of the employee and other members of the organisation, or the avoidance of similar occurrences in the future.

ACAS guidelines for disciplinary action suggest that an employee should not be dismissed from his or her job for a first offence, except in the case of gross misconduct (such as serious theft, or violence against another employee). Many enterprises have accepted the idea of progressive discipline, which provides for increasing severity of the penalty with each repeated offence: a bit like the yellow card (warning), red card (sent off) system used in football. The following are the suggested steps for progressive disciplinary action.

(a) *The informal talk*

If the offence is of a relatively minor nature and if the employee's record shows no previous discipline problems, an informal, friendly talk may clear up the situation.

(b) *Oral warning or reprimand*

The manager emphasises the undesirability of repeated violations, and warns the offender that it could lead to more serious penalties.

(c) *Written or official warning*

At this stage, the ACAS Code of Practice comes into effect. A written warning is a formal matter, and becomes a permanent part of the employee's record. (It may also serve as evidence in case of protest against the later dismissal of a repeated offender.)

(d) *Disciplinary lay-offs, or suspension*

Disciplinary lay-offs usually extend over several days or weeks. Some employees may not be very impressed with oral or written warnings, but they are likely to find a disciplinary lay-off (without pay) a rude awakening.

(e) *Dismissal*

This should be reserved for the most serious offences.

ACAS Code of Practice

Disciplinary procedures should:

(a) be in written form (the ACAS code of practice does not extend to informal 'first' warnings);

(b) specify to whom they apply (all, or only some of the employees);

(c) be capable of dealing speedily with disciplinary matters;

(d) indicate the forms of disciplinary action which may be taken (such as dismissal, suspension or warning);

(e) specify the appropriate levels of authority for the exercise of disciplinary actions;

(f) provide for individuals to be informed of the nature of their alleged misconduct;

(g) allow individuals to state their case, and to be accompanied by a fellow employee (or union representative);

(h) ensure that every case is properly investigated before any disciplinary action is taken;

(i) ensure that employees are informed of the reasons for any penalty they receive;

(j) state that no employee will be dismissed for a first offence, except in cases of gross misconduct;

(k) provide for a right of appeal against any disciplinary action, and specify the appeals procedure.

FOR DISCUSSION

How would you handle the following 'cases'? Discuss the disciplinary issues, and the consequences of any courses of action you recommend.

- An employee is persistently 15 minutes late for work.
- An employee persistently uses the office telephone for personal calls, despite clear policies.
- An employee is found smoking in a chemical storage area, despite clear safety warnings.
- An employee slaps his supervisor in the course of an argument.

---

3 REDUNDANCY

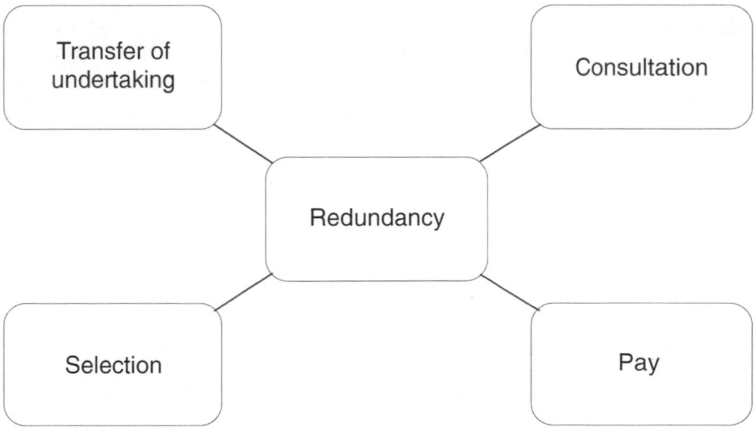

Definition

Redundancy is defined by the Act as dismissal where:

(a) the employer has ceased to carry on the business;

(b) the employer has ceased to carry on the business in the place where the employee was employed;

(c) the requirements of the business for employees to carry out work of a particular kind have ceased or diminished, or are expected to.

3.1 Redundancy pay

Redundant employees are entitled to compensation, in the form of redundancy pay:

(a) for loss of security; and

(b) to encourage them to accept redundancy without damage to industrial relations.

The employee is not entitled to redundancy pay if:

(a) the employer has made a 'suitable' offer of alternative employment and the employee has unreasonably rejected it. The offer must be of alternative employment in the same capacity, at the same place and on the same terms and conditions as the previous employment. It must be made before the end of the old employment, to take effect within four weeks of its end;

(b) the employee is of pension age or over, or has less than two years' continuous employment;

(c) the employee has resigned voluntarily;

(d) the employee has been dismissed for misconduct.

3.2 Consultation

From a purely humane point of view, it is obviously desirable to consult with employees or their representatives, and to give warning of impending redundancies. Beyond this, the employer has a statutory duty to consult with any trade union which is independent and recognised (in collective bargaining) by the employer as representative of employees. The consultation must begin 'at the earliest opportunity', defined as:

(a) a minimum of 90 days before the first dismissal, if 100 or more employees are to be dismissed at any one establishment;

(b) a minimum of 30 days before the first dismissal of 10–99 employees;

(c) at the earliest opportunity before even one (but not more than nine) employees are to be dismissed for redundancy.

These rules are applied to the total number involved and cannot be evaded by making essential dismissals in small instalments. The employer must within the same periods notify the Secretary of State in writing of proposed redundancies, with details of consultations with the trade union: a copy of this notice is given to the union representative.

In giving notice to the trade union the employer must give certain details in writing, including the reasons for the dismissals, the numbers employed and the number to be dismissed, the method of selecting employees for dismissal and the period over which the dismissals will take place. Information should be accurate, clear, realistic and positive as far as possible. Ideas for retraining and redeployment, benefits and potential for voluntary redundancies or retirements should be far enough advanced for some good news to be mixed with the bad. The employer should allow the trade union time in which to consider what has been disclosed and to make representations or counter proposals.

Activity 5 **(10 minutes)**

What measures might a personnel manager consider in order to avoid or reduce the numbers of forced redundancies that have to be made?

Where enforced redundancies are necessary, the legal provisions discussed above come into force, together with such collective bargaining procedures as may exist. Where possible, procedures and benefit packages should be planned for well in advance as a contingency measure, rather than as a reactive measure in the context of cost-cutting and industrial conflict. (This also benefits the employee, since benefits are likely to be higher if they are set before the use of economy measures which commonly necessitate workforce reduction.)

3.3 Selection for redundancy

There are various approaches to selection for redundancy. If demand for a particular type of work has disappeared completely, the situation is relatively clearcut: all those previously contracted to perform that work can be dismissed. Where management have to choose between individuals doing the same work, they may take the following approaches.

(a) Enforced or early retirement.

(b) Seeking volunteers, who would be willing to take their chances elsewhere on good redundancy terms.

(c) Value to the organisation, or retention by merit – keeping those who perform well and dismissing less effective workers (although this may be harder to justify to individuals and their representatives).

(d) 'Last in, first out' (LIFO). Newcomers are dismissed before long-serving employees. This may sound fair (especially in a seniority culture such as characterises Japanese big business), but may not meet the organisation's need for 'young blood' or for particular skills or merit in the individual.

Some large organisations provide services and benefits well in excess of the statutory minimum, with regard to consultation periods, terms, notice periods, counselling and aid with job search, training in job-search skills and so on. However, many reduce staffing levels in order to cut costs or take advantage of technological advances, without counting the cost in human terms, in times of high unemployment.

Organisations are now beginning to take more care of their 'survivors' (those people who remain in employment after redundancy programmes).

Definition

> The survivor syndrome has been coined as a term for a psychological state which involves long-term anxiety about job loss, increased loyalty to co-workers and reduced loyalty to the employer.

3.4 Transfer of undertaking

When an 'undertaking' - a business in the UK or a part of it - is transferred, the employees in the business are automatically transferred (on the same terms and with unbroken service) to the employment of the new owner. The Court of Appeal has considered the permissible scope to vary employees' terms or conditions upon transfer of an undertaking. Such a variation is effective if there is an 'ETO reason' (that is, an 'economic, technical or organisational reason') for the termination of the employees' contracts and their re-engagement on different terms and conditions.

> *Wilson and Others v St Helens Borough Council 1997*
> *The facts*: The running of a boys' home was transferred to St Helens BC from Lancashire County Council. Lancashire made the staff redundant, and they were re-employed by St Helens at lower rates of pay.
>
> *Held*: The Court of Appeal ruled that the dismissals were for an ETO reason in that neither Lancashire nor St Helens had the resources to run the home unless it was reorganised. Therefore both the dismissals by Lancashire and the variation in terms by St Helens were valid.

An employee cannot be compelled to accept continued employment in the service of a new employer. But his **refusal would be a resignation** which disentitles him from recovering redundancy pay or compensation for unfair dismissal.

If he does go over to the service of the transferee of the business, the employee has continuity of service.

The meaning of 'economic, technical or organisational reason' which renders a dismissal a fair dismissal for which no compensation must be given is not clear-cut. Meanwhile two limitations on the effect of the regulations should be noted.

(a) **There must be a real change in the ownership of the business**. If the business is carried on by a company and ownership is changed just by selling the share capital, rather than the business assets as a whole, the regulations do not apply.

(b) **There must be continuity in the business before and after the transfer**.

An employee does not have to know of the fact of the transfer and the identity of the transferee before his employment contract can be transferred: *Secretary of State for Trade and Industry v Cook and Others 1997*

The above rules on transfer of undertaking apply both to commercial ventures and to government, local authority, NHS and other 'public sector' undertakings.

4 EUROPEAN INFLUENCES

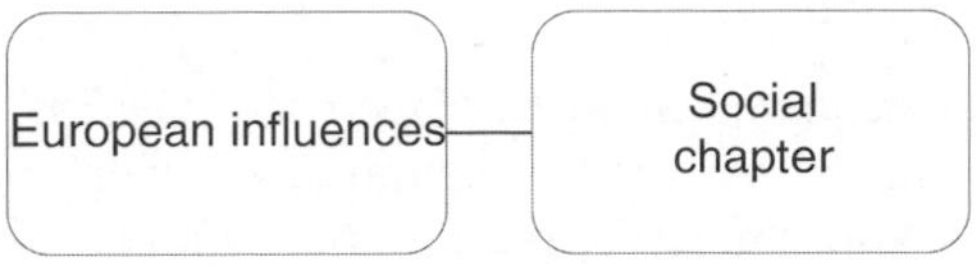

Employers and employees in this country are increasingly influenced by European Union legislation, case law and policy-making. We will here briefly introduce some of the issues on which European influences are brought to bear.

European Union rulings can have important implications for employment practices in nation states. Such rulings take the form of:

- *Regulations* which are binding on all member states without recourse first to national parliaments;
- *Directives* which are binding on all member states but where the methods of implementation and compliance are left to national discretion;
- *Decisions* which are more specifically focused and are binding on those addressed (Member States, organisations or individuals); and
- *Recommendations and Opinions* which are not binding.

Directives are often used where the method of implementation varies at national level and has to be related to existing laws.

In addition, case law – decisions in the European Court of Human Justice – sets precedents and defines how directives will be applied in practice.

4.1 The Social Chapter

The provisions of the Social Chapter, the key body of EU legislation, can be seen to originate in the various treaties which created the EU, such as the Treaties of Rome and Paris (1952 and 1957), and which included the aim of improving the working and living conditions of citizens of EU countries.

The main provisions of the Social Chapter are as follows.

(a) *Freedom of movement*. All workers should be able to move freely within the community.

(b) *Employment and remuneration*. Workers should be paid a fair wage.

(c) *Improvement of living and working conditions*. This provision covers the organisation of working time and holidays, and procedures for dealing with redundancy and bankruptcy.

(d) *Social protection*. Workers in the community must have access to adequate social benefits and those outside the labour market must receive adequate financial assistance.

(e) *Freedom of association and collective bargaining*. This includes for example the right to join, or not to join, a trade union; the right to negotiate and conclude collective agreements and the right to collective action such as strikes.

(f) *Vocational training*. Every worker should have access to suitable vocational training.

(g) *Equal treatment for men and women* with respect to access to employment, remuneration, working conditions, social protection, education and training and career development.

(h) *Information, consultations and participation of workers*. Changes that affect the workforce, such as new technology, working practices, mergers, restructuring and collective redundancy, should involve prior consultation with employees.

(i) *Health protection and safety at the workplace*. Every employee has the right to a safe and healthy working environment, and moves must be taken to ensure harmonisation of conditions in this area.

(j) *Protection of children and adolescents in employment*. The minimum employment age must not be lower than the school leaving age and neither of these must be lower than fifteen years of age. Duration of work must be limited, and night work prohibited, under eighteen years of age. Adequate remuneration and training must be made available.

(k) *Elderly persons*. At the age of retirement, every worker should be entitled to a decent standard of living and have recourse to social assistance where necessary.

(l) *Disabled persons*. Additional measures should be taken to improve the social and professional integration of disabled people. These include transport, housing, training and mobility.

The Social Chapter was included in the Treaty of Maastricht of 1993. The UK opted out of a number of its provisions, but with a change of government in 1997 began to adopt some of them.

5 EMPLOYEES AND INDEPENDENT CONRACTORS

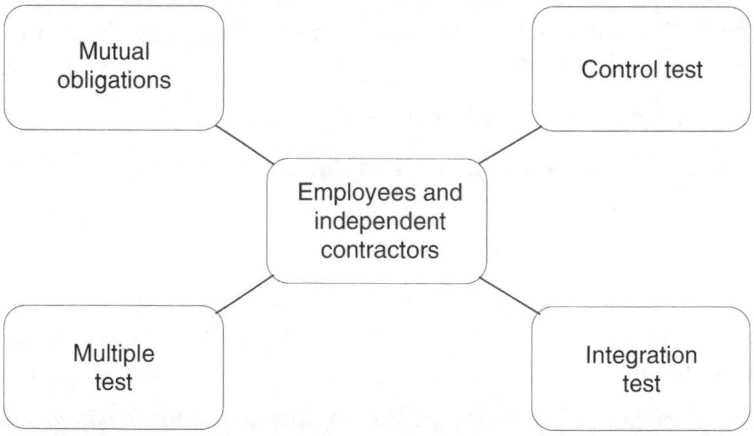

It is important for a number of reasons to determine whether a **contract of employment** exists. The court will look at the reality of the situation, rather than the form of the arrangement. If someone works for an organisation, but is not an employee, he is sometimes referred to as an independent contractor.

5.1 Examples

Ferguson v John Dawson & Partners 1976
The facts: a builder's labourer was paid his wages without deduction of income tax or National Insurance contributions and worked as a self-employed contractor providing services. His 'employer' could dismiss him, decide on which site he would work, direct him as to the work he should do and also provided the tools which he used. He was injured in an accident and sued his employers on the basis that they owed him legal duties as his employer.

Held: on the facts taken as a whole, he was an employee working under a contract of employment.

Where there is some doubt as to the nature of the relationship the courts will then look at any agreement between the parties.

Massey v Crown Life Assurance 1978
The facts: the claimant was originally employed by an insurance company as a departmental manager; he also earned commission on business which he introduced. At his own request he changed to a self-employed basis. Tax and other payments were no longer deducted by the employers but he continued to perform the same duties. The employers terminated these arrangements and the claimant claimed compensation for unfair dismissal.

Held: as he had opted to become self-employed and his status in the organisation was consistent with that situation, he must abide by his decision. His claim to be a dismissed employee failed.

5.2 Tests applied by the courts

It can be unclear whether a person is an employee or an independent contractor. The tests of **control, integration** into the employer's organisation, and **economic reality** (or the multiple test) are applied in such cases.

(a) *The control test*

Has the employer **control** over the way in which the employee performs his duties?

Mersey Docks & Harbour Board v Coggins & Griffiths (Liverpool) 1947
Stevedores hired a crane with its driver from the harbour board under a contract which provided that the driver (appointed and paid by the harbour board) should be the employee of the stevedores. Owing to the driver's negligence a checker was injured. The case was concerned with whether the stevedores or the harbour board were vicariously liable as employers.

Held: in the House of Lords, that the issue must be settled on the facts and not on the terms of the contract. The stevedores could only be treated as employers of the driver if they could control in detail how he did his work. But although they could instruct him what to do, they could not control him in how he operated the crane. The harbour board (as 'general employer') was therefore still the driver's employer.

(b) *The integration test*

If the employee is so skilled that he cannot be controlled in the performance of his duties, was he **integrated** into the employer's organisation?

Cassidy v Ministry of Health 1951
The full-time assistant medical officer at a hospital carried out a surgical operation in a negligent fashion. The patient sued the Ministry of Health as employer. The Ministry resisted the claim arguing that it had no control over the doctor in his medical work.

Held: in such circumstances the proper test was whether the employer appointed the employee, selected him for his task and so integrated him into the organisation. If the patient had chosen the doctor the Ministry would not have been liable as employer. But here the Ministry (the hospital management) made the choice and so it was liable.

(c) *The multiple test*

Is the employee **working on his own account**?

Ready Mixed Concrete (South East) v Ministry of Pensions & National Insurance 1968
The driver of a special vehicle worked for one company only in the delivery of liquid concrete to building sites. He provided his own vehicle (obtained on hire purchase from the company) and was responsible for its maintenance and repair. He was free to provide a substitute driver. The vehicle was painted in the company's colours and the driver wore its uniform. He was paid gross amounts (no tax etc deducted) on the basis of mileage and quantity delivered as a self-employed contractor. The Ministry of Pensions claimed that he was in fact an employee for whom the company should make the employer's insurance contributions.

Held: in such cases the most important test is whether the worker is working on his own account. On these facts the driver was a self-employed transport contractor and not an employee.

(d) *Other factors*

Other significant factors are as follows.

(i) Does the employee use his **own tools and equipment** or does the employer provide them?

(ii) Does the alleged employer have the power to **select or appoint** its employees, and may it dismiss them?

(iii) **Payment of salary** is, as mentioned above, a fair indication of there being a contract of employment.

(iv) **Working for a number of different people** is not necessarily a sign of self-employment. A number of assignments may be construed as 'a series of employments': *Hall v Lorimer 1994*.

In difficult cases, the court will also consider whether the employee can delegate all his obligations (in which case, there is no contract of employment), whether there is restriction as to place of work, whether there is a **mutual obligation** and whether holidays and hours of work are agreed.

O'Kelly v Trusthouse Forte Plc 1983
The employee was a 'regular casual' working when required as a waiter. There was an understanding that he would accept work when offered and that the employer would give him preference over other casual employees. The

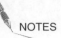

NOTES

Employment Appeal Tribunal held that there had been a sequence of contracts of employment on each occasion.

Held: the Court of Appeal disagreed with this finding and held that there was no contract, as there was no mutuality of obligation. Whether there is a contract of employment is a question of law but it depends entirely on the facts of each case.

5.3 Mutual obligations

There is no one test for ascertaining status, but the fundamental prerequisite of a contract of employment is that there must be **mutual obligations** on the employer to provide work for the employee and on the employee to perform work for the employer. In the case of *Clark v Oxford Health Authority 1998* the question of employment status was examined. Clark worked for the health authority on a no fixed hours basis. When they wanted her to work they asked her to do so, and paid her in relation to the hours worked. The Court of Appeal decided that there was no 'mutuality of obligation' between the parties – the employer was not obliged to offer work and the worker was not obliged to accept it.

6 THE SIGNIFICANCE OF THE DISTINCTION

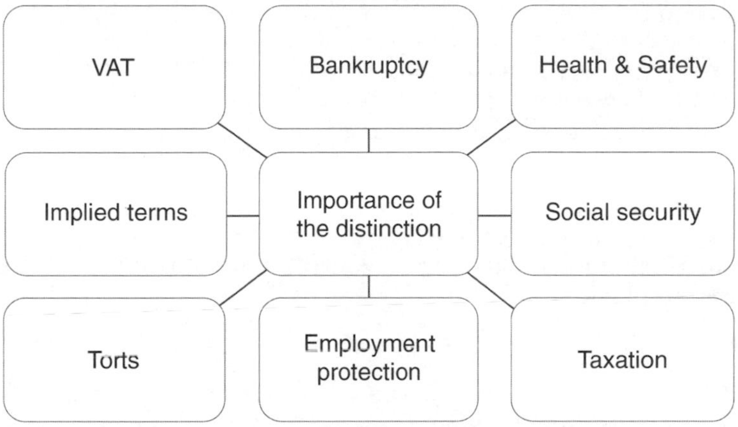

There are several reasons why the distinction between a contract of service (employee) and a contract for services (independent contractor) is important.

6.1 Social Security

The **contribution rates payable** under the social security legislation **differ** as between the employed (under a contract of service) and the self-employed, or independent contractor (under a contract for services). An employer must pay secondary Class 1 contributions (the employee making primary contributions on an earnings-related basis). Self-employed earners pay Class 2 and Class 4 contributions.

There are also differences in entitlement to benefits and statutory sick pay. Further, the employer may be required to pay a levy for industrial training purposes if he employs someone under a contract of service.

6.2 Taxation

Deductions must be made by an employer for income tax under Schedule E (known as **PAYE**) from salary paid to employees under a contract of service, whereas the self-employed are taxed under Schedule D and are directly responsible to the Inland Revenue for all taxation due.

6.3 Employment protection

There is much **legislation** which confers protection and benefits upon employees under a contract of service. This provides for minimum periods of notice, remedies for unfair dismissal and for redundancy payments.

The EAT has said that a controlling shareholder cannot usually be an employee for the purposes of employment protection legislation: *Buchan v Secretary of State for Employment 1997*, although this is not a rule of law.

6.4 Tortious acts

The **employer** is generally **vicariously liable** for tortious acts (civil wrongs) committed by his employees during the course of their employment, but such liability is severely restricted in the case of a contract for services. The employer will normally only be liable in such circumstances if he delegated performance to another.

6.5 Implied terms

The implied rights and duties which apply in the employer/employee relationship under a contract of service would not apply to the same degree to a contract for services. This is important since it will affect such things as copyright and patents.

6.6 VAT

An independent subcontractor may have to register his business for VAT and charge VAT on services supplied.

6.7 Bankruptcy

Should the employer go into liquidation or become bankrupt, the employee under a contract of service has preferential rights as a creditor for payment of outstanding salary and redundancy payments, up to certain limits.

6.8 Health and safety

The common law duty of an employer to provide a safe working environment for his employee has been extended to cover independent contractors, so in that respect the distinction between a contract of service and a contract for services is not as significant as it once was.

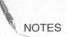

7 MATERNITY LEAVE

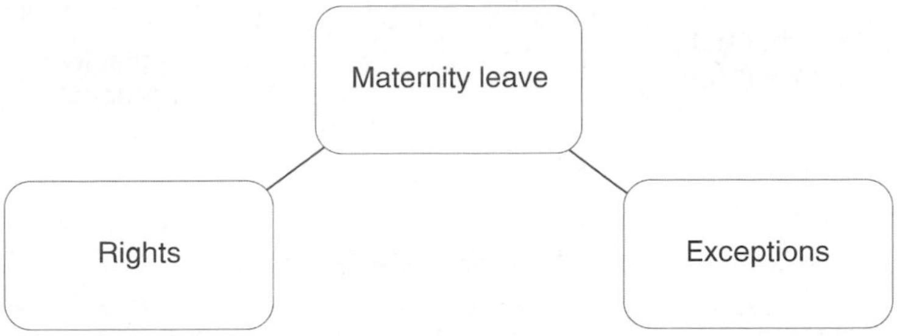

A woman who has completed the required period of continuous employment in the service of an employer has the following rights.

(a) The right to take paid time off for ante-natal care

(b) Protection against dismissal because of a pregnancy-related illness, or for taking maternity leave or for recent childbirth

(c) An entitlement to up to 11 weeks before the birth and up to 29 weeks' leave after having her baby (40 weeks in total), of which 18 weeks is leave with statutory maternity pay

(d) A right to return to her old job with no less favourable pay, seniority and pension rights than before. In order to preserve her right to return to work, the employee must let her employer have a letter or other document at least 21 days before her absence begins, stating her intention to return to work. She must also give at least 21 days' advance notice in writing of the date on which she proposes to return, or the employer may assume that she will not return: *Crouch v Kidsons Impey 1996*.

7.1 Examples

In *Brown v Rentokil Ltd 1998* the ECJ ruled that contractual terms allowing an employer to dismiss a worker after a certain stipulated period of absence are discriminatory when applied to a pregnant woman who is absent with a pregnancy related illness. Similarly in *Halfpenny v IGE Medical Systems Ltd 1999* it was decided that a woman who had served her notice to return to work, but could not do so because of post natal depression, was unlawfully dismissed and entitled to damages.

In *Eley v Huntley Diagnostics Ltd 1998* it was held that an employer's refusal to allow a receptionist to change her working hours on return from maternity leave when she was having difficulties with child care was justified, as the company and its customers needed to be able to rely on a full time receptionist who was familiar with the company's products.

7.2 Exceptions

There are two exceptions to the right to return.

(a) It does not necessarily apply to small businesses with five or fewer employees.

(b) If her job is made redundant, the employer need not take her back but must offer her suitable alternative employment on terms not substantially less favourable than the original contract. Unfair dismissal can be claimed by those to whom no such offer is made where it is possible to make one.

8 HEALTH AND SAFETY

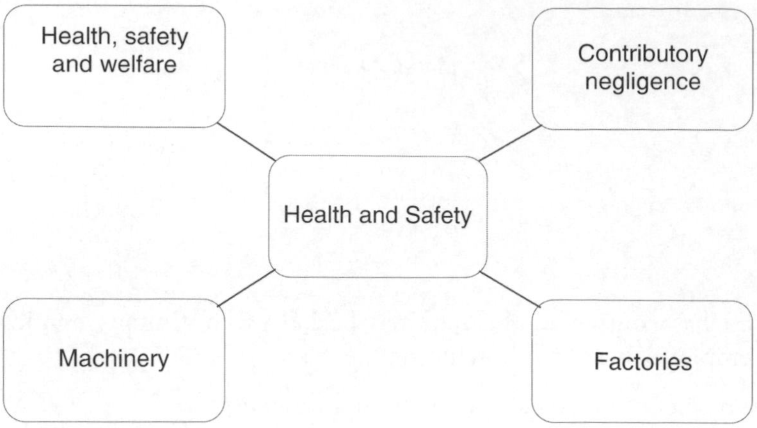

As well as a common law duty of care, the employer has statutory duties under the Factories Act 1961 and the Health and Safety at Work Act 1974 to **provide safe working premises** (particularly regarding machinery). The employer has strict liability for injuries caused by breach of his statutory duties. He is also required to insure against liability to employees for personal injury arising in the course of employment: Employer's Liability (Compulsory Insurance) Act 1969.

8.1 Contributory negligence

Due allowance is made for ordinary human failings. In particular the following principles apply.

(a) An employee is not deemed to consent to the risk of injury because he is aware of the risk.

(b) Employees can become inattentive or careless in doing work which is monotonous or imposes stress.

(c) It is not always a sufficient defence that the employer provided safety equipment. The employer has some duty to encourage if not to insist on its proper use.

(d) Many dangers can be caused by carelessness or other fault of an otherwise competent employee, possibly by his mere thoughtlessness.

(e) The employer's duty is to take reasonable care for employee safety in all acts which are normally and reasonably incidental to the day's work.

Davidson v Handley Page 1945
The facts: an employee went to wash her tea-cup after use. She slipped on a wet surface and was injured.

Decision: the employer had failed in his duty to take reasonable care to provide safe premises.

8.2 Factories

The Factories Act 1961 applies only to a factory, which is a place where manufacturing or processing work is done. Premises are not a factory unless:

(a) The substantial purpose for which the premises are used include **manual labour**. For example, a chemist's shop was not a factory although one member of its staff was a porter doing manual work; and

(b) The work is done in the **course of trade for purposes of gain**. An industrial laboratory for testing materials is part of the factory, but a laboratory at a technical college which tests materials is not a factory.

8.3 Duty to fence in machinery

The occupier of a factory has an absolute duty to fence securely all machines which provide power, say by driving belts to the manufacturing machinery, all transmission machinery and every dangerous part of any machinery.

> *Close v Steel Company of Wales 1961*
> *The facts*: the claimant was using an electric drilling machine. The drill shattered and a fragment flew into his eye.
>
> *Held*: it was not dangerous machinery since the harm caused was not reasonably foreseeable. It is not generally necessary to fence so as to prevent fragments of machinery or material from flying out.

Among particular points the following should be noted.

(a) It is no defence to show that there is no practicable means of fencing the machines.

(b) The fencing should be **substantial** and kept in position at all times when the machine is in motion.

(c) Machines brought into a factory for repair or similar purpose are not part of the factory machinery and there is no duty to fence them in.

(d) The duty to fence may apply to a moveable machine such as a mobile crane.

(e) It is only the dangerous parts which need to be fenced.

(f) A fence is sufficiently secure even when it does not prevent reckless employees from circumventing it.

> *Carr v Mercantile Produce Co 1949*
> *The facts*: a woman employee forced her hand through a small hole to remove dough from a moving part of a machine and her fingers were injured.
>
> *Held*: the machine was securely fenced and the employer was not liable for her injuries, which had arisen from her own recklessness.

8.4 Health, safety and welfare

Under s 2 of the Health and Safety at Work Act 1974 it is the duty of every employer, as far as is practicable, to ensure the health, safety and welfare of all his employees.

(a) Provide and maintain plant and systems of work which are safe and without risk

(b) Make arrangements to ensure health and safety in relation to the use, handling, storage and transport of articles and substances

(c) Provide adequate information, instruction, training and supervision

(d) Maintain safe places of work and ensure there is adequate access in and out

(e) Provide a safe and healthy working environment

The employer can be liable for **psychological damage** caused to an employee. Where it should be reasonably foreseeable to an employer that an employee might suffer a nervous breakdown because of his or her workload, the employer will be under a duty of care, not to cause the employee psychiatric damage by reason of the work which the employee is required to perform: *Walker v Northumberland County Council 1995*

8.5 Duty to visitors

Although the 1974 Act is intended mainly to safeguard employees it also imposes duties to avoid creating risks to visitors or those nearby. There are also rules to control or prohibit pollution of the environment by industrial processes.

9 FURTHER HEALTH AND SAFETY REGULATIONS

As well as the Health and Safety at Work Act, the 1990s saw published numerous additional Regulations (which effectively supplement the Act) on specific detailed aspects of health and safety. Many of these have been issued as a result of European Community Directives.

9.1 The Management of Health and Safety at Work Regulations 1992

Under the Management of Health and Safety at Work Regulations 1992 *employers* now have the following additional general duties.

(a) They must carry out risk assessment, generally in writing, of all work hazards. Assessment should be continuous.

(b) They must introduce controls to reduce risks.

(c) They must assess the risks to anyone else affected by their work activities.

(d) They must share hazard and risk information with other employers, including those on adjoining premises, other site occupiers and all subcontractors coming onto the premises.

(e) They should revise safety policies in the light of the above, or initiate safety policies if none were in place previously.

(f) They must identify employees who are especially at risk.

(g) They must provide fresh and appropriate training in safety matters.

(h) They must provide information to employees (including temps) about health and safety.

(i) They must employ competent safety and health advisers.

Employees are also given an additional duty under the 1992 regulations to inform their employer of any situation which may be a danger. This does not reduce the employer's responsibilities in any way, however, because his/her risk assessment programme should have spotted the hazard in any case.

NOTES

Under the *Health and Safety (Consultation with Employees) Regulations 1996,* employers must consult all of their employees on health and safety matters (such as the planning of health and safety training, any change in equipment or procedures which may substantially affect their health and safety at work or the health and safety consequences of introducing new technology). This involves giving information to employees and listening to and taking account of what they say before any health and safety decisions are taken.

9.2 The Workplace (Health, Safety and Welfare) Regulations 1992

The workplace regulations deal with matters that have been statutory requirements for many years in the UK under legislation such as the Offices, Shops and Railway Premises Act 1963, although in some cases the requirements have been more clearly defined. The following provisions are made.

(a) *Machinery and equipment.* All equipment should be properly maintained and fenced if dangerous.

(b) *Ventilation.* Air should be fresh or purified.

(c) *Temperature.* The temperature must be 'reasonable' inside buildings during working hours. This means not less than 16°C where people are sitting down, or 13°C if they move about to do their work.

(d) *Lighting* should be suitable and sufficient, and natural if practicable. Windows should be clean and unobstructed.

(e) *Cleaning and decoration.* Floors, walls, ceilings, furniture, furnishings and fittings must be kept clean.

(f) *Room dimensions and space.* Each person should have at least 11 cubic metres of space, ignoring any parts of rooms more than 3.1 metres above the floor or with a headroom of less than 2.0 metres.

(g) *Floors, passages and stairs* must be properly constructed and maintained (without holes, not slippery, properly drained and so on).

(h) *Falls or falling objects.* These should be prevented by erecting effective physical safeguards (fences, safety nets, ground rails and so on).

(i) *Glazing.* Windows should be made of safe materials and if they are openable it should be possible to do this safely.

(j) *Traffic routes.* These should have regard to the safety of pedestrians and vehicles alike.

(k) *Doors and gates.* These should be suitably constructed and fitted with any necessary safety devices (especially sliding doors and powered doors and doors opening in either direction).

(l) *Lifts, escalators and travelators* should function safely and be regularly maintained.

(m) *Sanitary conveniences and washing facilities* must be suitable and sufficient. This means that they should be properly ventilated and lit, properly cleaned and separate for men and women. 'Sufficient' means that undue delay is avoided!

(n) *Drinking water.* An adequate supply should be available with suitable drinking vessels.

(o) *Clothing*. There should be suitable accommodation for outdoor clothing, which should be able to dry out if wet. Facilities for changing clothing should be available where appropriate.

(p) *Rest facilities and eating facilities*. These must be provided unless the employees' workstations are suitable for rest or eating, as is normally the case for offices.

(q) *Fire precautions* should be taken, and appropriate firefighting equipment and clearly marked and unobstructed escape route should be provided. Fire alarms should be installed and tested.

(r) *First aid equipment* should be provided, under the charge of a responsible person who should be trained in first aid, if there are more than 150 employees.

Activity 6 **(60 minutes)**

Look at your own college (or workplace) from a health and safety perspective. Compare the provisions (a) to (r) above with what you see within your college/workplace. Make a note of areas where health and safety provisions fall short of requirements.

9.3 Other regulations

- *The Health and Safety (First Aid) Regulations 1981* require employers to provide adequate and appropriate equipment, facilities and personnel to enable first aid to be given to employees if they are injured or become ill at work. The minimum contents that should be found in a first aid box, for example, consist of dressings (plasters) and bandages of various sizes.
- *The Health and Safety (Young Persons) Regulations 1997* require employers to take into account the lack of experience, absence of awareness of existing or potential risks and/or the relative immaturity of young employees (aged under 18) when assessing the risks to their health and safety.
- *The Health and Safety (Safety Signs and Signals) Regulations 1996* describe the safety signs and signals that should be provided in the workplace, how they should be used and also require employers to instruct employees on their use and meaning.

In addition to legislation, you need to be aware of helpful guidance on health and safety from other sources. The instruction manual to a piece of equipment or machinery, for example, makes all the difference between a help and a hazard. The Health and Safety Commission issues helpful booklets on matters such as working with VDUs, smoking and alcohol. But there is no substitute for common sense: care in handling chemicals, lifting heavy objects, operating machinery, moving around the workplace (and playing practical jokes) is part of every employee's own 'Safety Policy'.

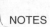

NOTES

Chapter roundup

- Employers and employees have rights and obligations under the contract of employment and employment protection and other legislation.
- Organisations need clear policies to deal with discipline, dismissal and redundancy.
- The Employment Rights Act 1996 provides for employment protection, particularly in the case of dismissal and redundancy. It defines situations when dismissal may be considered fair, and situations where dismissal may be considered to be unfair.
- European Union legislation can have important implications for employment practices in nation states. This is very much 'work in progress' and should be continually monitored.

Quick quiz

1 What is contained in an employment contract?

2 What is the difference between wrongful dismissal and unfair dismissal?

3 What reasons may an employer rely on in seeking to show that a dismissal was fair?

4 Describe circumstances when redundancy would be legal.

5 List five main provisions of the Social Chapter.

Answers to quick quiz

1 Names
Date of commencement
Continuous period of employment
Pay
Hours of work
Holiday entitlement
Sick leave/sick pay entitlement
Pensions
Notice period
Title
Disciplinary/grievance procedures (see para 1.1)

2 Wrongful dismissal arises when the dismissal is carried out in some wrongful way (eg not enough notice given) (see paras 2.3, 2.4)

3 Redundancy
Legal impediment
Lack of capability
Misconduct
Another 'substantial' reason (para 2.4)

4 When the employer has ceased to carry on the business.

When the employer has changed the location.

The requirement for an employee to be doing the sort of work has gone. (para 3)

5 Freedom of movement
Social protection
Freedom of association and collective bargaining
Vocational training
Equality between men and women (para 4.1)

Answers to activities

1 (a) Legal intention. Employer and employee intend to be legally bound by contract terms, and are aware that legal remedies/penalties apply in the event that the agreement is broken. Most commercial transactions are assumed to operate on this basis – but most social, domestic and family agreements are not. If a son agrees to paint the bathroom in the family home, this would not be a contract of employment.

(b) Offer and acceptance. This typically consists of the would-be employee being sent a letter offering a job on stated terms (offer) and telephone or writing back to accept, or simply turning up for work at the agreed time (acceptance). If the would-be employee failed to communicate any acceptance of a job offer to the employers, they could not claim the agreement had been broken if (s)he did not turn up for work: no contract would have been formed.

(c) Capacity. The employee must (usually) be of legal age, and of sound mind. (Employment contracts made to the benefit of a minor are, however, an important exception to the rule that contracts entered into by minors are invalid and unenforceable.) The employer must be authorised to make the offer of employment. This may be an issue if, for example, the offer is made by a recruitment agency.

(d) Consideration. This consists of the employee's 'promise' to work for the employer in exchange for a 'promise' to pay an agreed amount in remuneration. If a window-cleaner promised, as a special promotion, to clean your windows free of charge on the following day, and then failed to turn up, you could not sue for breach of contract, because there is no contract: no consideration was provided.

2 The answer to this activity depends on your own research and interests.

3 (a) Alan's only option is to require Sheerbrow Ltd to provide him with an amended copy of the particulars (within one month). The written particulars are merely evidence of the employment contact's terms – they do not represent the contract itself, so an amendment of an error cannot be said to be a breach.

(b) The publisher has breached the contract, because of the express contract terms of two year's work in a particular post: the employer also had the implied duty to supply the work, and failed to do so.

(c) Ambrose cannot claim that the company is in breach of contract for failure to provide work, or pay for work done, because no contract existed in the first place! There was no offer made – although Ambrose 'accepted' what he thought was an offer, by turning up to work.

4 (a) Bernie was fairly dismissed by reason of legal impediment.

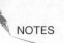

(b) Berenice was fairly dismissed by reason of lack of 'capability': she is clearly incompetent compared to the standard of performance required by the job.

(c) Bernadette was fairly dismissed: failure to accept necessary reorganisation is a 'substantial' reason.

(d) Benedict was unfairly dismissed, because he was trying to enforce his employment rights in a reasonable manner.

5 (a) retirement of staff over the normal retirement age;

(b) offering early retirement to staff approaching normal retirement age;

(c) restrictions or even a complete ban on recruitment, so as to reduce the workforce over time by natural wastage;

(d) dismissal of part-time or short-term contract staff, once contracts come to sensible break-off points or conclusions;

(e) offering retraining and/or redeployment within the organisation;

(f) seeking voluntary redundancies.

6 This will depend on your college or workplace. If the list is extensive, perhaps you should draw it to someone's attention!

Assignment 9 **(45 minutes)**

Exe Ltd carries on a food packaging and distribution business. The company's business premises are separated into an office section, which deals with the administration of the business, and a factory section, where the packaging and distribution take place.

Exe Ltd has always operated a 'no smoking' policy in the factory section, although there is no reference to this in any employee's contract of employment. Smoking is permitted, however, in the office section, and this is a cause of resentment between office and office factory staff, and for those office workers who do not smoke.

Advise Exe Ltd:

(a) whether R, a factory worker, and S, an office worker, may be justifiably dismissed by the company for smoking at work;

(b) whether T, an office worker, may be justifiably dismissed for poor attendance due to illness which is considered to be largely attributable to his heavy smoking over many years;

(c) how the company should proceed in order to ban smoking throughout its premises.

PART D

FORMATION, MANAGEMENT AND DISSOLUTION OF BUSINESS UNITS

BPP PUBLISHING

Chapter 13 :

BUSINESS ORGANISATIONS AND COMPANY FORMATION

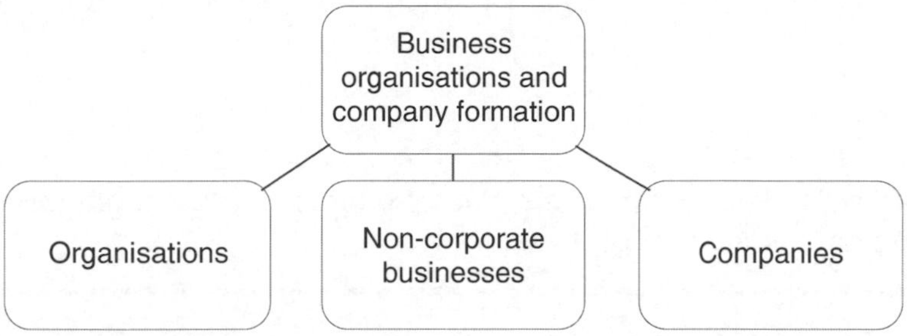

Introduction

All sorts of business unit exist. Each is formed by a group of people with a common aim. Many organisations are in the *private sector*, that is, they are privately owned and exist primarily to make profits. Some private sector organisations are *privatised* and *regulated* firms that used to be in the *public sector* (for example, British Gas and possibly your college). Organisations that are still in the public sector include local authorities. Still other organisations operate on a *not-for-profit* basis; these include clubs and charities.

Not all members of an organisation necessarily ever meet. For example, shareholders in a large public company many ever attend the annual general meeting yet are bound together by their membership of the group. Many large charities such as Greenpeace have a common sense of identity and yet recruit contributors by post. Other groups may meet regularly; for example, football teams, aerobics clubs, staff in a supermarket, Post Office workers and Members of Parliament. All these are clearly recognisable as organisation groupings and yet you would be able to identify them.

Your objectives

In this chapter you will learn about the following.

(a) The main types of business organisation and the differences between them

(b) How a partnership operates and its principal features

(c) The meaning of the term 'limited liability'

(d) The advantages and the disadvantages of corporate status

(e) The difference between public and private companies

1 ORGANISATIONS

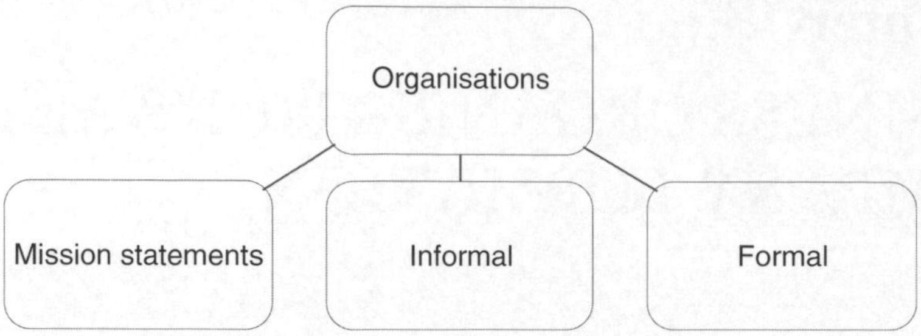

Definition

> *Organisation*: a clearly definable group of people who act together to achieve a common goal or set of objectives.

Membership of an organisation is defined by setting clear boundaries. Such boundaries may be paid employment, owing shares, paying a subscription or turning up at meetings.

> **Activity 1** **(20 minutes)**
>
> (a) List all the organisations you have come across in the last two days. You may have:
>
> - participated in them;
> - used their services or products;
> - heard or read about them.
>
> (b) Now write down what kind of organisation you think each one is: profit making, voluntary, public service, subscription and so on.

1.1 Why have organisations?

We have seen that organisations exist to achieve a purpose. The overall purpose, or mission, is achieved by meeting a series of objectives. The mission is sated in broad, general terms and a hierarchy of objectives set out in specific actions.

Formal and informal organisations

People join in organisations because they can achieve more by co-operating with others than they can on their own. Informal groups have to develop into a formal organisation is they are to be effective. Chester Barnard said that people had to accept a group purpose to co-ordinate their activities. A formal organisation comes into being when:

(a) people are willing to contribute to a common purpose:

(b) they communicate with each other.

People are prepared to co-operate because they accept the common purpose. Communication is essential to translate this purpose into action. The common purpose is achieved in practice through specific actions carried out by small subgroups of people called units. The size of a unit in an organisation depends on the complexity of its purpose and the technology it uses. Larger organisations consist of greater numbers of units.

EXAMPLE: BPP PUBLISHING

The employees of the publisher of this book accept that their common purpose is to publish books which will provide a return on the investment of the owners of BPP Publishing. To achieve that common purpose the company is divided into large units: sales/marketing and production. The two units communicate at director, management and executive levels, both formally and informally. Within those large units there are small units whose purpose is specifically to market and produce these texts. These are people who commission, edit, typeset, proof and organise the printing of the book (the production unit) and who disseminate information, take orders, store pack and distribute the book (the sales/marketing unit).

In organisations, people interact on a personal level in systematic ways that become organised into an informal organisation existing alongside the formal one; the informal organisation provides an individual with an essential communication channel and an escape from the routine and rigidity of the formal organisation.

1.2 Mission and objectives

Many organisations, especially those in the public sector, have a mission statement that sets out their purpose. For any organisation to survive, its members must continue to accept its purpose, so the mission is usually general and acceptable to all.

FOR DISCUSSION

What is your college's (or your work organisation's) mission statement?

Do the staff and students find it acceptable or unacceptable?

Most organisations exist for the long term. Many objectives have a time horizon (of a year, say) so new objectives have to be set regularly so the organisation can continue to fulfil its mission.

Forming an organisation can be as simple a process as people getting together to form a darts team because their objective is to play in a local league. Alternatively, it can be a complex process involving many people and procedures – for example, forming a public company with the objective of providing courier services world wide. The darts team achieves its general purpose by playing specific matches. The courier company's units may aim to open a new route, deliver faster to Paris, carry more parcels to Dallas or buy a new plane; all fit into the mission of providing global service.

Activity 2 **(5 minutes)**

Could your college achieve its purpose without establishing a formal organisation? Write down a brief reason for your answer.

The rest of this chapter examines private-sector organisations. We start by looking at two kinds or organisation that are not incorporated: sole traders and partnerships.

2 NON-CORPORATE BUSINESSES

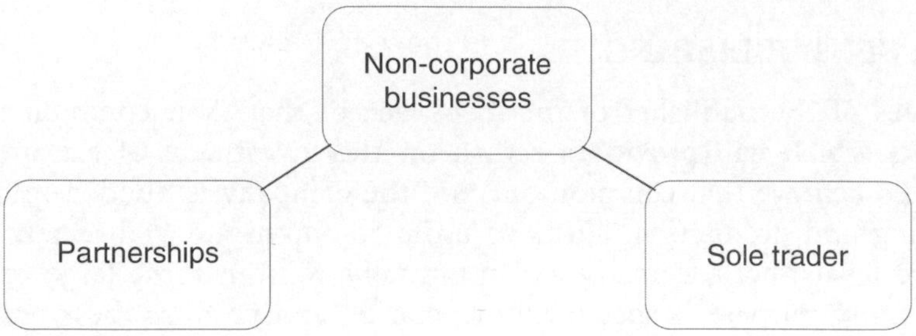

Definition

> Private sector: that sector of the economy comprising all activities that are not government owned. Business organisations in the private sector that exist to make a profit include sole traders, partnerships and private and public companies.

2.1 Sole traders

Also known as sole proprietors, a sole trader may be just that: a one person business. On the other hand, in theory, a sole tradership can employ many people and even have a fairly complicated management structure.

In a sole trader organisation, one person has ownership and control of the business and the ultimate power to make decisions. Management and decision making may be delegated, but the owner remains in control. The owner provides the finance and remains responsible for the success of failure of the business.

A sole trader business is not a legal entity separate from the owner. This means that the proprietor has unlimited liability and legally all contracts with the business are in fact made with the individual proprietor. If the firm fails, the proprietor could lose everything; all personal assets as well as the business assets could go to satisfy creditors.

Despite this risk, thousands of people start up new sole traderships every year. Anyone can set up as a sole trader without any formal procedures, except where a license is required to operate (for example, to retail wines and spirits or for consumer credit). Around eight per cent of UK businesses are sole traderships. They flourish in business sectors where:

- (a) personal expertise is important;
- (b) there are no great economies of scale;
- (c) little capital is required.

Sole traders tend to serve a local market, where they are often important to the community.

Definition

> Economies of scale: economies that arise within a firm as output increases and average total cost falls. The economies arise from technical factors (such as employing larger, more efficient machines) and from managerial factors such as specialisation, bulk buying and mass marketing.

> **Activity 3** **(30 minutes)**
>
> Look at six different local sole proprietors or businesses. List the factors necessary for them to start up.

Some individuals set up in business as sole traders, perhaps under a different name (for example, 'Joe Bloggs trading as Excelsior') and with a separate bank account, invoice and premises. Although legally speaking the affairs of Joe Bloggs and *Excelsior* are the same, there are a number of advantages in treating the business as a separate entity including:

(a) the need to create an identifiable presence in the market;

(b) the need to satisfy regulations on tax and employment;

(c) the need for a business entity to deal with bankers, suppliers and customers;

(d) the informality of establishing the business

(e) the informality of running the business – there is not requirement to publish accounts or to keep records except for tax purposes;

(f) the desire to be one's own boss.

2.2 Partnerships

When two or more people join in a business venture, they often create a partnership. Partnerships are the preferred form or organisation for professional practices such as lawyers.

Forming a partnership increases the financial resources and widens the range of expertise available to a business. Each new partner may bring in new capital and new skills. However, every new partner has a say in running the business and can take decisions binding the others whether or not they agree or even know of it.

The Companies Act 1985, and later amendments, limits the number of partners to twenty, but exempts from the limit qualified and practising accountants and solicitors and the business members of a recognised stock exchange.

A partnership like a sole proprietorship, is not a separate legal entity. Two or more persons carrying on a business together constitutes a partnership. It does not require any formal written agreement: a verbal arrangement is sufficient. Any partner can bind the partnership to a contract with third parties. The partnership is automatically dissolved by the withdrawal, bankruptcy or death of a partner.

Informality can be dangerous. Unless there are procedures set down for operating and dissolving the partnership, the individual members can be suddenly faced by all the financial difficulties caused by unlimited liability for all the debts of the partnership. In fact, partnerships are usually regulated by a formal agreement that covers the terms for subscribing capital, the division of profits and losses, duties, salaries and procedures for dissolving the partnership. It is very unwise to carry on business without such an agreement. Partnerships do not have to publish accounts so they can maintain secrecy of their profitability, or lack of it.

In rare cases, because limited companies are more attractive, there can be a limited partnership where:

(a) limited (or sleeping) partners' liabilities are limited to the capital contributed by them;

(b) limited partners take no part in running the business;

(c) there must be at least one general partner.

The partnership form of an organisation has particular attraction for accountants because the partners, in even the largest firm like Deloitte and Touche, can keep their own clients, have a say in running the business and enjoy the advantages of large scale. However, recent very large judgements against the top firms for negligence in auditing accounts and for bad advice have caused them to query the advantages of being a partnership and consider incorporation or moving to Jersey where large limited partnerships are possible.

Partnerships flourish in the same areas as sole traders. They appeal especially to professional people who can retain a lot of individual freedom of action and maintain their personal relationship with clients while gaining the advantage of larger capital and more expertise. They appeal to clients because the principle of professional responsibility and accountability is retained.

Activity 4 **(30 minutes)**

Identify four local partnerships.

For each, suggest three advantages of them being a partnership as opposed to a sole trader.

3 COMPANIES

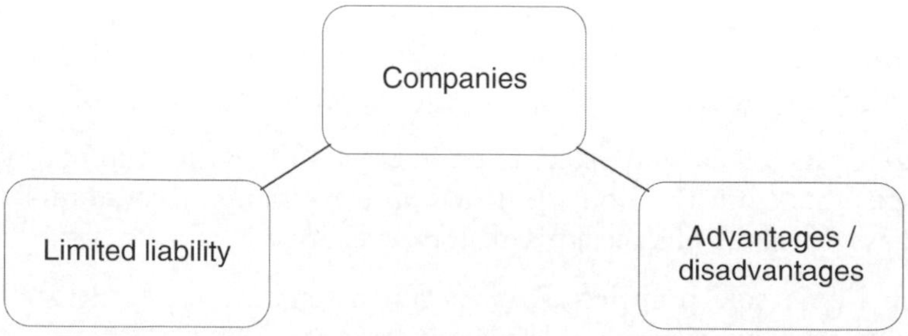

The principle of joint stock companies brought together venturers for centuries – people risked their capital jointly with others in the stock of the company. But joint ownership brought all the risks of a big partnership in terms of bearing losses until the principle of limited liability was recognised in 1855. The Companies Act introduced general limited liability for shareholders in companies and made it possible for firms to raise large amounts of capital with only limited risk to their owners. It took many years for people to trust companies, but by the end of the last century the structure of businesses had been transformed as limited liability companies made the risk of forming large firms acceptable to investors.

3.1 Limited liability

Definition

> Limited liability is an arrangement by which owners of a business that fails have their individual responsibility for its debts limited in some way. The most common situation is where shareholders in a company are responsible for the unpaid debts only to the extent of any unpaid amount for their shares. For example, they may have paid up only 50p per share. Should the firm fail they would be called upon for only 50 pence for each share owned, no matter how large the size of the company's outstanding debt. The liability to pay has no relation to the ability to pay.

Given that most shareholders pay the full nominal value of the shares, it means that in most cases they have no liability for the debts of the company.

Corporations can be established in various ways and are of different types:

(a) Royal Charter, once the only method, now used for special cases
(b) Act of Parliament, used for public corporations;
(c) registration under the Companies Act (by far the most common).

3.2 Advantages and disadvantages of companies

The advantages of forming a company are as follows:

(a) It has a separate legal entity from the shareholders, who, therefore cannot be sued for the actions of the company beyond the amount outstanding on their shares.

(b) There is limited liability. The liability of the members is limited to the amount (if any) which remains unpaid on their shares.

(c) Ownership and management of the business are separated so that investors can put money into shares without taking any responsibility for running the company.

(d) Large amounts of capital can be raised from large numbers of investors (private companies can approach only a limited number of members)

(e) Stocks are shares can easily be transferred so that investors can recover their capital (there are restrictions in private companies).

(f) The continuation and legal standing of a company director are not affected by the death of a member of the withdrawal of a director).

There are also some disadvantages

(a) The procedures for setting up a company are costly and complicated compared to starting up as a sole trader or partnership

NOTES

(b) Detailed annual accounts have to be prepared, audited and submitted to the Registrar, an Annual Report, made to shareholders and a register of shareholdings has to be maintained; these can all be inspected by the public (smaller companies, in terms of turnover, have a lesser burden in this respect).

(c) Shareholders have little control of Plcs in practice as individual shareholdings tend to be small and most shares are held by the pension funds and insurance companies etc. (investing institutions), which have rarely taken an interest in the management of the firms where they have holdings.

(d) Public companies are vulnerable to take-over bids.

(e) Managers are unlikely to put in as much effort as the sole traders or partners.

(f) Incentive schemes for directors and senior managers have been severely criticised as being too generous to the extent that in the late 1990s there were moves by groups of investing institutions to join in voting against proposals at AGMs.

(g) Small and new companies may have difficulty in getting credit because their limited liability makes suppliers and lenders wary (directors of private companies often have to give personal guarantees or security for loans).

4 PUBLIC AND PRIVATE COMPANIES

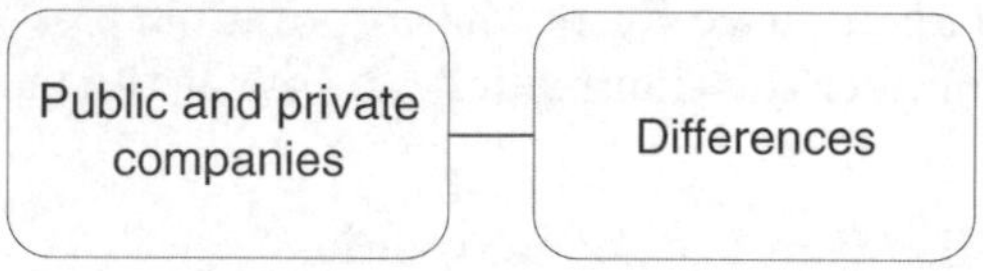

A public company is a company registered as such under the Companies Acts with the Registrar of Companies. Any company not registered as public is a private company: s 1(3). A public company may be one which was originally incorporated as a public company or one which re-registered as a public company having been previously a private company.

A public company is such because the Registrar of Companies (referred to as 'the registrar' in the remainder of this text) has issued a certificate that the company has been registered or re-registered as a public company.

The main feature of a public company is that it can issue its shares to the public. It does not have to however, and there are many public companies which are entirely in private hands.

4.1 Differences between private and public companies

The more important differences between public and private companies imposed by law relate to the following factors.

(a) *Directors*. A public company must have at least two directors but a private company needs only one: s 282. The rules on loans to directors are much more stringent in their application to public companies and their subsidiaries than to private companies: s 330. A public company, except by ordinary resolution with special notice, may not appoint a director aged over 70: s 293.

BPP PUBLISHING

(b) *Members*. A public company must have at least two members. A private company need only have one. There is no upper limit on the number of members of either public or private companies.

(c) *Capital*. The main differences are:

  (i) minimum amount of £50,000 for a public company, no minimum for a private company;

  (ii) a public company may raise capital from the general body of investors by offering its shares or debentures to the public; a private company is prohibited from doing so.

(d) *Dealings in shares*. In practice only a public company can obtain a Stock Exchange or other investment exchange listing for its shares. Not all public companies however are listed. There are additional rules of company law relating to listed securities.

(e) *Accounts*

  (i) A public company has seven months from the end of its accounting reference period in which to produce its statutory audited accounts. The period for a private company is ten months: s 244(1).

  (ii) A private company, if qualified by its size, may have partial exemption from various accounting provisions. These remissions are not available to a public company or to its subsidiaries (even if they are private companies): ss 246, 248 and 250.

(f) *Commencement of business*. A private company can commence business as soon as it is incorporated. A public company if incorporated as such must first obtain a certificate from the registrar who must be satisfied that the company has allotted at least £50,000 of its share capital, paid up as to at least a quarter of its nominal value and the whole of any premium: s 372.

(g) *Identification as public or private*

  (i) the word 'limited' or 'Ltd' in the name denotes a private company; 'public limited company' or 'plc' must appear at the end of the name of a public company: s 25;

  (ii) the *memorandum of association* of a public company must include a clause describing it as a public company. Nothing of this kind is prescribed for a private company.

Activity 5 **(10 minutes)**

In what ways do the rules which differ between public and private companies give extra protection to investors in public companies? Why should such extra protection be given?

5 HOLDING AND SUBSIDIARY COMPANIES

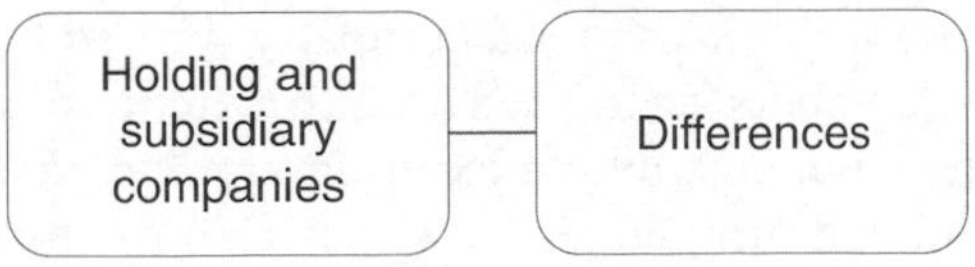

A further subdivision of companies arises depending on the type of limited liability.

A company will be the subsidiary company of another company, its holding company, if:

(a) the latter holds the majority of the voting rights in the former;

(b) the latter is a member of the former and in addition has the right by voting control to remove or appoint a majority of its board of directors; or

(c) the latter is a member of the former and controls a majority of the voting rights, pursuant to an agreement with other members or shareholders; or

(d) the former is a subsidiary of a company which is itself a subsidiary of the latter company: s 736 (1).

A company (A) is a wholly-owned subsidiary of another company (B) if it has no other members except B and its wholly-owned subsidiaries, or persons acting on B's or B's subsidiaries' behalf: s 736 (2).

The importance of the holding and subsidiary company relationship is recognised in company law in a number of rules.

(a) A holding company must generally prepare group accounts in which the financial situation of holding and subsidiary companies is consolidated as if they were one person: s 227.

(b) A subsidiary may not ordinarily be a member of its holding company or give financial assistance for the purchase of the shares of its holding company: s 23 and s 151(1).

(c) Since directors of a holding company can control its subsidiary some rules designed to regulate the dealings of a public company with its directors also apply to its subsidiaries even if they are private companies, particularly loans to directors: s 330.

Activity 6 **(10 minutes)**

A Ltd holds 60% of the shares in B Ltd, which holds 60% of the shares in C Ltd. A Ltd thus effectively holds 60% × 60% = 36% of C Ltd. Consider whether C Ltd is a subsidiary of A Ltd. Give reasons for your answer.

6 COMPANIES LIMITED BY SHARES AND BY GUARANTEE

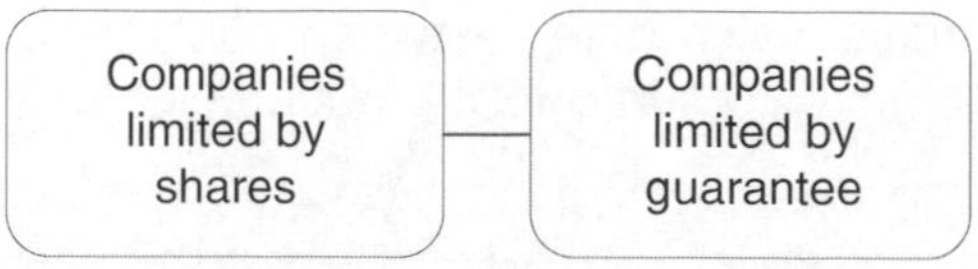

As you have seen, the expression that a company is limited by shares means that the liability of the members is limited to the amount (if any) which remains unpaid on their shares.

Occasionally, however, you may encounter a company limited by guarantee. This means that the liability of the members is limited to the extent to which they individually guarantee the debts of the company. The maximum amount that they may contribute is set in the company's Memorandum, which is its basic constitution when it is created. It is usually some token amount such as £1, and they would only have to pay it in the event of the company being wound up and unable to pay its debts.

Charities are often companies limited by guarantee, as it means that the organisation gets all of the benefits of corporate status without the costs and disadvantages of issuing shares.

7 THE FORMATION OF A COMPANY

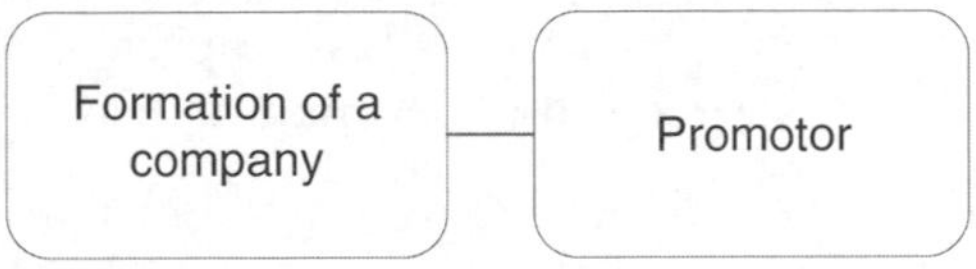

A company cannot form itself. It needs a promoter to undertake the task.

7.1 The promoter

If the promoter is to be the owner of the company, it does not matter if he obtains some personal advantage from the process of forming a company. If, however, anyone else buys some or all of the shares, the promoter is in a *fiduciary* position to the company and must disclose any advantage he will gain to an independent board of directors or to existing and prospective members. If he makes proper disclosure, the promoter may retain his profit, unless he is accountable to the company under some other principle.

A promoter can recover his expenses, by agreement, from the company. If, however, he enters into a contract before the company incorporates but purportedly on its behalf, he and not the company is personally liable on it: s 36(4). The company cannot retrospectively ratify the contract; the solution is to enter into a new contract on the same terms as the old one.

8 REGISTRATION PROCEDURES

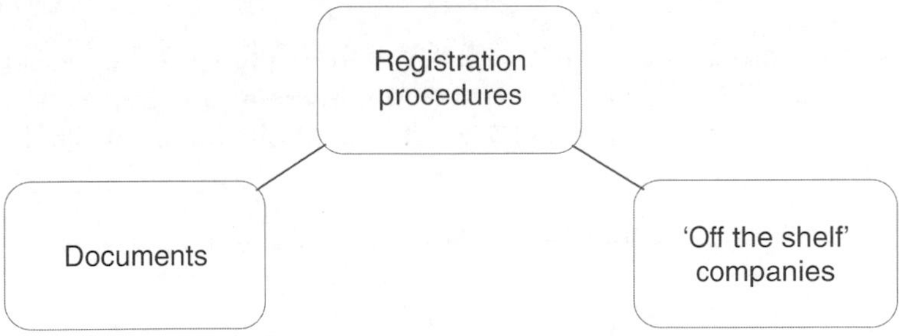

A company is formed by the issue of a certificate of registration by the registrar. The certificate identifies the company by its name and serial number at the registry and states (if it be so) that it is limited and (if necessary) that it is a public company.

To obtain the certificate of incorporation it is necessary to deliver to the registrar prescribed documents (see below) bearing the name of the proposed company.

8.1 The documents to be delivered to the registrar

(a) *A memorandum of association.* This is normally signed by at least two subscribers. However, in the case of single member private companies it is possible for only the one member to subscribe to the memorandum. The signature(s) must be dated and witnessed. Each subscriber agrees to subscribe for at least one share: s 1(1).

(b) *Articles of association* signed by the same subscribers, dated and witnessed. Alternatively the memorandum of a company limited by shares may be endorsed 'registered without articles of association'. The statutory Table A articles then become the company's articles in their entirety.

(c) *A statement in the prescribed form* (known as Form 10) giving the particulars of the first director(s) and secretary and of the first address of the registered office. The persons named as directors and secretary must sign the form to record their consent to act in this capacity. When the company is incorporated they are deemed to be appointed: ss 10 and 13.

(d) *A statutory declaration* (Form 12) by a solicitor engaged in the formation of the company or by one of the persons named as director or secretary that the requirements of the Companies Act in respect of registration have been complied with: s 12(3).

A registration fee is payable (currently £20).

The registrar considers whether the documents are formally in order and whether the objects specified in the memorandum appear to be lawful, since a company may only be registered if it has a lawful purpose: s 1. If he is satisfied, he gives the company a 'registered number' (s 705), issues a certificate of incorporation and publishes a notice in the London Gazette that it has been issued: ss 13 and 711.

8.2 Companies 'off the shelf'

Because the registration of a new company can be a lengthy business, it is often easiest for people wishing to operate as a company to purchase one 'off the shelf'. This is possible by contacting enterprises specialising in registering a stock of companies ready for sale when a person comes along who needs the advantages of incorporation.

Activity 7 **(10 minutes)**

'Off the shelf' companies cannot exist on the shelf, waiting to be bought, unless all the usual formalities of registration have already been complied with. What changes are the buyers of an off the shelf company likely to make immediately on purchase?

NOTES

9 THE MEMORANDUM AND ARTICLES

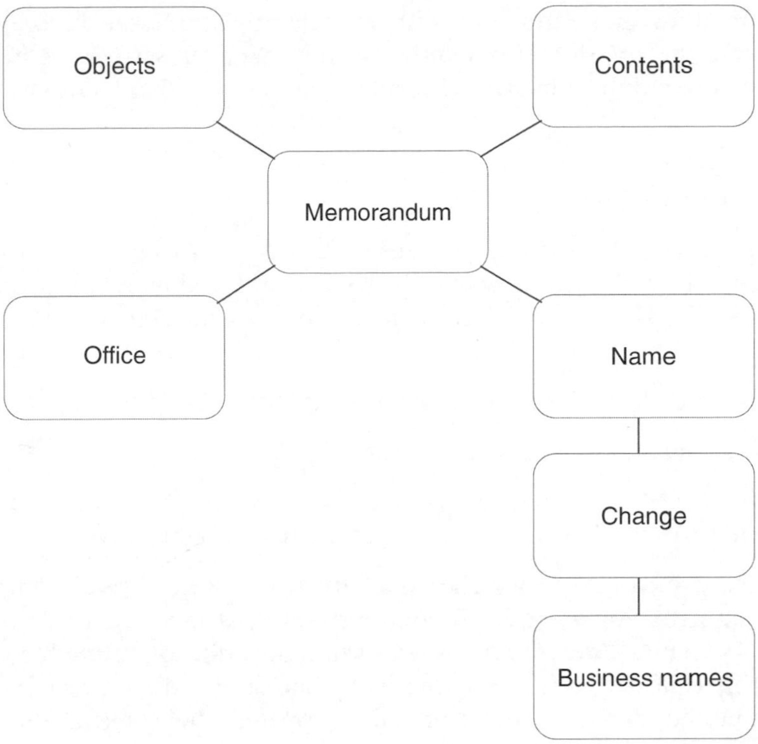

These two documents, which must be filed with the registrar on the formation of the company, form its basic constitution.

The purpose of the memorandum and articles of association (for short 'the memorandum' and 'the articles') is to define what the company is and how its business and affairs are to be conducted. The memorandum sets out the basic elements. The articles are mainly internal rules.

For historical reasons these are two separate documents. If there is any inconsistency between them the memorandum prevails.

The original memorandum must be presented to the registrar to obtain registration of the new company. It is usually signed by at least two persons (the subscribers) who agree to become the first members. In the case of single member private companies, however, it is now possible for only one member to subscribe to the memorandum of association. Whenever the memorandum is altered a copy of the complete altered text must be delivered to the registrar for filing: s 18.

9.1 Contents of the memorandum

The memorandum of a private company limited by shares is required by s 2 to state:

(a) the *name* of the company;

(b) whether the *registered office* is to be situated in England and Wales, or Scotland;

(c) the *objects* of the company;

(d) the *limited liability* of members;

(e) the *authorised share capital* and how it is divided into shares.

The items on this list are referred to in this chapter as 'compulsory clauses'.

The memorandum of a public company contains the above particulars and also a sixth statement (placed second in order) that the company is a public company: s 1(3).

Every memorandum must also end with a declaration of association by which the subscribers state their wish to form the company. Each subscriber must, opposite his signature, state the number of shares (in practice always one share only) which he agrees to take.

9.2 The company name

The name of the company serves to identify it and to distinguish it from any other company. For this reason, and to control the use of company names which might mislead the public, the registrar has statutory powers of control over the choice of names.

The choice of name of a limited company must conform to ss 25 to 31, as follows.

(a) The name must *end* with the word(s):

  (i) public limited company (abbreviated plc) if it is a public company; or
  (ii) limited (or Ltd) if it is a private limited company.

(b) No company may have a name which is the same as that of any existing company appearing in the statutory index at the registry. For this purpose two names are treated as 'the same' in spite of minor or non-essential differences; for instance the word 'the' as the first word in the name is ignored. 'John Smith Limited' is treated the same as 'John Smith & Company Ltd': s 26(3).

(c) No company may have a name the use of which would in the registrar's opinion be a criminal offence or which he considers offensive: s 26(1).

(d) No company may have a name which in the registrar's opinion suggests a connection with the government or a local authority or which is subject to control (unless of course its use is officially approved): s 26(2). Words such as 'International' or 'British' are only sanctioned if the size of the company matches its pretensions. A name which suggests some professional expertise such as 'optician' will only be permitted if the appropriate representative association has been consulted and raises no objection.

9.3 Change of name

A company may change its name by passing a special resolution (which requires a 75% majority of the shareholders who vote) and obtaining the registrar's certificate of incorporation that he has registered the company under a new name: s 28. The certificate makes the change effective from when it is issued, though the company is still the same legal entity as before.

The registrar can compel a company to change its name (within such time as he may allow) if:

(a) the name is the same as or in the registrar's opinion too like the name of another company which was or should have been on the register when the name was adopted, or if misleading information or assurances were given to secure registration: s 28; or

(b) the company's name gives so misleading an indication of its activities as to be likely to cause harm to the public: s 32.

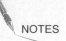

9.4 Business names other than the corporate name

Most companies trade under their own registered names. But a company may prefer to use some other name. If it does so it must:

(a) state its registered name and its address on all business letters, invoices, receipts, written orders for goods or services and written demands for payment of debts;

(b) display its name and address in a prominent position in any business premises to which its customers and suppliers have access;

(c) on request from any person with whom it does business give notice of its name and address.

9.5 Registered office

The memorandum does not state the address of the registered office but only that it will be situate in England and Wales. This fixes the domicile of the company which, unlike other matters comprised in the memorandum, is unalterable.

The first address of the registered office is given in the documents presented to secure incorporation.

At any time thereafter the directors may alter the address of the registered office. But the new address, like the old, must be within the country specified in the memorandum. The registered office need not have any close connection with the company. Some companies arrange with their accountants or solicitors to make the latter's office premises the registered office of the company.

If the address of the registered office is changed, notice of the new address must be given to the registrar and the change takes effect after the registration: s 287(3). Documents may still be served on the company at the former address for a further 14 days.

The importance of the registered office is that:

(a) if a legal document, such as a notice or writ to commence legal proceedings, has to be served on a company this may be done by delivering it at the registered office or by sending it by post (preferably recorded delivery) to that office: s 725. The company cannot then deny that it has received the document;

(b) various registers and other documents are held either at the registered office or in some cases at another address.

9.6 Objects

The objects clause sets out the 'aims' and 'purposes' of the company. It is usually very broadly drafted, so that the company's actions cannot be challenged as outside its objects. A clause ending as follows is not uncommon.

'to carry on any other business, trade or enterprise which may be advantageously carried out, in the opinion of the directors, in connection with or ancillary to the general business of the company'.

(a) *Objects and powers*

Also contained in the objects clause will be a list of permissible transactions (or express powers). These may include powers to lease and construct buildings, employ and remunerate staff, sub-contract work and so on. The most common and most important express powers are to borrow funds, to give security by creating charges over property, and to give guarantees.

The list of express powers may be long and detailed. This is to avoid the uncertainty caused by the fact that some powers to enter into transactions in the pursuit of the company's objects may only be implied. The danger here is that powers can only be implied to further the objects. Hence any action which does not promote the objects and is not an express power may not be effective as an implied power.

(b) *Object as a 'general commercial company'*

It is now possible to register a company with objects which merely state that the company's object is to 'carry on business as a general commercial company': s 3A. The legislation specifically states that this means that:

(i) the object of the company is to carry on any trade or business whatsoever; and

(ii) the company has power to do all such things as are incidental or conducive to the carrying on of any trade or business by it.

9.7 Alteration of objects

A company may by special resolution alter its objects (s 4(1)).

Section 5 provides a procedure for a dissenting minority to apply to the court to modify an otherwise valid alteration of the objects clause. The conditions are that:

(a) application to the court must be made within 21 days from the passing of the special resolution to alter the objects; and

(b) the applicants must hold in aggregate at least 15% of the issued share capital or 15% of any class of shares. They must not originally have voted in favour of the alteration or consented to it.

Once such an objection is made the alternative which was approved can only come into effect insofar as the court allows: s 4(2). The court can arrange for the parties to come to an agreement (s 5(4)) as it can, say, order the company to buy the dissenting minority's shares: s 5(5).

Activity 8 **(10 minutes)**

A company is set up with the object of making and selling computers, and with the power to borrow or lend money. Why would the directors not be empowered to run a moneylending business?

10 ARTICLES OF ASSOCIATION

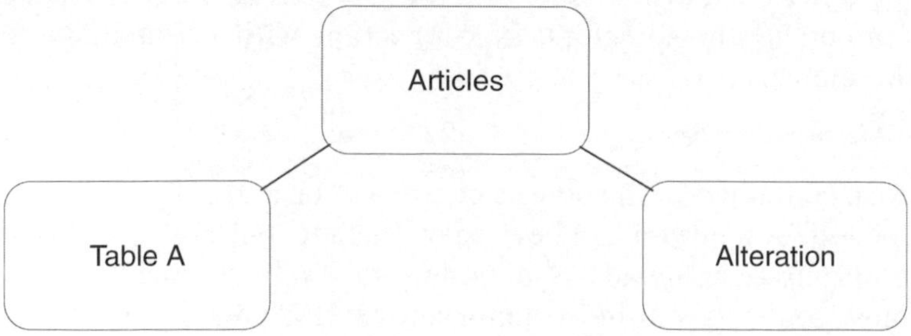

The articles of association deal mainly with the internal conduct of the company's affairs – the issue and transfer of shares; alterations of capital structure; calling general meetings and how they are to be conducted (including members' voting rights); appointment, powers and proceedings of directors; dividends; accounts and the issue of notices. If the company has more than one class of shares the rights of a class and the procedure for varying them is usually set out in the articles.

The memorandum differs from the articles in that it deals with the constitution of the company mainly as it affects outsiders. In cases of conflict the memorandum prevails over the articles. It is possible to alter the standard clauses of the memorandum (with one exception, namely the clause specifying country of origin) but special restrictions and procedures make it less easy to do so. The articles, however, may as a general rule be altered simply by passing a special resolution. Clauses which could be included in the articles may be placed in the memorandum in order to make it more difficult to alter them.

10.1 Table A articles

A company limited by shares may have its own full-length special articles, or it may adopt all or any part of the statutory standard model articles (known as Table A) made under s 8. Private companies usually have a short form of articles which state that Table A is to apply subject only to a few exclusions or modifications deemed desirable for the company.

As regards form, the articles must be printed and divided into numbered paragraphs: s 7(3). The first articles presented to obtain registration of a new company are signed by the subscribers to the memorandum, dated and witnessed. But if new or altered articles are adopted later the copy of the text to be delivered to the registrar need not be signed.

Whenever any alteration is made to the articles a copy of the altered articles must be delivered to the registrar within 15 days, together with a signed copy of the special resolution by which the alteration is made: ss 18 and 380.

10.2 Alteration of the articles

A company has a statutory power to alter its articles by special resolution: s 9(1). This means that if a special resolution is properly moved and carried at a general meeting by a 75% majority of votes cast, the alteration is valid and binding on all members of the company.

Alteration of the articles is restricted by the following principles.

(a) The alteration is void if it conflicts with the Companies Act or with the memorandum.

(b) In various circumstances, such as to protect a minority (s 459) or in approving an alteration of the objects clause (s 5(5)), the court may order that an alteration be made or, alternatively, that an existing article shall not be altered. The leave of the court is then required if the relevant article is later to be altered to vary it from the terms approved by the court.

(c) A member may not be compelled by alteration of the articles to subscribe for additional shares or to accept increased liability for the shares which he holds unless he has given his consent: s 16.

(d) An alteration of the articles which varies the rights attached to a class of shares may only be made if the correct variation procedure has been followed to obtain the consent of the class (s 125). A 15% minority may apply to the court to cancel the variation under s 127.

(e) An alteration may be void if the majority who approve it are not acting bona fide in what they deem to be the interests of the company as a whole (see below).

(f) A person whose contract is contained in the articles cannot obtain an injunction to prevent the articles being altered, but he may be entitled to damages for breach of contract.

Activity 9 **(10 minutes)**

R holds 10% of the shares in C Ltd. A special resolution is voted for by all the other shareholders (R voting against) to alter the articles so as to make each member liable to contribute an extra £10 per share. R is told that, as his holding is less than 15%, he must accept this. Is this true? Why?

11 THE MEMORANDUM AND ARTICLES AS CONTRACTS

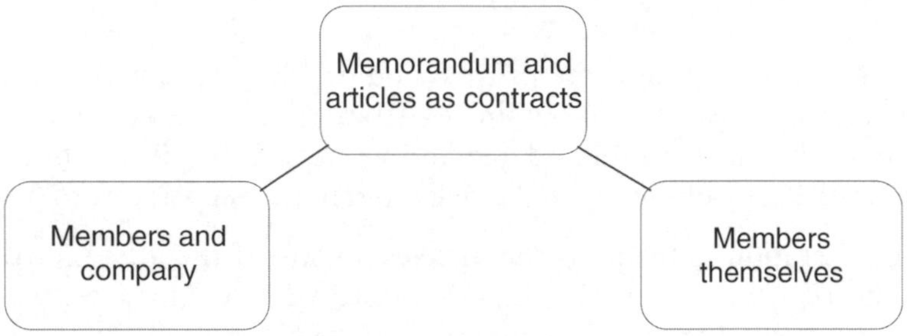

A company's memorandum and articles bind, under s 14:

(a) members to company;
(b) company to members (but see below);
(c) members to members; but not
(d) company to third parties.

The members are deemed to have separately covenanted to observe the articles and memorandum. The principle that only rights and obligations of members are covered by s 14 applies when a member seeks to rely on the articles in support of a claim made as an outsider.

> *Eley v Positive Government Security Life Assurance Co 1876*
> E, a solicitor, drafted the original articles and included a provision that the company must always employ him as its solicitor. E became a member of the company some months after its incorporation. He later sued the company for breach of contract in not employing him as a solicitor. The case turned partly on technical points which no longer arise since the law (the Statute of Frauds) has been changed.
>
> *Held:* E could not rely on the article since it was a contract between the company and its members and he was not asserting any claim as a member.

Section 14 gives to the memorandum and articles the effect of a contract made between (a) the company and (b) its members individually. It can also impose a contract on the members in their dealings with each other as illustrated by the case below.

NOTES

Rayfield v Hands 1958
The articles required that (a) every director should be a shareholder and (b) the directors must purchase the shares of any member who gave them notice of his wish to dispose of them. The directors, however, denied that a member could enforce the obligation on them to acquire his shares.

Held: there was 'a contract ... between a member and member-directors in relation to their holdings of the company's shares in its article' and the directors were bound by it.

12 COMMENCEMENT OF BUSINESS

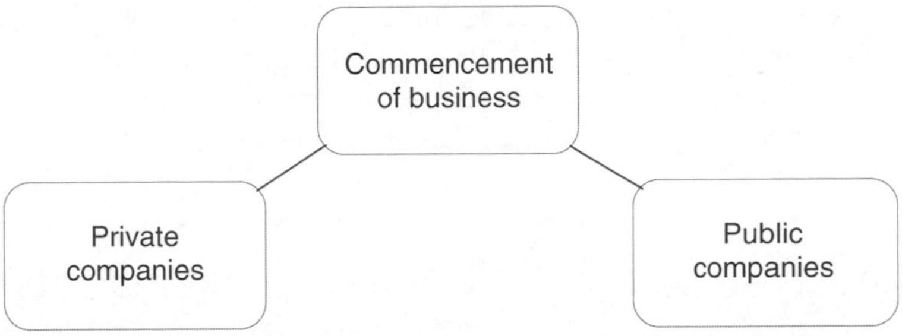

Public companies face additional restrictions before they can start trading.

12.1 Private companies

A *private company* may do business and exercise its borrowing powers from the date of its incorporation. It is normal practice to hold a first meeting of the directors at which the chairman, secretary and sometimes the auditors are appointed, shares are allotted to raise capital, authority is given to open a bank account and any other initial commercial arrangements are made. A return of allotments should be made to the registrar: s 88.

Within the first nine months of its existence the company should give notice to the registrar of the accounting reference date on which its annual accounts will be made up: s 224. If no such notice is given within the prescribed period, companies are deemed to have an accounting reference date of the last day of the month in which the anniversary of incorporation falls.

12.2 Public companies

A new *public company* may not do business or exercise any borrowing powers unless it has obtained a trading certificate from the registrar: s 117.

To obtain a trading certificate a public company makes application on Form 117 signed by a director or by the secretary with a statutory declaration made by the director or secretary which states:

(a) that the nominal value of the allotted share capital is not less than £50,000;

(b) the amount paid up on the allotted share capital, which must be at least one quarter of the nominal value and the entire premium if any: s 101;

(c) particulars of preliminary expenses and payments or benefits to promoters.

The registrar must notify receipt of Form 117 in the Gazette and may accept the declaration without investigation and issue a trading certificate which is conclusive evidence that the company is entitled to do business and to exercise its borrowing powers.

NOTES

13 COMPANY CONTRACTS

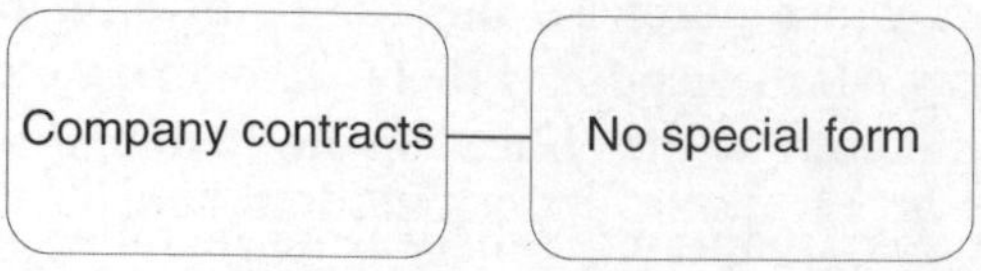

There is no special form of company contract – the same rules requiring use of written or sealed documents apply to companies as to individuals: s 36. The company must of course enter into contracts through agents. Its articles of association delegate wide powers to its directors and they may in turn permit employees to make commercial contracts under their general or specific authorisation.

A director, secretary or other authorised officer of a company may authenticate a document on the company's behalf: s 41. Provided the signature is made in this way and in the course of the company's business, that person's signature is treated as that of the company: *UBAF Ltd v European American Banking Corporation 1984.*

Activity 10 **(5 minutes)**

What key principle of company law is reflected in the fact that a company can make contracts in the same ways as an individual can (albeit through agents)?

Chapter roundup

- An individual trading alone is a sole trader, while two or more people trading together form a partnership.
- Both sole traders and partners incur personal liability for the debts of the business.
- The two main features of corporate personality are limited liability, in that the liability of the shareholders is limited to any amount unpaid on their shares, and separate legal personality, which means that the company is separate in the eyes of the law from its shareholders.
- A public company (plc) must be registered as such, and is subject to more stringent regulations in many cases than a private company.
- A public company can issue its shares to the public, while a private company cannot.
- A company is formed by its promoters. They have a fiduciary duty to the company.
- A company cannot be a party to a pre-incorporation contract, but such a contract can be replaced by a new contract which the company is a party to.
- Several documents must be submitted in order to obtain a registration certificate for a new company.
- A private company may commence business without further formality, but a public company must obtain a trading certificate.
- A company may make contracts in the same way as an individual, although it must do so through agents such as its directors.

Quick quiz

1 What is a mission statement?

2 What sort of liability does a sole trader have?

3 Why do people like to trade in partnerships?

4 What is meant by limited liability?

5 Write down two advantages and two disadvantages of forming a limited company.

6 Name two ways in which a private company is different from a public company.

7 What is a promoter?

8 What documents must be sent to the registrar to form a company?

9 What additional step must a public company take before it commences business?

Answers to quick quiz

1 A document which sets out an organisation's purpose. (see para 1.2)

2 Unlimited, ie personal liability. (para 2.1)

3 Privacy (no need to publish accounts)
Informality (no need to follow Companies Act)
Participation by partners
Freedom of action (para 2.2)

4 That the liability is the shareholders is limited to the amount (if any) unpaid on their shares. (para 3.1)

5 Separate legal personality
Limited liability
Detailed accounts
Subject to company law (para 3.2)

6 Directors: public company must have 2
private company needs only 1

Capital: minimum of £50,000 for a plc
No minimum for a private co (para 4.1)

7 The person who establishes the company in law. (para 7.1)

8 Memorandum
Articles
Form 10
Statutory declaration
Fee (8.1)

9 Obtain a trading certificate. (para 12.2)

Answers to activities

1 Your list might include some of the following: your college – a corporation that provides a service and tries, at least, to avoid a loss; supermarkets, a newsagents or other shops – profit making businesses; a sports club – an organisation based on subscription members; street lighting – a profit making electricity company and public service local authority. You may easily have listed 50 or more organisations.

2 Your college would be unlikely to achieve much without a formal organisation. Individual teachers could hold classes, but there would be timetabling clashes and problems about paying for resources, among other disadvantages.

3 You might have chosen, for example, your local newsagent, hairdresser, plumber, dentist, car mechanic and window cleaner. They all require personal qualities, such as the desire to be their own boss and willingness to work on their own and make decisions. They need varying amounts of capital depending on the premises, equipment and stock they must have. They require certain skills and training. Dentists must be qualified and registered. It is desirable for hairdressers, plumbers and car mechanics to be qualified and trained and to belong to recognised bodies. Shop keepers need expertise to run the business. Window cleaners need skill and knowledge to handle long ladders, for example.

4 Accountants, doctors, solicitors and dentists are the most likely partnerships. They benefit from more capital and shared expertise, premises and support services.

5 The need for two directors may make it difficult for a single dishonest director to defraud investors.

A public company must produce accounts more quickly than a private company.

A public company must raise substantial capital before it can trade. It must therefore ensure that many investors (or a few wealthy investors) accept that it is reputable.

The extra protection is needed because capital may be raised from investors who have no prior contact with or knowledge of the company.

6 Yes: C Ltd is a subsidiary of B Ltd, which is in turn a subsidiary of A Ltd.

7 The buyers are likely to change the company's name and its directors.

8 The power is restricted to use in connection with the company's object.

9 No: a member may not be compelled to accept increased liability for his shares.

10 Separate legal personality.

Assignment 10 **(45 minutes)**

Tom has carried on business for a number of years as a sole trader selling electrical goods to the public. Tom has now decided to incorporate his business.

(a) Explain the advantages and disadvantages of purchasing an 'off the shelf' company (ie a company already registered but not trading) compared with registering a new company.

(b) To what extent will Tom need to bring in another person in order to satisfy the law relating to the membership and management of a private company limited by shares?

(c) What are the possible consequences for a person carrying on business through a private company limited by shares, if he orders goods and omits to state the name of the company?

Chapter 14 :
SHARE CAPITAL AND DIVIDENDS

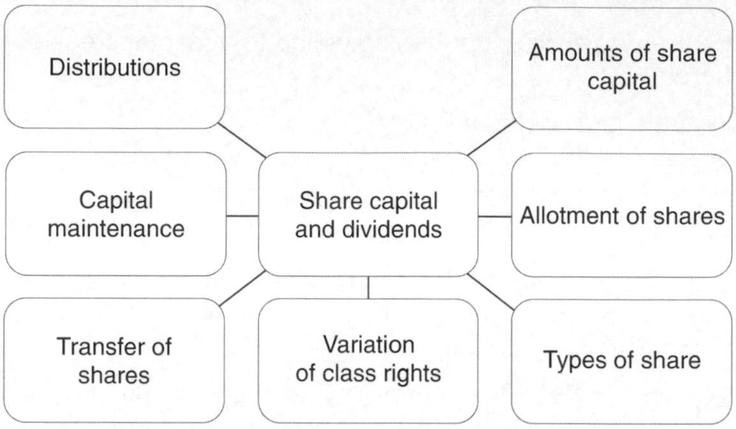

Introduction

A company's capital is the funds it has available for use in the business and represents its assets. Some, if not all, of a company's capital is provided by its members subscribing for shares. That is the subject of this chapter.

Share capital is elaborately regulated by law; in particular there are special rules relating to maintenance of capital in order to protect the 'creditors' buffer'.

Capital provided by lenders is dealt with separately.

Your objectives

In this chapter you will learn about the following.

(a) The different amounts of share capital which may be stated

(b) How shares are allotted

(c) What consideration for shares is acceptable

(d) Rights issues and bonus issues

(e) The difference between ordinary shares and preference shares

(f) How class rights may be varied

(g) How shares are transferred and how transfers may be restricted

(h) The significance of share certificates

(i) The concept of maintenance of capital

(j) How a company is prevented from reducing its capital except in restricted circumstances

(k) The powers of directors in relation to dividends

(l) What profits may be distributed and the consequences of paying excessive dividends

1 TYPES OF CAPITAL

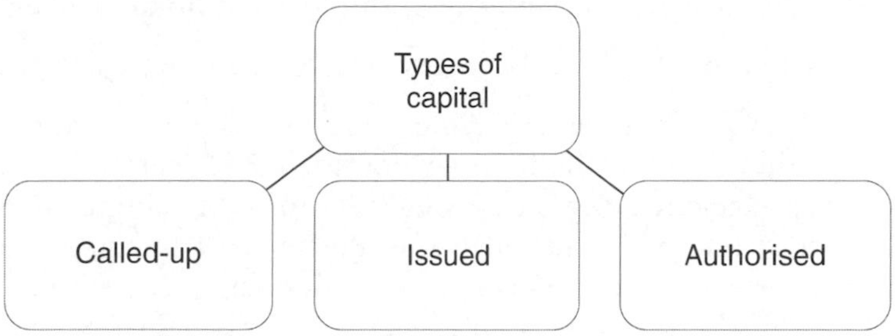

The term 'capital' is used in several senses.

1.1 Authorised share capital

This is the total amount of share capital which the company is authorised to issue by the capital clause of its memorandum. This total must be divided into shares of fixed amount (called the nominal or par value of the shares). It can be increased as prescribed in the articles (usually an ordinary resolution suffices).

1.2 Issued share capital (or allotted share capital)

This is the nominal value of the shares which have been allotted and issued to members. A company need not issue all its share capital at once. If it retains part this is unissued share capital.

1.3 Called up share capital

This is the aggregate amount of calls for money or other consideration which members are required to pay (or have paid in applying for shares): s 737. If, for example, a company has issued 70 £1 (nominal) shares, has received 25p per share on application and has called on members for a second 25p, its called up share capital is £35 (50p per share). When the members pay the call the paid up share capital is then £35 also. Capital not yet called is uncalled capital.

2 ALLOTMENT OF SHARES

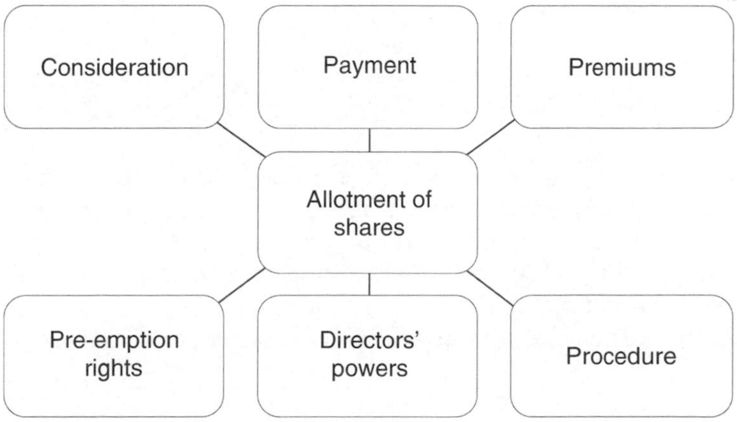

The allotment of shares is a form of contract. The intending shareholder applies to the company for shares. This is an offer which the company accepts by allotting shares to him.

2.1 Procedure for allotment of shares

The allotment of shares of a private company is a simple and immediate matter.

Public companies listed on The Stock Exchange usually follow a two-stage procedure.

(a) They first issue a renounceable allotment letter (or similar document) which the original allottee may for a limited period (up to six weeks) transfer to another person by signing a form of renunciation (included in the letter) and delivering it to the transferee. The original allottee or the ultimate renouncee, sends in the allotment letter with a completed application for registration of the shares in his name. No entry is made in the register of members when the allotment letter is first issued.

(b) On receipt of the application for registration the company enters the name of the applicant in the register of members and delivers a return of allotments to the registrar made up to show who is then on the register. The applicant becomes a member by entry on the register and receives a share certificate from the company.

Except where renounceable allotment letters are issued, the name of the allottee is usually entered in the register soon after, and as a direct consequence of, the allotment of shares to him. He then becomes a member: s 22.

Subscribers to the memorandum become members of the company as soon as it is incorporated and their names should be entered in the register of members without any decision to allot shares to them.

2.2 Directors' powers to allot shares

It is long established practice to delegate to the board of directors (as part of their general management functions) the decision on the terms of the contract of allotment and the power to allot shares. The directors may only exercise the power of allotment if they are properly authorised to do so, either by the articles or by ordinary resolution passed in general meeting.

Section 80 requires of a public company that the authority to allot shall be given until a specified date and for a specified period of not more than five years. A private company may confer authority to allot shares for an indefinite period, or for a fixed period longer than five years.

2.3 Pre-emption rights: s 89

Activity 1 **(10 minutes)**

Z Ltd has an authorised share capital of 20,000 £2 shares. It issues 60% of these shares, but only calls upon members to pay 70% of the nominal value, in three equal annual instalments. All members pay the amounts required on time. Calculate the company's paid up share capital after the second instalment has been paid.

If a company proposes to allot shares described as 'equity securities' wholly for cash it has a statutory obligation (subject to certain exceptions) to offer those shares to holders of similar shares in proportion to their holdings: s 89.

The offer must be made in writing in the same manner as a notice of a general meeting is sent to members. It must specify a period of not less than 21 days during which the offer may be accepted. If not accepted within that period the offer is deemed to be declined: s 90.

Equity securities subject to the rules just explained are broadly ordinary shares whenever issued for cash. But subscribers' shares, preference shares, bonus issues and shares allotted under an employees' share scheme are exempt from these restrictions which would be inappropriate to them: s 94.

Equity securities which have been offered to members in this way but are not accepted may then be allotted on the same (or less favourable) terms to non-members.

A private company may by its memorandum or articles permanently exclude these rules so that there is no statutory right of first refusal: s 91.

Any company may, by special resolution, resolve that the statutory right of first refusal shall not apply: s 95. For public companies, the period of disapplication is limited to five years.

2.4 Consideration for shares

Every share has a nominal value and may not be allotted at a discount. In allotting shares every company is required to obtain in money or money's worth consideration of a value at least equal to the nominal value of the shares: s 100. To issue shares 'at par' is to obtain equal value, say, £1 for a £1 share. If shares are allotted at a discount on their nominal value the allottee must nonetheless pay the full nominal value with interest at the appropriate rate (5%).

The no-discount rule only requires that, in allotting its shares, a company shall not fix a price which is less than the nominal value of the shares. It may leave part of that price to be paid at some later time by whoever then holds the shares.

2.5 Payment for shares

The price for the shares may be paid in money or 'money's worth', including goodwill and know-how: s 99. It need not be paid in cash and the company may agree to accept a 'non-cash' consideration of sufficient value. For instance, a company may issue shares in payment of the price agreed in the purchase of a property. The allotment of shares as a bonus issue is for full consideration since reserves, which are shareholders' funds, are converted into fixed capital and used to pay for the shares: s 99(4).

(a) *Private companies*

A private company may allot shares for inadequate consideration by acceptance of goods or services at an over-value. This loophole has been allowed to exist because in some cases it is very much a matter of opinion whether an asset is or is not of a stated value.

EXAMPLE: VALUING A PRIVATE COMPANY

K and M have sold their business and the assets used in it to a newly incorporated private company at a price of £56,300. The price was paid by the allotment of £20,000 in shares and the balance in cash and debentures. The company goes into liquidation and the liquidator, S, contends that the value of the business was overstated by about £18,000. S contends that K and M should be treated as having failed to provide adequate consideration for their shares, so that he could recover their excess value. However K and M argue that the business was valued by an expert at £56,300.

The courts would not overrule the directors in their valuations of the business as it appeared reasonable and honest.

(b) *Public companies*

The more stringent rules which apply to public companies regarding consideration and payment are as follows.

(a) Future services are not to be accepted as consideration: s 99(2).

(b) The company must, at the time of allotment, receive at least one quarter of the nominal value of the shares and the whole of any premium.

(c) Non-cash consideration may not be accepted as payment for shares if an undertaking contained in such consideration is to be, or may be, performed more than five years after the allotment: s 102.

(d) Any non-cash consideration accepted must be independently valued (except when shares are being issued in return for shares in a company being taken over): s 103.

(e) Within two years of receiving its certificate under s 117, a public company may not receive a transfer of non-cash assets from a subscriber to the memorandum, unless its value as consideration is less then 10% of the issued nominal share capital and it has been independently valued and agreed by an ordinary resolution: s 104.

2.6 Allotment of shares at a premium

A company may be able to obtain consideration for new shares in excess of their nominal value. The excess, called 'share premium', must be credited to a share premium account (s 130) to which certain restrictions apply. For example, shares with a nominal value of £1 may be issued for £1.50. The premium on each share is therefore 50p.

2.7 Return of allotments

Within one month of allotting shares, a company must deliver to the registrar a return of allotments in the prescribed form showing what shares have been allotted, to whom and for what consideration: s 88.

2.8 Rights and bonus issues

A *rights issue* is an allotment (or the offer of it by renounceable allotment letter) of additional shares made to existing members. If the members do not wish to subscribe for additional shares under a rights issue they may be able to sell their rights to other persons and so obtain the value of the option.

A *bonus issue* is more correctly but less often called a capitalisation issue (also called a scrip issue). The articles of a company usually give it power to apply its reserves (including its undistributed profits) to pay up unissued shares and then to allot these shares as a bonus issue to members.

> **Activity 2** **(10 minutes)**
>
> How might existing members of a company be unfairly treated if pre-emption rights did not exist, even assuming that all new shares were issued for their full market value?

3 THE NATURE OF SHARES AND TYPES OF SHARE

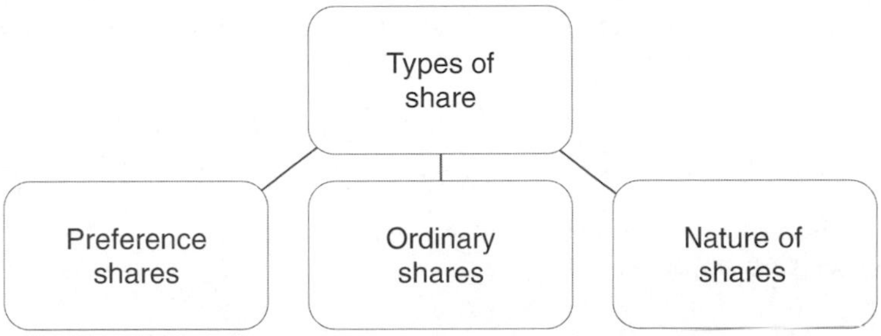

A share is a form of property, carrying rights and obligations. It is by its nature *transferable*. A member who holds one or more shares is by that fact a shareholder.

If no differences between shares are expressed it is assumed that all shares have the same rights. It is unnecessary to classify them as ordinary shares since there are no others. But there is no objection to doing so.

A company may at its option attach special rights to different shares, for example as regards dividends, return of capital, voting or, less often, the right to appoint a director. Any share which has different rights from others is grouped with the other shares carrying identical rights to form a class in distinction from shares with different rights included in another class.

The most common classes of share capital with different rights are *preference shares* and *ordinary shares*; there may also be ordinary shares with voting rights and ordinary shares (often distinguished as 'A' ordinary shares) without voting rights.

The essential characteristic of any preference share is that it carries a prior right to receive an annual dividend of fixed amount, say a 6% dividend. There are no other implied differences between preference and ordinary shares, though there are often express differences between them. For example, preference shares may carry a priority right to return of capital.

> **Activity 3** **(10 minutes)**
>
> J Ltd has some £1 8% preference shares and some £1 ordinary shares in issue. Nothing is stated about the rights attaching to the preference shares. A holds 100 preference shares and 500 ordinary shares. In years 1 and 2 no dividend is paid. In year 3 a 9% dividend is declared on the ordinary shares.
>
> Calculate how much A will receive in year 3.

NOTES

4 VARIATIONS OF CLASS RIGHTS

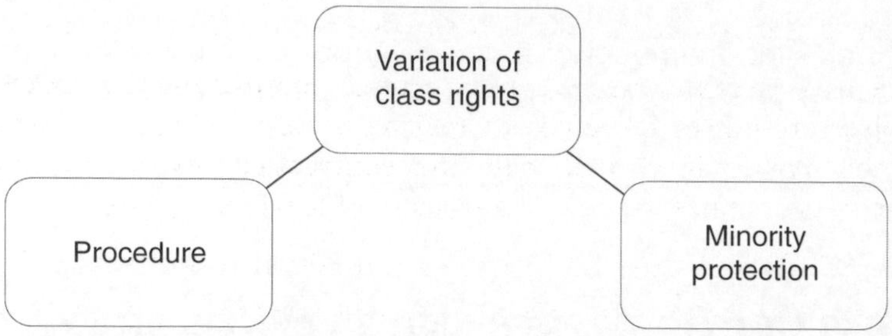

The holders of issued shares have vested rights which can only be varied by the company with the consent of all the holders or with such consent of a majority as is specified in the articles.

The usual procedure for variation of class rights requires that an extraordinary resolution (giving approval) shall be passed by a three-quarters majority cast either:

(a) at a separate meeting of the class, or
(b) by written consent: s 125(2).

4.1 Minority appeals to the court

Whenever class rights are varied under a procedure contained in the memorandum or articles a minority of holders of shares of the class may apply to the court to have the variation cancelled: s 127. The objectors together must:

(a) hold not less than 15% of the issued shares of the class in question;

(b) not themselves have consented to or voted in favour of the variation; and

(c) apply to the court within 21 days of the consent being given by the class: s 127 (2) and (3).

The court can either approve the variation as made or cancel it as 'unfairly prejudicial': s 127 (4). It cannot, however, modify the terms of the variation or approve it subject to conditions. To establish that a variation, although approved by a three-quarters majority of the class, is 'unfairly prejudicial' to the class, it must generally be shown that the majority who voted in favour were seeking some advantage to themselves as members of a different class instead of considering the interests of the class in which they were then voting.

5 THE TRANSFER OF SHARES

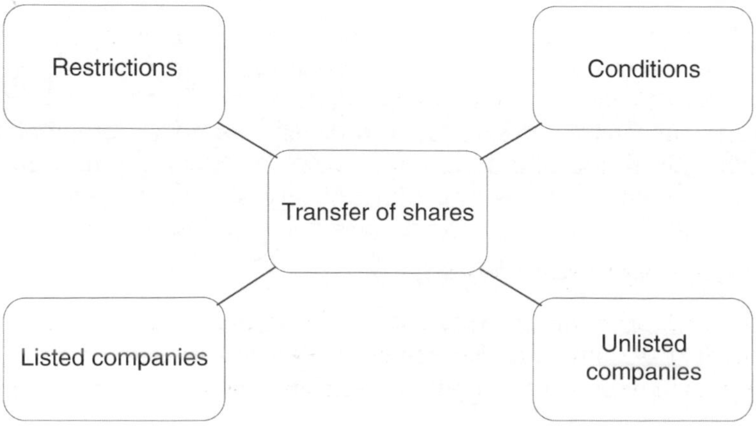

To obtain transfer of the legal ownership of shares two conditions must be satisfied.

(a) A 'proper instrument of transfer' must be delivered to the company which may not enter the transfer in its register until this is done: s 183(1).

(b) If, as is general practice with private companies, the articles give to the directors power to refuse to register a transfer and the directors exercise their power in proper way, the contractual restriction imposed by the articles operates to prevent a transfer of legal ownership.

It is standard practice in unlisted companies nowadays to use the stock transfer form authorised for general use by the Stock Transfer Act 1963: s 1. This can be used to transfer fully paid shares irrespective of any provision in the articles requiring some other form and must be signed but not sealed: s 2 Stock Transfer Act 1963. Transactions on The Stock Exchange are effected using sold transfer and bought transfer forms.

5.1 Transfer procedures in unlisted companies

The unlisted company transfer procedure is that the registered holder (the 'seller') completes and signs the stock transfer form and delivers it with his share certificate to the transferee (the 'buyer') who completes the transfer and pays stamp duty before delivering it together with the seller's share certificate to the company for registration. The buyer becomes the holder and legal owner of the shares only when his name is entered in the register of members: s 22. The company issues to him a new share certificate within two months (s 185) and cancels the old one.

5.2 Transfer procedure for Stock Exchange transactions

Since 1996, listed companies have been able to make their shares eligible for CREST, the Stock Exchange's electronic shareholding and transfer system. The members of the company are entitled to reject membership of CREST.

The main feature of CREST is that anyone dealing on the stock market will be able to hold shares in electronic form, rather than on paper. Electronic holdings can be quickly, cheaply and safely exchanged for money in CREST when shares are bought and sold.

The CREST system operator will instruct the company secretary to amend the share register when a transaction occurs. The company secretary must follow the instructions and must confirm to the CREST system operator that this has happened.

Activity 4 **(10 minutes)**

In Re Holders Investment Trust Ltd 1971, a scheme to substitute unsecured loan stock for preference shares was voted through by the holders of the vast majority of preference shares, because they (as holders of 52% of the ordinary shares) would benefit overall. On what ground to you think the court forbade the change in preference shareholders' rights?

5.3 Restrictions on transfer of shares

Although it is no longer legally necessary to do so the articles of private companies usually provide that the directors may refuse to register a transfer of any share, whether fully or partly paid. The articles of a public company may impose this restriction but the company cannot have a Stock Exchange listing for its shares if the transfer of fully paid shares is restricted.

If the directors have a power under the articles to refuse a transfer they should exercise that power properly. Otherwise the transfer must be registered and the court may order rectification of the register for that purpose.

(a) To exercise their power the directors must consider the transfer and take an active decision to refuse to register it.

(b) The directors in reaching their decision must act bona fide in what they consider to be the interest of the company. But the court is reluctant to intervene.

(c) The articles should either authorise the directors to refuse in their absolute discretion to register a transfer, or specify grounds of refusal.

(d) The power of refusal must be exercised within a reasonable time from the receipt of the transfer. A company is required to give notice of any refusal within two months: s 183(5).

In *Popely v Planarrive Ltd 1996* the court reinforced the rule that they would uphold provisions in a company's articles giving directors the right to refuse share transfers, provided they act bona fide within their powers. The fact that the directors are ill-disposed towards the transferee is irrelevant.

The articles may also restrict the right of transfer of shares by giving to members a right of first refusal of the shares which other members may wish to transfer. Any such rights are strictly construed. A member who wishes to accept such shares must observe the terms of the articles; a member wishing to sell shares will not be permitted to evade his obligation to make the offer.

6 SHARE CERTIFICATES

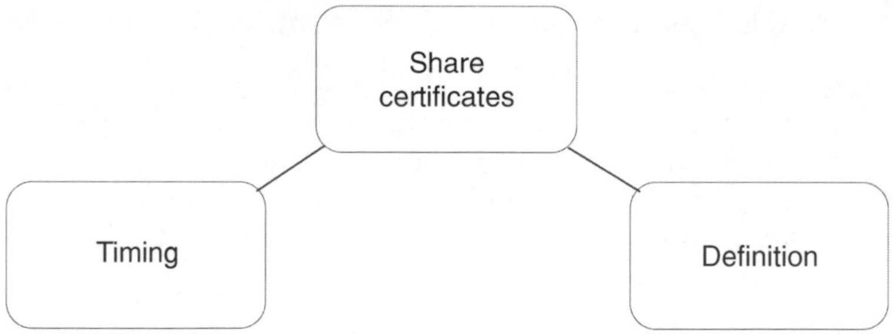

Within two months of allotting shares or receiving a transfer a company must have ready for delivery a certificate of the shares allotted or transferred (unless the transfer is rejected). This is a formal written declaration that the person named is entered in the register as the holder of the shares specified: s 185. A company listed on The Stock Exchange has the shorter time limit of 14 days.

A share certificate is not a document of title but is prima facie evidence of ownership: s 186. The company therefore requires the holder to surrender his certificate for cancellation when he transfers all or any of his shares.

Activity 5 **(10 minutes)**

In Re Hackney Pavilion Ltd 1924, a company's two directors were unable to agree on whether to register a share transfer, and neither had a casting vote. How would this situation be resolved?

7 MAINTENANCE OF CAPITAL

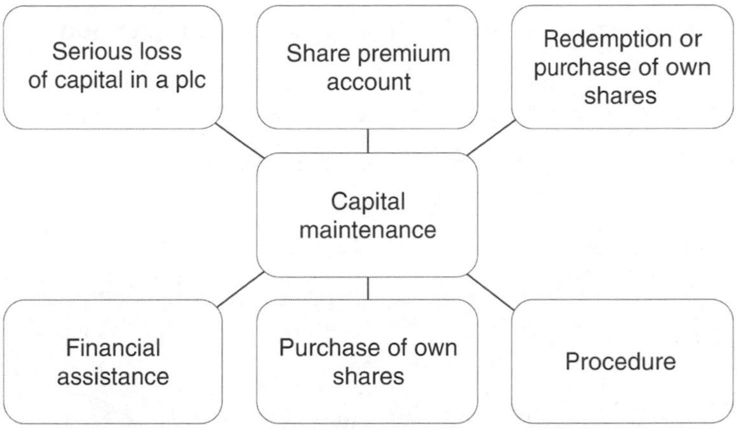

The capital which a limited company obtains from its members as consideration for their shares (and its right to call for payment of the balance (if any) still owing on its shares) is sometimes called 'the creditors' buffer'. No one can prevent an unsuccessful company from losing all or part of its capital by trading at a loss. But insofar as subscribed capital remains in the hands of the company it must be held for the payment of the company's debts and may not be returned to members (except under procedures which safeguard the interest of creditors). That is the price which members of a limited company are required to pay for the protection of limited liability. They cannot be compelled to pay more than the amount due on their shares but they cannot recover what they or their predecessors have subscribed for the shares unless the company's debts have been paid.

7.1 Share premium account

A company which obtains for its shares a consideration in excess of their nominal value must transfer the excess to a share premium account: s 130.

The permitted uses of share premium are:

(a) to make an issue of fully paid bonus shares;

(b) to make an authorised reduction of capital. Such reductions are strictly controlled;

(c) to pay capital expenses, such as the preliminary expenses of forming the company;

(d) to pay a discount on the issue of debentures;

(e) to pay a premium (if any) on the redemption of shares or debentures: s 130(2).

Private companies (but not public companies) may also use a share premium account in purchasing or redeeming their own shares out of capital. This procedure is strictly controlled.

7.2 Redemption or purchase by a company of its own shares

There is a general prohibition against any voluntary acquisition by a company of its own shares, though there is no objection to accepting a gift: s 143.

The prohibition is subject to exceptions. A company may:

(a) purchase its own shares in compliance with an order of the court;

(b) issue redeemable shares and then redeem them (out of distributable profits or the proceeds of a new issue);

(c) purchase its own shares under certain specified procedures; and

(d) forfeit or accept the surrender of its shares.

7.3 Purchase of own shares

Companies are allowed to purchase shares provided certain safeguards are followed. A limited company may now purchase its own shares (whether issued as redeemable or irredeemable):

(a) out of profits or the proceeds of an issue of new shares; or
(b) if it is a private company, out of capital.

For redemption or purchase of shares out of capital there is a long and involved procedure which includes the following steps.

(a) A statutory declaration must be made by the directors (supported by a report of the auditors) to the effect that after the payment is made the company will be able to pay its debts and to carry on its business for at least a year to come: s 173; these must also be delivered to the registrar: s 195.

(b) Shareholders must approve the payment by passing a special resolution. In this decision any vendor of shares may not use the votes attached to the shares which he is to sell to the company: s 173.

(c) A member who did not vote for the resolution and a creditor (for any amount) may within five weeks apply to the court to cancel the resolution (which may not be implemented until the five weeks have elapsed): s 176.

(d) A notice must be placed in the London Gazette and in an appropriate national newspaper, or every creditor must be informed: s 175.

If the company goes into insolvent liquidation within a year of making a payment out of capital the persons who received the payment and the directors who authorised it may have to make it good to the company.

Activity 6 **(10 minutes)**

Why are elaborate precautions not needed when a company buys its own shares out of profits or the proceeds of an issue of new shares?

7.4 Financial assistance for purchase of own shares

Giving financial assistance to a third party to enable him to buy the company's shares can take many forms. Hence it is difficult to prohibit altogether or to regulate. The relevant rules (ss 151-158) comprise:

(a) a general prohibition;

(b) a procedure by which a private company may give such assistance;

(c) a complex set of definitions and exceptions intended to determine which transactions are or are not prohibited.

Subject to exceptions it is not lawful for a company to give any financial assistance for the purpose of the acquisition of shares either of the company or of its holding company or to discharge liabilities incurred in making the acquisition. The prohibition applies to assistance given either directly or indirectly, before or after, or at the time of the acquisition. 'Financial assistance' is elaborately defined to mean a loan, a guarantee or indemnity or security, purchase of such rights from a third party and 'any other financial assistance given by a company which reduces to a material extent, its net assets': s 152.

Two main tests have to be applied to any suspect transaction.

(a) What was its purpose? It is not objectionable if its principal purpose was not to give financial assistance for the purchase of the shares nor if it was an incidental part of some larger purpose of the company: s 153(1)(a).

(b) What was the state of mind of the directors in approving the transaction? Did they act in good faith in what they deemed to be the interests of the company and not of a third party?: s 153 (1)(b).

A private company may give financial assistance for the acquisition of its own shares or the shares of its holding company, subject to the following conditions of ss 155-158.

(a) The financial assistance given must not reduce the net assets of the company or, if it does, the financial assistance is to be provided out of distributable profits.

(b) There must be a statutory declaration of solvency by the directors of the company (with a report by the auditors) of the same type as is prescribed when a private company purchases its own shares by a payment out of capital.

(c) A special resolution must be passed to approve the transaction. Normally this is a resolution of the company which gives the assistance. But if that company is a wholly owned subsidiary which assists the acquisition of shares of its holding company the members of the latter company must pass the resolution.

(d) A right to apply to the court is given to members holding at least 10% of the issued shares (or of a class of shares). To permit them to exercise this right there is a four week delay in the implementation of the resolution.

Three other specific exceptions are made. A company is not prohibited from entering into any of the following transactions: s 153(4).

(a) Making a loan, if lending is part of its ordinary business and the loan is made in the ordinary course of its business. This exception is restricted to money-lending companies, but it would permit a bank to make a loan to a customer on standard terms even though he then used the money to invest in shares of the bank;

(b) Providing money in good faith and in the best interests of the company for the purpose of an employees' share scheme or for other share transactions by bona fide employees or connected persons;

(c) Making loans to persons (other than directors) employed in good faith by the company with a view to those persons acquiring fully paid shares in the company or its holding company to be held by them as beneficial owners.

7.5 Loss of capital in a public company

If the net assets of a public company are half or less of the amount of its called up share capital there must be an extraordinary general meeting: s 142. This is because the company has large accumulated losses.

The duty to call the meeting arises as soon as any of the directors comes to know of the problem. When the directors' duty arises they must issue a notice to convene a meeting within 28 days of becoming aware of the need to do so. The meeting must be convened for a date within 56 days of their coming to know the relevant facts. The purpose of this procedure is to enable shareholders to consider 'whether any, and if so what, measures should be taken to deal with the situation'.

Activity 7 **(10 minutes)**

A borrows money to buy shares in a manufacturing company, which is a public company and is not her employer. The loan is for five years, but the lender may demand early repayment. The lender does so, because he is concerned that A may soon become unable to pay her debts. The lender suggests that A asks the company to guarantee the loan, in return for which he will not demand early repayment. He says that the use made of the loan is immaterial, because the purchase of shares has already been made. Would the company be allowed to give the guarantee? Give reasons for your answer.

8 DIVIDENDS

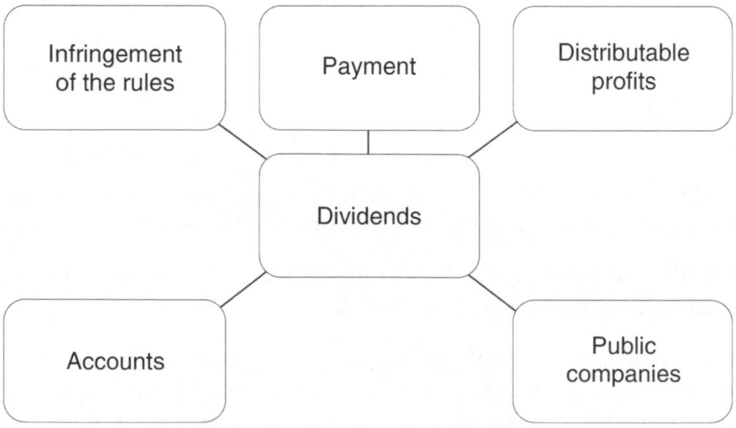

NOTES

8.1 Payment of dividends

Dividends may only be paid by a company out of profits available for the purpose: s 263. The power to declare a dividend is given by the articles which usually follow the model of Table A.

(a) The company in general meeting may declare dividends but no dividend may exceed the amount recommended by the directors: Table A Article 102.

(b) The directors may declare such interim dividends as they consider justified: Article 103.

(c) A dividend may be paid otherwise than in cash: Article 105. Without such a provision, payment must be in cash.

A shareholder (including a preference shareholder) is not entitled to a dividend unless it is declared in accordance with the procedure prescribed by the articles and the declared date for payment has arrived.

8.2 Distributable profits

The profits which may be distributed as dividend are 'accumulated realised profits, so far as not previously utilised by distribution or capitalisation, less accumulated realised losses, so far as not previously written off in a reduction or reorganisation of capital duly made': s 263(3).

The word 'accumulated' requires that any losses of previous years must be included in reckoning the current distributable surplus.

8.3 Dividends of public companies – the full net worth test

The above rules on distributable profits apply to all companies, private or public. A public company is subject to an additional rule which may diminish but cannot increase its distributable profit as determined under the above rules.

A public company may only make a distribution if its net assets are, at the time, not less than the aggregate of its called-up share capital and undistributable reserves. The dividend which it may pay is limited to such amount as will leave its net assets at not less than that aggregate amount: s 264(1).

Undistributable reserves are defined in s 264(3) as:

(a) share premium account;

(b) capital redemption reserve;

(c) any surplus of accumulated unrealised profits over accumulated unrealised losses (known as a revaluation reserve);

(d) any reserve which the company is prohibited from distributing by statute or by its memorandum or articles.

8.4 Relevant accounts

The question of whether a company has profits from which to pay a dividend is determined by reference to its 'relevant accounts' which are generally the latest audited annual accounts: s 270. Relevant accounts must be properly prepared in accordance with the requirements of the Companies Acts. If the auditor has qualified his report on the accounts he must also state in writing whether, in his opinion, the subject matter of his qualification (if it relates to statutory accounting requirements) is material in determining whether the dividend may be paid: s 271.

8.5 Infringement of dividend rules

Any member of a company may apply to the court for an injunction to restrain the company from paying an unlawful dividend. A resolution passed in general meeting to approve it is invalid and does not relieve the directors of their liability.

The company is entitled to recover an unlawful distribution from its members if at the time of receipt they knew or had reasonable grounds for knowing that it was unlawful: s 277. If only part of the dividend is unlawful if it exceeds the distributable profits by a margin, it is only the excess which is recoverable. If a member knowingly receives an improperly paid dividend a derivative action cannot be brought by him against the directors.

The directors are liable to make good to the company the amount unlawfully distributed as dividend if they caused an unlawful dividend:

(a) if they recommend or declare a dividend which they know is paid out of capital;

(b) if without preparing any accounts they declare or recommend a dividend which proves to be paid out of capital;

(c) if they make some mistake of law or interpretation of the memorandum or articles which leads them to recommend or declare an unlawful dividend. But in such cases the directors may well be entitled to relief under s 727 (acts performed 'honestly and reasonably').

The directors may however honestly rely (in declaring or recommending a dividend) on proper accounts which disclose an apparent distributable profit out of which the dividend can properly be paid. They are not liable if it later appears that the assumptions or estimates used in preparing the accounts, although reasonable at the time, were in fact unsound.

Activity 8 **(10 minutes)**

In year 1 H Ltd suffers a realised loss of £1,000. In year 2 it has a realised profit of £9,000 and pays dividends totalling £4,700. In year 3 it suffers a realised loss of £500.

What total dividend could be paid at the start of year 4? How is this calculated?

Chapter roundup

- Every company has an authorised share capital, an issued share capital, a called up share capital and a paid up share capital. All of these amounts may differ.
- Shares may be allotted to investors immediately on application, or alternatively renouncable allotment letters may be issued. The directors normally have power to allot shares, but in a public company they may not be given authority to allot for more than five years at a time. Existing members have pre-emption rights in relation to ordinary shares issued wholly for cash unless these rights have been disapplied.
- The consideration for shares need not be cash, but some forms of consideration are excluded or subject to special restrictions in the case of public companies.
- Shares may be allotted at a premium. A return of allotments must be made. Shares may be issued in rights issues and bonus issues.
- Shares may have different rights attaching to them. The most common distinction is between ordinary shares and preference shares. Preference shareholders have certain standard rights in comparison to ordinary shareholders unless the contrary is stated.
- Class rights may be varied, but a minority may have a right of objection to the court.
- There are standard procedures for the transfer of shares. The directors of a company may be given the power to refuse to register a transfer, but they must exercise such a power properly.
- A share certificate is prima facie evidence of ownership of shares, and a company may be estopped from denying its correctness.
- The paid up capital of a limited company is the investment of the members to which the creditors may have recourse if need be. Its reduction is therefore carefully controlled. Shares may be issued as redeemable and then redeemed, and shares may be purchased, but only in such a way as to maintain the company's capital. A private company may purchase its own shares out of capital subject to certain safeguards designed to ensure the company's continued solvency. The giving of financial assistance by a company for the purchase of its own shares is severely restricted. If a public company suffers a severe loss of capital the members must consider the situation.
- The directors of a company determine what dividends, if any, are to be declared. The members have no right to insist on the payment of a dividend.
- Dividends may only be paid out of accumulated realised profits less accumulated realised losses. Public companies are subject to a further restriction, the full net worth test. The permissible level of dividend payments is determined by reference to the 'relevant accounts'. Excessive dividends may in certain cases be recovered from the members or from the directors.

Quick quiz

1 Distinguish between authorised, issued and called up share capital.

2 What are the statutory rules under which directors may be authorised to allot shares?

3 In respect of which share issues must a company give to its members a right of first refusal?

4 What is a return of allotments?

5 What is (a) a rights issue and (b) a bonus issue?

6 What is the main way in which preference shares differ from ordinary shares?

7 What statutory right of objection exists in favour of the minority of a class who have been outvoted at a class meeting held to approve a variation of class rights?

8 In what ways may funds standing to the credit of the share premium account be used?

9 What resources may (a) a public company and (b) a private company use to purchase its own shares?

10 Give examples of transactions expressly excepted from the prohibition on giving 'financial assistance' for the purchase of the company's shares.

11 What are the duties of the directors of a public company whose assets fall to half or less of its called up share capital?

12 What profits may lawfully be distributed as dividends?

13 What is the position of the directors if, after payment of a dividend, it is discovered that they have recommended or declared a dividend which is not covered by sufficient distributable profits?

Answers to quick quiz

1 Authorised – what the company can issue

Issued – the nominal value of what has been issued

Called-up – the amount of money called up and received for the shares issued (see para 1.1-1.3)

2 Directors must be authorised
Must observe pre-emption rights
Must take proper consideration (para 2.2)

3 Equity shares issued wholly for cash. (para 2.3)

4 A form showing what shares have been allotted, to whom and for what consideration. (para 2.7)

5 Rights issue: allotment of additional shares to existing members, for a payment.

Bonus issue: reserves are used to capitalise issued shares and allot them free of charge to members.

6 Right of dividend
Right of return of capital
Rights to vote at company meetings (para 3)

7 Holders of 15% of the issued shares of the class in question can apply to court within 21 days. (para 4.1)

8 Issue of fully paid bonus shares
Authorised reduction of capital
Preliminary expenses of formation
Discount on issue of debentures
Premium on issue of shares or debentures (para 7.1)

9 Public company: profits or the proceeds of a new issue
Private company: the above plus capital (para 7.3)

10 Making a loan in the normal course of business
Employee share schemes
Loans to buy shares in the company (para 7.4)

11 To call a meeting to discuss the problem within 28 days of becoming aware of it. (para 7.5)

12 Accumulated realised profits less accumulated realised losses. (para 8.2)

13 May have to make good the loss to the company. (para 8.5)

Answers to activities

1 20,000 x £2 x 60% x 70% x 2/3 = £11,200.

2 A new member could obtain control of the company if enough shares were issued to him.

3 100 x 8% x 3 + 500 x £1 x 9% = £69.

4 The holders of the vast majority of the preference shares sought an advantage as members of a different class (the ordinary shareholders).

5 The directors did not take an active decision to refuse to register and therefore the company would be forced to register.

6 There is no reduction of non-distributable capital.

7 No: assistance after the acquisition of shares is forbidden.

8 £(– 1,000 + 9,000 – 4,700 – 500) = £2,800.

NOTES

Assignment 10 **(60 minutes)**

(a) What are the statutory 'pre-emption rights' of the ordinary shareholder where a company proposes to make a new issue of shares? To what types of share issue do pre-emption rights not apply and to what extent can they be excluded?

(b) DEF plc, a company regulated by Table A, has an authorised share capital of £750,000 out of which 250,000 fully paid £1 shares have been issued. The three directors Doris, Edith and Francis each hold 50,000 £1 shares and the remaining shares are divided equally between ten other shareholders. The directors realise that the company is undercapitalised and a fresh issue of shares is necessary. They ask you to attend a board meeting at which they inform you that they are proposing to make a rights issue of a further 250,000 £1 shares.

They ask your advice on the following points.

(i) Do they need authority to issue the new shares? If so, how do they obtain that authority?

(ii) As they, as shareholders, intend to take advantage of the pre-emption provisions, does the fact that they are also directors present any difficulties and, if so, how should they deal with the situation?

(iii) What registration requirements will they have to observe on the assumption that the issue is successfully effected?

Chapter 15 :
LOAN CAPITAL AND CHARGES

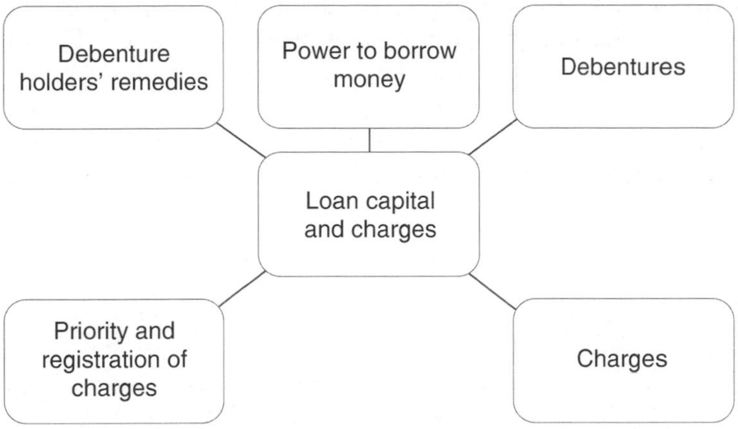

Introduction

In the previous chapter we looked at aspects of share capital. You should be aware that capital is also provided by lenders who provide loan capital by taking debentures or debenture stock.

Loan capital is less closely regulated than share capital. Furthermore, it will become apparent in this chapter that the interests and position of a provider of loan capital are very different from those of a shareholder.

Your objectives

In this chapter you will learn about the following.

(a) The powers a company has to borrow money

(b) Debentures and the role of a debenture trust deed

(c) Fixed and floating charges

(d) The rules on the priority of charges and on the registration of charges

(e) The ways in which debentureholders may enforce a company's obligations to them

1 BORROWING

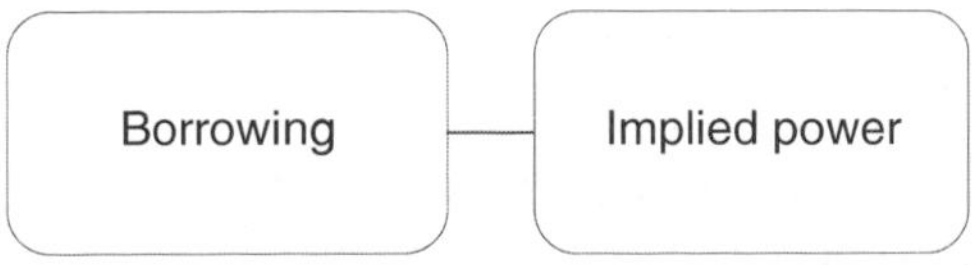

A company whose objects are to carry on a trade or business has an implied power to borrow for purposes incidental to the trade or business. The objects clause, however, nearly always contains an express power to borrow. It is usual not to impose any maximum amount on the company's capacity to borrow (though it is possible to do so). In delegating the company's power to borrow to the directors it is usual, and essential in the case of a company whose shares are listed on The Stock Exchange, to impose a maximum limit on the borrowing arranged by directors.

If there is a power to borrow there is also a power to create charges over the company's assets as security for the loan.

A public company initially incorporated as such cannot borrow money until it has obtained a certificate under s 117. Only a public company may offer its debentures to the public and any such offer is a prospectus; if it seeks a listing on The Stock Exchange then the rules on listing particulars must be followed.

2 DEBENTURES

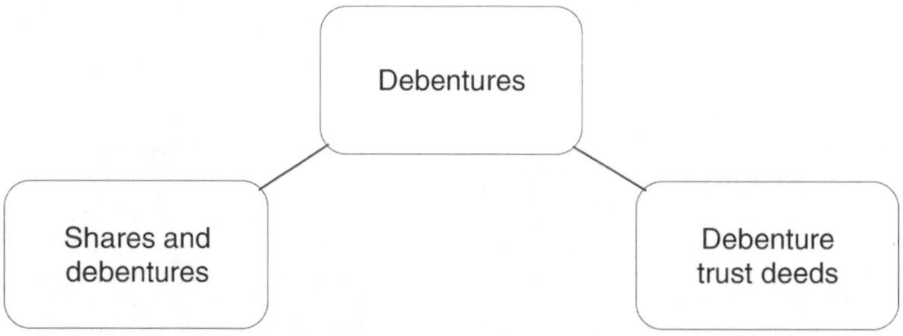

Any document which states the terms on which a company has borrowed money is a debenture (a written acknowledgement of a debt): s 744. It may create a charge over the company's assets as security for the loan. However, a document relating to an unsecured loan is also a debenture in company law (though often called an unsecured loan note in the business world to distinguish it from a secured debenture).

2.1 Debenture trust deeds

A company may create a debenture trust deed. It is usually a long and elaborate legal document whose main elements are as follows.

(a) A trustee for prospective debentureholders is appointed.

(b) The nominal amount of the debenture stock is defined, which is the maximum amount which may be raised then or later. The date or period of payment is specified, as is the rate of interest and interest payment dates.

(c) If the debenture stock is secured the deed creates a charge or charges over the assets of the company (and often of its subsidiaries which are parties to the deed for that purpose).

(d) The trustee is authorised to enforce the security in case of default and, in particular, to appoint a receiver with suitable powers of management.

(e) The company enters into various covenants, for instance to keep its assets fully insured or to limit its total borrowings; breach is a default by the company.

(f) There are provisions for a register of debentureholders, transfer of stock, issue of stock certificates, and meetings of debentureholders at which extraordinary resolutions passed by a three-quarters majority are decisions binding on all debentureholders.

2.2 Comparison of shares and debentures

There are important differences between shares and debentures.

(a) A shareholder is a proprietor or owner but a debentureholder is a creditor of the company. As a member a shareholder may vote at general meetings; a debentureholder has no such right, though exceptionally he may have votes if the Articles and the deed allow.

(b) In the event of liquidation debentures, like other debts, must be repaid in full before anything is distributed to shareholders.

(c) Interest at the agreed rate must be paid on debentures even if it is necessary to pay out capital in doing so. A shareholder only receives dividends if they can be paid out of distributable profits and the company decides to declare a dividend.

(d) A company has no statutory restriction on redeeming or purchasing its debentures (unless prohibited by the terms of the debenture). It may usually re-issue debentures which have been redeemed. There are elaborate rules to regulate the redemption or purchase by a company of its own shares.

Activity 1 **(10 minutes)**

A company offers 10% preference shares and 7% debentures to investors. Ignoring tax considerations and the repayment of capital, why might an investor prefer the debentures?

3 CHARGES

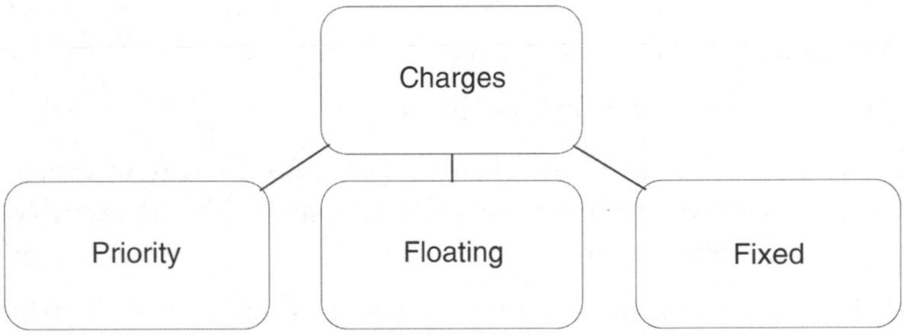

A charge over a company's assets gives to the creditor (called the 'chargee') a prior claim (over other creditors) to payment of his debt out of those assets. Charges are of two kinds.

(a) Fixed or specific charges attach to the relevant asset as soon as the charge is created. A fixed charge is best suited to fixed assets which the company is likely to retain for a long period, because the company is not allowed to trade those assets without the consent of the chargeholder.

(b) Floating charges do not attach to the relevant assets until the charges crystallise.

A floating charge attaches to all the company's assets of the relevant description at the time of crystallisation, so it may be given over current assets. A floating charge over 'the undertaking and assets' of a company (the most common type) applies to fixed assets as well as to current assets. Assets which are the subject of a floating charge can be traded by the company (for example stocks).

EXAMPLE: TYPES OF CHARGE

B plc obtained a substantial loan from A plc on 1 January 2000. The loan is secured by the following charges which are set out in the bank's standard form of debenture document and which were registered at Companies House on 18 January 2000.

(a) A charge over the company's freehold land. The company is not free to sell, lease or in any way deal with the land without A's express permission.

(b) A charge over the company's book debts now and from time to time owing to the company. The company shall immediately pay all moneys received in respect of such debts into the company's bank account and the company may not otherwise deal with the book debts without A's express permission.

(c) A charge over all the company's other assets and undertaking. The company may deal freely with these in the ordinary course of business.

Charge (a) is clearly a fixed charge because the company is not free to deal with the land, and it is a charge over a specific piece of property.

Similarly, charge (b) is a fixed charge because the company is not free to deal with the debts.

Charge (c), however, is a floating charge because the company may carry on business and deal with the assets.

Crystallisation of a floating charge means that it is converted into a fixed charge on the assets owned by the company at the time of crystallisation. Events causing crystallisation are:

(a) the liquidation of the company;

(b) cessation of the company's business;

(c) active intervention by the chargee, generally by way of either appointing a receiver over the assets of the company subject to the security or exercising a power of sale;

(d) if the charge contract so provides, when notice is given by the chargee that the charge is converted into a fixed charge;

(e) automatically on the occurrence of some specified event, without notice from the chargee, if the charge contract so provides;

(f) the crystallisation of another floating charge if it causes the company to cease business.

3.1 Priority of charges

If different charges over the same property are given to different creditors it is necessary to determine their priority so that it is clear whose debt would be repaid first. Leaving aside the question of registration, the main points in connection with the priority of any charges are as follows.

(a) Legal charges (legal mortgages of land or of shares) rank according to the order of creation.

(b) An equitable charge (any charge other than a legal mortgage of land or of shares) created before a legal charge will only take priority over the latter if, when the latter was created, the legal chargee had notice of the equitable charge.

(c) A legal charge created before an equitable one has priority.

(d) Two equitable charges take priority over each other according to the time of creation.

It is always possible to vary these rules by agreement of both creditors.

If a floating charge is created and a fixed charge over the same property is created later, the fixed charge will rank first since it attached to the property at the time of creation but the floating charge attaches at the time of crystallisation.

4 REGISTRATION OF CHARGES

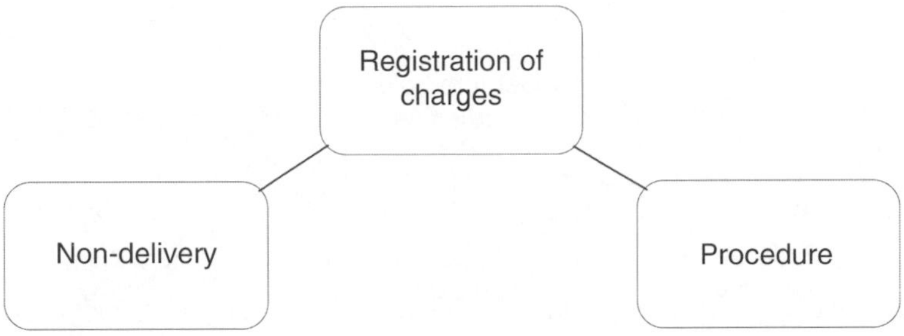

If a company creates a fixed or floating charge over its assets the charge should usually be registered within 21 days of its creation: s 398(1). It is primarily the duty of the company to register thc chargc but particulars may also be delivered by another person interested in the charge: s 398(1).

The registrar files the particulars in the 'companies charges register' which he maintains (s 397) and notes the date of delivery. He then sends copies of the particulars and of the note of the date of registration delivered to the company and chargee: s 398(5).

4.1 The effect of non-delivery

Non-delivery within 21 days results in the charge being void (ie of no legal effect) against an administrator, liquidator or person acquiring an interest in the charged property.

(a) The charge will be void even if insolvency proceedings or the acquisition of an interest in the property occur within the 21 days prescribed for delivery, if the particulars are not in fact delivered during this period: s 399(1).

(b) Creditors who subsequently take security over property and duly register their charge within 21 days will take precedence over a previous unregistered charge. This will be the case even if the later chargee had actual notice of the previous unregistered charge (unless the later charge was expressed as being subject to the earlier charge).

Non-delivery of a charge means that the sum secured by it is payable forthwith on demand, even if the sum so secured is also the subject of other security: s 407(1).

Activity 2 **(15 minutes)**

On 1 January, a company mortgages its factory to A as security for a £50,000 loan. On 1 February the same factory is mortgaged to B as security for a £40,000 loan. On 1 March C takes a floating charge over all the company's assets as security for a £60,000 loan, and on 1 April D takes a floating charge over all the company's assets as security for a £20,000 loan. All charges are registered within 21 days of creation, except that C's charge is not registered.

On 1 August, the company goes into liquidation. The factory is worth £120,000 and the company's other assets are worth £12,000. The company has no other liabilities. How much do each of A, B, C and D receive? Why is this so?

5 DEBENTURE HOLDERS' REMEDIES

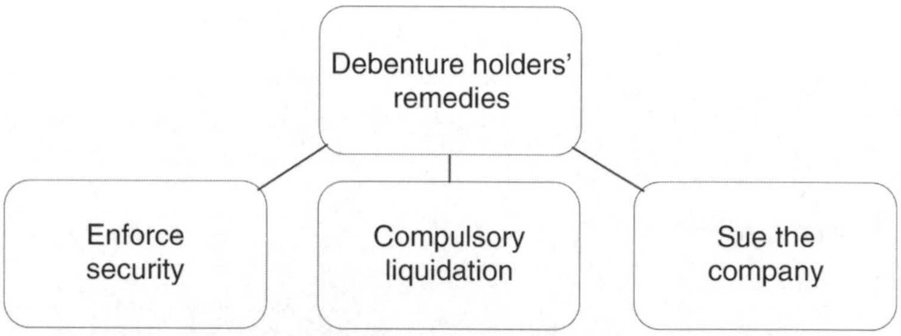

Any debentureholder is a creditor of the company with the normal remedies of an unsecured creditor. He could:

(a) sue the company for debt and seize its property if his judgement for debt is unsatisfied;

(b) present a petition to the court for the compulsory liquidation of the company;

(c) present a petition to the court for an administration order.

A secured debentureholder (or the trustee of a debenture trust deed on behalf of secured debentureholders) may enforce the security. He may:

(a) take possession of the asset subject to the charge if he has a legal charge (if he has an equitable charge he may only take possession if the contract allows);

(b) sell it (provided the debenture is executed as a deed);

(c) apply to the court for its transfer to his ownership by foreclosure order (rarely used and only available to a legal chargee);

(d) appoint a receiver of it.

6 RECEIVERS

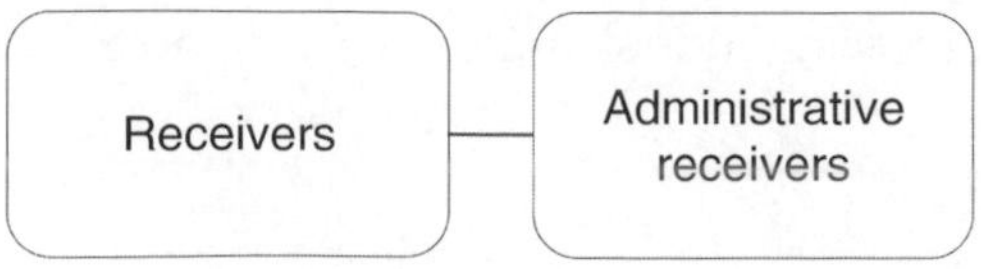

The debenture (or debenture trust deed) usually gives power to the debentureholders (or their trustee) to appoint a receiver in specified circumstances of default by the company. The debenture also provides that the receiver, when appointed:

(a) shall have suitable powers of management and disposal of the assets under his charge; and

(b) shall be an agent of the company and not of the debentureholders by whom he is appointed. The purpose of this stipulation is to safeguard the debentureholders against liability for any wrongful act of the receiver.

A receiver may be appointed under a fixed or a floating charge. He takes control of the assets subject to the charge as a means of enforcing the security for the benefit of the secured creditor by or for whom the receiver is appointed.

6.1 Administrative receivers

A receiver who is appointed under a floating charge extending over the whole or substantially the whole of the company's property is called an administrative receiver. He is in charge of the company's business and therefore he has to manage it, and he must be a qualified insolvency practitioner.

An administrative receiver is automatically given a long list of statutory powers, unless the debenture provides to the contrary. These include powers:

(a) to borrow money and give security;

(b) to carry on the business of the company;

(c) to sell the company's property;

(d) to transfer the business of the company (or part of it) to a subsidiary.

Unless appointed by the court, the receiver is an agent of the company unless or until it goes into liquidation. As agent:

(a) he is personally liable on contracts made in the course of his duties as receiver;

(b) he is entitled to an indemnity for that liability out of the company's assets; and

(c) he can bind the company by his acts.

An administrative receiver is also liable on employment contracts, adoption of which does not require any formal act. Once the contracts have been adopted, for example by continuing to pay wages, regardless of any disclaimer, such contracts have a first charge on the company's assets: *Powdrill & Another v Watson & Another 1994*, better known as the Paramount case. However, the Insolvency Act 1994 restricts liability to certain 'qualifying liabilities' such as wages and salaries, sickness and holiday pay and pension contributions.

The function of a receiver is to manage or to realise the assets which are the security with a view to paying out of those assets what is due to the debentureholders whom he represents (plus the expenses, including his own remuneration). If he is able to discharge these debts he vacates his office of receiver and the directors resume full control.

Activity 3 **(10 minutes)**

A lender to a company takes a fixed legal charge over the company's only premises and a floating charge over the company's assets and undertaking. The company defaults at a time when its premises are worth much less than the debt but the company's inventory is very valuable. How should the lender proceed?

Chapter roundup

- Companies generally have powers to borrow and to create charges over assets.
- A debenture is a written acknowledgement of a debt. An issue of debentures may be accompanied by a debenture trust deed, appointing a trustee to look after the interests of the debentureholders and imposing constraints on the issuing company.
- A debentureholder is a creditor of the company, and the company must pay interest and repay capital on the due dates. A shareholder has no automatic right to the payment of dividends, and share capital is normally only repaid on a liquidation.
- A company may create fixed or floating charges over its assets as security for money borrowed. A fixed charge is given over specific assets, whereas a floating charge attaches to whatever assets of a given class the company has at the time of crystallisation.
- Charges must be registered within 21 days of their creation. There are rules on the priority of charges, and late registration may cause a charge to lose its priority.
- Debentureholders have the usual remedies of any creditor if amounts owing to them are not paid on time. Secured debentureholders may take and sell the assets they have a charge over, or they may appoint a receiver.

Quick quiz

1 State three matters on which a debenture trust deed normally makes provision.

2 What are the characteristics of a floating charge?

3 In what circumstances does a floating charge crystallise and what is the effect of its doing so?

4 In what circumstances will a fixed charge created later than a floating charge take priority over the floating charge?

5 What is the effect of non-delivery of particulars of a charge?

6 What remedies are available to (a) a secured and (b) an unsecured debentureholder?

Answers to quick quiz

1 Appointment of trustee
Amount of debenture stock
Details of charges (see para 2.1)

2 Attaches to assets at time of crystallisation
Assets can be traded
Rank behind fixed charges (para 3)

3 Liquidation of the company
Cessation of company business
Intervention of the chargee
On specified other events (para 3)

4 Always, unless the parties agree otherwise. (para 3.1)

5 The charge will be void. (para 4.1)

6 Secured: take possession and sell the asset, or appoint a receiver
Unsecured: sue the company; act for compulsory liquidation (para 5)

Answers to activities

1 Interest must be paid on time even if the company makes a loss. Dividends need not be paid, even if the company makes a profit.

2 A receives £50,000 and B receives £40,000 because A has the first fixed charge on the factory and B the second. D's charge than takes priority over C's unregistered charge and therefore D receives £20,000 and C receives what is left (£22,000).

3 The lender should appoint a receiver under the floating charge to sell as much of the inventory as is needed to pay the debt.

Assignment 12 **(30 minutes)**

Explain the meaning of the following terms in company law.

(a) (i) Fixed charges
(ii) Floating charges

(b) How do floating charges crystallise?

Chapter 16 : DIRECTORS

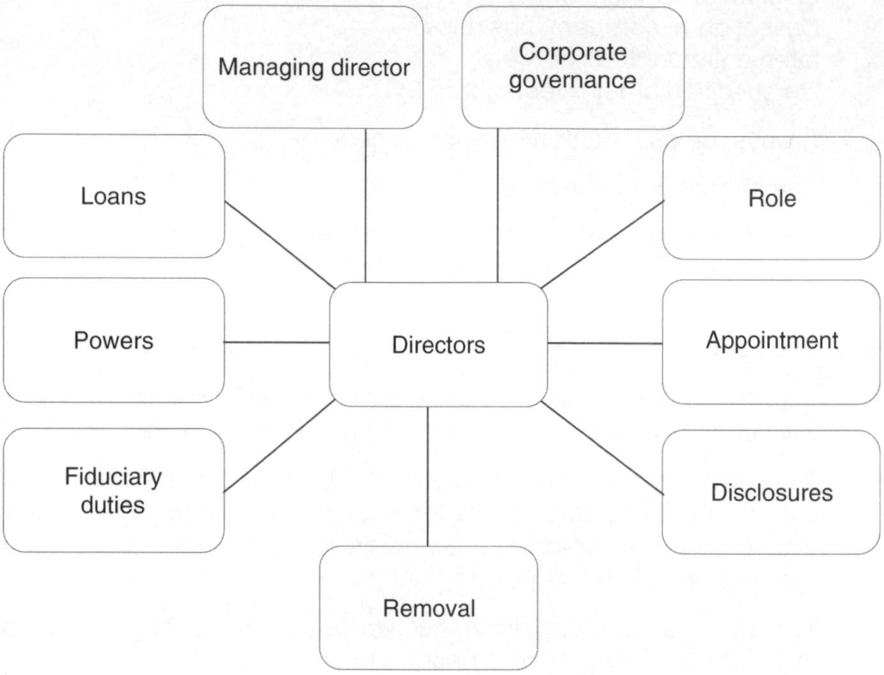

Introduction

Earlier in this book, the idea of a company as an abstract legal person was discussed. As an abstract person, a company cannot manage itself. Company law therefore requires that every company must have one or more directors.

Since directors are in control of the assets of another person (the company) they are subject to an elaborate code of rules. These rules derive mainly from statute and case law, but recently the Cadbury Code and subsequent reports on corporate governance have started to have an influence on directors of listed companies.

Your objectives

In this chapter you will learn about the following.

(a) The role of directors

(b) How directors may be appointed

(c) The rules on the disclosure of directors' shareholdings

(d) The other required disclosures concerning directors

(e) How a director's term of office may come to an end

(f) When a person may be disqualified from being a director

(g) The fiduciary position of directors

(h) The extent of directors' duty of care

(i) The restrictions on directors' interests in company contracts and on loans to directors

(j) The extent of directors' powers and the rules on board meetings

(k) The position of a managing director

(l) How members can control directors

(m) What is meant by corporate governance

(n) The position of outsiders when directors exceed their actual authority

(o) The role of the company secretary

1 WHO AND WHAT IS A DIRECTOR?

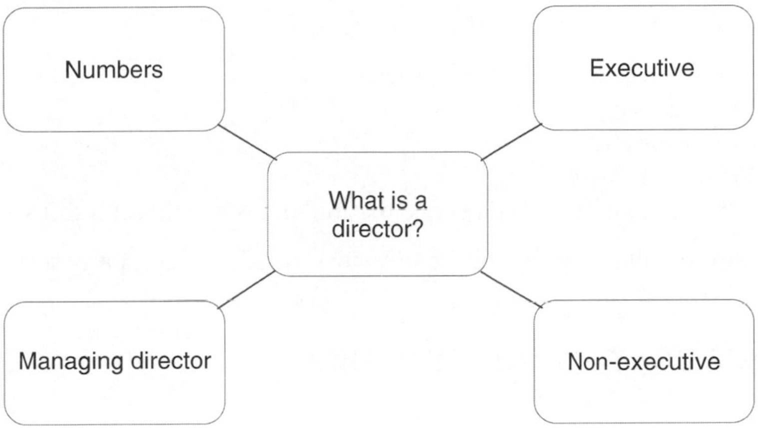

Any person who occupies the position of a director is treated as such: s 741. The test is one of function.

Any person (except a professional adviser) by whose directions the board is accustomed to act (but who is not officially a director) is called a shadow director.

A person appointed by a director to attend board meetings and vote on his behalf is an alternate director.

A director who merely sits on the board, with no additional management duties, is a non-executive director.

If the articles provide for it, a managing director may be appointed.

Every company must have at least one director, and for a public company, the minimum is two: s 282. There is no statutory maximum.

2 APPOINTMENT OF DIRECTORS

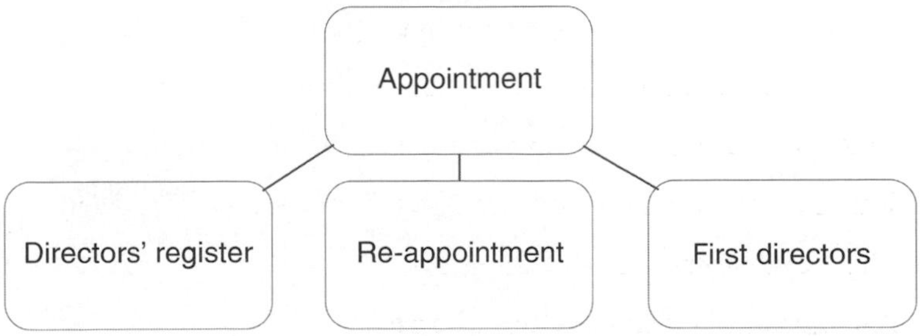

The documents delivered to the registrar to form a company include a form giving particulars of the first directors and signed by them to signify their consent: s 13(5). On the formation of the company those persons become the first directors.

Once a company has been formed any appointment of directors in addition to or in replacement of previous directors is made as the articles provide. Most companies follow Table A in providing for co-option of new members by existing directors and election of directors in general meeting. Table A also provides (Articles 73 – 80) for rotation (retirement and re-election) of directors. However, the articles may exclude retirement by rotation or permit some person, such as the holding company or a major shareholder, to appoint one, several or all directors. It is a matter of choosing whichever procedure is convenient.

2.1 Register of directors and secretaries

A company must keep at its registered office, where any person may inspect it, a register of its directors and secretaries showing:

(a) the name of each director/secretary;
(b) his address;
(c) his nationality;
(d) his date of birth;
(e) particulars of his business occupation and other directorships.

Items (c), (d) and (e) above apply only to directors, not to the company secretary.

3 DIRECTORS AS SHAREHOLDERS

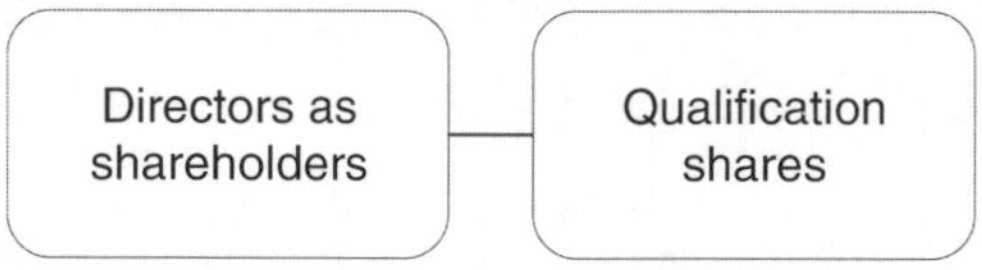

There is no general rule that a director must be a shareholder nor any rule which prohibits him from being one. The articles may however require that each director shall be the registered holder of a specified number of shares (called 'qualification shares').

If a director does hold shares or debentures, he is required to give notice to the company and the company must enter the information in a register of directors' interests which is kept with the register of members (normally at the registered office) and is similarly open to public inspection.

4 DISCLOSURES CONCERNING DIRECTORS

4.1 Loans to directors

A company may not (subject to exceptions) enter into a loan or similar transaction with a director of the company or of its holding company nor (in the case of a public company or its subsidiary) with a person connected with such a director. If any such loan (whether prohibited or permitted) existed during the year prescribed particulars must be included (subject to limited exceptions) in the annual accounts for the year: s 232.

4.2 Directors' interests in contracts

There are similar requirements for disclosure in the annual accounts of transactions in which a director had a material interest either directly or indirectly (for example through another company): Sch 6 para 1. The other directors may decide whether a director's interest is 'material' (and so requires disclosure).

A company must make available for inspection by members a copy or particulars (if there is no written service agreement) of contracts of employment between the company or a subsidiary with a director of the company: s 318.

There are two exceptions to the general rule (s 319).

(a) If the service contract requires the director to work wholly or mainly outside the UK only brief particulars (the director's name and the duration of the contract) need to be given.

(b) If the contract will expire or if the company can terminate it without compensation within a year, no copy or particulars need be kept available for members' inspection.

More detailed rules now apply to listed companies.

The copy or particulars must be available either at the registered office, or at the principal place of business in England.

Prescribed particulars of directors' emoluments must be given in the accounts and also particulars of any compensation for loss of office and directors' pensions: Sch 5.

5 THE TERMINATION OF DIRECTORSHIPS

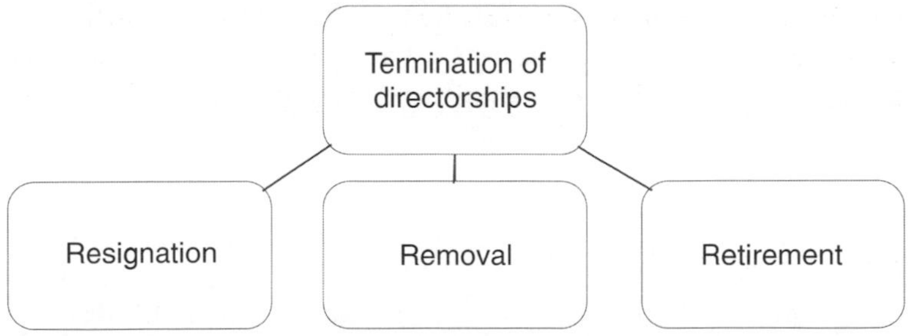

A director may always vacate his office by resignation (Table A Article 81 provides for resignation by notice in writing given to the company) or by not offering himself for re-election when his previous term of office ends under the rotation rules. Obviously office is also vacated on the death of a director or on the dissolution of the company. In addition there are statutory provisions for removal from office and for disqualification.

The articles may provide for the removal of a director from office. But if the director also has a service agreement he may still be entitled to compensation for its breach by his dismissal.

NOTES

In addition to any provisions of the articles for removal of directors, a director may be removed from office by ordinary resolution of the members (passed by a simple majority) of which special notice to the company has been given by the person proposing it: s 303. On receipt of the special notice the company must send a copy to the director who may require that a memorandum of reasonable length shall (unless it is defamatory) be issued to members; he also has a right to address the meeting at which the resolution is considered: s 304.

This statutory power of removal overrides the articles and any service agreement (but the director may claim damages for breach of the agreement). The power is, however, limited in its effect in two ways.

(a) A member who gives special notice to remove a director cannot insist on the inclusion of his resolution in the notice of a meeting unless he qualifies by representing members who either have one-twentieth of the voting rights or are at least 100 members on whose shares an average of at least £100 has been paid up: s 376.

(b) A director may be irremovable if he has weighted voting rights and can prevent the resolution from being passed.

Retirement of directors

A director of a public company is deemed to retire at the end of the AGM following his 70th birthday: s 293(3). This rule is disapplied if the articles permit him to continue or if his continued appointment is approved by the general meeting. It is the duty of directors to disclose their ages to the company for the purposes of this rule: s 294.

> **Activity 1** **(10 minutes)**
>
> In Bushell v Faith 1969, the company had three members who were also the directors and each held 100 shares. On a resolution to remove a director, that director was to have three votes per share while other members were to have one vote per share. Could a director prevent a resolution to remove him from being put forward? Could he prevent it from being passed?

6 DISQUALIFICATION OF DIRECTORS

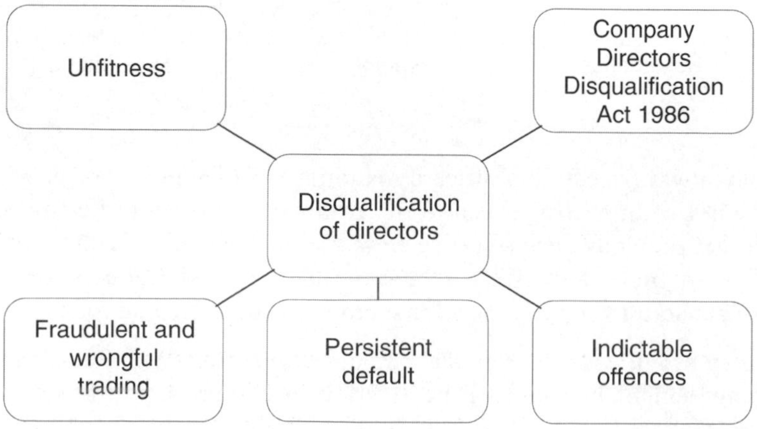

Table A Article 81 provides that a director must vacate office:

(a) if he is disqualified by the Act or any rule of law (for example, if he ceases to be the registered holder of qualification shares);

(b) if he becomes bankrupt or enters into an arrangement with his creditors;

(c) if he becomes of unsound mind;

(d) if he resigns by notice in writing;

(e) if he is absent for a period of six consecutive months from board meetings held during that period without obtaining leave of absence and the other directors resolve that he shall on that account vacate office.

6.1 Statutory disqualification of directors

The Company Directors Disqualification Act 1986 (CDDA) provides that a court may disqualify any person from being without leave of the court a director (including a shadow director), liquidator, administrator, receiver or manager of a company's property or in any way directly or indirectly being concerned or taking part in the promotion, formation or management of a company: s 1. The terms of the disqualification order are thus very wide. They have been held to include acting as a consultant to a company.

The court *may* make an order on any of the following grounds.

(a) *Where a person is convicted of an indictable offence in connection with the promotion, formation, management or liquidation of a company* or with the receivership or management of a company's property: s 2. An indictable offence is an offence which may be tried at a crown court; it is therefore a serious offence. It need not actually have been tried on indictment (at the crown court) but if it was, the maximum period for which the court can disqualify is 15 years compared with only five years if the offence was dealt with summarily (at the magistrates court): s 5. Either the court which convicted the person or the court with jurisdiction in regard to the insolvency (if there is one) may make the disqualification order.

(b) *Where it appears that a person has been persistently in default in relation to provisions of company legislation* requiring any return, account or other document to be filed with, delivered or sent, or notice of any matter to be given to the registrar of companies: s 3. Three defaults in five years are conclusive evidence of persistent default. The maximum period of disqualification under this section is five years.

(c) *Where it appears in the course of the winding up of a company that a person has been guilty of fraudulent trading* (the person does not actually have to have been convicted of fraudulent trading) or has otherwise been guilty, while an officer or liquidator of the company or receiver or manager of its property, of any fraud in relation to the company or of any breach of his duty as such officer, etc: s 4. The maximum period of disqualification under this section is 15 years. The first case to be brought under this section was Re Samuel Sherman plc 1991. The director of a public company had committed a number of persistent and deliberate breaches of important statutory provisions. The period of disqualification chosen was five years.

(d) *Where the Secretary of State acting on a report made by the inspectors or from information or documents obtained under the Companies Act, applies to the court* for an order believing it to be expedient in the public interest. If the court is satisfied that the person's conduct in relation to the company makes that person unfit to be concerned in the management of a company then it may make a disqualification order: s 8. Again the maximum is 15 years.

(e) *Where a director has participated in wrongful trading:* s 10. Maximum 15 years.

Fraudulent and wrongful trading are discussed later in the context of winding up of companies.

The court *must* make an order where it is satisfied:

(a) that a person has been a director of a company which has at any time become insolvent (whether while he was a director or subsequently); and

(b) that his conduct as a director of that company makes him unfit to be concerned in the management of a company: s 6 CDDA.

In such cases disqualification is mandatory, and the fact that alternative remedies are available will not justify refusing to disqualify.

Activity 2 **(10 minutes)**

S was a director of a company which, a month after her resignation, became insolvent. She was also responsible for wrongful trading while a director of another company.

Consider whether she would be disqualified from being a director, if a court considered the matter.

7 FIDUCIARY DUTIES OF DIRECTORS

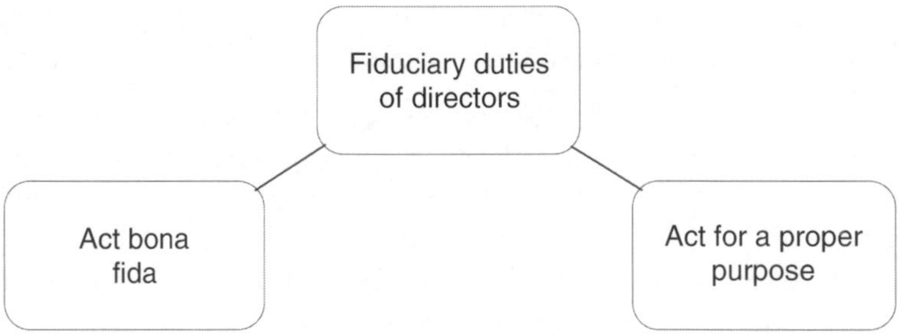

Directors are said to hold a fiduciary position (a position in which they must serve faithfully) since they make contracts as agents of the company and have control of its property.

The directors owe a fiduciary duty to the company to exercise their powers bona fide in what they honestly consider to be the interests of the company. The effect of this rule is seen in cases on gifts made to persons not employed by the company.

Re W & M Roith Ltd 1967
The controlling shareholder and director wished to make provision for his widow, but did not want to leave her shares. His service agreement therefore provided her with a pension for life on his death.

Held: the object of this was to benefit the widow, not the company, and hence could be rescinded.

In exercising the powers given to them by the articles the directors have a fiduciary duty not only to act bona fide but also only to use their powers for a proper purpose.

The directors owe a fiduciary duty to avoid a conflict of duty and personal interest. It is unnecessary to show that the company has been prejudiced in any way by the conflict of interest.

A director may not obtain any personal advantage from his position of director without the consent of the company for whatever gain or profit he has obtained.

> *Industrial Development Consultants Ltd v Cooley 1972*
> C was managing director of the company which provided consultancy services to gas boards. A gas board declined to award a contract to the company but C realised that he personally might be able to obtain it. He told the board of his company that he was ill and persuaded them to release him from his service agreement. On ceasing to be a director of the company C obtained the contract. The company sued him to recover the profits of the contract.
>
> *Held:* C was accountable for his profit.

Activity 3 **(10 minutes)**

In Regal (Hastings) Ltd v Gulliver 1942, the company had an investment opportunity, but insufficient capital. It formed a subsidiary and subscribed some of the necessary capital, while the directors and others subscribed the rest. The result was that the directors made a substantial profit, and the company had lost nothing because it could not have made the investment without their help. However, the directors still had to account to the company for their profit. Which of the above rules on directors' duties was applied?

8 DIRECTORS' DUTY OF CARE

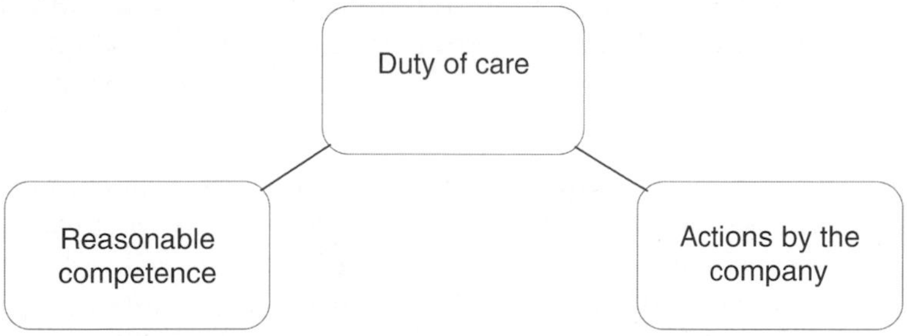

Directors have a common law duty of care to show reasonable competence. A director is expected to show the degree of skill which may reasonably be expected from a person of his knowledge and experience: the standard set is personal to the director.

In the absence of ground for suspicion and subject to normal business practice, he is entitled to leave the routine conduct of the business in the hands of its management and may trust them, accepting the information and explanation which they provide, if they appear to be honest and competent.

8.1 Company's action against negligent directors

The company may recover damages from its directors for loss caused by their negligence. But something more than imprudence or want of care must be shown. It must be shown to be a case of gross negligence.

9 DIRECTORS' DEALINGS WITH THEIR COMPANY

There are several statutory rules forbidding or restricting transactions affecting or involving directors.

9.1 Directors' interests in company contracts

A director shall always 'declare the nature of his interest', direct or indirect, in a contract or proposed contract with the company: s 317. The disclosure must be made to the first meeting of the directors at which the contract is considered or (if later) the first meeting held after the director becomes interested in the contract.

The requirement to declare his interest at a meeting of the company directors also applies in the case of a sole director: *Re Neptune (Vehicle Washing Equipment) Ltd 1995*. In this case it was held that it was especially important for a sole director to consider any conflict of interest and, furthermore, that the word 'meeting' did not exclude sole directors. Compliance with s 317 could be achieved by either holding a meeting alone or with, say, a company secretary. Any declaration must be minuted.

The shareholders' approval is required for any contract or arrangement by which the company buys from or sells to a director of the company or of its holding company or a person connected with any such director property which exceeds £100,000 in value or (if less) exceeds 10% of the company's net assets (subject to a minimum of £2,000 value): s 320.

A company must disclose in the annual report and accounts any contract or arrangement with the company (or a subsidiary) in which a director, directly or through a connected person, has an interest which is material. The other directors may decide that a director's interest in a contract is not material for disclosure. But contracts of a value not exceeding £1,000 or (if greater) not exceeding 1% of the company's assets (subject to a maximum of £5,000) are exempt from this disclosure requirement: s 232 and Sch 6.

If a director's service contract extends for longer than five years and under its terms the company either cannot terminate by notice or can only terminate it in specified circumstances (s 319(6)), the company can in fact terminate it at any time with reasonable notice. However, such a contract will only be valid if it is first approved by an ordinary resolution: it cannot later be ratified.

9.2 Loans to directors (ss 330-338)

Every company is prohibited by s 330 from:

(a) making a loan to a director of the company or of its holding company;

(b) guaranteeing or giving security for a loan to any such director;

(c) taking an assignment of a loan which, if made originally by the company, would have been contrary to (a) and (b);

(d) providing a benefit to another person as part of an arrangement by which that person enters into a transaction forbidden to the company itself by rules (a), (b) or (c).

There are the following general exceptions to these rules.

(a) A company may make a loan or give a guarantee or security in respect of a loan to a director which is also its holding company: s 336.

(b) A company may fund a director to enable him to perform his duties provided that the money is approved in general meeting before or afterwards; if it is made available before approval is obtained, it must be approved at or before the next AGM and must be repaid within six months of that AGM if not so approved: s 337.

(c) A money-lending company may advance money to a director, provided it is done in the normal course of business and the terms are not more favourable than the company would normally allow: s 338.

(d) A company may make a loan of up to £5,000: s 334.

(e) Group members may lend to each other: s 333.

(f) A holding company may make loans to directors of its subsidiaries, provided they are not directors of, nor connected to directors of, the holding company.

Relevant companies

There are more stringent rules for 'relevant companies' which include any public company and any private company which is a member of a group which includes a public company. The same basic rules apply to relevant companies as to other companies. In addition:

(a) the exceptions described in (b) and (c) above are limited to a maximum of £10,000 and £100,000 respectively, although a bank is only restricted to the £100,000 limit if the loan is to buy a residence: s 338;

(b) there are restrictions on indirect means of enabling a director to obtain goods or services on credit;

(c) a company transaction with a third party who is connected with one of its directors is subject to the same rules as apply to its transactions with a director himself.

Activity 4 **(10 minutes)**

A company is to buy from a director a piece of land worth £3,500. The company's net assets are worth £80,000. The other directors consider that the director's interest is material. Must the shareholders approve the contract? Must the contract be disclosed in the annual report and accounts?

10 DIRECTORS' POWERS

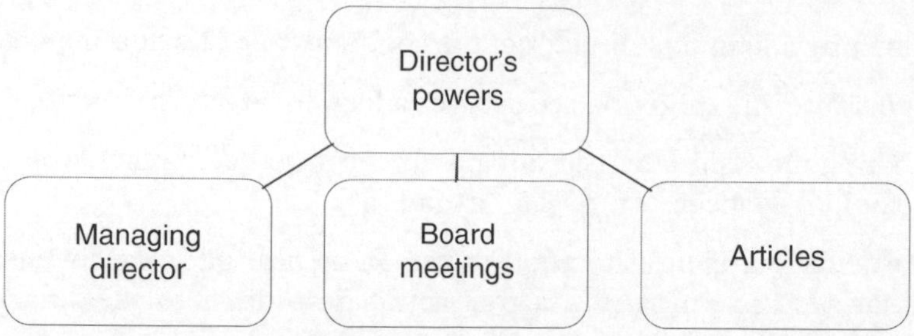

The powers of the directors are defined by the articles. It is usual (Table A Article 70) to authorise the directors 'to manage the business of the company' and 'to exercise all the powers of the company'. They may then take any decision which is within the capacity (as defined by the objects clause) of the company unless either the Act or the articles themselves require that the decision shall be taken by the members in general meeting.

10.1 Board meetings

The articles confer powers on the directors collectively and not upon individual directors (unless appointed as managing directors). The directors should therefore exercise their powers by holding board meetings at which collective decisions are taken.

The articles usually leave the directors free to decide when and how board meetings shall be held. No period of notice is prescribed by law nor need a notice of a board meeting disclose the business to be transacted. Any member of the board may call, or require the secretary to call, a meeting. Reasonable notice should be given to all members sufficient to enable them to attend unless the articles (Table A Article 88) provide that directors who are abroad are not entitled to receive notice.

Minutes must be kept of the proceedings of board meetings and when signed by the chairman are evidence of those proceedings. The directors (and also the auditors for the purpose of their audit) have a right to inspect the minute book. No one else has the right of inspection nor need the minute book be kept at any particular place: s 382.

The directors are usually authorised by the articles (Table A Article 72) to delegate any of their powers to a committee of the board or to a single director either for a specific transaction or as managing director.

10.2 Managing and other working directors

If the articles provide for it (as they usually do) the board may appoint one or more directors to be managing directors. In his dealings with outsiders the managing director has apparent authority as agent of the company to make business contracts. No other director, even if he works full time, has that apparent authority as a director, though if he is employed as a manager he may have apparent authority at a slightly lower level. The managing director's actual authority is whatever the board gives him, and the board may change the limits of that authority, if necessary breaching his service agreement to do so.

11 MEMBERS' CONTROL OF DIRECTORS

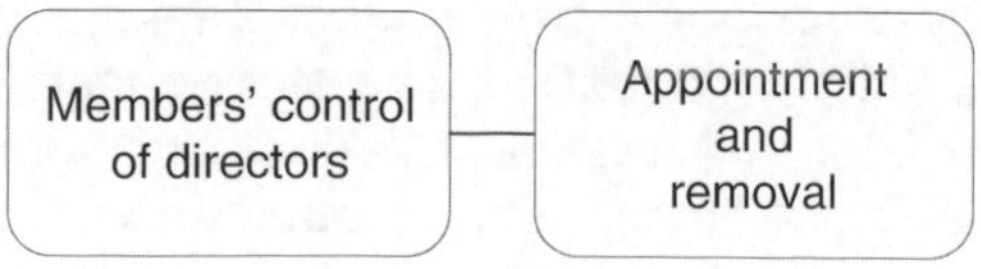

The members of a company appoint the directors and may remove them from office under s 303. They can also, by altering the articles, re-allocate powers between the board and the general meeting. The members therefore have some control over the directors. But the directors are not agents of the members who can be instructed by the members in general meeting as to how they should exercise their powers.

Salmon v Quin and Axtens Ltd 1909
The articles provided that certain transactions should require the approval of both the two joint managing directors. One of them dissented from a resolution which the board wished to pass. The company in general meeting passed an ordinary resolution to 'ratify' the board resolution.

Held: this was 'an attempt to alter the terms of the contract (the articles) between the parties by a simple resolution instead of by a special resolution'. The general meeting could not override a veto given to a managing director by the articles.

John Shaw & Sons (Salford) Ltd v Shaw 1935
In exercise of their general management powers given by the articles the directors began legal proceedings in the name of the company. The defendants, who were shareholders and directors convened an EGM to pass a resolution that the action against them should be discontinued. The board challenged this decision.

Held: the general body of shareholders 'cannot themselves usurp the powers which by the articles are vested in the directors'. The resolution passed by the EGM was therefore invalid.

Activity 5 **(10 minutes)**

In Holdsworth & Co v Caddies 1955 a managing director had a service agreement under which his duties related to several companies in a group. The board confined his duties to one subsidiary. Were they entitled to do so?

12 CORPORATE GOVERNANCE

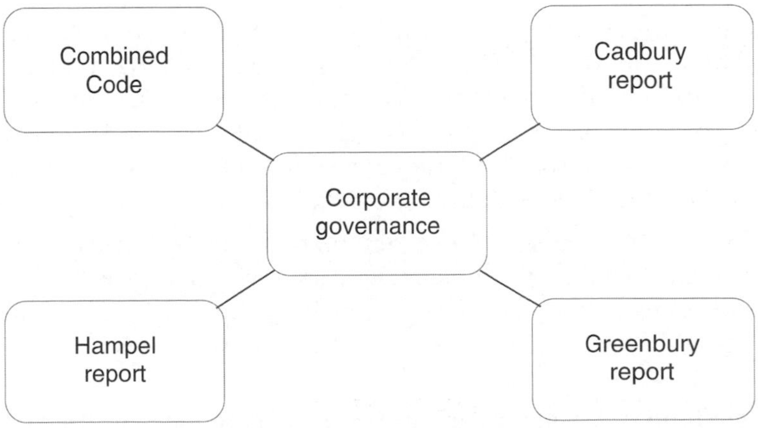

Corporate governance can be defined as the accountability of those who control and manage large public companies to do so for the benefit of the shareholders.

NOTES

12.1 The Cadbury Report

The Cadbury Report defines corporate governance as the system by which companies are directed and controlled, and identifies the three elements of governance as the board of directors, the shareholders and the auditors.

The Cadbury report, with its accompanying Code of Best Practice ('the Code') seeks to clarify and redress the balance between the respective roles and responsibilities of the directors, the shareholders and the auditors. The directors are responsible for corporate governance, the shareholders must see that an appropriate governance structure is in place and the auditors must provide an external and objective check.

The Code itself covers the role and structure of the board of directors, the appointment and independence of non-executive directors, the determination of the executive directors' remuneration and the financial reporting and controls to be exercised by the board.

All Stock Exchange listed companies must now comply with the Code, although it is applicable to many companies, whether public or private.

12.2 The Greenbury report

In 1995, the Greenbury committee's report on directors' remuneration was published. It contained the following recommendations.

(a) **Greater disclosure** in the published accounts of remuneration packages, including full details of options and bonus arrangements

(b) **Remuneration committees** publishing reports to explain why and how they arrived at their decisions for each executive

(c) That **executive share options** are not banned, but made subject to new rules. Proposals include stopping options being offered at a discount and for option prices to be fixed as much as two years after flotation

(d) No **ceiling on commissions** or bonuses payable to directors

It still remains to be seen whether the above proposals will be an adequate remedy for the alleged abuses by 'fat cat directors'.

12.3 The Hampel Report

In January 1996, the remit and composition of the committee on corporate governance formed to succeed Cadbury was announced, the Hampel committee.

The Hampel committee produced a final report in January 1998. The committee followed up matters raised in the Cadbury and Greenbury reports, aiming to restrict the regulatory burden on companies and substituting principles for detail whenever possible. The introduction to the report also stated that whilst the Cadbury and Greenbury reports concentrated on the prevention of abuses, Hampel was equally concerned with the positive contribution good corporate governance can make.

The introduction to the report pointed out that the primary duty of directors is to shareholders, to enhance the value of shareholders' investment over time. Relationships with other stakeholders were important, but making the directors responsible to other stakeholders would mean there was no clear yardstick for judging directors' performance.

The Hampel committee was also against treating the corporate governance codes as sets of prescriptive rules, and judging companies by whether they have complied. The report stated that there can be guidelines which will normally be appropriate, but the differing circumstances of companies mean that sometimes there would be valid reasons for exceptions.

The major recommendations of the report were as follows.

(a) *Directors*

Executive and non-executive directors should continue to have the same duties under the law.

The majority of **non-executive directors** should be **independent**, and boards should disclose in the annual report which of the non-executive directors are considered to be independent. Non-executive directors should comprise at least one third of the membership of the board.

The roles of **chairman** and **chief executive** should generally be **separate**.

All directors should submit themselves for **re-election** at least once **every three years**.

Boards should **assess the performance** of individual directors and collective board performance.

(b) *Directors' remuneration*

Boards should establish a **remuneration committee**, made up of independent non-executive directors, to develop policy on remuneration and devise remuneration packages for individual executive directors.

Boards should try to **reduce directors' contract periods** to one year or less.

The accounts should **include** a **general statement** on remuneration policy, but this statement should not be the subject of an AGM vote.

(c) *Shareholders and the AGM*

Companies should **consider providing** a **business presentation** at the AGM, with a question and answer session.

Shareholders should be able to **vote separately** on each **substantially separate issue**; and that the practice of 'bundling' unrelated proposals in a single resolution should cease.

Companies should **propose a resolution** at the AGM relating to the report and accounts.

(d) *Accountability and audit*

Each company should establish an **audit committee** of at least three non-executive directors, at least two of them independent. The audit committee should keep under review the overall financial relationship between the company and its auditors, to ensure a balance between the maintenance of objectivity and value for money.

Directors should report on internal control, but should not be required to report on effectiveness of controls. Auditors should report privately on **internal controls** to directors.

Companies which do not already have a separate internal audit function should consider the need for one.

(e) *Reporting*

The accounts should contain a statement of how the company applies the corporate governance principles, and should explain their policies, including any circumstances justifying departure from best practice.

(f) *Criticisms of the Hampel report*

Some commentators have criticised the Hampel report for stating that the debate on accountability has obscured the first responsibility of a board, to enhance the prosperity of a company over time. Critics have argued that accountability and prosperity should be seen as compatible. In addition

Hampel has been criticised for dropping the requirement for the board to report publicly on the effectiveness of internal controls and for the auditors to report publicly on the statement made by the board.

12.3 Combined Code

In June 1998 a combined governance code, which was derived from the recommendations of the Cadbury, Greenbury and Hampel reports, was issued. The Stock Exchange Listing Rules were amended to take account of the recommendations of the Combined Code.

The Stock Exchange requires listed companies to include in their accounts:

(a) a **narrative statement** of how they applied the principles set out in the combined code, providing explanations which enable their shareholders to assess how the principles have been applied;

(b) a **statement** as to whether or not they **complied throughout** the **accounting period** with the provisions set out in the Combined Code. Listed companies that did not comply throughout the accounting period with all the provisions must specify the provisions with which they did not comply, and give reasons for non-compliance.

Listed companies are also required to include a **statement** on **directors' remuneration**, which must contain a statement of the company's policy on the remuneration of executive directors, the amount of each element in the remuneration package for the period under review (including salary, benefits in kind, bonuses compensation for loss of office and other information about share options, pensions and service contracts).

12.4 Future developments

At the time of writing, indications are that the government is contemplating certain statutory changes to reinforce the work of the corporate governance committees, but will otherwise let the approach of voluntary compliance alone for now. However Margaret Beckett, when she was Trade and Industry Secretary, stated that there should be an emphasis on growth, investment, accountability and transparency.

13 LIABILITY OF THE COMPANY FOR UNAUTHORISED ACTS OF DIRECTORS

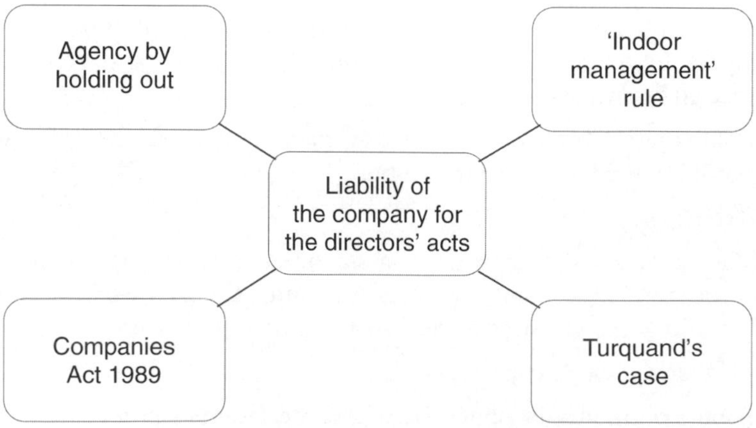

The powers given to 'directors' by the articles are only vested in persons who are directors. If they have not been properly appointed or if they have ceased to be directors they do not have the directors' powers under the articles. But a person who deals with a company through persons who appear to be and who act as directors can usually enforce the contract. It is provided that the acts of a director or manager are valid notwithstanding any defect that may afterwards be discovered in his appointment or qualification: s 285 and Article 92. But to bring this statutory rule into operation there must be an appointment which is later found to be defective. It does not extend to a case where no appointment at all is made or the 'director' has ceased to be a director.

13.1 The 'indoor management' rule

The articles may reserve to the company in general meeting power to authorise certain transactions or impose on the directors some rule of procedure such as fixing a quorum of two or more for board meetings. The rule in Turquand's case is that the outsider who deals with the directors (or apparent directors):

(a) is deemed to be aware of the requirements or restrictions imposed by the articles; but

(b) is entitled to assume (unless he knows or should suspect the contrary) that these internal rules have been observed.

Royal British Bank v Turquand 1856
Under the articles the directors could only borrow for the company such amounts as might be authorised by ordinary resolution passed in general meeting. A resolution was passed but it was defective since it did not specify the amount which the directors might borrow. The directors issued to the bank a debenture for £2,000 believing that they had authority to do so. The bank did not know of the defective terms of the resolution and had no legal right to inspect it since no copy of an ordinary resolution (of this type) is filed at the registry. The company went into liquidation and the liquidator (Turquand) argued that the company had no obligation to repay the loan since the loan contract (debentures) had been made without the authority required by the articles (of which the bank must be deemed to be aware – the doctrine of constructive notice of a company's basic public documents).

Held: the bank must be deemed to be aware that the directors needed authority to borrow but it was also entitled to assume that authority had been properly given since the bank had no means of discovering whether a valid resolution had been passed.

13.2 Turquand's case and the Companies Act 1989

The status of the rule in Turquand's case is questionable in the light of the amendments made to the Companies Act 1985 by the Companies Act 1989. The new ss 711A, 35(1), 35A and 35B all impact on this position. Section 711A abolishes the doctrine of constructive notice as it applies to documents held by the registrar, or made available to the company for inspection. This strikes out a basic premise of Turquand's case. However, s 711A(2) specifically provides that the abolition does not affect the question of whether a person is affected by notice of any matter by reason of a failure to make such enquiries as ought reasonably to be made: that is, a person is deemed to have constructive notice if he did not bother to make reasonable enquiries.

The combined effect of the new provisions certainly overlaps with the rule in Turquand's case. An ultra vires act is now almost always validated. In relation to intra vires actions beyond the delegated powers of directors, it is clear that s 35A covers very similar situations to Turquand's case, and that it applies in some situations where Turquand's case does not.

> **Activity 6** **(10 minutes)**
>
> How might the outcome in Turquand's case have differed if the bank had been a member of the debtor company?

13.3 Agency by holding out

Holding out is a basic rule of the law of agency: if the principal (the company) holds out a person as its authorised agent it is estopped (against a person who has relied on the representation) from denying that he is its authorised agent and so is bound by a contract entered into by him on the company's behalf.

This situation usually results from the board of directors permitting a director to behave as if he were a managing director duly appointed when in fact he is not. As explained above a managing director does, by virtue of his position, have apparent authority to make commercial contracts for the company. If the board allows a director to enter into contracts, being aware of his dealings and taking no steps to disown him, the company will usually be bound.

14 THE COMPANY SECRETARY

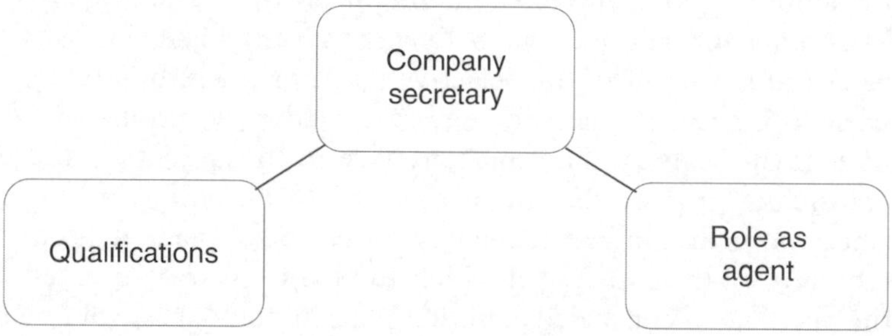

Every company must have a secretary and a sole director must not also be the secretary. The directors of a public company must take all reasonable steps to ensure that the secretary is suitably qualified for his post by his knowledge and experience. Under s 286, a public company secretary may be anyone who:

(a) was the secretary or his assistant on 22 December 1980; or

(b) has been a public company secretary for at least three out of the five years previous to appointment; or

(c) is a member of the Institute of Chartered Secretaries and Administrators or of one of several accountancy bodies; or

(d) is a barrister, advocate or solicitor in the UK; or

(e) is a person who, by virtue of holding or having held any other position or being a member of any other body, appears to the directors to be capable.

The Act does not define the general duties of a company secretary since these will vary according to the size of the company and of its headquarters. The standard minimum duties of the secretary are:

(a) to make the arrangements incidental to meetings of the board of directors. The secretary usually convenes the meetings (Table A Article 88), issues the agenda (if any), collects or prepares the papers for submission to each meeting, attends the meeting, drafts the minutes and communicates decisions taken to the staff of the company or to outsiders, for instance a refusal of the directors to approve the transfer of shares;

(b) to maintain the register of members (unless this work is contracted out to professional registrars), to enter in transfers of shares and to prepare share certificates for issue to members. The secretary also keeps the other statutory registers and prepares the notices, returns and other documents which must be delivered to the registrar.

14.1 The secretary as agent

It is a general principle of agency law that if a person is employed in a capacity in which he does certain things for his principal he has apparent authority to bind his principal by such actions on his behalf, unless the principal has denied him that authority and the other party has notice of the restriction. In 1971 the Court of Appeal applied this principle and recognised that it is a normal function of a company secretary to enter into contracts connected with the administration of the company.

> *Panorama Developments (Guildford) Ltd v Fidelis Furnishing Fabrics Ltd 1971*
> B, the secretary of a company, ordered cars from a car hire firm, representing that they were required to meet the company's customers at London Airport. Instead he used the cars for his own purposes. The bill was not paid, so the car hire firm claimed payment from B's company.
>
> Held: B's company was liable, for he had apparent authority to make contracts such as the present one, which were concerned with the administrative side of its business. The decision recognises the general nature of a company secretary's duties. The court also said that, if the issue had arisen, it might not have treated the secretary as having apparent authority to make commercial contracts such as buying or selling trade goods, since that is not a normal duty of the company secretary.

The Cadbury Report stated that the company secretary also has an important role in corporate governance.

The report states that the secretary has a key role in ensuring that board procedures are observed and regularly reviewed.

The point was also made that the company secretary may be seen as a source of guidance on the responsibilities of the board and its chairman under the new regulations, and on the implementation of the Code of Best Practice laid down in the report.

Activity 7 **(10 minutes)**

Would a company secretary ordering office stationery be likely to be treated as acting with apparent authority in a plumbing company? Why?

Chapter roundup

- A director is a person who takes part in making decisions by attending board meetings, whether or not he is called a director. Directors may also be employees of their company, with contracts of employment. A private (but not a public) company may have only one director, but a sole director may not also be the company secretary.
- Directors are generally elected by the members. Table A provides for the rotation of directors.
- Directors need not be members unless the articles require them to be, but they may be members. Any shareholdings must be disclosed in a register of directors' interests.
- Loans to directors, directors' interests in contracts and the terms of directors' service contracts must all be disclosed.
- A director may resign. He may also be removed from office, either in accordance with the articles or by an ordinary resolution of the members.
- A director may be required by the articles to vacate office in certain circumstances. Any person may be disqualified from being a director under the Company Directors Disqualification Act 1986.
- A director holds a fiduciary position, and must act in the best interests of his company. If he makes a personal profit from his position he may be required to account for it to the company.
- A director has a duty of care, and is expected to show the degree of skill which may reasonably be expected from a person of his knowledge and experience.
- A director must declare any interest he has in a contract with the company, and such interests may have to be disclosed in the annual report and accounts. There are severe restrictions on loans by companies to their directors.
- Directors have the power to manage their company. This power is exercised in board meetings. A managing director has apparent authority to make contracts for the company on his own.
- The members of a company cannot tell the directors how to exercise their powers, but they can remove the directors.
- The acts of an irregularly appointed director are valid. Under the indoor management rule, an outsider is entitled to assume that internal formalities required by a company's articles have been observed. However, this rule is now less important than it was because of legislation contained in the Companies Act 1989.
- If a director is allowed to represent that he is a managing director, he may come to have the apparent authority of a managing director.
- Every company must have a company secretary, and the secretary of s public company must be appropriately qualified. The secretary is effectively the company's chief administrative officer. He has apparent authority to bind the company in administrative contracts.

Quick quiz

1. What is meant by the expressions (a) 'shadow director' and (b) 'alternate director'?
2. What are the rules about the number of directors?
3. What information is available to members concerning the terms of employment of directors?
4. What are the practical limitations on the members' statutory powers to remove a director from office?
5. Give the grounds, included in the Table A model articles, for disqualification of a director from continuing to hold office in the company.
6. Upon what grounds may a director be disqualified by a court order from holding office? When must the court disqualify him?
7. What are the main elements of a director's fiduciary duty?
8. What standard of competence is expected of directors?
9. What are the main exceptions to the general rule against a company making a loan to one of its directors?
10. What is the standard (Table A) formula by which the powers of the directors are defined?
11. Are members in general meeting allowed to exercise powers which under the articles are delegated to the directors?
12. What is 'corporate governance'?

Answers to quick quiz

1. Shadow director – a person by whose directions the directors normally act

   Alternate director – a person appointed by a director to attend board meetings and vote on his behalf (see para 1)
2. All companies must have at least 1
   Plcs must have at least 2 (para 1)
3. A copy of the contract of employment. (para 4.2)
4. The members must form the appropriate minority to table a resolution. The director might have weighted voting rights. (para 5)
5. Disqualified
   Bankrupt
   Unsound mind
   Resigns

   Absent from board meetings for 6 months without consent (para 6)
6. Conviction for an indictable offence

   Persistent default over company documents

   Fraudulent trading

   Wrongful trading

   Must disqualify: conduct as a director of an insolvent company makes him unfit to be a director. (para 6.1)

7 Exercise powers bona fide
Avoid a conflict of interest (para 7)

8 Standard which could be expected from a person of his knowledge and experience. (para 8)

9 Business expenditure
Money-lending company in normal course of business
Up to £5,000 (para 9.2)

10 'To manage the business of the company' and 'to exercise all the powers of the company'. (para 10)

11 No, although they can direct that the Articles be altered. (para 11)

12 The accountability of those who control and manage large public companies to the shareholders of those companies. (para 12)

Answers to activities

1 A resolution to remove a director could be put forward against his wishes, but he could prevent it from being passed (by 300 votes to 200).

2 S might be disqualified, but she need not be (unless her conduct while a director of the insolvent company makes her unfit to be concerned in the management of a company).

3 The rule that directors must not obtain any personal advantage or profit from their position.

4 The shareholders need not approve the contract, but it must be disclosed in the annual report and accounts.

5 Yes: the board may change the limits of his authority despite the consequent breach of his contract.

6 The bank would have known that the required resolution had not been passed, so it would probably have lost its right to repayment of the loan.

7 Yes, because the contract is connected with the administration of the company. If the company traded as a stationer, the contract might be a commercial contract outside the company secretary's apparent authority.

Assignment 13 **(60 minutes)**

Robert and Stephen are the directors of Fabric Ltd. They are the controlling shareholders of the company. Last year Robert and Stephen negotiated a valuable contract with Cotton Ltd, but they diverted this contract to a partnership of which they are the partners. This action was recently disclosed to a general meeting of Fabric Ltd, which duly approved it by passing an ordinary resolution. Both Robert and Stephen voted for the resolution.

Philip and Quentin are directors in Weft Ltd. Last March, Thomas, a senior manager in the company, was discovered to have stolen some office equipment which belonged to Weft Ltd. He was subsequently convicted of theft and fined by the court. In a general meeting the members of Weft Ltd directed that the directors of the company take legal action to recover the office equipment, but Philip and Quentin have so far not done so and appear reluctant to initiate action against Thomas.

Ursula is a minority shareholder in both Fabric Ltd and Weft Ltd and seeks your advice as to what, if any, action she may take in relation to the above two matters. Advise her.

Chapter 17 : SHAREHOLDERS

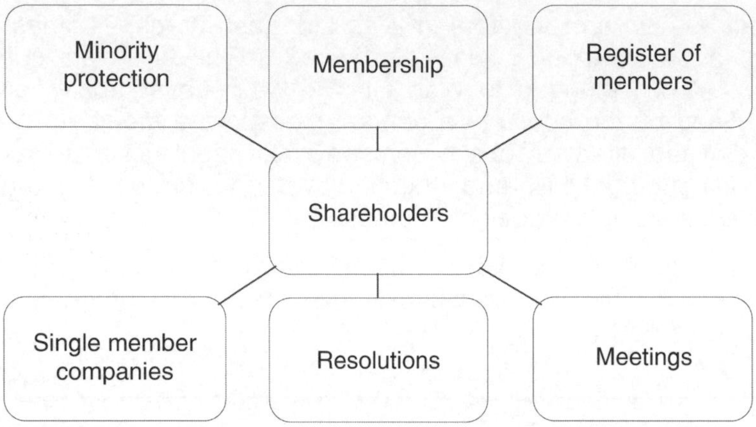

Introduction

In the previous chapter we considered the people who run the company, the directors. We now turn to consider the position of the people who own the company, the shareholders. They may be considered from various different angles, the two main ones being the administration of shareholders via the shareholders' register and the protection of their rights by the use of meetings and resolutions and minority protection.

Your objectives

In this chapter you will learn about the following.

(a) How someone becomes and ceases to be member of a company

(b) The register of members and its contents

(c) The difference between annual and extraordinary meetings

(d) The difference between ordinary, extraordinary and special resolutions

(e) The rules governing elective and written resolutions

(f) The special rules applying to single member companies

(g) How minority shareholders are protected

1 BECOMING A MEMBER

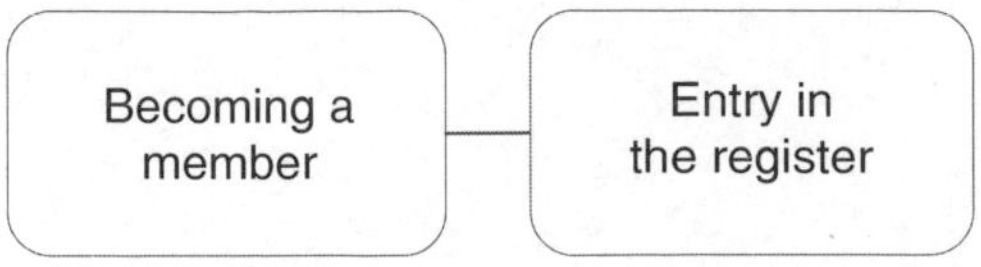

A member of a company is a person who has agreed to be a member and whose name has been entered in the register of members: s 22(2). Entry in the register is essential. Mere delivery to the company of a transfer does not make the transferor a member.

Subscribers to the memorandum are deemed to have agreed to become members of the company. The subscribers are liable to pay an amount equal to the nominal value of their shares unless the company waives its rights against them by allotting all the authorised share capital to other persons.

2 CEASING TO BE A MEMBER

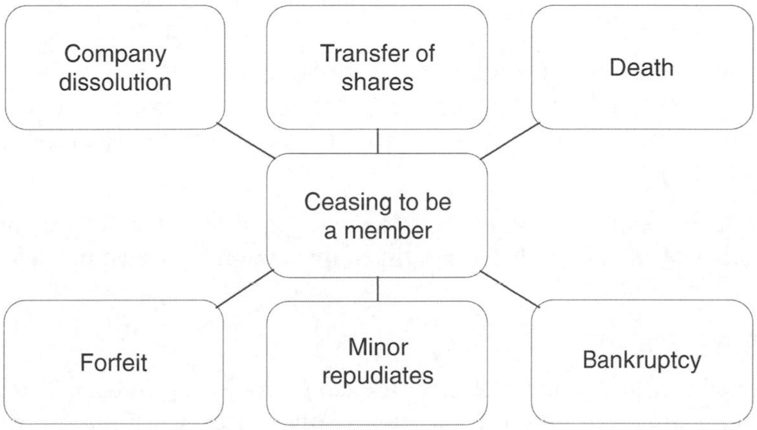

A member ceases to be a member if:

(a) he transfers all his shares to another person and the transfer is registered;

(b) he dies;

(c) he becomes bankrupt and his shares are registered in the name of his trustee;

(d) he is a minor who repudiates his shares;

(e) he is the trustee of a bankrupt member and disclaims his shares;

(f) the company forfeits or accepts the surrender of shares or sells them under a lien;

(g) the company is dissolved and ceases to exist.

3 THE REGISTER OF MEMBERS

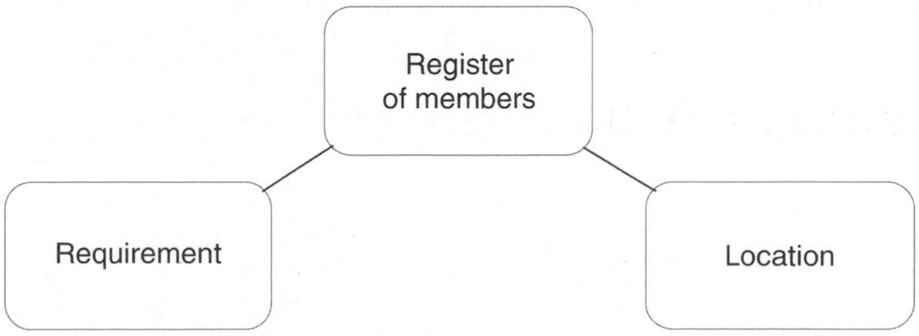

Every company must, under s 352, keep a register of members and enter in it:

(a) the name and address of each member and the class (if more than one) to which he belongs, unless this is indicated in the particulars of his shareholding;

(b) if the company has a share capital, the number of shares held by each member. In addition:

   (i) if the shares have distinguishing numbers, the member's shares must be identified in the register by those numbers; and

   (ii) if the company has more than one class of shares, the member's shares must be distinguished by their class, such as preference or ordinary shares;

(c) the date on which each member became and eventually the date on which he ceased to be a member. The company must preserve entries relating to former members for 20 years from the date of their ceasing to be a member: s 352(6).

Any member of the company can inspect the register of members of a company without charge; a member of the public has the right of inspection but must pay a fee.

3.1 Location of register

To make the right of inspection effective, the company is required to hold its register of members either at its registered office or at any other place at which the work of making up the register is done. But if the register of members is kept elsewhere than at the registered office:

(a) notice of the place at which the register is held must be sent to the registrar (and notice of any change of that address). It must also be shown in the annual return; and

(b) the alternative address at which the register is kept must be within the same country as the registered office.

Activity 1 **(10 minutes)**

J sells all her shares in a company to S. The contract for the sale is made on Monday, S pays J on Wednesday and the transfer is registered on Friday. Which of the two is a member on Thursday?

Why is this the case?

4 SUBSTANTIAL SHAREHOLDINGS

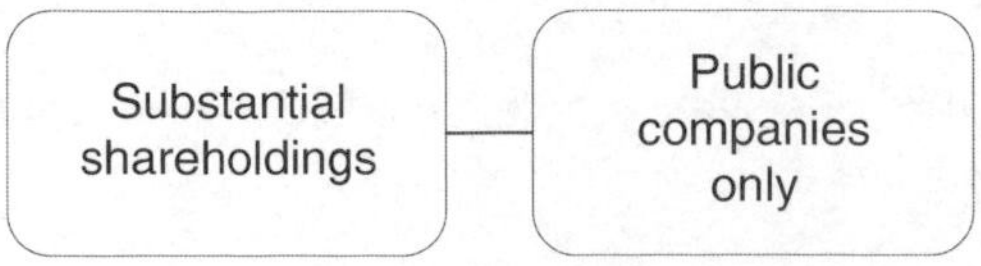

Any person who acquires a notifiable interest in voting shares of a public company must give notice (with prescribed particulars) to the company of his interest: s 198. Thereafter so long as his interest is above the minimum he must give similar notice of all changes: s 202. The company on receiving the information must enter it in a register of interests in shares which is open to public inspection: s 211.

A person has a notifiable interest when he is interested in at least 3% of the shares: ss 198201. Disclosure must be made to the company within two days: s 202. A person has an interest even if shares are held in someone else's name: thus substantial investors cannot conceal themselves by using nominees to hold their shares.

The company may (and on the requisition of 10% or more (in share value) of its members, must) call on anyone (not necessarily a member) to declare whether he has a notifiable interest: s 212 and s 214.

Activity 2 **(10 minutes)**

On 1 June L buys 500 shares in a company with 50,000 shares in issue. On 4 June she buys a further 400 shares, on 12 June she buys a further 700 shares and on 20 June she buys a further 2,000 shares. By what date must she disclose her interest to the company? Why?

5 COMPANY MEETINGS

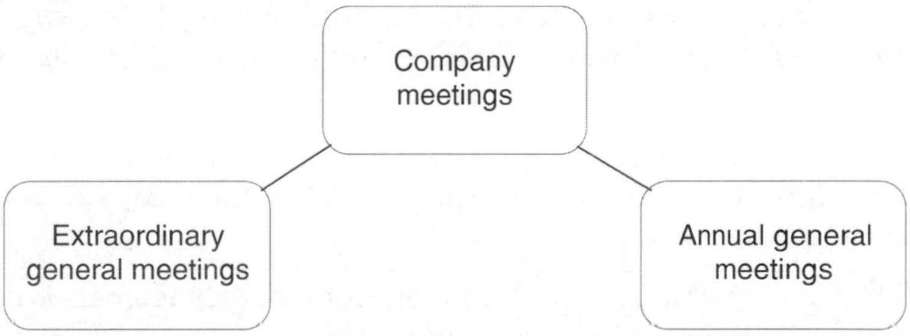

Although the management of a company is in the hands of the directors, the decisions which affect the existence of the company, its structure and scope, are reserved to the members in general meeting.

There are two kinds of general meeting of members of a company, annual general meetings (AGMs) and extraordinary general meetings (EGMs).

5.1 Annual general meetings

The rules are as follows.

(a) Every company must hold an AGM in each (calendar) year.

(b) S 366A allows a private company to dispense with the holding of an AGM by the passing of an elective resolution. An election has effect for the year in which it is made and subsequent years. In any such year affected by the resolution any member, by notice to the company not later than three months before the end of the year, may require the holding of an AGM in that year.

(c) Not more than 15 months may elapse between meetings. But provided that the first AGM is held within 18 months of incorporation, the company need not hold it in the year of incorporation or in the following year.

(d) If a default is made, the Department of Trade and Industry on application of any member may call the AGM and give whatever directions are necessary, even to modify the articles or fix a quorum of one. In this case the company may resolve that this meeting also constitutes the AGM of the year in which it is held: s 367.

(e) A notice convening an AGM must be in writing and in accordance with the articles. At least 21 days' notice should be given; shorter notice is valid only if all members entitled to attend agree.

(f) The notice must specify the meeting as an AGM.

It is usual, but not obligatory, to transact at an AGM the 'ordinary business' of the company if so described in the articles.

5.2 Extraordinary general meetings

The directors have power to convene an EGM whenever they see fit: Table A Article 37.

The directors may be required to convene an EGM by requisition of the members. The rules (s 368) are as follows.

(a) The requisitionists must hold at least 10% of the paid up share capital carrying voting rights.

(b) They must deposit at the registered office a signed requisition stating the objects of the meeting, that is the resolutions which they intend to propose.

(c) If the directors fail within 21 days of the deposit of the requisition to convene the meeting, any reasonable expenses of the requisitionists in convening the meeting are then payable by the company and recoverable from the directors.

(d) The date for which an EGM on requisition of the members is called must be within 28 days of the issuing of the notice.

Activity 3 **(10 minutes)**

Give some examples of events which might lead to an EGM, bearing in mind that the ordinary management of a company is entrusted to the directors and not the members.

Why might the position differ if the company traded as a stationer?

NOTES

6 CONVENING A MEETING

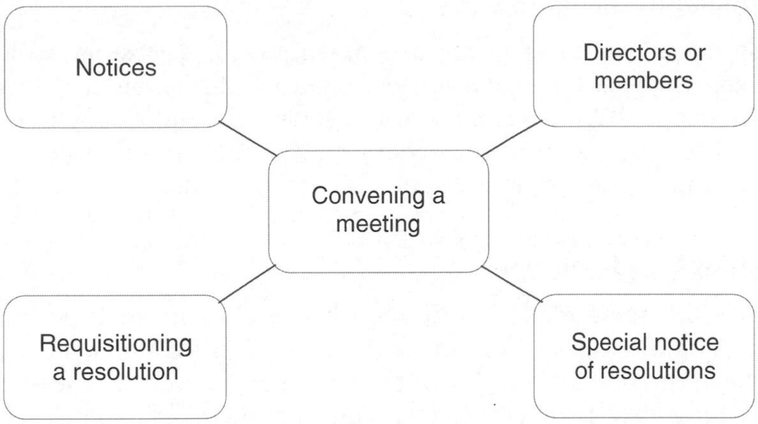

A meeting cannot make valid and binding decisions until it has been properly convened.

(a) The meeting must be called by the board of directors or other competent person or authority. If, however, there is some irregularity in the board meeting which convenes a general meeting and the members in general meeting nonetheless pass the resolutions proposed, this may be taken as a waiver of irregularity.

(b) The notice must be issued to members in advance of the meeting so as to give them 14 days' notice of the meeting (21 days if a special resolution is to be proposed). The members may agree to waive this requirement.

(c) The notice must be sent to every member (or other person) entitled to receive it, but it need not be sent to a member whose only shares do not give him a right to attend and vote (as is often the position of preference shareholders), nor need it usually be sent to a joint holder of voting shares who is not the first named holder on the register. If, however, the business to be done must by law be disclosed to all members (for example proposals to pay compensation to directors for loss of office requiring approval under s 312) then notice of it must be sent even to members who are not entitled to vote on it).

(d) The notice must include any information reasonably necessary to enable shareholders to know in advance what is to be done.

6.1 Special notice of a resolution

Special notice must be given to the company of the intention to propose a resolution:

(a) to remove an auditor or to change the auditor;
(b) to reappoint a director aged more than 70 where the age limit applies;
(c) to remove a director from office or to appoint a replacement after removal.

When special notice is given under s 379 the sequence is as follows.

(a) The member gives special notice of his intention to the company at least 28 days before the date of the meeting at which he intends to move his resolution. If, however, the company calls the meeting for a date less than 28 days after receiving the special notice that notice is deemed to have been properly given.

(b) On receiving special notice the company may be obliged under s 376 to include the resolution in the AGM notice which it issues. But in other circumstances the company (the directors) may refuse to include it in their notice. If the company gives notice to members of the resolution it does so by a 21 day notice to them.

(c) If special notice is received of intention to propose a resolution for the removal from office of a director (under s 303(2)) or to change the auditor (under s 391A) the company must forthwith send a copy to the director or auditor so that he may exercise his statutory right to defend himself by issuing a memorandum and/or addressing the meeting in person.

6.2 Requisitioning a resolution

It usually rests with the directors to decide what resolutions shall be included in the notice of a meeting. But (apart from the requisition of an EGM) members can take the initiative if they represent at least 5% of the voting rights or are at least 100 members holding shares on which there has been paid up an average per member of at least £100. These members may:

(a) by requisition delivered at least six weeks in advance of an AGM require the company to give notice to members of a resolution which they wish to move;

(b) by requisition delivered at least one week in advance of an AGM or EGM require the company to circulate to members a statement not exceeding 1,000 words in length (unless the court declares it to be defamatory).

In either case, the requisitionists must bear the incidental costs unless the company otherwise resolves. The company need not comply if the court is satisfied that the procedure is being used to obtain needless publicity for defamatory material.

6.3 Content of notices

The notice of a general meeting must give the date, time and place of the meeting, and an AGM or a special or extraordinary resolution must be described as such. Information must be given of the business of the meeting sufficient to enable members (in deciding whether to attend or to appoint proxies) to understand what will be done at the meeting.

Activity 4 **(10 minutes)**

D, a shareholder in Q Ltd, wishes to include a resolution in the notice of an AGM about to be sent to members. The directors do not wish to include his resolution. He holds 4% of the votes, but his paid up share capital is £15,000. Can he force the inclusion of his resolution? Why not?

7 PROXIES

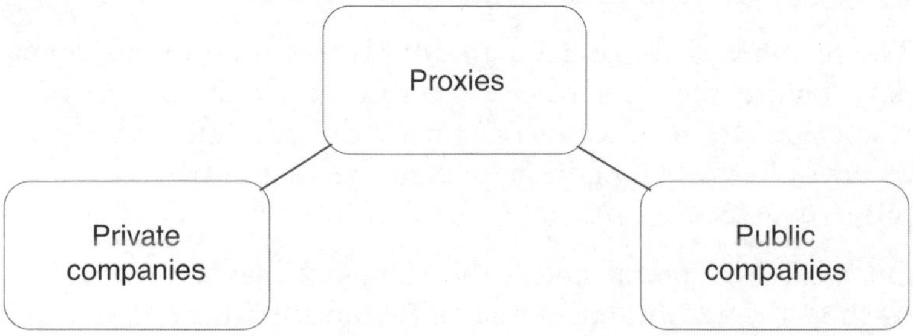

Any member of a company which has a share capital, if he is entitled to attend and vote at a general or class meeting of the company, has a statutory right (s 372) to appoint an agent (called a proxy) to attend and vote for him. The rules are as follows.

(a) A meeting of a *private company* may only appoint one proxy who may, however, speak at the meeting.

(b) A member of a *public company* (who may be a nominee of two or more beneficial owners of the shares whose voting intentions conflict) may appoint more than one proxy but his proxy has no statutory right to speak at the meeting (this is to prevent the use of professional advocates at large meetings).

(c) The proxy need not himself be a member of the company.

(d) Whether it is a private or a public company the proxy may vote on a poll but not on a show of hands.

The articles may vary condition (a) for private companies. Both public and private company articles may vary condition (d): proxies voting on a show of hands.

8 TYPES OF RESOLUTION

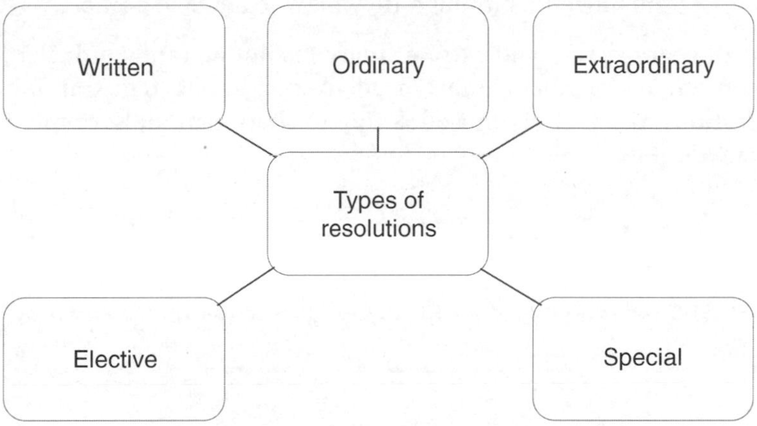

A meeting reaches a decision by passing a resolution. There are five kinds of resolution.

(a) An *ordinary resolution:* is carried by a simple majority of votes cast (over 50%).

(b) An *extraordinary resolution* is carried by a 75% majority of votes cast.

(c) A *special resolution* is carried by a 75% majority of votes cast.

Twenty-one days' notice is required for a meeting at which a special resolution is to be put forward, but only 14 days' notice is required if only ordinary and extraordinary resolutions are to be put forward.

However, remember that there are some ordinary resolutions which require special notice, for example to remove a director.

(d) An *elective resolution* may be passed by a private company (*not* a plc):

(i) to confer authority to issue shares indefinitely or for a fixed period which may exceed five years;

(ii) to dispense with the laying of accounts before a general meeting, unless a member or the auditors require it;

(iii) to dispense with holding an AGM unless a member requires it;

(iv) to reduce the 95% majority needed to consent to short notice to a figure of not less than 90%;

(v) to dispense with the annual appointment of auditors (so that the incumbent auditors are automatically reappointed).

To pass such a resolution, all the members entitled to attend and vote must agree. Twenty-one days' notice is required and the resolution must be registered within 15 days. An elective resolution may be revoked by ordinary resolution but this must also be registered.

(e) A *written resolution* is available again only to private companies. Anything that a private company could do by a resolution of a general meeting or a class meeting may be done by a written resolution. All members entitled to attend and vote must sign the resolution. Note the following restrictions.

(i) A written resolution cannot be used to remove a director or auditor from office, since such persons have a right to speak at a meeting.

(ii) A written resolution must be sent to the auditors at the same time as or before it is sent to the shareholders. However, auditors are no longer able to object to written resolutions. In addition, if the company's officers fail to send the auditors a copy the resolution will remain valid, although they may be liable to a fine.

A signed copy of every special and extraordinary resolution (and equivalent decisions by unanimous consent of members) must be delivered to the registrar for filing. Some ordinary resolutions, particularly those relating to share capital, have to be delivered for filing, but many do not.

Activity 5 **(10 minutes)**

Distinguish special resolutions from resolutions requiring special notice.

9 VOTING AND POLLS

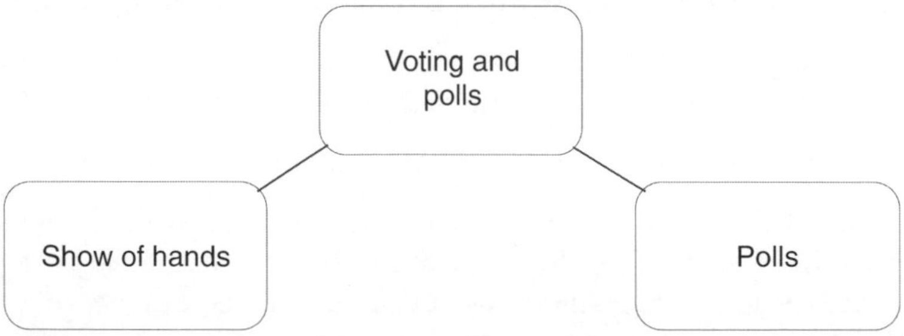

The rights of members to vote and the number of votes to which they are entitled in respect of their shares are fixed by the articles. One vote per share is normal but some shares, for instance preference shares, may carry no voting rights in normal circumstances. To shorten the proceedings at meetings the procedure is as follows.

(a) *Voting on a show of hands*. On putting a resolution to the vote the chairman calls for a show of hands. One vote may be given by each member present in person: proxies do not vote. The chairman declares the result. Unless a poll is then demanded, the chairman's declaration (duly recorded in the minutes) is conclusive.

NOTES

(b) *Voting on a poll*. If a real test of voting strength is required a poll may be demanded. The result of the previous show of hands is then disregarded. On a poll every member and also proxies representing absent members may cast the full number of votes to which they are entitled. A poll need not be held forthwith but may be postponed so that arrangements to hold it can be made.

A poll may be demanded as provided by the articles, but in any case:

(a) by not less than five members;

(b) by member(s) representing not less than one tenth of the total voting rights;

(c) by member(s) holding shares which represent not less than one tenth of the paid-up capital.

10 SINGLE MEMBER PRIVATE COMPANIES

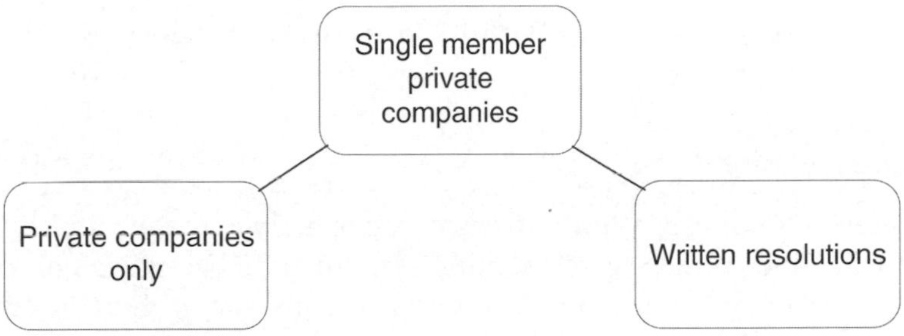

A private company can be formed and operate with only one member. One effect of the regulations is that, following s 382B, if the sole member takes any decision that could have been taken in general meeting, that member shall (unless it is a written resolution) provide the company with a written record of it. This allows the sole member to conduct members' business informally without notice or minutes.

Filing requirements still apply, for example, in the case of alteration of articles. Furthermore, the single member company must hold an annual general meeting unless it has opted out by elective resolution.

Single member companies may conduct business by written resolution, provided they follow the formalities of s 381A.

11 MINORITY PROTECTION

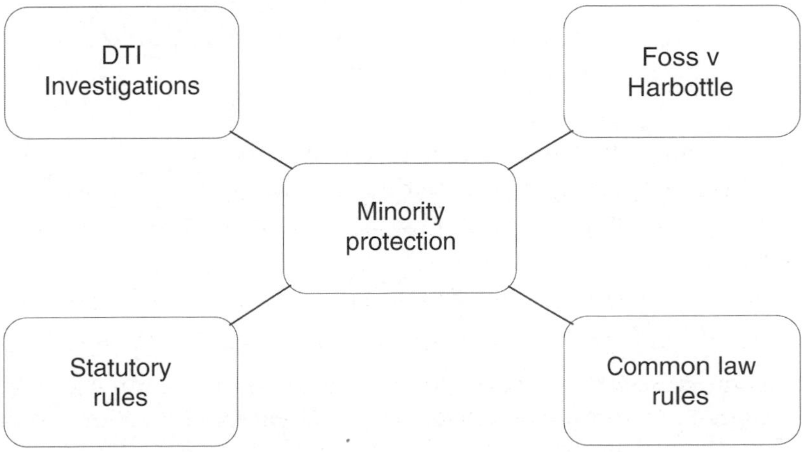

BPP PUBLISHING

NOTES

11.1 The rule in Foss v Harbottle

Ultimate control of a company rests with its members voting in general meeting since (among other things) the directors are required to lay annual accounts before a general meeting and may be removed from office by a simple majority of votes. But if the directors hold a majority of the voting shares or represent a majority shareholder the minority has no remedy unless the rules of minority protection apply.

Foss v Harbottle 1853
A shareholder (Foss) sued the directors of the company alleging that the directors had defrauded the company by selling land to it at an inflated price. The company was by this time in a state of disorganisation and efforts to call the directors to account at a general meeting had failed.

Held: the action must be dismissed since:

(a) the company as a person separate from its members is the only proper claimant in an action to protect its rights or property; and

(b) the company in general meeting must decide whether or not to bring such legal proceedings.

11.2 Common law rules

Case law recognises a number of limitations to the principle of majority control (the rule in *Foss v Harbottle*) and in those cases permits a minority to bring legal proceedings. The decisions are not entirely consistent but the principles are generally summarised as follows.

(a) No majority vote can be effective to sanction an act of the company which is illegal. Illegal decisions taken in general meeting are not binding because a majority of members cannot decide that the company shall break the law. If they attempt to do so any member may apply to the court for a declaration that the decision is void and (if necessary) for an injunction to restrain the company from acting on the decision.

(b) If the law or the company's articles require that a special procedure shall be observed, say alteration of the articles by special resolution, the majority must observe that procedure and their decision is invalid if they do not do so.

(c) A minority may also apply to the court for a remedy if a meeting is convened by a notice which does not, as the articles usually require (Table A Article 38), disclose in sufficient detail 'the general nature of the business' to be done: *Kaye v Croydon Tramways* and *Baillie v Oriental Telephone Co*. But a mere technical irregularity of procedure in convening a meeting may not suffice to invalidate its decisions.

Bentley-Stevens v Jones 1974
A director complained that he had not been given notice of a board meeting held to convene a general meeting at which a resolution was duly passed to remove him from office. In all other respects the correct procedure had been observed.

Held: the members of the company could waive any irregularity in convening the general meeting and the court would not intervene.

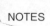

If the directors exercise powers given to them by the articles for an improper purpose a member may challenge them in the courts. But the court is likely to remit the matter back to the company in general meeting for decision by majority vote: *Bamford v Bamford 1970*.

(d) If the company under majority control deprives a member of his individual rights of membership, he may sue the company to enforce his rights.

Pender v Lushington 1877
The articles gave members one vote for each ten shares held by them but subject to a maximum of 100 votes for each member. A company which was a large shareholder transferred shares to the claimant to increase its voting power. At the meeting the chairman rejected the claimant's votes. The claimant sued and the company relied on the argument that only the company itself could object to an irregularity of voting procedure.

Held: the claimant's votes were a 'right of property' which he was entitled to protect by proceedings against the company.

(e) If those who control the company use their control to defraud it (or possibly to act oppressively towards a minority) the minority may bring legal proceedings against the fraudulent (or oppressive) majority. Otherwise a wrong would be without remedy since the majority would prevent the company from taking action.

The exception to the rule in *Foss v Harbottle* over fraud by a controlling majority is to protect the company by a member's action since the company cannot protect itself. It must be shown that:

(i) what was taken belonged to the company;

(1) it passed to those against whom the claim is made; and

(2) those who appropriated the company's property are in control of the company.

To divert away from the company profitable contracts which it was about to make is to deprive it of its property (for the purposes of this rule).

Cook v Deeks 1916
The directors, who were also controlling shareholders, negotiated a contract in the name of the company. They took the contract for themselves and passed a resolution in general meeting declaring that the company had no interest in the contract. A minority shareholder sued them as trustees for the company of the benefit of the contract.

Held: the contract 'belonged in equity to the company' and the directors could not, by passing a resolution in general meeting, bind the company to approving this action of defrauding it.

If the property of the company passes to a third party that may be negligence – it is not fraud. But if it passes to those who are controlling shareholders, that is equivalent to 'fraud' even though no dishonesty is shown.

Pavlides v Jensen 1956
The claimant, a minority shareholder, alleged that the directors who represented the controlling shareholder, had negligently sold the principal asset, a mine worth £1m (in his opinion) to a third party for a mere £182,000.

Held: there could be no fraud unless the controlling shareholder benefited. Merely to allege negligence was not enough to justify a minority action to protect the company's rights. The company in general meeting must decide

NOTES

whether to hold the directors liable for mismanagement or alternatively it could exonerate them. The judge described the directors as 'an amiable bunch of lunatics' – they were not fraudsters.

Daniels v Daniels 1977
The company was controlled by its two directors, husband and wife. It bought land for £4,250 (probate value) from the estate of a deceased person and later resold it at the same price to the lady director. She resold it for £120,000. A minority shareholder sued the directors but did not allege fraud. Objection was raised that a member could not sue the directors on the company's behalf for negligence (*Pavlides*' case above) but only for fraud.

Held: the circumstances required investigation and a member might sue the directors and controlling shareholders for negligence if one of them secured benefit from the company by reason of it.

There are also procedural intricacies in bringing a minority shareholders' action.

(a) The claimant may bring a derivative action on behalf of the company to enforce its rights or recover its property. Any benefit obtained will accrue to the company since the claim is derived from and made on behalf of the company. The court is prepared to order the company to pay the claimant's legal costs (and may do so even if he fails in his action). In the Newman Industries case the action was at first a derivative one but subsequently was adopted by the whole company.

(b) The claimant usually combines a derivative action with a representative action – he asserts that he sues on behalf of all other shareholders (except the defendants). He may however combine this form of action with a personal claim for damages provided that he can show that he has suffered actual loss.

(c) In the Newman Industries case the claimant combined a derivative action with a personal claim for damages for the loss which it was alleged the claimant had suffered.

The matter is further confused by the practice, even in a derivative action, of making the company a defendant, so that any order made by the court may be binding on it. If this were not done the controlling shareholders might continue to use their control of the company to avoid some of the consequences of a court decision against them.

Activity 6 **(15 minutes)**

A Ltd has three directors. D, B and C. Together they own 85% of the shares in the company. They agree to sell a plot of land to W for £50,000 which is what they honestly believe it to be worth. They do not, however, have the land professionally valued until later when it is shown to be worth nearer £100,000. E and J are two minority shareholders who are considering bringing an action against the directors and the company.

Advise E and J whether they are likely to be successful.

11.3 Statutory rules

Any member may now apply to the court for relief under s 459 on the grounds that the company's affairs are being or have been conducted in a manner which is unfairly

BPP PUBLISHING

prejudicial to the interests of the members generally or of some part of the members. Application may also be made in respect of a particular act or omission which has been or will be prejudicial. It is not necessary to show that there has been bad faith or even an intention to discriminate against the minority. But the complaint must be based on prejudice to the member as a member and not, for example, as an employee or as an unpaid creditor.

Whatever the basis of the petition the court will take account of the surrounding circumstances and conduct of the parties.

Re R A Noble & Sons (Clothing) Ltd 1983
B had provided the capital but left the management in the hands of N, the other director, on the understanding that N would consult B on major company matters. N did not do so and B confined himself to enquiries to N on social occasions; he accepted N's vague assurances that all was well. The petition followed from a breakdown of the relationship.

Held: B's exclusion from discussion of company management questions was largely the result of his own lack of interest. His petition was dismissed.

Re Jermyn Street Turkish Baths Ltd 1971
The petitioners were the executors of a deceased member who had been a guarantor of the company's overdraft. At the time of his death the company was in poor financial shape. The controlling shareholder, who took over at this point, pulled the company round and among other things paid off the overdraft. The value of the deceased's shareholding increased. The complaint was that the controlling shareholder had allotted more shares to herself and had also taken most of the profits as commission (under a pre-agreed formula) so that no dividends were paid.

Held: on balance there had been no 'oppression' (and presumably would be no 'unfair prejudice' under the current formula). The petition was dismissed.

Re a Company 1983
The petitioners' grievance was the directors' refusal to put forward a scheme of reconstruction or a proposal to purchase their shares (by the company). The directors were preoccupied with plans for diversification of the business.

Held: the directors' duty was to manage the company to its advantage as they saw it. It was not a case of 'unfair prejudice'.

Re London School of Electronics Ltd 1985
The other shareholders had removed the petitioner from his directorship after he had alleged that they were diverting business from the company to themselves. He then set up a rival business and took part of the company's connection with him.

Held: he had a right to relief even though he did not have 'clean hands'. The majority had to buy out the minority without any discount for the fact that his were minority shares and therefore of less value.

Re McGuinness and Another 1988
Disputes arose among board members after one company had taken over another. The petitioners, who included the MD and a minority shareholder, requisitioned on 4 November an EGM to consider a resolution to remove two directors and appoint others, including one of the petitioners. The board notified them on 23 November that the EGM would be held in seven months' time.

Held: this was not a breach of s 368 but was unfairly prejudicial to the minority and hence a s 459 claim succeeded. The court ordered an earlier meeting. Note that the company did not have a 1985 set of Table A articles and hence were not constrained by Article 37 to hold the EGM within eight weeks; nor had s 368 yet been amended to impose the new 28-day limit, which effectively solves the problem.

When a petition is successful the court may make whatever order it deems fit – though the petitioner is required in presenting his petition to state what relief he seeks. It may include, under s 461:

(a) an order regulating the future conduct of the company's affairs: for example, that a controlling shareholder shall conform to the decisions taken at board meetings (Re H R Harmer Ltd 1958);

(b) an authorisation to any person to bring legal proceedings on behalf of the company. The company is then responsible for the legal costs;

(c) an order requiring the company to refrain from doing or continuing an act complained of;

(d) provision for the purchase of shares of the minority by either the controlling shareholder or the company;

(e) inclusion in the memorandum or articles of provisions which may only be altered or removed thereafter by leave of the court.

Two recent cases have considered the scope of s 459 and the availability of the rare remedy of requiring the majority to sell to the minority.

Re Brenfield Squash Racquets club Ltd 1996
Eighty-six per cent of the shares in Brenfield were held by FMR Ltd and 14% by S and his family. S was appointed Managing Director of the company and the remaining directors were nominated by FMR. The nominees failed to distinguish between the affairs of FMR and the company, treating the company's assets as available for FMR's benefit.

Relations between the directors broke down and S was replaced by M as Managing Director, and eventually removed from the board.

Held: s 459 had been made out. The new MD had deliberately set out to conceal information from S and to remove him from his company position. FMR was ordered to sell its share to the minority.

However, in *Re a company 1996* the same remedy was refused. The judge said that the order was rare and would not be available in this case as the applicant was 85 and had not played a recent part in the company's affairs. The action was thus struck out as the majority had offered to buy out the minority's shares, thus giving him all the relief he could expect from a successful petition.

11.4 Investigations by the Department of Trade and Industry

The Department of Trade and Industry (the DTI) has statutory power to appoint an inspector to investigate the affairs or ownership of a company.

The DTI must appoint inspectors if a court so orders. In addition, it may appoint inspectors to investigate the affairs of a company:

(a) if the company itself applies;

(b) if application is made by members who are not less than 200 in number or who hold at least one tenth of the issued shares (or, if the company has no share capital, by at least one fifth of the members). The applicants may be required to produce evidence to show good reasons for their application and to give security (not exceeding £5,000) for the costs of the investigation;

(c) if the DTI considers that the affairs of the company have been conducted in a fraudulent or unlawful manner (or that it was formed for a fraudulent or unlawful purpose) or in a manner unfairly prejudicial to some part of its members or that members have not been given all the information with respect to its affairs which they might reasonably expect: s 432.

Activity 7 **(10 minutes)**

The controlling shareholders of a company resolve to replace the directors with new directors who will work to increase efficiency by reducing the number of employees. John, a minority shareholder and senior employee, is made redundant by the new directors. Could he apply for relief under s 359. Why?

Chapter roundup

- A person becomes a member of a company by being entered in the register of members. He ceases to be a member when he dies, when the company ceases to exist or when all of his shares are registered in the name of another person.
- The shareholdings of all members are recorded in the register of members. No notice of a trust may be included in the register, but the position of a beneficiary may be protected by serving a stop notice on the company.
- Any person interested in at least 3% of a company's shares must notify the company.
- Major decisions affecting a company are taken by the members in general meeting. Every company must hold AGMs, except for private companies which have decided not to by elective resolution. EGMs may be called by the directors or requisitioned by a sufficiently large number of the members.
- A meeting must be properly convened. Certain resolutions can only be included in the agenda if special notice has been given to the company. The directors can exclude a resolution unless a sufficiently large number of the members force its inclusion.
- Any member entitled to attend and vote may send a proxy to the meeting instead.
- Resolutions may be ordinary, extraordinary or special. A private company may also pass an elective resolution or a written resolution.
- Voting is normally by a show of hands, although a poll may be demanded.
- In general, majority rule prevails, but this principle is restricted to protect minorities. There are several common law restrictions, and under statute law any member may apply for relief if the company's affairs are conducted in a way which is unfairly prejudicial to some or all of the members.
- The Department of Trade and Industry may appoint inspectors to investigate a company.

Quick quiz

1. In what ways may a person (a) become and (b) cease to be a member of a company?
2. What particulars must be entered in a register of members?
3. Who may inspect a register of members?
4. What are (a) the intervals and (b) the period of notice fixed by law for an AGM?
5. How may an EGM be convened?
6. For what purposes may a private company use an elective resolution?
7. What are the two ways of voting at a company meeting?
8. Who may demand a poll?

NOTES

9 What is the rule in Foss v Harbottle?

10 When may the DTI appoint inspectors to investigate a company's affairs?

Answers to quick quiz

1 Becoming a member: by subscription
by buying shares

Ceasing to be a member: sale of shares
death
bankruptcy
forfeit
company dissolution (see para 1, 2)

2 Name and address
Class of shares
Number of shares
Dates

3 Any member: no charge
Any member of the public: for a fee (para 3)

4 Every calendar year
No more than 15 months apart
Notice: 21 days (para 5.1)

5 By directors
By appropriate minority of members (para 5.2)

6 Indefinite authority to issue shares
Dispense with laying of accounts
Dispense with holding an AGM
Reduce 95% needed for short notice to 90%
Dispense with annual appointment of auditors (para 8)

7 Show of hands or a poll. (para 9)

8 At least 5 members, or the holders of one tenth of the voting rights or the holders of one tenth of the paid-up capital. (para 9)

9 Control of the company rests with a majority of the members in a general meeting. (para 11.1)

10 When asked by:

- the company
- at least 200 members, or holders of one tenth of the issued shares

or the DTI warrants it. (para 11.4)

Answers to activities

1 J (she is on the register on Thursday).

2 50,000 x 3% = 1,500 shares, so L must disclose her interest by 14 June (two days after 12 June).

3 The directors might all die or otherwise become incapable of acting.

It might become impossible for the company to carry on its business, because of (say) a fire or a change in the law.

You can probably think of other examples.

4 No: he does not hold 5% of the votes.

BPP PUBLISHING

5 A special resolution is passed by a 75% majority, and needs 21 days' notice *to the members*.

Special notice of a resolution (which may be an ordinary resolution) is given *to the company* at least 28 days before the relevant meeting.

6 The type of action open to E and J would be a derivative action, that is one brought by E or J on behalf of the company, with the directors as defendants. However, they would be unlikely to succeed. The facts of this case resemble those of Pavlides v Jensen 1956. In this case it was held that mere negligence did not justify a minority action to protect the company's rights. Thus, in the absence of fraud, the sale could legitimately be approved by a majority of the shareholders.

7 No: he would be applying as an employee and not as a member.

Assignment 14 **(60 minutes)**

(a) What are the statutory requirements in respect of holding annual general meetings? State the ordinary business usually transacted at such meetings. What action can the members of a company take if the directors fail to call an annual general meeting?

(b) The annual general meeting of Broadway plc, a company regulated by Table A, will consider the following special business:

(i) to change the name of the company to Broadway (Manchester) plc;

(ii) to increase the authorised share capital of the company to £500,000;

(iii) to allot one fully paid bonus share to members for every five ordinary shares held.

Advise the company secretary of the types of resolutions required to give effect to these proposals and the registration requirements he must attend to, provided that the resolutions are passed.

(c) Tom, a shareholder in Broadway plc, has entered into a contract to sell his shares to Harry, although no transfer has been completed or registered. The company secretary who is aware of the contract sends the notice of the annual general meeting to Harry rather than to Tom.

Explain, giving reasons, what effect (if any) the secretary's action may have on the proceedings of the annual general meeting.

Chapter 18 :
DISSOLUTION OF BUSINESS UNITS

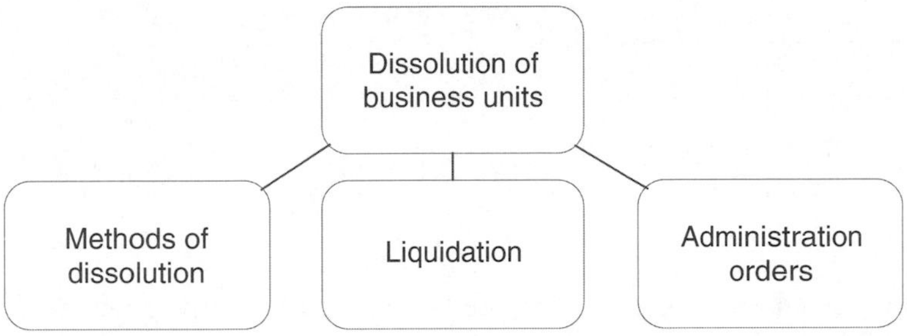

Introduction

This chapter completes your studies of company law with an insight into liquidations and other insolvency procedures.

Liquidations and receiverships have been in the news all too frequently in recent years, and you will enhance your understanding of a potentially dry and technical topic by relating it to real life events.

Liquidation is expensive and unconstructive; alternatives have therefore been put forward in the form of administration and voluntary arrangements.

Your objectives

In this chapter you will learn about the following.

(a) How a company may come to be dissolved

(b) The effects of a decision to liquidate a company

(c) The grounds for compulsory liquidation

(d) The difference between a members' and a creditors' voluntary liquidation

(e) How each type of liquidation proceeds

(f) The role of a liquidation committee

(g) The position of contributories

(h) The powers and duties of liquidators

(i) The effects of an administration order and the position of an administrator

Statutory references in this chapter are to the Insolvency Act 1986 unless otherwise stated. 'CA' denotes the Companies Act 1985.

1 METHODS OF DISSOLUTION

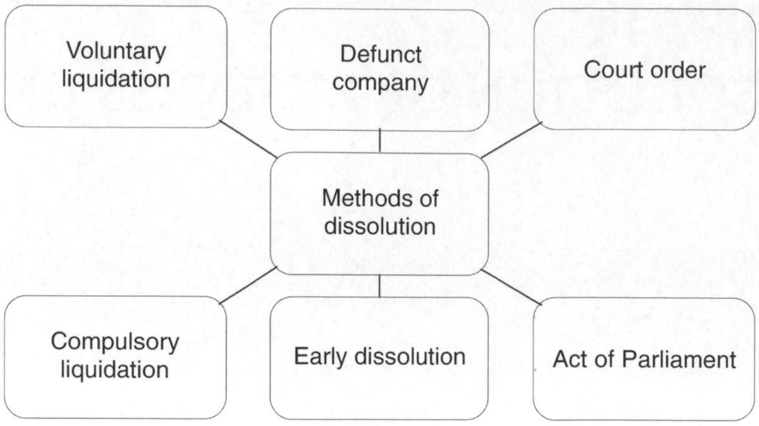

Dissolution occurs when a company's name is removed from the register. At this point it ceases to exist. There are several ways in which this may be done.

(a) By the registrar, under s 652 CA, if it appears to him that the company is defunct;

(b) By order of the court under s 427(3)(d) CA following a scheme of arrangement under s 425: no winding up is necessary as the company is transferring its business;

(c) By Act of Parliament (very rarely used);

(d) On application by the official receiver for early dissolution: s 202;

(e) On completion of a compulsory liquidation;

(f) On completion of a voluntary liquidation.

2 LIQUIDATIONS

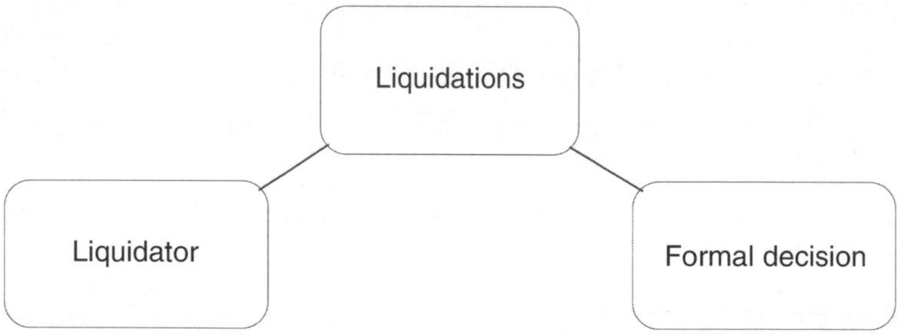

Most dissolutions follow liquidation or 'winding up' (the terms are used synonymously). The assets are realised, debts are paid out of the proceeds, and any surplus amounts are returned to members.

Liquidation begins with a formal decision to liquidate. If the members in general meeting resolve to wind up the company, that is a voluntary liquidation. This may be either a members' or a creditors' voluntary liquidation, depending on whether the directors believe that the company will or will not be able to pay its debts in full.

A company may also be obliged to wind up by a compulsory liquidation, ordered by the court on a petition usually presented by a creditor or a member.

NOTES

Whether liquidation is voluntary or compulsory it is in the hands of the liquidator (or joint liquidators), who takes over control of the company from its directors. No further share dealings or changes in membership will be permitted (unless the court sanctions a rectification or other change); and all invoices, orders, letters and other company documents must state prominently that the company is in liquidation.

Activity 1 **(5 minutes)**

What is the point of requiring that all documents state that a company is in liquidation, given that the members and creditors are likely to be aware of that fact?

3 COMPULSORY LIQUIDATION

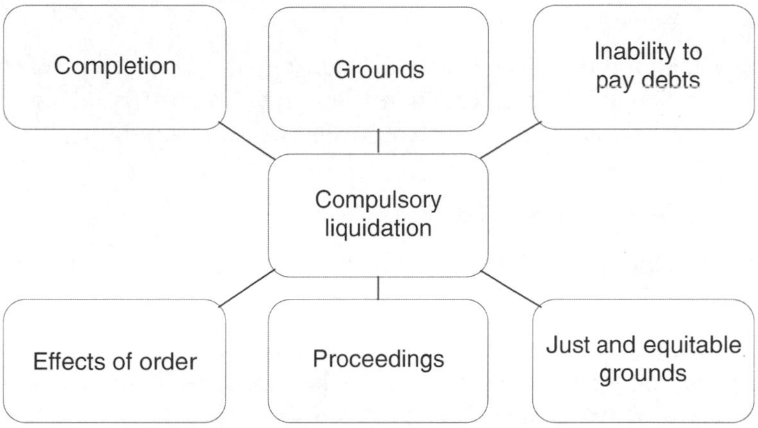

A petition is presented to the Chancery Division of the High Court (or, if the company has an issued and paid up share capital not exceeding £120,000 in the county court of the district in which the registered office is situated): s 117. The petition will specify the ground for compulsory winding up and be presented (usually) either by a creditor or by a member (called a 'contributory' in the context of liquidation). The standard grounds for compulsory liquidation are listed in s 122.

(a) The company has by special resolution resolved that it should be wound up by the court.

(b) The company, incorporated as a public company, has failed within a year to obtain a trading certificate.

(c) The number of members of a public company has been reduced to below two.

(d) The company has not commenced its business within a year of incorporation or has suspended its business for a year.

(e) The company is unable to pay its debts: s 122(1)(f). This is the most common ground.

(f) The court considers that it is just and equitable to wind up the company: s 122(1)(g). This ground may be used by a dissatisfied member.

3.1 Company unable to pay its debts

A creditor who petitions on the grounds of the company's insolvency may rely on any of three situations to show that the company is unable to pay its debts: s 123.

(a) A creditor (or creditors) to whom the company owes more than £750 serves on the company at its registered office a written demand for payment and the company neglects, within the ensuing 21 clear days, either to pay the debt or to offer reasonable security for it.

(b) A creditor obtains judgement against the company for debt, and attempts to enforce the judgement but is unable to obtain payment because no assets of the company have been found and seized.

(c) A creditor satisfies the court that, taking into account the contingent and prospective liabilities of the company, it is unable to pay its debts. The creditor may be able to show this:

   (i) by proof that the company is not able to pay its debts as they fall due: the *commercial insolvency test*; or

   (ii) by proof that the company's assets are less than its liabilities: the *balance sheet test*.

At the hearing other creditors of the company may oppose the petition. If so, the court is likely to decide in favour of those to whom the larger amount is owing. But the court may also consider the reasons for the differences between the creditors.

3.2 The just and equitable ground

Orders have been made for liquidation on the just and equitable ground in the following situations.

(a) The substratum of the company has gone: the main object of the company can no longer be achieved. This is less likely now that a company can have a very broadly-termed objects clause.

(b) The company was formed for an illegal or fraudulent purpose or there is a complete deadlock in the management of its affairs.

(c) The understandings between members or directors which were the basis of the association have been unfairly breached by lawful action.

(d) The directors deliberately withheld information so that the shareholders have no confidence in the company's management.

Activity 2 **(10 minutes)**

In Re a Company (No 003729 of 1982) 1984, the petitioner for compulsory liquidation had demanded a sum due under a contract from the company. The company had disputed the amount due, and had only paid part of the sum demanded. The petitioner therefore claimed that the company had neglected to pay a debt. Why do you think the petitioner failed?

3.3 Proceedings for compulsory liquidation

When a petition is presented to the court a copy is delivered to the company in case it objects. It is advertised so that other creditors may intervene if they wish.

Once the court has received a petition, it may appoint a provisional liquidator: s 135. The Official Receiver is usually appointed, and his powers are conferred by the court. These usually extend to taking control of the company's property and applying for a special manager to be appointed (ss 144 and 177).

3.4 Effects of an order for compulsory liquidation

The effects of the order, which may be made some time after a provisional liquidator is appointed, are as follows.

(a) The Official Receiver (an official of the DTI whose duties relate mainly to bankruptcy of individuals) becomes liquidator: s 136.

(b) The liquidation is deemed to have commenced at the time (possibly several months earlier) when the petition was first presented. If compulsory liquidation follows voluntary liquidation already in progress liquidation runs from the commencement of the voluntary liquidation: s 129.

(c) Any disposition of the company's property and any transfer of its shares subsequent to the commencement of liquidation is void unless the court orders otherwise: s 127. The court will decide whether to validate a disposition made under s 127.

(d) Any legal proceedings in progress against the company are halted (and none may thereafter begin) unless the court gives leave. Any seizure of the company's assets after commencement of liquidation is void: ss 130 and 128.

(e) The employees of the company are automatically dismissed. The provisional liquidator assumes the powers of management previously held by the directors.

(f) Any floating charge crystallises.

The assets of the company may remain the company's legal property but under the liquidator's control – unless the court vests the assets in the liquidator. The business of the company may continue but it is the liquidator's duty to continue it with a view only to realisation, for instance by sale as a going concern.

Within 21 days of the making of the order for winding up (or of the appointment of a provisional liquidator) a statement of affairs must be delivered to the liquidator verified by one or more directors and by the secretary. The statement shows the assets and liabilities of the company and includes a list of creditors with particulars of any security which creditors may hold and how long it has been held: s 131.

Meetings of contributories and creditors

The Official Receiver has 12 weeks to decide whether or not to convene separate meetings of creditors and contributories. The purpose of these meetings would be to provide the creditors and contributories with the opportunity to appoint their own nominee as permanent liquidator to replace the official receiver, and a liquidation committee as their representative to work with the liquidator. (In cases of conflict, the creditors' nominee takes precedence over the members' nominee.) If the Official Receiver believes there is little interest and that the creditors will be unlikely to appoint a liquidator he can dispense with a meeting, informing the court, the creditors and the contributories of the decision. He must then call a meeting if at least 25% in value of the creditors require him to do so: s 136.

If the creditors do hold a meeting and appoint their own nominee he automatically becomes liquidator subject to a right of objection to the court: s 139. Any person appointed to act as liquidator must be a qualified insolvency practitioner.

At any time after a winding up order is made, the Official Receiver may ask the Secretary of State to appoint a liquidator. Similarly, he may request an appointment if the creditors and members fail to appoint a liquidator: s 137.

3.5 Completion of compulsory liquidation

When the liquidator completes his task he reports to the DTI, which examines his accounts. He may apply to the court for an order for dissolution of the company. The order is sent to the registrar who gives notice of it in the London Gazette and dissolves the company: s 205.

Activity 3 **(10 minutes)**

Following an order for compulsory liquidation of a company with debts of £120,000, meetings of the creditors and contributories are held. The creditors nominate P as liquidator, whereas the contributories nominate S. P claims that he can realise the company's assets within a month for £100,000, whereas S claims that she can run the business and sell it as a going concern for £140,000 within six months. If nobody reconsiders his or her position, who will be appointed liquidator? Why is this?

4 VOLUNTARY LIQUIDATION

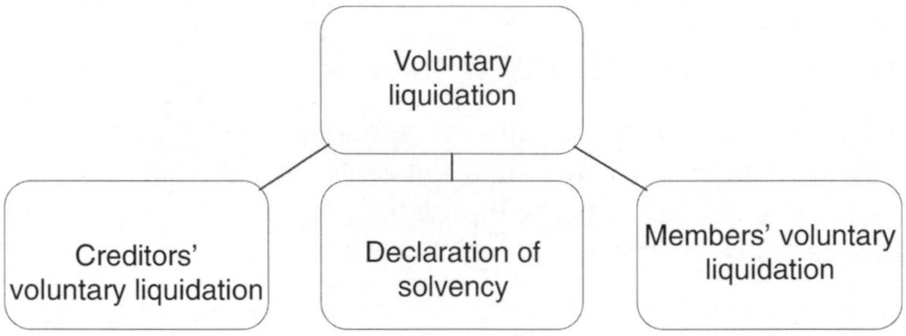

There are two types of voluntary liquidation, a members' voluntary liquidation (where the company is solvent) and a creditors' voluntary liquidation (where the company is insolvent and the members resolve to liquidate in consultation with creditors).

4.1 Members' voluntary liquidation

The type of resolution to be passed varies with the circumstances of the case: s 84. A company may by extraordinary resolution resolve to wind up because it cannot, by reason of its liabilities, continue its business. This enables an insolvent company to go into liquidation on a 14 day notice. A company may, by special resolution (giving no reasons), resolve to wind up.

The winding up commences on the passing of the resolution. A liquidator is usually appointed by the same resolution (or a second resolution passed at the same time).

4.2 Declaration of solvency

A voluntary winding up is a members' voluntary winding up only if the directors make and deliver to the registrar a declaration of solvency: s 89. This is a statutory declaration that the directors have made full enquiry into the affairs of the company and are of the opinion that it will be able to pay its debts, together with interest (at the rate applicable under s 189(4)) on those debts, in full, within a specified period not exceeding 12 months. If the liquidator later concludes that the company will be unable to pay its debts he must call a meeting of creditors and lay before them a statement of assets and liabilities: s 95.

The liquidator calls special and annual general meetings of contributories to whom he reports. Within three months after each anniversary of the commencement of the winding up the liquidator must call a meeting and lay before it an account of his transactions during the year: s 93. When the liquidation is complete the liquidator calls a meeting to lay before it his final accounts: s 94.

After holding the final meeting the liquidator sends a copy of his accounts to the registrar who dissolves the company three months later by removing its name from the register: s 201.

4.3 Creditors' voluntary liquidation

If no declaration of solvency is made and delivered to the registrar the liquidation proceeds as a creditors' voluntary liquidation even if in the end the company pays its debts in full: s 96.

To commence a creditors' voluntary liquidation the directors convene a general meeting of members to pass an extraordinary resolution. They must also convene a meeting of creditors (s 98), giving at least seven days' notice of this meeting. The notice must be advertised in the London Gazette and two local newspapers. The notice must either:

(a) give the name and address of a qualified insolvency practitioner to whom the creditors can apply before the meeting for information about the company; or

(b) state a place in the locality of the company's principal place of business where, on the two business days before the meeting, a list of creditors can be inspected.

The meeting of members is held first and its business is to resolve to wind up, to appoint a liquidator and to nominate up to five representatives to be members of the liquidation committee.

The creditors' meeting should preferably be convened on the same day at a later time than the members' meeting, or on the next day, but in any event within 14 days of it. One of the directors presides at the creditors' meeting and lays before it a full statement of the company's affairs and a list of creditors with the amounts owing to them. The meeting may (if the creditors so wish) nominate a liquidator and up to five representatives to be members of the liquidation committee. If the creditors nominate a different person to be liquidator, their choice prevails over the nomination by the members.

4.4 The effect of voluntary winding up

Unlike a compulsory winding up, there is no automatic stay of legal proceedings against the company and the employees are not automatically dismissed.

Activity 4 **(10 minutes)**

Why do the creditors of a company ordinarily have no role in a members' voluntary liquidation?

5 LIQUIDATION COMMITTEE

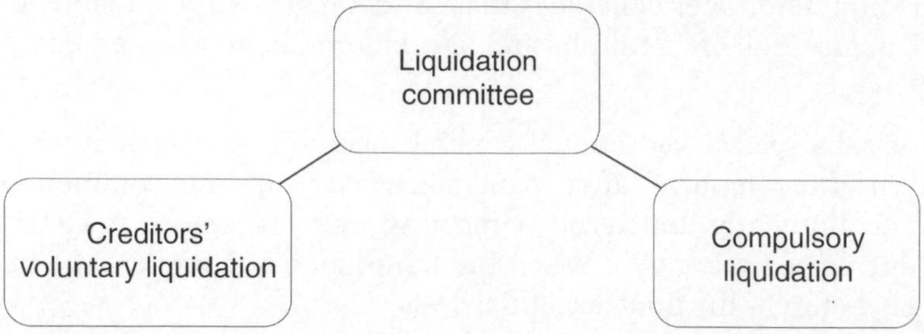

A liquidation committee may be appointed in a compulsory liquidation and in a creditors' voluntary liquidation. It usually comprises an equal number of representatives of members and of creditors (in a creditors' voluntary liquidation it is limited to a maximum of five from each side). The committee meets once a month unless otherwise agreed and may be summoned at any time by the liquidator or by a member of the committee.

The general function of the committee is to work with the liquidator, to supervise his accounts, to approve the exercise of certain of his statutory powers and to fix his remuneration. Like the liquidator himself members of the committee are in a fiduciary position and may not secure unauthorised personal advantages, for example by purchase of the company's assets.

6 CONTRIBUTORIES

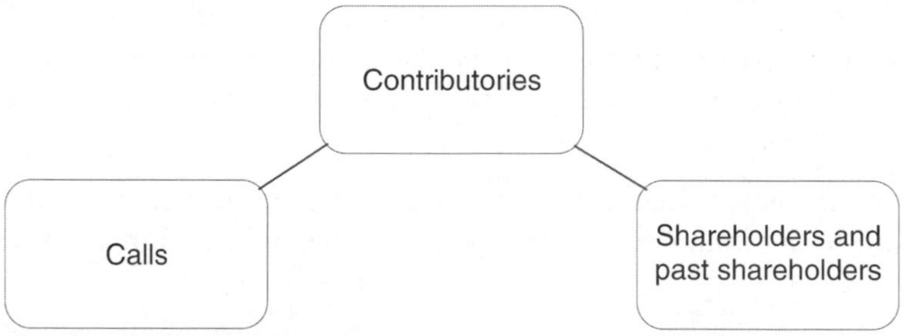

Shareholders and past shareholders are called contributories. A contributory may have to contribute funds to meet a company's debts if the shares which he holds or previously held are partly paid or if it is found that the rules on consideration have been breached in the allotment of the shares as fully paid.

If it is necessary to make calls on contributories the liquidator draws up an 'A' List of contributories who were members at the commencement of the winding up and a 'B' List of contributories who were members within the year preceding the commencement of winding up. A B List contributory has liability limited by the following principles.

(a) He is only liable to pay what is due on the shares which he previously held and only so much of the amount due on those shares as the present holder (an A List contributory) is unable to pay.

(b) He can only be required to contribute (within the limits stated in (a) above) in order to pay those debts of the company incurred before he ceased to be a member which are still owing.

No contributory who ceased to be a member more than a year before the commencement of liquidation can be liable.

7 POWERS OF LIQUIDATORS

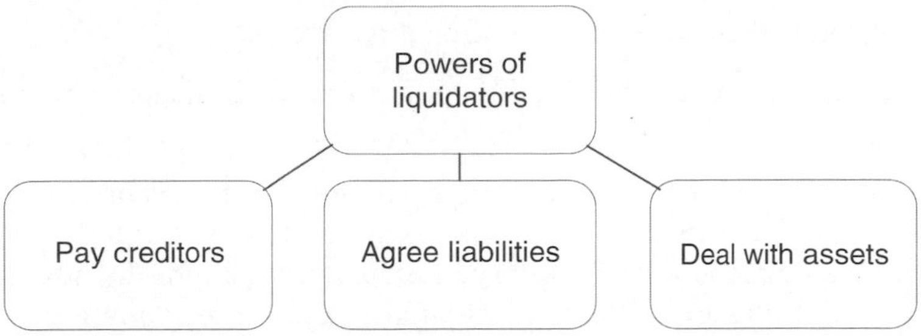

In order to perform his function satisfactorily, the liquidator is given certain powers, contained in Sch 4. His basic function is to obtain and realise the company's assets to pay off its debts.

All liquidators may, with the relevant sanctions:

(a) pay any class of creditors in full;

(b) make compromises or arrangements with creditors;

(c) compromise any debt or questions relating to assets;

(d) take security;

(e) bring or defend legal proceedings (without sanction in a voluntary liquidation)

(f) carry on the business in a way beneficial to the winding-up (without sanction in a voluntary liquidation).

His subsidiary powers, given to enable him to perform the above, include selling assets, giving receipts (often under seal), receiving dividends, drawing bills of exchange, raising money, appointing agents and doing any other necessary things.

8 DUTIES OF LIQUIDATORS

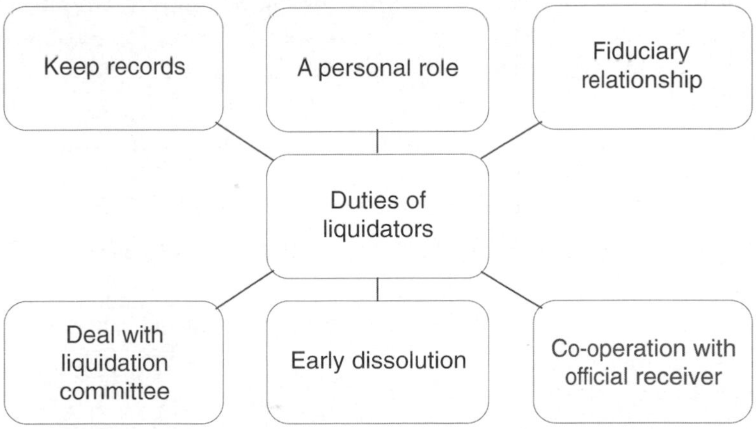

Given the wide-ranging powers invested in a liquidator, he has certain duties.

(a) He must exercise his discretion personally. Although he may delegate clerical tasks and those which he cannot perform personally (for which he can appoint agents), a liquidator cannot delegate his duty to use his judgement, even to the court. However, if it is in the interest of the company's creditors and contributories, and in any case if the nature of the business requires it, a liquidator may ask the court to appoint a manager with special skills.

(b) He stands in a fiduciary relationship to the company, its creditors and contributories.

(c) He must co-operate with the official receiver.

(d) He must notify the liquidation committee of (i) dispositions to a connected person, and (ii) all matters of concern.

A liquidator must keep records of proceedings. He must keep a record of all receipts and payments and, if the company continues trading, a trading account should be kept. An account must be submitted to the Secretary of State every 12 months, the first one being accompanied by a summary statement of affairs and an explanation of why assets referred to therein have not been disposed of. A final account must be submitted within 14 days of leaving office. On request, creditors and contributories are entitled to free copies of accounts, and the Secretary of State may order them to be audited.

A liquidator must act quickly in carrying out his duties, and not delay for lack of obvious funds.

Liquidators must keep minutes of the proceedings and resolutions of creditors', contributories' and liquidation committee meetings.

After six months of voluntary liquidation, the liquidator must pay the balance of funds not required for day-to-day running of the liquidation into a special account at the Bank of England (the Insolvency Services Account). Money received in a compulsory liquidation must be paid into this account immediately, unless the liquidator has express authority from the DTI to operate a local bank account.

The registrar is entitled to receive reports on a voluntary liquidation at the end of 12 months and every six months thereafter.

Activity 5 **(10 minutes)**

J Ltd is in liquidation with debts of £70,000. The company has one asset, a building. Tony would pay £100,000 for the building, but he refuses to deal with a company in liquidation. The building is therefore sold to a company owned by the liquidator for £90,000, and then re-sold to Tony for £100,000. All the creditors of J Ltd are paid in full. What duty, if any, has the liquidator breached?

9 APPLICATIONS OF ASSETS IN A WINDING UP

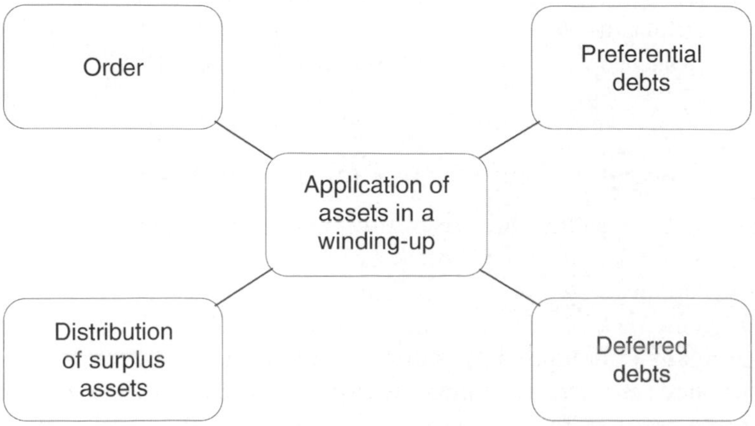

A secured creditor obtains payment (to the extent that his security is adequate) because he has a valid prior claim to that security. Unsecured creditors are paid out of the remaining assets, being the aggregate of:

(a) any surplus value obtained by secured creditors in realising assets which represent their security and are then paid over to the liquidator; and

(b) any assets which are not subject to charges given to secured creditors.

9.1 Order of application

The order of application of assets in liquidation is as follows.

(a) *Secured creditors* who have *fixed charges* are entitled to be paid out of their security so far as it suffices. If the security is insufficient in value to pay the debt in full the creditor ranks as an unsecured creditor for the balance. Therefore if the secured asset does not realise the amount of debt the secured creditor will only get the amount realised.

(b) The *costs of winding up* are paid next; they rank before floating charges.

(c) *Preferential unsecured debts* are paid next.

(d) *Debts secured by floating charges* come next in order.

(e) *Unsecured non-preferential debts* come next.

(f) *Deferred debts* come last in order.

Any money left would then be used to repay the shareholders their capital.

9.2 Preferential debts

Preferential debts rank *pari passu* or equally. If there are insufficient funds to pay them all, they are all pro-rated. The most important preferential debts are:

(a) PAYE income tax deducted, and other social security contributions, for the last 12 months and VAT referable to the period of 6 months before the 'relevant datc'. The relevant date is defined as:

  (i) the date of the *order for compulsory liquidation* (or an earlier order for appointment of a provisional liquidator); or

  (ii) the date of passing a resolution to wind up voluntarily.

(b) Wages and salary of an employee, such as a clerk, servant, workman or labourer (including commission or piece work payments) for the four months up to the relevant date limited to a maximum of £800 owed to each individual employee, accrued holiday pay and employer's national insurance contributions. A director is not an employee in respect of a claim for unpaid fees but he may be in respect of salary if he has a service contract.

9.3 Deferred debts

A debt owed to a member as member, say an unpaid dividend, is a *deferred debt* and is paid only when ordinary unsecured debts have been paid in full.

9.4 Distribution of surplus assets

If the debts are paid in full the liquidator should apply what remains in repayment of capital paid on shares and then distribute any residue to those entitled to the surplus. Unless otherwise stated all shares rank equally. However the articles often provide that preference share capital is to be repaid in priority (with the implication that preference shares do not carry a right to participate in any surplus left after all paid up share capital has been repaid).

10 ALTERNATIVES TO LIQUIDATION

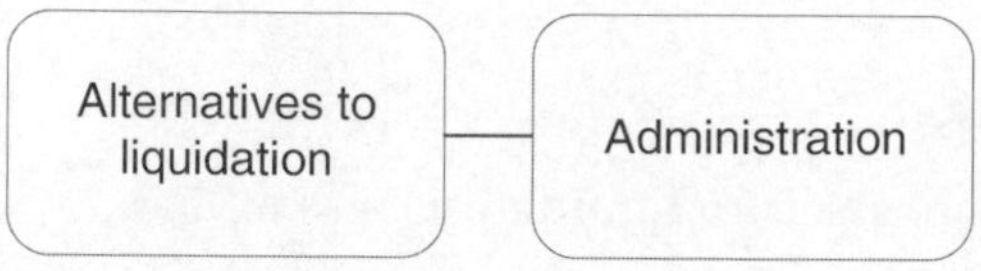

Winding up a company is a fairly drastic step involving the cessation of trading, the disposal of assets and the final dissolution of the company. There are alternatives to liquidation when a company is insolvent to some degree. One of the main alternatives is the granting of an administration order. Under this procedure a moratorium is imposed by the court on creditors' actions against the company while an insolvency practitioner attempts to solve the problem.

11 ADMINISTRATION ORDERS

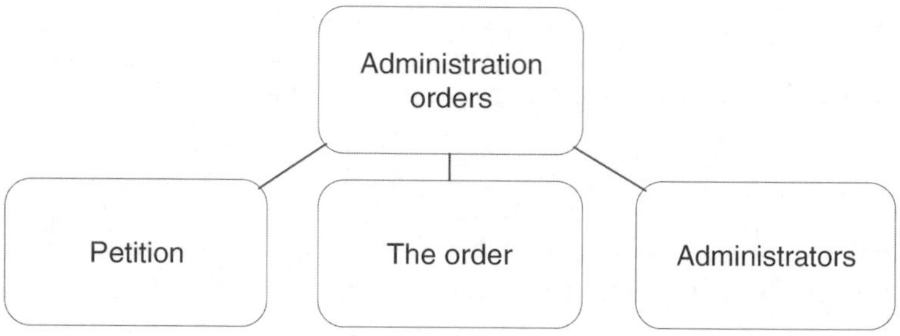

If a company is not yet in liquidation but is already, or is likely to become, unable to pay its debts the company itself, its directors, or any of its creditors, including unsecured creditors, may present a petition to the court to make an administration order in respect of the company: s 9(1). The broad effect of such an order is to put an insolvency practitioner in control of the company with a defined programme, and meanwhile to insulate it from pressure by creditors. The administration order provides an alternative for the unsecured creditor to suing for the debt in the courts or petitioning for winding up. For the secured creditor it is an alternative to both these solutions and to putting in a receiver.

Effectively the secured creditors have a right of veto over the making of an administration order. This is because anyone petitioning for an administration order must give notice of the fact to anyone who is entitled to put in a receiver or to anyone who has actually put one in. The secured creditor on receiving the notice can then appoint a receiver. If he does, an administration order cannot be made. If a receiver is already in place and the secured creditor does not consent to that receiver stepping down, then again an administration order cannot be made. On the other hand once an administration order is made it is no longer possible for a creditor to appoint a receiver.

Once a winding up resolution has been passed or the court has ordered the company to be wound up, an administration order can no longer be made. On the other hand once an administration order has been made it will no longer be possible to petition the court for a winding up order.

11.1 The petition for administration

The first step is to present a petition to the court for an administration order: s 9. In order to make an order the court must be satisfied that:

(a) the company is or is likely to become unable to pay its debts; and

(b) the making of an administration order is likely to achieve one or more of:

  (i) the survival of the company and its undertaking as a going concern;

  (ii) the approval of a voluntary arrangement;

  (iii) the sanctioning of a scheme of arrangement under s 425 CA;

  (iv) a more advantageous realisation of the company's assets than would be effected in a liquidation.

The effect of the administration petition is to impose a standstill on any move:

(a) for voluntary liquidation;

(b) for seizure of the company's goods in execution of a judgement for debt;

(c) to re-possess goods obtained on hire purchase, rental or retention of title arrangements;

(d) for the institution of any legal proceedings against the company.

It does not, however, prevent the presentation of a petition for compulsory liquidation, though no order may be made while the petition for an administration order is pending, nor does it prevent a receiver from being appointed.

Activity 6 **(10 minutes)**

A petition for an administration order is made on 1 August, and the order is made on 15 August.

(a) Could a receiver have been appointed on 8 August?

(b) Could a petition for compulsory liquidation have been presented on 8 August?

11.2 The administration order

If the administration order is made, the above temporary measures become permanent; in addition no petition may be presented for compulsory liquidation nor may any administrative receiver be appointed: s 11. Other effects of an administration order are as follows.

(a) In addition to the powers given to a receiver an administrator may challenge past transactions of the company with a view to having them reversed by court order.

(b) An administrator may, with the sanction of the court or with the charge-holder's agreement, sell property of the company subject to a fixed charge: s 11. He may also sell property subject to a floating charge and in this case the charge is then transferred to the proceeds of sale: s 15.

(c) A supplier of goods on hire purchase or retention of title terms may not, unless the administrator consents or the court gives leave, re-possess those goods: s 11(3). The powers of sale described in (b) extend to goods in this category: s 15(2).

(d) The administrator acts as the company's agent (s 14), but he does not have statutory liability on contracts. A person dealing with an administrator in good faith is entitled to assume that he is acting within his powers: s 14(6).

(e) As regards contracts, the administrator can be prevented by injunction from refusing to carry on with a contract made by the company.

(f) Under the Insolvency Act 1994, the administrator's liability under employment contracts is restricted to certain qualifying liabilities, as for administrative receivers.

11.3 The administrator

The court appoints an insolvency practitioner to be the administrator of the company; in that capacity he has all the statutory powers of an administrative receiver. In addition he may remove any director from office, appoint directors and call meetings of creditors and of members: s 14. With the approval of the court he may also dispose of, free of encumbrance, property of the company until then subject to a charge and also property in its possession under a hire purchase, rental or retention of title agreement. But if he does so, a sum equal to the market value of the property (the net proceeds topped up if necessary) must be applied in repayment of the previously secured debt, or in meeting the claims of the persons whose goods have been sold: s 15.

The order must be publicised.

(a) All company correspondence and documentation must bear the administrator's name and state that an order has been made: s 12.

(b) The administrator must give notice to the company (immediately), to the registrar (within 14 days) and to the creditors (within 28 days): s 21.

An administrator is entitled to receive a statement of affairs. Within three months (or such longer time as the court may allow) he must produce and circulate a statement of his proposals for implementing the purpose of the administration order. Copies go to the creditors; members receive copies or a notice is published to inform them where they may apply for a copy. The administrator next calls a meeting of creditors, on 14 days' notice, to consider and, if thought fit, approve his proposals. He then reports to the court on the result of the meeting. If the proposals have been approved, the administration order will continue in force so that they may be implemented. If the proposals have not been approved the court is likely to discharge the order: s 24(5).

In approving the administrator's proposals, the creditors' meeting may resolve to appoint a creditors' committee to work with the administrator: s 26. They may modify his proposals, but only if he agrees to each change: s 24.

Activity 7 **(10 minutes)**

An administrator of a company with three factories proposes to close and sell one factory and to buy new equipment for the two remaining factories. The creditors are generally in favour of the proposed sale, but will not under any circumstances agree to spending money on new equipment. The administrator will not agree to the sale unless new equipment is to be bought. What is the likely outcome?

Chapter roundup

- When a company is dissolved, it is removed from the register and ceases to exist. This can happen in several ways, but the most common way is liquidation. In a liquidation, a company's assets are disposed of, its debts are paid so far as possible and any surplus is paid to the members.
- A compulsory liquidation may be petitioned for on any of several grounds, but the most common ground is that the company is unable to pay its debts. A provisional liquidator (usually the Official Receiver) is appointed on the presentation of a petition and, if the court is satisfied, an order for winding up is granted. A statement of affairs is prepared and meetings of contributories and creditors may be held in order to appoint a replacement liquidator. The liquidator reports to the DTI on the completion of his work.
- If a company is solvent, it may go into members' voluntary liquidation. The liquidator holds meetings of contributories, and prepares final accounts once he has finished his work.
- A creditors' voluntary liquidation is also instigated by the members, but a meeting of the creditors must also be held. The creditors may nominate a liquidator and their choice prevails over the members' choice. A liquidation committee may be appointed to work with the liquidator.
- In any liquidation, contributories may be called upon to provide funds to meet the company's debts if they hold partly paid shares or if they disposed of such shares within the year preceding the commencement of the winding up.
- A liquidator may pay and compromise debts, and may conduct legal proceedings. He stands in a fiduciary relationship to the company, and he must exercise his discretion personally and keep records.
- If a company is in temporary difficulty, it, its directors or any of its creditors may apply for an administration order. Once an administration order has been made, a receiver cannot be appointed and the court cannot be petitioned for a winding up order. The administrator then has time to devise a scheme to save the company from insolvency.

Quick quiz

1. Describe how a company may be dissolved.
2. Give three grounds on which an order may be made by the court for compulsory liquidation of a company.
3. What grounds may be asserted in a creditor's petition to establish that the company is unable to pay its debts?
4. Give two examples of circumstances which can provide 'just and equitable' grounds for compulsory winding up.
5. What meetings are called by the Official Receiver?
6. What type of resolution is passed to put a company into voluntary liquidation?
7. What is a liquidation committee?
8. What are the main powers of liquidators?
9. What accounting records must a liquidator keep?

10 Who may act as an administrator?

Answers to quick quiz

1 By registrar, if defunct
By court order
By Act of Parliament
Early dissolution
After liquidation (see para 1)

2 Special resolution
Unable to pay debts
Just and equitable to wind up (para 3)

3 Written demand for payment of at least £750 remains unpaid for 21 days. (para 3.1)

4 Substratum failed
No confidence by shareholders (para 3.2)

5 The meetings to commence a compulsory liquidation. (para 3.4)

6 Extraordinary resolution. (para 4.1, 4.3)

7 Consists of representatives of members and creditors. Main function: to work with the liquidator and fix his fees. (para 5)

8 Pay creditors
Deal with assets
Carry on business (para 7)

9 Receipts and payments
Trading account (if applicable) (para 8)

10 A licensed insolvency practitioner. (para 11.3)

Answers to activities

1 Persons with no previous dealings with the company need to be warned before they make contracts with the company.

2 The company had not neglected to pay: it was deliberately disputing the amount due.

3 P: the creditors' choice prevails.

4 It is expected that all creditors will be paid in full, so there is no need for them to interfere.

5 He has breached his fiduciary duty to the company by making a profit from his position.

6 (a) Yes: the petition for an administration order does not prevent a receiver from being appointed.

(b) Yes: the petition for an administration order does not prevent a petition for compulsory liquidation, although an order may not be granted.

7 The court will discharge the administration order.

NOTES

Assignment 15 **(30 minutes)**

Explain the sanctions open to the courts for directors who fail to run their company properly in the period leading up to the insolvent liquidation of their company.

Chapter 19 :
PARTNERSHIPS

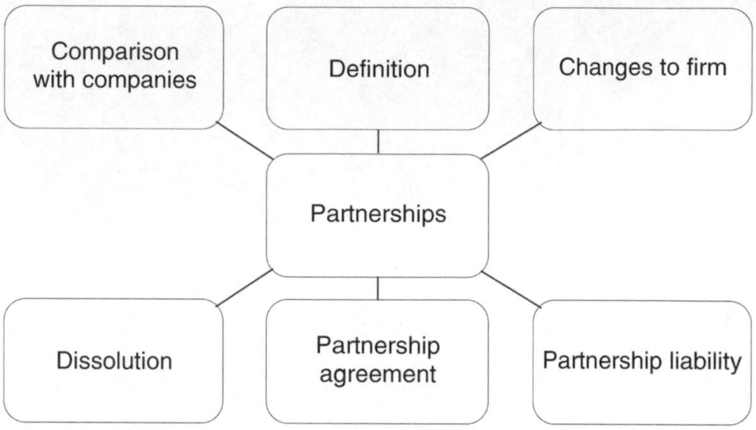

Introduction

Outcome 3 of the syllabus for this unit refers to the 'legal provisions concerned with the formation, management and dissolution of business units'. So far, this book has concentrated almost exclusively on company law although from time to time reference has been made to partnerships as another form of business unit.

This chapter draws together some of the aspects of partnership which you have already seen, and discusses further aspects of partnership, so that you have a complete picture of the law relating to partnerships. This will also mean that you appreciate the differences between the two forms of business unit.

Your objectives

In this chapter you will learn about the following.

(a) The definition of a partnership

(b) What happens when there is a change in the partnership

(c) The nature of partnership liability

(d) The contents of a partnership agreement

(e) The procedure on the dissolution of a partnership

(f) The main differences between partnerships and companies

1 PARTNERSHIP

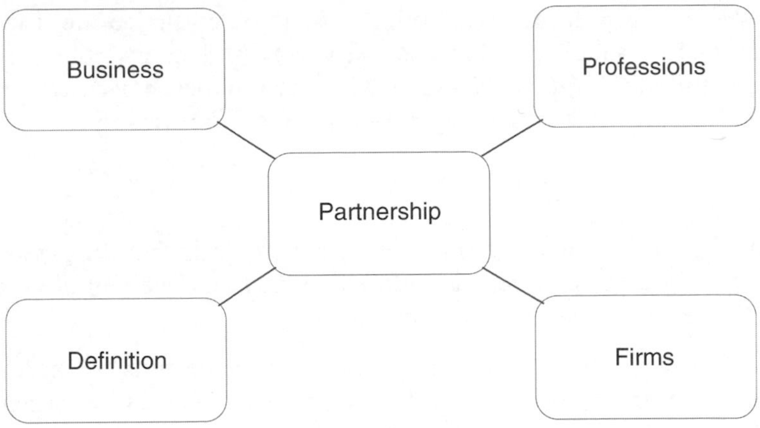

Partnership is the normal organisation in the professions but is less common in commerce. This is because most professions prohibit their members from carrying on practice through limited companies. Businessmen are not so restricted and generally prefer to trade through a limited company so that, if it becomes insolvent, they are not liable for its debts. A partner is personally liable for all the debts of the firm (incurred while he is a partner and sometimes even after he has ceased to be a partner).

The word 'firm' is correctly used to denote a partnership. It is not correct to apply it to a registered company (though the newspapers often do so). The word 'company' may form part of the name of a partnership firm, eg 'Smith & Company'. But 'limited company' or 'registered company' is only applied to a company incorporated under the Companies Act 1985. You are advised to avoid using the word 'company' in connection with a partnership (and you should never use the words 'limited company' in that connection) as it may suggest that you are unable to distinguish a partnership from a registered company.

1.1 Definition of partnership

In most cases there is no doubt about the existence of a partnership. The partners declare their intention by such steps as signing a written partnership agreement and adopting a firm name. But these outward and visible signs of the existence of a partnership are not essential - a partnership can exist without them. The main consequence of a partnership is that there is no separate legal person as distinct from its members. A partnership exists whenever the facts satisfy the statutory definition (s 1 Partnership Act 1890), which is as follows:

'Partnership is the relation which subsists between persons carrying on a business in common with a view of profit'.

1.2 The relation which subsists between persons

(a) Partnership is *the relation which subsists between persons*. 'Person' includes a corporation such as a registered company as well as an individual living person.

(b) There must be at least two partners. If, therefore, two men are in partnership, one dies and the survivor carries on the business he is a sole trader - there is no longer a partnership.

(c) The standard maximum number of partners permitted by law is 20: s 716 Companies Act 1985. The intention of this rule is that if more than 20 persons wish to carry on a commercial business they should form a registered company for that purpose.

(d) As professional practice cannot usually be carried on by a registered company, solicitors, chartered surveyors and many other professions are permitted to form partnerships with any number of partners; the limit of 20 only applies to commercial, not professional partnerships.

1.3 Carrying on a business

The next point in the statutory definition of a partnership is that the persons concerned are *carrying on a business.* Business is defined to include 'every trade, occupation or profession': s 45. But three points should be noted.

(a) A business is a *form of activity.* If two or more persons are merely the passive joint owners of revenue-producing property, such as investments or rented houses, that fact of itself does not make them partners: s 2(1).

(b) A business can consist of a *single transaction.* These situations are often described as 'joint ventures' - the partners associate solely for the purpose of completing one deal, such as a joint speculation in buying potatoes wholesale for resale: *Mann v Darcy 1968.*

(c) Carrying on a business must have a *beginning and an end.* A partnership begins when the partners begin their business activity: it does not make any difference if they entered into a formal partnership agreement with effect from some earlier or later date. Similarity, statements that the individuals involved are partners does not establish a business. Courts will decide whether a business is being carried on in common by reviewing the facts: *Kahn and Others v Miah and Others 1997.*

(d) Making preparations to carry on a partnership, such as obtaining finance, is *not* the same as carrying it on. Thus in the *Kahn v Miah* case partnership could not commence until the Indian restaurant the partnership was set up to run had actually opened.

1.4 In common

To constitute a partnership the partners must also carry on business *in common.* Broadly this phrase means that the partners must be associated in the business as joint proprietors. The evidence that this is so is found in their taking a share of the profits.

1.5 A view of profit

The persons must have a *view of profit.* If persons enter into a partnership with a view to making profits but they actually suffer losses, it is still a partnership. The test to be applied is one of intention.

1.6 Liability of the partners

Every partner is liable *without limit* for the debts of the partnership. It is possible to register a limited partnership in which sole partners have limited liability, but the limited partners may not take part in the management of the business: Limited Partnerships Act 1907.

NOTES

2 CHANGES OF MEMBERSHIP

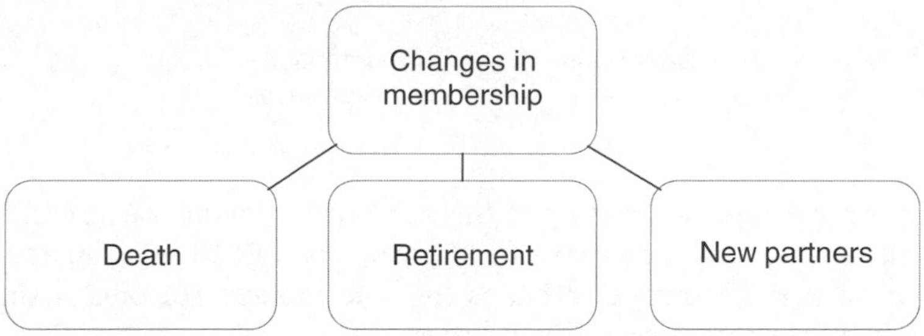

2.1 Death of a partner

The death of a partner may itself dissolve the partnership (s 33 so provides unless otherwise agreed). This is usually avoided by expressly agreeing that so long as there are two or more surviving partners the partnership shall continue. The estate of a deceased partner is only liable for debts of the partnership incurred *before* his death.

2.2 Retirement of a partner

The effect of retirement is that the partner who retires:

(a) is still liable for any outstanding debts incurred while he was a partner unless the creditor has agreed to release him from liability; and

(b) is also liable for debts of the firm incurred after his retirement if the creditor knew him to be a partner (before retirement) and has not had notice of his retirement. This is due to the principle that a person who was previously known to be a partner continues to be an 'apparent member' of the partnership and liable for all its debts until notice is given that he is no longer a partner; s 36.

2.3 Notice of retirement

To avoid being still an 'apparent member' of the firm after his retirement the retiring partner should give notice of his retirement.

(a) To creditors who had dealings with the firm while he was a partner, he should give actual notice of his retirement. This need not be an express notice. If for example the firm reprints its letterhead to omit him from the list of partners and writes a letter on the new letterhead to a creditor that is sufficient notice to the creditor of the change.

(b) To persons who may have known that he is a partner (before his retirement) but who begin to have dealings with the firm for the first time after his retirement, the retired partner cannot easily give actual notice since he does not know (at his retirement) who they may prove to be. But sufficient notice is given to them if he advertises the fact of his retirement in the London Gazette: s 36(2). They are then deemed to have notice even if they have not read the advertisement.

2.4 New partner

A new partner admitted to an existing firm is liable for debts incurred only after he becomes a partner. He is not liable for debts incurred before he was a partner unless he agrees to become liable.

BPP PUBLISHING

3 PARTNERSHIP PROPERTY

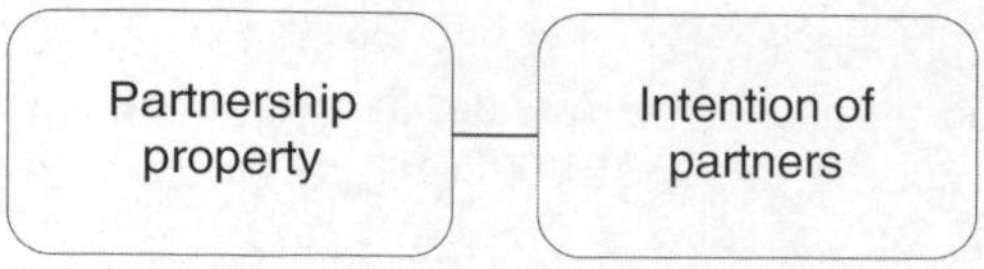

The initial property of the partnership is that which the partners expressly or impliedly agreed shall be partnership property. It is quite possible that property used in the business is not partnership property but is the sole property of one of the partners; it depends entirely on the intention of the partners.

4 A PARTNER'S AUTHORITY AS AGENT OF THE FIRM

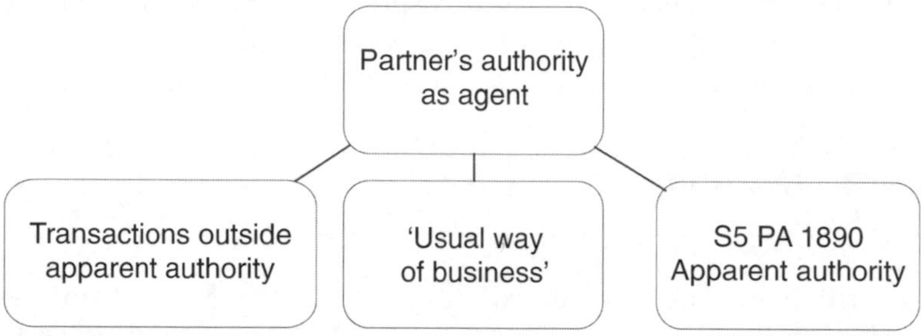

The Partnership Act 1890 defines the apparent authority of a partner to make contracts as follows. The definition is found in section 5 which is one of the most important sections in the Act.

'Every partner is an agent of the firm and his other partners for the purpose of the business of the partnership; and the acts of every partner who does any act for carrying on in the usual way business of the kind carried on by the firm of which he is a member bind the firm and his partners, unless the partner so acting has in fact no authority to act for the firm in the particular matter, and the person with whom he is dealing either knows that he has no authority, or does not know or believe him to be a partner': s 5.

The Act also states that the partnership is only bound by acts done by a partner in the firm's name and not apparently for the partners personally: ss 6 and 7.

4.1 Apparent authority

Sometimes a single partner enters into a transaction which the other partners wish to repudiate on the ground that it is outside the limits of the *business of the kind carried on by the firm*. It is indeed usual to specify in a partnership agreement what is the nature of the firm's business. But unless the person with whom a partner deals is aware of the agreed limits he may hold the firm bound by a transaction which would appear to him (and other outsiders) to be the kind of business which such a firm ordinarily carries on.

> *Mercantile Credit v Garrod 1962*
> P and the defendant entered into partnership to let lock-up garages and repair cars. P ran the business and the defendant was a sleeping partner. Their partnership agreement provided expressly that the firm would not buy and sell cars. But P sold a car which the firm did not own to a finance company (the claimant) so that it might be let on hire purchase to a customer. The claimant sued the defendant to recover the £700 which it had paid P for the car. The defendant denied liability on the ground that P in selling the car had been acting outside the agreed limits of the firm's business and so P had no

actual or apparent authority from him. Evidence was given that other garage businesses of the type carried on by P and the defendant did deal in cars.

Held: the test of what is the firm's business is not what the partners agreed it should be but 'what it appeared to the outside world' to be (established by the practice of 'businesses of a like kind'). By that test P appeared to the claimant to be carrying on business of the kind carried on by such a firm. Buying and selling the firm's goods is within the authority of a single partner.

4.2 The 'usual way' of business

The second test of s 5 is that a partner is agent of the firm in carrying on the firm's business *in the usual way*. What is usual in any particular business must always depend partly on the general practice of businesses of a similar type and size. In particular a distinction is made between commercial firms which trade in buying and selling goods and non-commercial firms (including of course professional partnerships) which do not do so. A single partner of a commercial firm (acting on behalf of the firm and within the apparent limits of its kind of business) is deemed to have the authority of the other partners to engage in any of the following transactions.

(a) To buy and sell goods in the course of the firm's business (including the purchase of fixed assets for use in the business such as a typewriter or a delivery van).

(b) To receive payment of debts owed to the firm and to issue receipts.

(c) To engage employees to work in the firm's business.

(d) To sign cheques drawn on the firm's bank account.

(e) To sign bills of exchange as drawer acceptor or endorser.

(f) To borrow money and to give security by pledging the firm's goods or by deposit of title deeds etc relating to the firm's land and buildings.

4.3 Transactions outside a partner's apparent authority

The following transactions are not within the apparent authority of a single partner in any kind of partnership.

(a) To execute a deed such as a legal mortgage of property; for this he requires a power of attorney executed by all the partners.

(b) To give a guarantee of another person's debt unless it is the custom in the firm's trade to do so.

(c) To submit a dispute to arbitration.

(d) To accept property, eg fully-paid shares of a company, in satisfaction of a debt owed to the firm.

Activity 1 **(10 minutes)**

Andrew, Brian and Cecil are in partnership as antique dealers and repairers. Cecil entered a contract with Tom to repair a grandfather clock belonging to Tom. Once it was repaired, Cecil sold the clock and has disappeared with the money. Do you think Tom has any course of action against Andrew and Brian?

5 THE PARTNERSHIP AGREEMENT

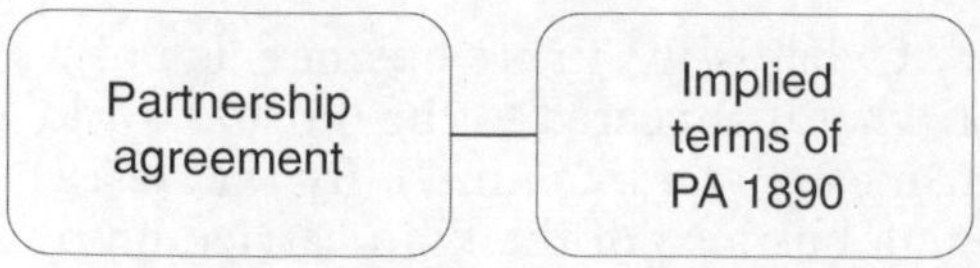

There is no legal requirement for a written partnership agreement. A partnership may be established without formality by oral agreement or even by conduct. But in practice there are advantages in setting down in writing (signed by the partners) the terms of their association. This is called a 'partnership agreement' or 'articles of partnership'.

(a) It fills in the details which the law would not imply - the nature of the firm's business, the firm name, and the bank at which the firm will maintain its bank account.

(b) A written agreement serves to override terms otherwise implied by the Partnership Act 1890 which are inappropriate to the partnership. The Act for example implies (unless otherwise agreed) that partners share profits equally. But in many firms the older partners take a larger profit share than the younger ones.

5.1 Terms implied by the Partnership Act 1890

The partnership agreement is often used as a way of codifying the relationship and can exclude terms implied by the Partnership Act 1890. Some of the more important areas covered by this Act are as follows.

(a) *Freedom of variation*. Under s 19 Partnership Act 1890, the partnership agreement may be varied with the consent of all the partners. This may be formal or informal.

(b) *Good faith*. There is a duty of utmost good faith once the partnership is established, although the contract of partnership is not itself *uberrimae fidei* ('of the utmost good faith').

(c) *Profits and losses*. These are shared equally in the absence of contrary agreement. However, if the partnership agreement states that profits are to be shared in certain proportions then, prima facie, losses are to be shared in the same proportions.

(d) *Interest on capital*. None is paid on capital except by agreement. However, a partner is entitled to 5% interest on advances beyond his original capital.

(e) *Indemnity*. The firm must indemnify any partner against liabilities incurred in the ordinary and proper conduct of the partnership business or in doing anything necessarily done for the preservation of the partnership property or business.

(f) *Management*. Every partner is entitled to take part in managing the firm's business; ordinary management decisions can be made by a majority of partners.

(g) *Change in business*. Any decision on changing the nature of the partnership's business must be unanimous.

(h) *Remuneration*. No partner is entitled to remuneration such as salary for acting in the partnership business.

(i) *Records and accounts*. These must be kept at the main place of business, and must be open to inspection by all partners.

(j) *New partners*. New partners must only be introduced with the consent of all existing partners.

(k) *Expulsion*. A partner may only be expelled by a majority of votes when the partnership agreement allows; even then, the power must only be used in good faith and for good reason.

(l) *Misrepresentation*. When a partner is induced to enter into a partnership by misrepresentation he remains liable to creditors for obligations incurred whilst a partner, but he has several remedies against the maker of the statement including, for example, rescission and/or damages (reflecting the basic contractual rules on misrepresentation which you encountered earlier).

(m) *Dissolution*. The authority of the partners after dissolution continues so far as is necessary to wind up the partnership affairs and complete transactions already begun. On dissolution, any partner can insist on realisation of the firm's assets (including goodwill), payment of the firm's debts and distribution of the surplus, subject to any contrary agreement.

(n) *Capital deficiency*. A distinction is made between a loss (including a capital loss such as the sale of a fixed asset for less than its book value) and a capital deficiency. It can happen that as a result of normal losses a partner's capital is exhausted and in addition he becomes (by reason of his share of the losses) a debtor to the firm. If in those circumstances he is unable to pay what he owes to the firm, there is a capital deficiency. If there are two or more solvent partners with credit balances on capital account the assets (less the irrecoverable sum owed by the insolvent partner) will be less than the aggregate of those balances. They share the deficiency not as a loss but in ratio to the amounts of capital which they originally contributed to the firm. This is the rule in *Garner v Murray 1904*.

6 DISSOLUTION

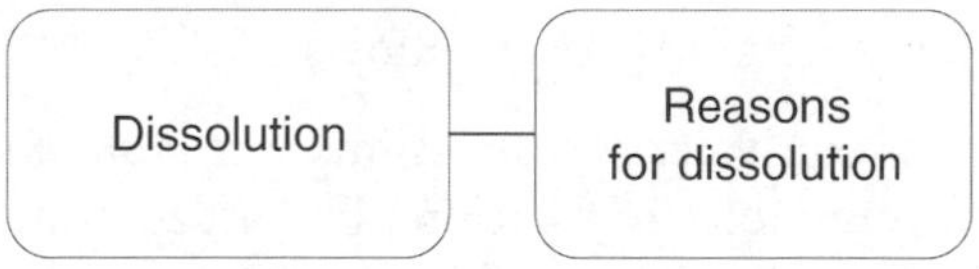

Dissolution of a partnership occurs in the following situations.

(a) By *passing of time*, if the partnership was entered into for a fixed term.

(b) By *termination of the venture*, if entered into for a single venture.

(c) By the *death or bankruptcy* of a partner, unless the partnership agreement otherwise provides.

(d) By *subsequent illegality*, such as an event which makes it unlawful to continue the business.

(e) By *notice* given by a partner if it is a partnership of indefinite duration.

(f) By *order of the court* granted to a partner, for one or several reasons - for example the permanent incapacity of a partner or because it is just and equitable to order dissolution.

NOTES

7 SUPERVISION

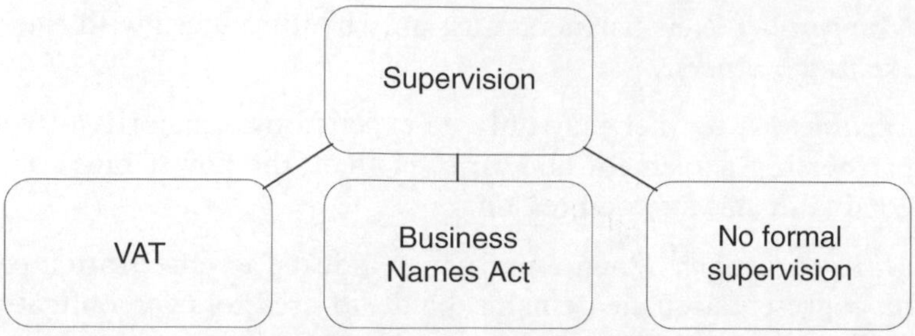

There is no formal statutory supervision of partnerships. Their accounts need not be in prescribed form nor is an audit necessary. The public has no means or legal right of inspection of the firm's accounts or other information such as companies must provide.

Partnerships are not subject to the stringent rules governing companies as set out in the Companies Act 1985 and the Insolvency Act 1986.

If, however, the partners carry on business under a firm name which is not the surnames of them all, say, 'Smith, Jones & Co', they are required to disclose the names of the partners on their letterheads and at their places of business. Business Names Act ss 1 and 4. They are required to make a return of their profits for income tax and usually to register for VAT.

8 OTHER MATTERS

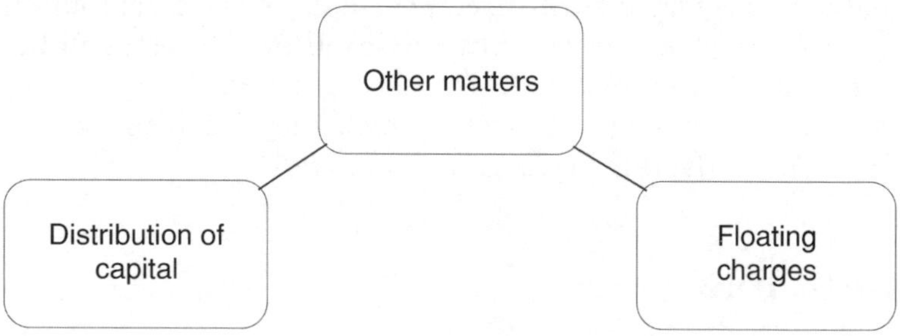

Other matters relevant to partnerships are as follows.

(a) There are no equivalent restrictions on *distribution of capital* to those contained in companies legislation. The assets transferred as capital are the partners'; there is no exchange for shares.

(b) A partnership, unlike a company, cannot create a *floating charge* over its assets - such as stock in trade or book debts - as security for a loan.

9 DIFFERENCES BETWEEN COMPANIES AND PARTNERSHIPS

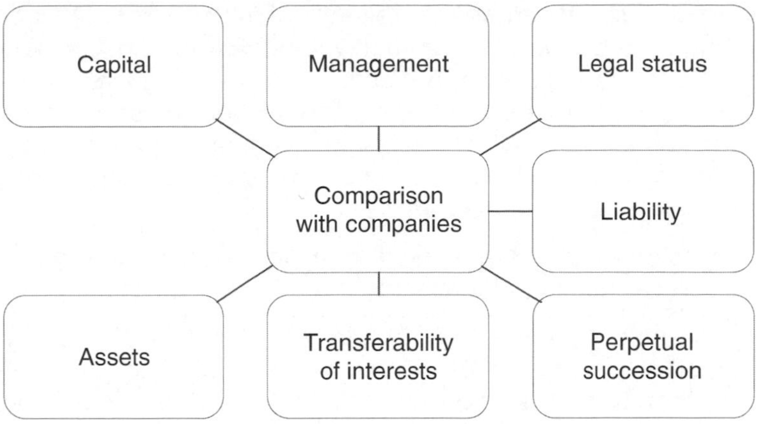

The owners of a small business have a choice whether to trade as a partnership or as a company although, as noted above, some professions, including solicitors, do not permit their members to practise as companies. The choice is often determined by the amount of tax likely to be paid under one alternative or the other. There are however a number of other factors of comparison.

The crucial factors (apart from tax) which often swing a decision as to whether to incorporate or to remain a partnership are *limited liability* and *privacy*. The former is clearly an advantage for anyone seeking to invest money or who wishes to protect himself against further outlay. The lack of privacy, however, may be offputting; even a small company must prepare annual accounts, have them audited and (usually) lay them before a general meeting. However the exemption for a requirement for an annual audit is currently being extended to companies with a turnover of less than £1m.

The principal differences between companies and partnerships can be summarised under the following headings.

(a) Legal entity.
(b) Liability of members/partners.
(c) Perpetual succession.
(d) Transferability of interest.
(e) Ownership of assets.
(f) Repayment of capital.
(g) Management.
(h) Written constitution.
(i) Accounts and audit.
(j) Security/charges.

Activity 2 **(20 minutes)**

Using the above headings, draw up a table which sets out the differences between companies and partnerships. You will need to think back to what you learned about company law.

Chapter roundup

- Partnership is defined as 'the relation which subsists between persons carrying on a business in common with a view of profit'. A partnership is not a separate legal person distinct from its members - it is merely a 'relation' between persons. Each partner (there must be at least two) is personally liable for all the debts of the firm. A partnership may exist without any formal documentation or procedure (although many firms do have such a formal agreement).
- In the absence of express terms in a partnership agreement, the 1890 Act implies a number of terms into the relationship.
- Each partner is an agent of the firm when he acts in carrying on in the usual way business of the kind carried on by the firm, although his authority may be restricted by the other partners. The authority of an individual partner varies depending on whether the firm is commercial or non-commercial.

Quick quiz

1 What definition of partnership is given by the Partnership Act 1890?

2 To what type of partnership does the 20 partner limit apply?

3 What happens if a partner dies?

4 Explain the importance of S5 Partnership Act 1890.

5 What is meant by the 'usual way of business'?

6 Give three implied terms of the Partnership Act 1890.

7 Is the general public entitled to access to the accounts of a partnership?

Answers to quick quiz

1 'The relation which subsists between persons carrying on a business in common with a view of profit'. (para 1.1)

2 Commercial partnerships. (para 1.2)

3 The partnership dissolves unless there is an agreement to the contrary. (para 2.1)

4 It sets out the concept of apparent authority of a partner to bind the firm acting in the usual way of business. (para 4.1)

5 What the firm could normally be expected to do. (para 4.2)

6 Act in good faith

No right of remuneration

New partners to be introduced with the consent of existing partners (para 5.1)

7 No. One of the main advantages of partnership. (para 7)

Answers to activities

1 Yes, as Cecil was acting in the normal course of business of the firm and he had apparent authority to bind the firm.

2

	Company	*Partnership*
(a)	Separate entity	No separate entity
(b)	Members' liability may be limited	Partners' liability usually unlimited
(c)	Perpetual succession - no cessation by change of membership	A change of partners is a termination of the old firm and the beginning of a new one
(d)	Members own transferable shares	A partner can assign his interest but the assignee does not become a partner
(e)	Company (not members) own assets	Partners jointly own partnership property
(f)	Capital subscribed by shareholders may only be repaid to them under certain rules	Partners may (by mutual agreement) withdraw capital as they wish
(g)	A company must have one or more directors. A member has no involvement in management	Partners are entitled to participate in management and are agents of the firm
(h)	A company always has a written constitution	A partnership may exist without any written partnership agreement
(i)	Usually, a company must deliver annual accounts, annual returns and other notices to Registrar of Companies	A partnership must disclose the names of the partners. But no one except a partner has any right to inspect accounts
(j)	A company may offer security by way of floating charge over its assets	Partners cannot usually provide security by a floating charge on goods

NOTES

Assignment 16 **(60 minutes)**

Complete the table below giving any relevant information on each feature for each type of organisation. Find any information not in this chapter from books in any library.

Comparisons of business organisation

Features	Sole trader	Partnership	Private company	Public company
Creation				
Legal status				
Liability				
Publicity				
Audit				
Reporting of results				
Ownership				
Control				
Management				
Transfer of membership				
Duration				
Ownership of assets				

ANSWERS TO ASSIGNMENTS

NOTES

Answer to assignment 1 (Chapter 3)

> **Tutorial note**. A straightforward question on basic contract law. Outline the courts' approach to deciding whether an offer has been accepted by reference to the appropriate case law.

An *agreement* constituted by an offer (or definite promise to be bound on specific terms) and acceptance of that offer, is one of the essentials of a contract, the others being an intention to create legal relations and consideration. The courts will generally take an objective approach to deciding whether an offer has been legally and validly accepted and the following considerations will be important.

The acceptance must be an unqualified agreement to the terms of the offer. If it in fact introduces new terms then it is a *counter offer* and not an acceptance (which might then be accepted by the original offeror). Thus in *Hyde v Wrench 1840*, where an offer was made to sell land for £1000 and the plaintiff made a counter offer of £950 but later sought to accept the original offer, it was held that the plaintiff's counter offer had terminated the original offer.

A response to an offer which is actually a request for further information or an enquiry as to a variation of terms (*Stevenson v McLean 1880*) will not constitute acceptance. Acceptance made 'subject to contract' will not amount to a valid acceptance until the proposed formal contract has been signed (cf *Branca v Cobarro 1947*).

Since an invitation for tenders is considered an invitation to treat and not an offer, it follows that the making of a tender is not an acceptance but itself the offer which can then be accepted in the same way as any other offer, unless the tender is to supply or perform a series of things (ie a standing offer) which is accepted by each order (creating a separate contract in each case).

The acceptance may be by express words or by action (*as in Carlill v Carbolic Smokeball Co 1893*) or be inferred from conduct (*Brogden v Metropolitan Rly Co 1877*). There must be some act on the part of the offeree, however, as mere silence or passive inaction is not capable of constituting acceptance (*Felthouse v Bindley 1862*).

The acceptance must be *communicated* to the offeror before it can be effective unless the offeror expressly waives the need for communication. Such waiver can either be express or inferred from the circumstances. In Carlill's case, it was held sufficient for the offeree to act on the offer without previously notifying his acceptance of it (this was termed a unilateral contract). Similarly, acceptance by conduct is sufficient in reward cases. The offeror may stipulate that communication must be made in a particular way. Unless he stipulates that such means is the only way then acceptance by some other means equally expeditious would constitute a valid acceptance (*Tinn v Hoffmann 1873*). Acceptance of an offer can only be made by the offeree or a person authorised to make it (*Powell v Lee 1908*).

The *postal rule* provides that an acceptance is effective once posted and not once it arrives at the offeror's address, assuming it was correctly stamped, addressed and actually posted and that acceptance by post was reasonably in the contemplation of both parties (*Adams v Lindsell 1818*). If the offer is made by post, it will be assumed that acceptance by post was intended (*Household Fire and Carriage Accident Insurance Company v Grant 1879*). Again, if a particular mode of communication is stipulated in the offer which is inconsistent with the postal rule, then the rule will not apply (*Holwell Securities v Hughes 1974*). If two identical offers cross in the post there is no acceptance and thus no contract (*Tinn v Hoffman 1873*).

NOTES

Answer to assignment 2 (Chapter 4)

> **Tutorial note**. In part (a) you had to explain the requirement that consideration must be 'real', ie not vague/illusory/indefinite. It is not necessary, however, that the 'price of the promise' (consideration) should be adequate. The law allows the parties to arrive at their own 'bargain'. In part (b) you had to explain the extent to which an existing legal obligation can amount to sufficient consideration for a contract, for example an existing contractual or public duty. This is sufficient consideration only when the promisee performs an act in excess of the existing obligation.

(a) The first half of the statement, that consideration must be real, is often phrased to say that consideration must be adequate. The meaning of each is the same - what is meant is that what is given as consideration must be capable in law of being regarded as consideration. The second half of the statement, that consideration need not be adequate, means that consideration does not have to be equal to the consideration received in return.

These two halves of the statement provide two overlapping rules in the law of consideration. This means that although consideration does not have to be equal in value to the consideration received, it does have to be capable of being regarded as consideration. The courts will not enquire into the adequacy of consideration. It is generally presumed that each party is capable of serving his own interests, and the courts will not seek to weigh up the comparative value of the promises or acts exchanged.

When it is said that consideration does not have to be adequate, what is meant is that it does not have to be a fair price for the contract. The law demands that there be an element of bargain but it does not require a good bargain. In *Chappell & Co v Nestle Co 1960*, a company offered to supply a record to anyone sending in a small sum of money and three chocolate wrappers from its products. It was held that the wrappers were valuable consideration as they were of some commercial value to the company, even though they were of no economic value. They therefore formed adequate consideration. Another case in which the monetary value of consideration was very low is *Thomas v Thomas 1842*. By his will, a husband expressed the wish that his widow should have the use of his house during the rest of her life. His executors let it to her in accordance with her husband's wishes and in return for her agreeing to pay them £1 per annum. They later sought to show that the husband's wish did not constitute adequate consideration. It was held that the husband's wish was not consideration for the let, but the payment of money was, even though £1 was clearly not a good economic rent.

Consideration must be sufficient in that it must be capable of being regarded in law as consideration. This means that it must be of some value. A promise to give up a hopeless claim or a purely moral claim is not good consideration as it is of no value. A promise to forbear from exercising a legal right is capable of being good consideration as the party given it has given something of value, eg a bank agreeing not to enforce its rights to demand immediate repayment of an overdraft is good and valuable consideration: *Alliance Bank v Broom 1864*. The plaintiff seeking to rely on such a waiver to support a contract must show that the claim is a reasonable one, that he has an honest belief in its chance of success and that he has withheld no information which might affect the validity of the claim.

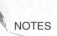

(b) The question may arise as to the extent to which performance of existing obligations can constitute consideration.

Performance of an existing obligation imposed by statute is no consideration for a promise of reward: *Collins v Godefroy 1831*. But if some extra service is given that will constitute sufficient consideration: *Glasbrook Bros v Glamorgan CC 1925*. In this case, at a time of industrial unrest, colliery owners, rejecting the view of the police that a mobile force was enough, asked for and agreed to pay for a special stationary guard on the mine. Later they repudiated liability saying that the police had done no more than perform their public duty of maintaining order, and that no consideration was given. It was held that the police had done more than perform their general duties. The extra service given, beyond what the police in their discretion deemed necessary, was consideration for the promise to pay. If the judgment of the police authorities had been that a stationary guard was necessary, they would not have been entitled to charge for it.

In this case, neither party could call off the strike, and so the threat to law and order was not caused, directly or indirectly, by them. Where one party's actions lead to the need for heightened police presence, and the police deem this presence necessary, they may still be entitled to payment: *Harris v Sheffield United FC Ltd 1988*, where the football club argued unsuccessfully that they did not have to pay for a large police presence at their home matches. It was held that they had voluntarily decided to hold matches on Saturday afternoons when huge attendances were likely, thus increasing the risk of disorder.

In the case in question, Snowden's decision to hold a concert is a voluntary one, and the weather has no bearing on this. It is likely that the court would follow the *Sheffield United* case and that Snowden would be liable to pay.

Answer to assignment 3 (Chapter 5)

A contract is a legally binding agreement. Hence a mere agreement is not a contract unless there is evidence, express or implied, of the intention of the parties that their agreement should give rise to legal relations or legally binding obligations.

Express statements

In making an agreement, the parties may expressly say that it is or it is not intended to create legal relations. In one leading case, a written agreement stated that 'this agreement is not entered into...as a formal or legal agreement': *Rose & Frank Co v J T Crompton and Bros Ltd 1925*.

As an example of the opposite case it is provided by statute that an agreement between an employer and a trade union on conditions of employment etc is not to be legally binding unless the parties state in writing that it shall be: s 179 Trade Union and Labour Relations (Consolidation) Act 1992.

Although an express statement of intention either way will always be accepted by the courts, it is not often possible to settle the matter in that way. The parties do not usually express any intention of this kind at all. In those circumstances the courts interpret the agreement which the parties have made by objective criteria, based on the words used, the subject-matter of the contract, the relationship of the parties and so on. In this way the courts seek to deduce what is the presumed but unexpressed intention of the parties.

Presumptions

In *commercial agreements*, the courts will normally infer that there is an intention to create legal relations unless there is evidence to the contrary. In *Edwards v Skyways 1964* an agreement entered into to make an 'ex-gratia' payment as part of a larger negotiation was held to be legally binding.

The issue may sometimes arise when a supplier of goods has published an advertisement which may be an offer to sell the goods or to give some guarantee in respect of them. In the well-known carbolic smoke ball case (*Carlill v Carbolic Smoke Ball Co 1893*) the manufacturer argued - unsuccessfully - that his offer to pay a sum of money to any user of his medicine (who was not protected by it) was a mere 'puff' not intended to create a legally binding agreement.

The court decided against him because his advertisement stated that as proof of the seriousness of his assurance he had deposited money in a bank account to meet claims. This fact overrode any deduction about the general effect of an advertisement.

At one time, it was considered that in an agreement made in a *domestic context* there was no implied intention to create legal relations if none had been expressed. Thus an agreement by a husband to pay an allowance to his wife during his absence abroad was not legally binding: *Balfour v Balfour 1919*.

However, the courts are now more readily disposed to assume that there is an intention to create legal relations in an agreement between husband and wife, especially if they are no longer living together: *Merritt v Merritt 1969*. But much also depends on how the parties express their agreement. In *Merritt's* case, the wife insisted that the agreement be in writing so that the husband should sign it. In another case, a husband on leaving home promised to pay £15 per week to his wife 'so long as I can manage it'; this commitment was held to be so vague that no intention to create a legal obligation should be assumed: *Gould v Gould 1969*.

In other relationships, the court is more readily disposed to assume that the parties, although relatives or friends, did intend that a financial agreement should be binding. This may apply if there is a 'mutuality of agreement' amounting to a joint enterprise, for example where persons jointly enter a competition: *Simpkins v Pays 1955*. In this case, a woman, her granddaughter and a paying lodger took part in a weekly competition in a newspaper, which they entered in the grandmother's name. One week they won £750 and the lodger was denied a third share. It was held that there was a mutuality of agreement and that this was not a friendly adventure but a contract.

Answer to assignment 4 (Chapter 6)

There are two important clauses to consider in Brian's encounter with the car park. The first is 'closed circuit television in operation' and the second is 'cars parked at owners' risk. No responsibility ... etc ...'. The status of the first clause is unclear. It could amount to a representation, inducing the formation of the contract but not becoming a contract term, or it could be construed as a term of the contract. The remedies available to Brian will differ depending on the position. The second clause is a notice which purports to exclude liability and may therefore have the status at law of an exclusion clause, by which the car park operator will, as is seen in the conversation between Brian and the attendant, seek to exclude any liability on its part for Brian's loss.

Taking the two matters in reverse order, as this is the sequence in which they are considered when Brian seeks a remedy from the car park operator, the following matters require consideration in relation to the exclusion clause. As exclusion clauses are open to abuse by a stronger party where the persons making the contract are of unequal bargaining power, the law departs from its usual position of allowing parties to govern their own contractual relations and imposes some restrictions on their use. Certain types of clause are void by statute, while others will be examined by the courts firstly to ensure that they are properly incorporated into the contract and secondly to interpret the clause.

Only in limited circumstances will the courts allow the incorporation of a term after the contract has been made. It may only be done by the mutual agreement of the parties. Thus a sign on a hotel room wall was not incorporated into the contract between hotel and client since it was not seen until after the contract was made: *Olley v Marlborough Court 1949*. The court will have regard to the nature of the liability which is being excluded when deciding whether a clause has been effectively incorporated. If the terms are particularly unusual or wide, a more prominent notice may be necessary. For example, in *Thornton v Shoe Lane Parking Ltd 1971* a notice excluding liability for injury in an automatic car park was not sufficiently displayed or referred to at the time the contract was made). The terms may be incorporated into the contract by the signature of the other party on a document bearing the terms. The signatory is taken to know of the terms, even if he could not read them: *L'Estrange v Graucob 1934*. Where the parties deal frequently in transactions of a similar nature and on the same terms, the courts are ready to hold that the exclusion clause has been incorporated into the latest agreement by virtue of its being present in the previous dealings. However, it is not enough that the other party ought to have known of the clause; he must actually be aware of it: *Hollier v Rambler Motors 1972*.

As well as controlling the incorporation of exclusion clauses into contracts, the courts have developed other restrictions on their use. They tend to interpret them strictly, in favour of the weaker party. This is the *contra preferentem* rule. They presume that the clause is not intended to defeat the main purpose of the contract. If the clause limits liability in general terms, the courts will construe its scope so as to give the party relying on it the minimum opportunity to escape liability. A general exemption will not usually be interpreted so as to cover negligence: *Hollier v Rambler Motors 1972*. Statute law also imposes some very important restrictions on the use of exclusion clauses. The Unfair Contract Terms Act 1977 divides these clauses into two types; those which are void and those which are valid only as far as they are reasonable. Liability for personal injury or death due to negligence may never be excluded. An exclusion for loss due to negligence in other circumstances will be valid only insofar as it is reasonable: s 2 UCTA 1977.

In standard term contracts made with a consumer, terms which seek to exclude liability for breach, or to allow substantially different performance, or no performance at all, are valid only insofar as they are reasonable: s 3. Reasonableness is to be considered with reference to the factors in s 11. The court will consider the relative strength of the parties' bargaining power, whether an inducement was offered to the consumer, whether the consumer knew or ought to have known of the exclusion clauses and whether compliance with the contract's terms so that the exclusion clause would never be needed was practicable (Sch 2).

The wording of the question makes it clear that there is a contract between Brian and Secure Car Parks Ltd (ie this is not a free car park). The first issue to consider is therefore whether the clause was incorporated into the contract or not. A notice of this type may be inadequate if not seen until after the contract was entered into: *Olley v Marlborough Court 1949*. However an analogy may be drawn with the printing of conditions on a railway ticket in *Thompson v LMS*

Railway 1930. Here, the ticket was given at the time the contract was made and, if the notice was visible at the same time, it is likely that the notice is part of the contract. If the ticket contained reference to the notice, as in *Thompson v LMS Railway 1930*, the notice may still be binding on Brian (although this is more likely to be so if Brian had used the car park previously and so had constructive and/or actual notice of it, and this appears to be his first visit).

As noted earlier there is a well-known case which actually concerns a car park - *Thornton v Shoe Lane Parking Ltd 1972*. Here it was held that a contract was formed before the plaintiff received the car park ticket: the 'parking' sign was an offer and his act of parking was acceptance. A notice disclaiming liability for damage to cars which was on display inside the car park after the ticket was received was therefore found not to be validly included in the contract.

Here, Brian has not yet got his ticket, but he is in the process of parking when he sees the sign. The case is not clear-cut, but will probably depend on, for example, whether or not he is able to turn his car round at this point. Assuming though that *Thornton* is followed, the act of parking may be held to be the critical point at which the contract is made and, since Brian is actually driving in to the car park and is about to take a ticket when he sees the sign, he therefore has notice of the clause before the contract is made. Secure Car Parks Ltd would therefore be able to rely on the clause.

As the term covers damage to property it must be decided whether it is reasonable within s 2 of the 1977 Act. This will depend on the criteria of Sch 2: the relative strength of the parties, the offer of inducements to enter into the contract, awareness of the effect of the contract and so on.

On being informed of the effect of the exclusion clause, Brian turns to the matter of the closed circuit television. Whether the sign is a representation or a contract term will depend on the following.

(a) The interval of time between the statement being made and the contract coming into effect. The later the statement is made the more likely it is to be a term of the contract.

(b) Whether the party making the statement is in a position of special knowledge. If he is, the statement is more likely to be a term of the contract.

In Brian's case, both these tests suggest that the statement is a contract term. Under normal circumstances, Brian would therefore have a claim against Secure Car Parks Ltd for breach of contract, and seek to claim damages against the company. However, if, as supposed above, the exclusion clause is a valid one, this may not be possible. Turning to s 3 of UCTA, this states that, in standard term contracts made with a consumer, terms which seek to exclude liability (of the person imposing the term) for breach, or to allow substantially different performance, or no performance at all, are valid only insofar as they are reasonable. The court will therefore have to consider further whether the exclusion clause is reasonable. The fact that there is an 'inducement' to enter the car park - in the form of the sign about closed circuit TV itself - may well count against the car park operator.

Answer to assignment 5 (Chapter 8)

> **Tutorial note**. In this question the mistake was made by the buyer; there was no representation by the seller. The buyer should have made enquiries before purchase and will be bound under the principle of *caveat emptor* (let the buyer beware).

There are relatively few circumstances when a contract will be void because of some mistake made by one or all of the parties to the contract. English law classifies legal mistake in one of two ways: it may be bilateral, meaning that both parties to the contract are mistaken in some way, or unilateral, meaning that only one party is mistaken. Bilateral mistake may further be classified as identical bilateral mistake (usually referred to as common mistake) or non-identical bilateral mistake (usually referred to as mutual mistake).

Common mistake occurs where both parties are in agreement but both are mistaken as to some fundamental point. The principles were set out in *Associated Japanese Bank v Credit du Nord 1988*. The common mistake must be held by both parties and thus may not be claimed where one party knows of the error and must relate to facts as they existed at the time of the agreement. The common mistake must be with regard to facts in existence when the contract was made and the subject matter of the contract must in fact be rendered essentially different from that contemplated. Thus, if the subject matter of the contract has ceased to exist, unbeknown to both parties, then there is no contract: *Couturier v Hastie 1852*. Similarly, a contract where one party purports to buy what he already owns will be void: *Cochrane v Willis 1865*. The former case is an example of res *extincta*, or non-existent subject matter, and the latter is an example of *res sua*.

The doctrine is strictly interpreted. A mistake as to 'quality' of the subject matter will not be sufficient to render the contract void: *Bell v Lever Bros 1932*. In that case, a contract cancelling a management agreement was held to be valid, even though it was claimed that there had been a mutual mistake as to the validity of the management agreement rendering the new agreement void. Common mistake can therefore be seen to operate where both parties to a contract have made the same mistake with regard to the contract. In such cases the contract will be void.

A mutual mistake occurs where the parties are at cross purposes as regards the subject matter of the contract. If the misunderstanding results in a failure to identify the subject matter at all then the contract may be void: *Raffles v Wichelhaus 1864*. More commonly, the mistake can be resolved in favour of one or other of the parties and the mistaken party is bound by his agreement: *Tamplin v James 1880*. As stated in the Associated Japanese Bank case, the court's role is to uphold agreements and the avoiding of a contract for common mistake is not lightly done. Again, if the subject matter is adequately identified, a misunderstanding concerning its qualities does not make the contract void. If each party is unaware that the other intends subject matter of a different quality, he may perform his side of the contract according to his intention even though the other party was expecting something different: *Smith v Hughes 1871*.

Unilateral mistake occurs when only one party makes the mistake (which may have been induced by a misrepresentation by the other party) and the other party is aware of his mistake. In a contract for sale, a unilateral mistake as to identity of the purchaser is usually only operative if the seller can show that he or she intended to sell to somebody other than the actual buyer: *Cundy v Lindsay 1878*. If, however, the seller is only mistaken as to the creditworthiness of the buyer, not his identity, this is not an operative mistake: *King's Norton Metal v Edridge Merrett & Co 1897*.

Turning to the situation of Alan and Graham, there is no suggestion that Alan is mistaken in any way which means that there is neither common mistake nor mutual mistake to render the contract void. The mistake made by Graham would appear to be merely a mistake concerning a quality of the vehicle which is not, in itself, sufficient to render the contract void. Further there is no evidence of misrepresentation by Alan nor is it is a case of mistaken identity so unilateral mistake is also not relevant. In the absence of mistake or misrepresentation the contract will be upheld and Graham is bound on the principle of *caveat emptor*. He should have protected his position by making enquiries of Alan before entering into an agreement with him.

Answer to assignment 6 (Chapter 9)

> **Tutorial note**. This question was based on discharge of a contract by breach and frustration. The circumstances related to examples of frustrating events such as subsequent illegality (*Re Fibrosa*) or self induced frustration (*Maritime National Fish v Ocean Trawlers*).

The doctrine of frustration was developed by the courts to give relief in appropriate circumstances from the sometimes harsh common law rule that there is an absolute duty to perform a contractual duty. The courts will generally, in contractual disputes, seek to uphold the contract. Only in special circumstances will they listen to the argument of one party to the contract that the existence of the contract itself should be called into question. At common law, 'where a party by his own contract creates a duty or charge upon himself, he is bound to make it good, notwithstanding any accident by inevitable necessity, because he might have provided against it by his contract': *Paradine v Jane 1647.*

Frustration can be described as the discharge of a contract by some outside event for which neither party is responsible which makes further performance impossible. If it appears that the parties assumed that certain underlying conditions would continue, the contract may be frustrated if these assumptions prove to be false. The change in underlying conditions must be of a fundamental nature, such as the accidental destruction of the subject matter of the contract. The doctrine of frustration provides a number of exceptions to the common law rule described above and provides a valid excuse for non-performance:

(a) when the subject matter of the contract is destroyed before performance falls due: *Taylor v Caldwell 1863*. This case gave rise to the doctrine of frustration and involved the accidental destruction by fire of a music hall which had been let to be used for a series of concerts. The plaintiff in this case sought damages from the owner of the concert hall on the basis that the owner had failed to provide the concert hall even though such provision had been agreed under a legally binding contract. The court held that as the concert hall, the subject matter of the contract, had been destroyed, the contract had been frustrated;

(b) when there is personal incapacity to perform a contract of personal service: *Condor v Barron Knights 1966*. For this to succeed, it must be shown that the presence of the individual is a fundamental requirement of the contract. Other examples include frustration by reason of an individual's death, imprisonment, call-up for national service or internment in time of war;

(c) where there is government intervention: *Metropolitan Water Board v Dick, Kerr & Co 1918*;

This is a common cause of frustration, particularly in times of war;

(d) where there is a case of supervening illegality: *Re Shipton, Anderson & Co 1915*;

(e) where an event which is the sole purpose of the contract does not occur: *Krell v Henry 1903.*

This case involved the hire of a room overlooking the route of the Coronation procession of Edward VII. When the Coronation was postponed due to the illness of the King, the defendant successfully pleaded frustration, as the room had been hired for the specific purpose of watching the procession. This case can usefully be compared and contrasted with *Herne Bay Steamboat Co v Hutton 1903*, which concerned the hire of a steamboat to carry passengers round the Spithead naval review and to cruise round the fleet. The naval review was cancelled due to the same circumstances, but it was held that the cruise round the fleet could still have taken place and so this was not a case of frustration.

There are also a number of well-established circumstances where frustration will not be held to apply.

(a) An alternative mode of performance is still possible: *Tsakiroglou v Noblee Thorl GmbH 1962.*

(b) Performance has simply become more expensive: *Davis Contractors v Fareham UDC 1956.*

(c) One party has accepted the risk that he will be unable to perform: *Budgett & Co v Binnington & Co 1981.*

(d) One party has induced frustration by his own choice between alternatives: *Maritime National Fish v Ocean Trawlers 1935.*

Turning to the circumstances surrounding the international billiards competition organised by Iggins Ltd, each person's situation can be considered in the light of the existing case law.

Brown is unable to attend because his passport had expired. This will be treated as 'self-induced' frustration and therefore, following the *Maritime National Fish* case, will not enable Brown to escape liability under his contract with Iggins Ltd.

Green is unable to attend because of an injury which prevents him from playing. This amounts to personal incapacity to perform a contract of personal service, and so Green will be able to demonstrate frustration of the contract with Iggins Ltd. He will not be liable to Iggins Ltd for breach of contract, although it is possible that Iggins Ltd may wish to investigate the possibility of a claim for negligence.

White is unable to travel through ill health and his position is therefore similar to that of Green, ie personal incapacity to perform a contract of personal service.

Black has no justification for failing to attend. It is perhaps possible to draw a parallel with the *Davis Contractors* case in that the decision not to perform his side of the contract is motivated by economic considerations. Black is liable to Iggins Ltd for breach of contract.

The question of Iggins Ltd's potential liability to the remaining competitors must also be considered. The 'Coronation cases' provide a useful parallel here - Iggins Ltd may seek to argue that the basis for the contract no longer exists, following *Krell v Henry*, but the remaining competitors will cite the *Herne Bay Steamboat* case and argue that the competition could still have taken place. It is submitted that they should have a strong case. If they succeed, they will be able to claim damages for breach of contract against Iggins Ltd.

Answer to assignment 7 (Chapter 10)

> **Tutorial note.** The provisions of the 1979 Sale of Goods Act and the implied conditions of title to the goods (s 12) and satisfactory quality (s 14) are relevant here. You should note that faults may arise earlier in second hand cars and therefore they will not be as fully protected as new vehicles under the legislation.

(a) The Sale of Goods Act 1979 implies certain terms into contracts for the sale of goods, though in certain circumstances the contracting parties may be able expressly to limit the application of the Act. These implied terms tend to displace the old principle of *caveat emptor*.

The first implied condition is that contained in section 12 which applies to both business and private sales and provides that the seller has the right to sell the goods (or that he will have that right at the time when the property is to pass) to the buyer who receives good title. The significance of the point is apparent where goods are sold by someone who does not in fact own them. The breach of condition as to title has been held to constitute a 'total failure of consideration' and the purchaser does not obtain the ownership of the goods which is the essential basis of the contract, with the result that the buyer is entitled to the return of the total price, even though he may have benefited by using the goods for a limited time (*Rowland v Divall 1923*).

Further, the seller gives a warranty - not a condition - that the buyer shall have quiet possession of the goods free of any encumbrance or challenge by a third party (unless disclosed to the buyer when the contract is made).

The Unfair Contract Terms Act 1977 entirely prohibits any exclusion or limitation by the terms of the contract of the condition as to title.

The contract between Jay and Rob is a contract for the sale of goods. S 12 implies a condition that Rob had title to pass to Jay but Rob is in clear breach of that condition. Jay is therefore entitled to recover the full price paid and Don is entitled to recover the goods since Rob never had title in them to pass to Jay.

(b) S 14(2) SGA 1979 (as amended by the Sale and Supply of Goods Act 1994) provides that 'where the seller sells goods in the course of a business, there is an implied condition that the goods supplied under the contract are of satisfactory quality' which means that they 'meet the standard that a reasonable person would regard as satisfactory, taking account of any description of the goods, the price (if relevant) and all other relevant circumstances'. The test of 'satisfactory quality' replaced one of 'merchantable quality'. S 14(2b) provides that the quality of goods includes their state and condition and that in appropriate cases the following matters will be relevant aspects of the quality of goods: fitness for all relevant purposes, appearance and finish, freedom from minor defects, safety and durability.

Price will also be relevant (*Shire v General Guarantee Corp 1988*) so that a higher degree of quality can be expected from a new or more expensive car (*Rogers v Parish (Scarborough) Ltd 1987*) and mere roadworthiness is not sufficient. If a low price is designed to allow for known defects then the test of satisfactory quality may be considered satisfied (*Bartlett v Sydney Marcus Ltd 1965*).

The condition in s 14(2) will not apply with regard to defects specifically drawn to the buyer's attention before the contract is made or, where the buyer examines the goods before entering into the contract, with regard to defects which that examination ought to reveal. Where the buyer does examine the goods before the contract is made, he shall be treated as having discovered all defects which are apparent on inspection whether or not he actually discovers them (*Thornett Fehr v Beers & Son 1919*).

Under s 14(3) SGA 1979 there is a further condition implied that the goods shall be fit for any particular purpose which the buyer expressly or by implication makes known to the seller. If the goods only have one obvious purpose, then by implication the buyer makes his purpose known to the seller simply by agreeing to buy the goods (*Priest v Last 1903*).

The Unfair Contract Terms Act 1977 prohibits any exclusion or limitation of the conditions in sections 13, 14 and 15 where the buyer is dealing as a consumer - that is, when he is not buying in the course of business and the seller is selling in the course of business. If the buyer is not dealing as a consumer, any exclusion or limitation of the conditions is only valid if it satisfies a test of reasonableness.

If Sarah bought her car from a person selling in the course of a business, there will be an implied condition in the contract under s 14 and there would appear to be a breach of that condition having regard to the price, age and mileage of the car and the serious nature of the mechanical failure. Sarah will be entitled to treat the contract as repudiated and claim damages. Any exclusion clause would not be valid. If, however, Sarah bought from a private seller, s 14 would not apply and the contract would need to be construed according to common law rules including the principle of *caveat emptor*.

Polly also has the benefit of the condition implied by s 14 SGA which provides that the car should be of satisfactory quality. However, in determining whether the test has been satisfied, the fact that the car is already 10 years old and has done 160,000 miles and cost only £1,200 will be relevant. The defect arose after 4 months when the seller stipulated that the car would be roadworthy for 6 months. This may tip the balance in Polly's favour in considering the test of satisfactory quality.

Answer to assignment 8 (Chapter 11)

> **Tutorial note**. Make sure you have presented your answer in report format. The key to a good answer here is familiarity with the relevant statutory protection for consumers. The chief area of protection is of course under the Consumer Protection Act 1987. Do not forget to consider the statutory defences open to Price Cutters Ltd, as that is what the board of directors will want to hear about as a possible course of action. The Sale of Goods Act 1979 implies a term of 'satisfactory quality' in all such contracts.

To: Board of Directors
From: Company Secretary
Date: December 1998
Re: *Electric fires*

There are several potential areas of liability to be considered in respect of the personal injury and damage to property suffered by Ashok and Indira, the principal area of liability being under the Consumer Protection Act 1987.

(a) CPA 1987. This Act imposes liability for any of the listed parties who make, import or supply a defective product as a result of which a consumer suffers damage resulting from the defect. The consumer does not have to prove negligence, nor any privity of contract between him and the person he is suing. The strict civil liability imposed by the Act cannot be excluded by any disclaimer.

A supplier (usually a retailer) can be liable under the Act. The other listed parties with potential liability are (i) the manufacturer of the end product, (ii) the manufacturer of a defective component, (iii) an importer into the EC and (iv) an 'own-brander'. It is true to say that usually a supplier will only be liable if he will not disclose the identity of the importer or manufacturer. The parties in the chain of distribution are entitled to adjust the liabilities between themselves subject to any common law or statutory controls.

The consumer must prove that (i) the product contained a defect, (ii) he suffered damage, (iii) the damage resulted from the defect and (iv) the defendant was one of the listed parties referred to above. It is up to the consumer to satisfy the court that the defect caused the damage and that the damage was reasonably foreseeable in order to succeed in his claim for damages.

All products are covered by the legislation including component parts and raw materials. A product is regarded as defective if it is found to be not as safe as it is reasonable to expect. This standard is measured taking into account all circumstances concerning the product, such as the way it is advertised, the time of supply, its anticipated normal use, the provision of instructions for use and the cost of making the product safer.

A consumer or other user, including the recipient of the defective product as a gift (as Indira was in this case) can bring a claim under the Act claiming compensation for damage, personal injury or damage to property other than the product itself (but not for economic loss). He or she must bring the claim within 3 years of the fault becoming apparent and within 10 years of the date of original supply. The amount of any damage to property must be over £275.

A defendant has possible statutory defences, namely:

(i) that the state of knowledge at the time of manufacture and supply was such that no manufacturer could have been expected to be aware of the fault;

(ii) that the defect did not exist when the goods were originally supplied;

(iii) that the product complies with mandatory legislative or EC safety standards;

(iv) that the supply was otherwise than in the course of a business;

(v) that the product was at no time supplied to another; and

(vi) that the defect was wholly attributable to the design of a subsequent product into which the product in question was incorporated.

It seems likely that the electric fires supplied would be considered defective products within the scope of this legislation and, as retailer, the company faces potential liability for their supply in respect of the personal injury and property damage suffered by Ashok and Indira (noting the minimum level of property damage of £275). It will be essential to identify the manufacturer and importer into the EC if relevant. The defences would not appear to be available to the company in this case.

NOTES

(b) Criminal liability is imposed on any suppler of consumer goods which fail to comply with a general safety requirement (Pt II of the same Act). This requirement applies to all consumer goods (unless more specific legislation applies) and means that goods must be reasonably safe taking into account the manner in which and the purposes for which they are marketed, any instructions or warnings provided in them, any publicised safety standards and the existence of any means by which it would have been reasonable to make the product safer.

Criminal liability is also imposed for contravention of safety regulations made by the DTI under CPA 1987 including the Electric Equipment (Safety) Regulations 1975 requiring that various items of electrical equipment comply with appropriate British Standards. These regulations are enforced by trading standards officers.

(c) Liability arises under s14 Sale of Goods Act 1979 which provides that a term shall be implied into all contracts for the sale of goods that the goods sold in the course of a business are of satisfactory quality. Satisfactory quality is met if the goods 'meet the standard that a reasonable person would regard as satisfactory, taking account of any description of the goods, the price (if relevant) and all other relevant circumstances'.

The Act lists some of the attributes which are to be taken into account in deciding whether the goods are of satisfactory quality, including fitness for the purpose, appearance and finish, freedom from minor defects, safety and durability. Breach of this provision would be a breach of condition of the contract entitling the consumer to reject the contract and treat it as repudiated (unless he has lost the right to do so) and to claim damages. Liability to a consumer for breach of this provision cannot be excluded (Unfair Contract Terms Act 1977).

(d) The purchaser of defective products may be able to recover damages in respect of damage caused by the negligence of the manufacturer or supplier. However to establish liability in tort it is necessary to show that the plaintiff was owed a duty of care by the defendant, that the defendant was in breach of that duty and the plaintiff suffered injury as a result. Given the strict liability imposed by the CPA 1987 it seems very unlikely that the consumers would pursue an action in tort rather than under that legislation.

Signed: Company secretary

Answer to assignment 9 (Chapter 12)

Tutorial note. This assignment requires you to provide 'basic employment law advice' on another topical issue - that of employer's obligations in respect of smoking at work. You may feel that the issue of smoking at work is a fairly specialist one, but most of the issues to be discussed here do not relate specifically to smoking and indeed only the *Dryden* case described in part (c) is specifically relevant to the issue of smoking, as opposed to any other activity in the workplace.

(a) When an employee is dismissed with a shorter period of notice than the employer is obliged to give either under the employment contract or by statute and wishes to claim against his former employer, there are two courses of action open. He may claim for damages at common law for wrongful dismissal. Alternatively, there may be grounds for a claim for unfair dismissal.

BPP PUBLISHING

Unfair dismissal is a concept created by employment protection legislation, and is also a possible route where proper notice has been given. An action for wrongful dismissal would be heard in the civil courts, while an action for unfair dismissal would be heard by an employment tribunal.

If sufficient notice is given by the employer, he will be open only to a claim for unfair dismissal and not to a claim for wrongful dismissal. If insufficient notice is given by the employer, he may be open to a claim for unfair dismissal or a claim for wrongful dismissal.

Company policy

Looking at the facts of the case, R's behaviour is in contravention of the 'no smoking' policy in the factory section, while S's behaviour appears to be permitted by the employer.

Wrongful dismissal

To prevent the risk of an action for wrongful dismissal, an employer should give the appropriate period of notice to an employee. Alternatively, the employer must show one of the following.

(i) *Wilful disobedience* of a lawful order suffices if it amounts to wilful and serious defiance of authority, serious enough to show that the employee is repudiating the essential basis of the employment agreement: *Pepper v Webb 1969.* A single incident may not suffice: *Laws v London Chronicle 1957.*

(ii) *Misconduct* in connection with the business or outside it if it is sufficiently grave. For example, acceptance of a secret commission, disclosure of confidential information, assault on a fellow employee or even financial embarrassment of an employee in a position of trust: *Pearce v Foster 1886*

(iii) *Dishonesty,* where the employee is in a position of particular trust: *Sinclair v Neighbour 1967.*

(iv) *Incompetence or neglect* insofar as the employee lacks or fails to use skill which he professes to have: *Taylor v Alidair Ltd 1978.*

(v) *Gross negligence,* depending on the nature of the job.

(vi) *Immorality*, only if it is likely to affect performance of duties or the reputation of the business.

(vii) *Drunkenness*, only if repeated or if it occurs in aggravated circumstances such as when driving a vehicle.

Unfair dismissal

Even if notice is given, an employee may be open to a claim for unfair dismissal. Dismissal may be justified in the following circumstances.

He must first show that he has acted reasonably, by applying the correct procedures, taking all circumstances into consideration and doing what any reasonable employer would have done. He must then show that the reason for dismissal related to one of the five categories set out in s 48 Employment Rights Act 1996. These are as follows.

(i) The capability or qualifications of the employee for performing work of the kind which he was employed to do.

(ii) The conduct of the employee.

(iii) Redundancy

NOTES

(iv) Legal prohibition or restriction by which the employee could not lawfully continue to work in the position which he held (eg if a doctor or a solicitor employed as such is struck off the relevant professional register).

(v) Some other substantial reason which justifies dismissal.

Conclusion

It is unlikely that R's behaviour is enough to warrant summary dismissal (dismissal without notice). Even though it could be classified as misconduct, it is unlikely that it is serious enough to fall into the category described above. It may be that Exe could show justifiable dismissal (with notice), as there is clearly a hygiene issue involving work with food. This misconduct, if proven, would probably justify dismissal. Exe Ltd would, of course, also have to show that it had acted reasonably in all the circumstances.

As regards S, it is extremely unlikely that Exe Ltd could show a justifiable reason for dismissal, and S could probably win a unfair dismissal claim.

(b) If an employer dismisses an employee, he may defeat a claim for unfair dismissal by showing that the contract of employment has in fact been frustrated.

Ill health

If the employer relies on ill health as the ground of incapability there must be proper medical evidence. The employer may make enquiries of the employee's doctor and also obtain an opinion from the company's medical adviser. In the event of long-term sickness, the employer can only be expect to act within sensible limits. He should consider the employee's situation, but is also entitled to consider his own business needs. In the event of a number of periods of short-term sickness, the employee should again act with sympathy, understanding and compassion. This involve cautions, confrontation with records and the granting of a period for improvement.

In *International Sports Ltd v Thompson 1980*, the employee had been away from work for around 25% of the time, suffering from a number of complaints, including dizzy spells, anxiety, bronchitis, viral infections, dyspepsia and flatulence, all of which were certified by medical certificates. She received a number of warnings. Following a final warning and prior to dismissal the company consulted their medical adviser. As the illnesses were unrelated and unverifiable, he did not consider an examination worthwhile. She was dismissed. It was held that the dismissal was fair.

Frustration

This is most likely to occur in two particular situations. If there is a long-term absence of the employee through accident or illness, this may frustrate the contract: *Notcutt v Universal Equipment Co (London) Ltd 1986*. If the employee is imprisoned, this is also frustration, even though it may appear that the imprisonment is effectively self-induced: *FC Shepherd & Co Ltd v Jerrom 1986*. Such cases will be judged according to a number of factors, including the length of absence, the necessity for the employer to obtain a replacement, length of service and position of the employee.

NOTES

Conclusion

Again, Exe Ltd should give notice to avoid a claim for wrongful dismissal. The company might be subject to a claim for unfair dismissal. As noted in (a), a claim for unfair dismissal might be defeated if the employee is not capable of performing work of the kind which he or she was employed to do. Exe Ltd should, of course, act reasonably in all the circumstances.

(c) The effect of a ban would be different in each part of the business.

Factory

The 'no smoking' policy is described as something which Exe Ltd has always operated. To this extent, it could be described as an implied term of the contract of employment. A spreading of the ban throughout the premises would effectively make this into a express term of the contract.

Office

There is currently no 'no smoking' policy. Therefore, the implementation of such a policy would constitute a *change* in contract terms.

Change in contract terms

Whenever any change in contract terms is made, the employer must, within one month, provide a written statement of the change. This can be done by means of an amendment of the written particulars of employment.

Because the extension of this policy amounts to a unilateral changing of contract terms, employees who disagree with it may have an action for breach of contract. They should register their disapproval by protesting or ignoring the ban; if they impliedly accept the ban by working according to it, they will lose this right.

The employer should, as above, act reasonably. This will include the provision to the employees of notice of the ban. An employee may still claim unfair dismissal, but this is unlikely to succeed.

In *Dryden v Greater Glasgow Health Board 1992*, Dryden, a heavy smoker, was accustomed to smoking cigarettes in areas of the hospital where she worked set aside for this purpose. Her employers decide to ban smoking throughout the hospital and, after extensive consultations, imposed a non-smoking ban. She decided that she could not continue to work without smoking, and resigned, claiming constructive dismissal. It was held that 'the right to smoke' was not an implied term of the contract.

Answer to assignment 10 (Chapter 13)

(a) Most of the advantages and disadvantages of purchasing an off the shelf company relate to the **formalities** required to incorporate a company and to **alter various details** that relate to existing companies.

Advantages

The principal advantages are as follows.

(i) Tom will **not need to file** the following documents with the Registrar of Companies:

(1) a **memorandum** and **articles**;

(2) a **statement** in the **prescribed form**;

(3) **statutory declaration**; and

(4) **fee**.

This will be a quicker, and very possibly cheaper, way of incorporating his business.

(ii) There will be **no risk** of **potential liability** arising from pre-incorporation contracts. Tom will be able to continue trading without needing to worry about waiting for the registrar's certificate of incorporation.

(iii) The **need to use** the services of **professionals** will be **decreased**, making incorporation cheaper.

Disadvantages

The disadvantages relate to the changes that will be required to the off-the-shelf company to make it compatible with Tom's needs.

(i) The **objects** set out in the company's memorandum may **not** be **appropriate** for Tom's business. They may need to be altered and the altered form lodged with the registrar. However, if, as is likely, the memorandum (in accordance with new provisions in the Companies Act 1989) describes its objects as those of a 'general commercial company', it is unlikely that any change would be needed.

(ii) The off-the-shelf company is likely to have **Table A articles**. Tom may wish to amend these, for example to give himself 'golden shares' which ensure he retains control. Revised articles would need to be filed with the registrar.

(iii) Tom may want to **change** the **name** of the company and, if so, would need to pass a special resolution and file this with the registrar.

(iv) The **subscriber shares** will need to be **transferred**, and the transfer recorded in the Register of Members. Stamp duty will be payable.

(v) **Tom** will have to have himself **appointed** as **company director**, and someone else as company secretary.

(vi) Tom may wish to have the **authorised share capital increased**. If so, an ordinary resolution sanctioning the increase would need to be passed and filed with the registrar along with Form G123.

On balance it is likely to be easier and quicker to purchase an off-the-shelf company, but it depends on how many changes will be required to make the company compatible with Tom's needs.

(b) Private companies may be formed with only one member.

Certain formalities are required of single member companies. The fact that it is a single member private company must be **stated** in the **register of members** and the member's name and address given. **Company resolutions** or decisions which normally decided in general meeting must be **evidenced in writing.** Any **contract between** the **company** and the **sole member/director** not made in the ordinary course of business must also be **in writing**.

S 282 provides that a private company need only have one director but a **sole director cannot be** the **company secretary**: (s 283(2)). Therefore Tom will need to bring in another person and appoint him or her to be company secretary though he may be sole member and sole director. The secretary does not need to own shares in the company.

(c) Every company is required to **exhibit** its **name** in its **correct form** outside **every place of business**, on its **seal**, **business letters**, **forms** and **other documents** including invoices and orders for goods: s 348 - 349. In the event of default, the company is liable to a fine and furthermore, the responsible officer of the company may be fined.

The fact that a company name is stated incorrectly will not necessarily render the document ineffective provided that it is clear that it was intended to name that company: *Bird (London) Ltd v Thomas Cook & Sons (Bakers) Ltd 1937.*

In the case of **bills of exchange**, **cheques** or **orders** for **money** or **goods in** which the company name is not stated as required by s 349(1) the courts have adhered to a strict view of s 349(4) and imposed **personal liability** on a responsible company officer: *Rafsanjan Pistachio Producers Co-operative v Reiss 1990.*

However in *Jenice Ltd v Dan 1993* the court interpreted s 349(4)'s purpose as being to **ensure outsiders** knew they were **dealing** with a **company** whose members had limited liability. Thus **typographical errors** such as missing out odd letters may **not now render** a **director liable**. **Omission** of the word **limited** will **render** the **company officer liable** if the company defaults: *Penrose v Martyr 1858.*

Answer to assignment 11 (Chapter 14)

(a) Pre-emption rights

If a company issues ordinary shares for cash, it has a statutory obligation to offer those shares to holders of similar shares in proportion to their holdings: s 89. If, for example, a company has an issued ordinary share capital of 400,000 £1 shares and it intends to issue 100,000 ordinary shares for cash, it should first offer the new shares to the existing shareholders in the ratio of one new share for every four shares already held.

The shares must be offered on terms at least as favourable as they would be offered to third parties.

The offer must be made in writing in the same manner as a notice of a general meeting is sent to members. It must specify a period of not less than 21 days during which the offer may be accepted. If not accepted within that period, the offer is deemed to be declined: s 90.

Exemption from pre-emption rights

Subscribers' shares, preference shares, bonus shares and shares allotted under an employees' share scheme are exempt from these restrictions, which would be inappropriate to them.

Exclusion of pre-emption rights

A private company may by its memorandum or articles permanently exclude these rules so that there is no statutory right of first refusal: s 91.

Any company may, by special resolution, resolve that pre-emption rights shall not apply: s 95. Such a resolution to 'disapply' the right may either:

NOTES

(i) be combined with the grant to directors of authority to issue shares under s 80. It is then restricted to a maximum duration of five years; or

(ii) it may simply permit an offer of shares to be made for cash to a non-member (without first offering the shares to members) on a particular occasion.

In case (ii) the directors, in inviting members to 'disapply' the right of first refusal, must issue a circular setting out their reasons, the price at which the shares are to be offered direct to a non-member and their justification for that price.

(b) (i) The directors may only exercise the power of allotment if they are properly authorised to do so, either by the articles or by ordinary resolution passed in general meeting: s 80. S 80 requires of a public company that the authority to allot shall be given until a specified date and for a specified period of not more than five years. The authority will state the maximum number of securities which may be allotted under it.

Since the company is regulated by Table A which does not contain such an authority, the directors will have to check the company minutes to see whether there is a current valid authority. If not, articles can be altered by special resolution so that they contain one. However, this process is probably unnecessary since the directors can simply call an extraordinary general meeting to pass an ordinary resolution to obtain authority.

(ii) The directors may, under Table A provisions, issue shares at board meetings. They are required, however, to declare their interest in their proposed purchase of the shares at the beginning of the meeting: s 317.

(iii) As regard the issue of shares, if the authority derives from the passing of an ordinary resolution, the resolution must be filed with the Registrar of Companies within 15 days.

If the authority was granted by altering the articles, the special resolution and the amended articles must both be submitted to the registrar within 15 days: s 380.

The company will also have to make a return of allotments to the registrar of companies on the appropriate form within one month: s 88.

The register of members will need to be updated to reflect the changes in the numbers of shares held by the members when the new shares have been taken up. In addition, the register of directors' interests will have to be amended to take account of the shares of Doris, Edith and Francis.

Answer to assignment 12 (Chapter 15)

(a) (i) A **fixed charge** attaches to a specific asset as soon as the charge is created. If the company goes into liquidation, the asset will be sold to realise the debt, and the proceeds of the sale will go to the fixed chargeholder in preference to preferential creditors and floating charges.

Examples of fixed charges are legal mortgages of shares or land, or equitable charges over other property.

The fact that a document is called a fixed charge will not be conclusive where in fact the company is still permitted to deal with the charge without reference to the chargee: *R in Right of British Columbia v Federal Business Development Bank 1988.*

(ii) A floating charge is:

(1) a charge on a **class of assets** of a company, present and future;

(2) which class is in the ordinary course of the company's business **changing** from time to time; and

(3) until the holders enforce the charge the company may **carry on business** and **deal** with the asset charged: *Re Yorkshire Woolcombers Association Ltd 1903.*

A floating charge can apply to fixed assets and current assets. It does not attach to any assets until crystallisation.

(b) **Crystallisation** of a floating charge means that the **charge** is **converted into a fixed equitable charge**, that is a fixed charge on the assets owned by the company at the time of crystallisation.

Crystallisation occurs on:

(i) the **liquidation** of the company;

(ii) **cessation** of the company's business;

(iii) **crystallisation of another floating charge** if it causes the company to cease business.

(iv) **active intervention** by the chargee, by appointing a reviewer or exercising a power of sale;

(v) if the **charge contract provides**, when notice is given by the chargee that the charge is converted into a fixed charge.

Answer to assignment 13 (Chapter 16)

Two aspects need to be considered here.

(a) Whether Ursula can bring the directors of either or both companies to account for **breach of duties**.

(b) Whether she can invoke the rules of **minority protection**.

Remedies against Robert and Stephen for breach of duty

Directors have a duty to avoid a conflict of duty and personal interest. They also have a duty not to profit from their position. Robert and Stephen seem likely to have failed in both duties. However the company in general meeting can ratify these breaches of duty (*Regal (Hastings) Ltd v Gulliver 1942*) and Fabric Ltd has done this.

Remedies against directors of Weft Ltd for lack of skill and care

Directors can also be liable for negligence, showing lack of skill and care.

However, gross negligence must be proved, and this is unlikely to apply here. Instead the courts are more likely to consider the rules on members' control of directors. In *John Shaw & Sons (Salford) Ltd 1935*) the members in general meeting instructed the directors to discontinue a legal action. The court held the general body of shareholders cannot usurp the directors' power of management and the directors' motion was thus invalid.

Thus, in neither instance is Ursula likely to bring an action against the directors under the breach of duties rules in company law. Her best chance of success appears to be bringing an action under the minority protection rules.

s 459 action

In either or both cases Ursula could bring an action under s 459. She would have to prove that the affairs of the company are being or had been conducted in a manner which is unfairly prejudicial to the members generally or some part of the members.

Action against Robert and Stephen

Ursula could claim under s 459 that the directors' action has deprived the members of the enhancement of their share value through the contract. A successful minority protection action was brought under s 459 against directors who had diverted a company's business to a director-controlled company: *Re Cumana Ltd 1986*.

Action against Phillip and Quentin

A claim by Ursula under s 459 is unlikely to succeed against Phillip and Quentin since the courts have been unwilling to invoke the minority protection rules in disputes against management, even bad management.

In *Re Five Minute Car Wash Ltd 1966,* a complaint that incompetent management had caused loss but was tolerated by the controlling shareholder was not upheld.

Common law action

Alternatively Ursula could bring an action in either or both instances under the common law minority protection rules.

(a) No **illegal action** of the company can be made lawful by a majority vote.

(b) If the law or the articles of a company require that a **special procedure** be observed then a majority decision which ignores that requirement will be invalid.

(c) A member may sue the company to **enforce his rights** where a majority decision deprives him of his individual rights of membership.

(d) If a controlling majority **defraud the company** in some way or act oppressively to a minority then the minority may bring an action against the fraudulent or oppressive majority.

Action against Robert and Stephen

The action of Robert and Stephen, by diverting the contract away from the company and for the benefit of their partnership, could be said to be a fraud on the minority in that it deprives the company of its property - although it is not clear whether the contract had been concluded first of all in the company's name or otherwise had become the property of the company. Furthermore, Ursula would need to show that those who appropriated the property, Robert and Stephen, are in control of the company and responsible for the ordinary resolution approving the action. That is to say that they were in a position to, and did, prevent an action being brought by the company itself (which would appear to be the case).

The case of *Cook v Deeks 1916* was brought on similar facts. The directors (and controlling shareholders) negotiated a contract in the company's name, took it for themselves and passed a resolution in general meeting to the effect that the company had no interest in the contract. A minority shareholder sued them as trustees for the company of the benefit of the contract. It was held that the contract 'belonged in equity to the company' and the directors could not bind the company to approving their action of defrauding it.

Even if Ursula cannot show that the directors' action was 'fraudulent' as such, it may be sufficient nonetheless to evidence that the company's property was, even negligently passed to benefit the controlling shareholders in order to make those shareholders accountable: Daniels v Daniels 1977.

Action against Phillip and Quentin

However Ursula is unlikely to succeed in a common law minority protection action against Phillip and Quentin since the facts do not appear to fit any of the common law minority protection exceptions.

Conclusion

Thus Ursula may succeed in an action under s 459 against Robert and Stephen; if she does the court will make whatever order it sees fit. She may also succeed under the common law minority protection rules against Roger and Stephen. She is unlikely to succeed against Phillip and Quentin.

Answer to assignment 14 (Chapter 17)

(a) **Holding an AGM**

There is a general requirement, contained in s 366, that every company must hold an AGM in each calendar year (unless it has passed an elective resolution to the contrary. This only applies to *private* companies, however). This is so unless it is the first AGM of a company, which must be held within 18 months of incorporation. In all cases, not more than 15 months may expire between AGMs.

There must be a notice given of the meeting, which must include the fact that the meeting is the AGM. The period of notice for an AGM is given by s 369, and is a minimum of 21 days notwithstanding anything to the contrary in the articles. Notice is required to be in writing.

Business at an AGM

In general, the ordinary business of an AGM will follow a reasonably standard form. It will comprise the following items:

(i) any declaration of a dividend;

(ii) the retirement, appointment or re-appointment of directors;

(iii) the presentation of the directors' report;

(iv) the presentation of the auditors' report;

(v) consideration of the accounts and balance sheets;

(vi) appointment or re-appointment of auditors, together with provision for their remuneration.

Failure to hold an AGM

A failure to hold an AGM as required results in any member being entitled to make an application to the Secretary of State to call such a meeting (or order that one be held). The Secretary of State has a wide discretion to make other directions as to the arrangements for the meeting or its conduct.

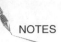

(b) The resolutions and registration requirements are as follows.

   (i) A change of company name requires a special resolution (s 28(1)), a copy of which must be sent to the Registrar within 15 days (s 380).

   (ii) An ordinary resolution is required to effect the increase in authorised share capital, under s 121 and Article 32. The Registrar of Companies must be notified of the increase within 15 days (s 123).

   (iii) The allotment of bonus shares can be achieved by ordinary resolution (Article 110). Form 88(2) will be required to be sent to the Registrar within one month of the allotment taking place (s 88) along with the contract between the members and the company. This is because the shares are being allotted for non-cash consideration.

(c) S 370 states that all persons entitled to receive a notice of a meeting must be sent one, in the manner prescribed by the articles. Failure to do so results in the resolutions passed at the meeting being invalid: *Young v Ladies Imperial Club 1920*, where the failure to give notice invalidated the proceedings of a meeting, even though the member concerned had already declared her intention not to attend any more meetings.

   Relief may be found from the strictness of these rules in article 39, which allows an 'accidental omission' to give notice not to invalidate the proceedings. Unfortunately, though, it is clear that the circumstances here do not comprise an accidental omission as required by the articles. There is a case called *Musselwhite v C H Musselwhite and Sons 1962*, the facts of which are almost exactly the same as the situation under discussion here, in that notice was not sent to a member who had agreed to sell his shares, but who had not yet been replaced on the register of members by the purchaser. This was not an accidental omission, it was an error of law, and the article did not act to validate the proceedings of the meeting. The proceedings at the AGM, it seems, are invalidated by the lack of notice to a member.

Answer to assignment 15 (Chapter 18)

The insolvency legislation of 1986 introduced a much more onerous regime for directors of companies which had gone into insolvent liquidation. Its main components were the Insolvency Act 1986 supported by the Company Directors' Disqualification Act 1986.

Misfeasance

S 212 is linked with breach of a director's fiduciary duty and relates to a director who has misapplied or retained or become accountable for any money or other property of the company. Often this involves the wrongful exercise of lawful authority as happened in *Flitcroft's Case 1882*, where the accounts were falsified in order for a dividend to be paid. In *Bishopsgate Investment Management Ltd v Maxwell 1993* the defendant was instrumental in transferring stock from the company pension fund to accounts privately controlled by the Maxwell family. He was ordered by the court to compensate the company to the extent of £5,000,000.

Fraudulent trading

Under s 213, if during a winding up it becomes apparent that there was an intention to defraud creditors, then the court can declare that the perpetrators of the fraud should make such contribution to the company's assets as they think proper. In addition to compensation a guilty director is liable to a fine or imprisonment or both. S 213 reinforces s 458 of the Companies Act which provides sanctions against carrying on business with intent to defraud creditors or for any other fraudulent purpose. Such an offence requires proof beyond all reasonable doubt. Since the affairs of the company may be exceedingly complex, it is only rarely pursued with any success.

Wrongful trading

Because of the long perceived difficulty in proving fraud s 214 introduced the new concept of wrongful trading by which the court can declare that a director can be declared liable to contribute to the company's assets. The application to the court is made by the liquidator, and unlike s 213 no criminal intent has to be proved.

Commonly before 1986 directors carried on trading and incurring additional debts long after the company was technically insolvent in the hope that better times were just around the corner. Now a director incurs personal liability for the additional debts if it can be shown that sometime before the commencement of the winding up the director knew or ought to have known that there was no reasonable prospect that the company would avoid going into insolvent liquidation. A director can avoid liability if it can be shown that he took reasonable steps to realise the potential loss to creditors. Nonetheless this section places a burden on directors that cannot safely be ignored.

Malpractice

Under s 218, if during the course of the winding up it appears that a director has been guilty of an offence for which there is criminal liability, the court may direct the liquidator to refer the matter to the prosecuting authority.

Disqualification

Apart from the specific matters referred above a disqualification order may be made by the court against a director. The maximum period of disqualification is 15 years. Some of the other matters that might result in such disqualification:

(a) persistent failure to comply with statutory filing requirements; s 3 CDDA. Three failures in five years are evidence of persistent failure.

(b) transactions at an undervalue: s 238. These are gifts or transactions in the two years prior to liquidation by which a company gives consideration of greater value than it receives, for instance a sale at less than full market price.

(c) transactions conferring an improper preference: s 239. A company gives preference to a creditor if it does anything by which his position will be benefited if the company goes into liquidation, and the company does this with the intention of producing that result. The relevant period is within six months before the commencement of liquidation to a person unconnected with the company, and two years for a person connected with the company.

(d) use of prohibited names: s 216. A director, who is involved with a company that goes into insolvent liquidation, should not be involved for the next five years with the management of a business which has an identical name to the original company, or a name similar enough to suggest a connection.

(e) unfitness relating to conduct generally contributing to the company's insolvency: CDDA s 9.

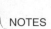

NOTES

Answer to assignment 16 (Chapter 19)

Your completed table should be as follows:

Comparisons of business organisations

Features	Sole trader	Partnership	Private company	Public company
Creation	Informal	Informal or deed	Register	Register
Legal status	Personal	Personal	Separate	Separate
Liability	Unlimited	Unlimited (except Ltd partner)	Limited	Limited
Publicity	No	No	Yes	Yes
Audit	No	No	Usually	Yes
Reporting of results	No	No	Yes	Yes
Ownership	Self	Partners	Shareholders	Shareholders
Control	Self	Partners	Shareholders	Shareholders
Management	Self	Partners	Board	Board
Transfer of membership	Sale	None	Sell shares	Sell shares
Duration	Temporary	Temporary	Permanent	Permanent
Ownership of assets	Self	Partners	Ordinary shareholders	Ordinary shareholders

GLOSSARIES OF BUSINESS LAW TERMS AND COMPANY LAW TERMS

NOTES

ACAS Advisory, Conciliation and Arbitration Service.

Acceptance A positive act by a person accepting an offer so as to bring a contact into effect.

Accord and satisfaction Agreement and consideration.

Actus reus Guilty act. One of the two requirements normally present in a crime, the other being *mens rea*.

Ad idem Of the same (mind or intention). A requirement for a valid contract.

Administrative tribunals Special 'courts' set up to settle disputes.

Agent A person authorised to act for another (the principal) and bring that other into legal relations with a third party.

Anticipatory breach Renunciation by party to a contract of his contractual obligations before the date for performance.

Appeal A request to a higher court by a person dissatisfied with a decision of a lower court that the previous decision be reviewed.

Arbitration A means of settling a dispute outside the courts.

Assignment Transfer of rights and liabilities.

Bill The draft of a proposed statute.

Bill of exchange A type of order to pay money.

Bona fide In good faith

Capacity The ability or power of a person to enter into legal relationships or carry out legal acts.

Care, duty of The care owed by one person to another which, if broken, may give rise to an action for negligence.

Case stated A particular form of appeal.

Caveat emptor Let the buyer beware.

Charge An encumbrance upon an asset which gives the holder certain rights over the asset. In particular a charge gives to the creator a prior claim over other creditors for payment of his debt out of the asset.

Charterparty A contract between the shipowner and the charterer whereby a ship is hired for a period of time or for a particular voyage.

Codification The replacement of common law rules by statute which embodies those rules.

Collective agreement An agreement between a trade union and an employer.

BPP PUBLISHING

Common law The body of legal rules developed by the common law courts and now embodied in legal decisions.

Condition Term vital to a contract. Breach of a condition destroys the basis of the contract.

Condition precedent Specific type of contract term.

Condition subsequent Specific type of contract term.

Consideration That which is given, promised or done by a party to a contract.

Consolidation The passing of an Act to 'tidy up the law'.

Constructive dismissal Serious breach of contract by an employer which forces an employee to leave.

Continuous employment Period of unbroken employment required for certain statutory rights to be available to the employee.

Contract An agreement which the law will recognise and enforce.

Control test Test used by the courts to determine whether a contract of employment exists.

Council on Tribunals Statutory body which overseas the workings of administrative tribunals.

Counsel's opinion The advice of a barrister on a specialised or difficult point of law which may be obtained by a solicitor before advising his or her client on whether or not to proceed with his or her action.

Counterclaim When court proceedings are begun by the claimant serving details of his claim upon the defendant, the defendant may reply with a counterclaim alleging that he or she is the injured party. For example, he or she may allege that he or she did not pay for the goods because they were defective.

County court Inferior civil court.

Court of Appeal Appeal court divided into two divisions.

Covenant A clause in a deed whereby a person promises to do, or refrain from doing, a specific act.

CRE Commission for Racial Equality.

Custom Unwritten law which formed the basis of common law.

Damages The sum claimed or awarded in a civil action in compensation for the loss or injury suffered by the plaintiff.

De facto As a matter of fact, disregarding questions of right or title.

De jure As a matter of law.

Decision Secondary source of European law.

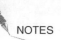

Defendant The person against whom a civil action is brought or who is prosecuted for a criminal offence.

Delegated legislation Rules of law made by subordinate bodies to whom the power to do so has been given by statute.

Directive Secondary source of European law.

Dismissal Termination by an employer of a contract of employment.

EOC Equal Opportunities Commission.

Equity A source of English law consisting of those rules which emerged from the Court of Chancery.

Estoppel If a person, by his words or conduct, leads another to believe that a certain state of affairs exists and that other alters his or her position to his or her detriment in reliance on that belief, the first person is estopped (prevented) from claiming later that a different state of affairs existed. Thus if a principal, by honouring contracts made by his or her agent, induces a third party to believe that the agent possesses certain authority, the principal will be bound by later contracts of a similar nature made by the agent even if they are unauthorised.

Exclusion clause Contract clause purporting to exclude or restrict liability.

Ex gratia By way of favour or gift.

Ex parte Of the one part or one side.

Executed That which takes place at the present time.

Executory That which is to take place at some future time.

Fraud Using misrepresentation to obtain an unjust advantage in the knowledge that it is untrue, without belief in its truth or recklessly, not caring whether it be true or false.

Frustration Discharge of contract by some outside event which makes further performance impossible in the form anticipated.

Fundamental breach Doctrine developed by the courts as a protection against unreasonable exemption clauses in contracts.

Good faith Fair and open action without any attempt to deceive or take advantage of knowledge of which the other party is unaware.

Guarantee A promise to answer for the debt or default of another.

High Court Civil court with extensive jurisdiction.

HSC Health and Safety Commission.

HSE Health and Safety Executive.

Implied term Term deemed to form part of a contract even though not expressly mentioned by the parties.

In personam An action *in personam* is one seeking relief against a particular person.

In rem An action *in rem* is one brought in respect of property.

Indemnity Security against or compensation for loss.

Independent contractor Self-employed person.

Industrial tribunals Local tribunal dealing with disputes between employer and employee.

Injunction An order of the court directing a person not to carry out a certain act.

Integration test Test used by the courts to determine whether a contract of employment exists.

Intention to create legal relations Element necessary for an agreement to become a legally binding contract.

Invitation to treat Indication that a person is prepared to receive offers with a view to entering into a binding contract.

Judgment The sentence or order of the court.

Law Commission Two Commissions were set up in 1965, for England and Wales and for Scotland, as permanent bodies charged with the task of keeping the law under review and proposing reforms where necessary. There are five full-time Commissioners, a High Court judge as chairman and four other legal practitioners or academic lawyers. Normal practice is to publish a working paper first to invite comment and then a final report, often with a draft bill included which embodies the proposed reforms.

Law Lords The name given to the ten life peers or Lords of Appeal in Ordinary who, together with the Lord Chancellor and any other peers who have held high judicial office, sit in the House of Lords as the final court of appeal. In practice, five will normally sit.

Law Reports The principal reports of decided cases

Law Society The statutory body governing the solicitors' branch of the legal profession.

Lien A right to retain possession of property until a debt has been paid.

Limitation of actions By statute, proceedings must be commenced within a certain period of time from the date when the action could first have been brought.

Mens rea Guilty mind.

Minor A person under the age of eighteen.

Misrepresentation False statement made with the object of inducing the other party to enter into a contract.

Multiple test Test used by the courts to determine whether a contract of employment exists.

National insurance State insurance scheme funded by deductions from earnings which provides for benefits to be paid in the event of unemployment, sickness, invalidity, industrial injuries etc.

Negligence This may refer to the way in which an act is carried out, that is carelessly, or to the tort which arises when a person breaches a legal duty of care that is owed to another, thereby causing loss to that other.

Negotiability Quality possessed by certain documents representing claims to money which may be transferred by delivery (and in some cases endorsement).

Negotiable instrument A document which is negotiable, for example a bill of exchange or a cheque.

Novation Transaction whereby a creditor agrees to release an existing debtor and substitute a new one in his or her place.

Obiter dictum Something said by the way.

Offer Express or implied statement of the terms on which the maker is willing to be contractually bound.

Past consideration Something already done at the time that a contractual promise is made.

Penalty clause Clause in a contract providing for a specific sum to be payable in the event of a subsequent breach.

Per se By itself.

Possession Actual physical control over property with the intention of maintaining that control.

Power of attorney An authority in the form of a deed which enables one person to act on behalf of another, if necessary by deed and, for example, convey property.

Precedent A previous court decision.

Presumption A rule of evidence.

Prima facie At first sight or on first impressions.

Privity of contract The relation between two contracting parties which allows either to sue the other for breach.

Pro rata In proportion to the value.

Promise Voluntary understanding by one person to another to perform or abstain from performing a certain act.

Quantum meruit As much as he has deserved.

Quasi contract Resembling a contract but not really a contract.

Ratio decidendi The reason for the decision.

Re In the matter of.

Rectification An equitable remedy.

Regulation A secondary source of EC law.

Remoteness of damage Relationship between a wrongful act and the resulting damage which determines whether or not compensation may be recovered. Different principles apply in contract and in tort.

Repudiation Rejection or renunciation.

Rescission The act of repudiation of a contract. An equitable remedy.

Restitutio in integrum Restoring to the original position.

Restraint of trade Restriction upon a trade or business which is *prima facie* void at common law.

Restrictive Practices Court A special court with High Court status.

Royal Assent Final stage in the process by which a Bill becomes an Act.

Sale of goods A contract whereby the seller transfers or agrees to transfer the property in goods for a money consideration called the price.

Specific performance A type of court order.

Standard form contract Contract where the terms are drawn up by the stronger party

Standard of proof The extent to which the court must be satisfied by the evidence presented.

Statute-barred Inability to pursue an action because proceedings were not started within the period prescribed by statute.

Statutory instrument Form of delegated legislation.

Subject to contract Qualified acceptance pending making of a more formal agreement.

Subpoena Under penalty (for refusal).

Summons Generally an order to appear before a court but used particularly of the document which begins County Court proceedings and of the order to appear before a Magistrates' Court when the accused is not arrested.

Tender Offer, particularly of goods or money.

Title Legal right to possession or ownership of property.

Tort A wrongful act.

Trade union An organisation of employees formed to regulate relations between employer and employees.

Trust An arrangement by which the legal owner of a property has an obligation to administer it for the benefit of the beneficiary who has an equitable interest in it.

Uberrimae fidei Of utmost good faith.

Ultra vires Beyond their powers. In company law this term is used in connection with transactions which are outside the scope of the objects clause and therefore, in principle at least, unenforceable.

Unenforceable Not actionable in a court

Unfair dismissal Termination of a contract of employment in breach of certain statutory rights given to the employee.

Vicarious liability Liability for the wrongful acts of another.

Void Having no legal effect.

Voidable Capable of being rendered void at the option of one of the parties, but valid until the option is exercised.

Waive Give up a claim or right, such as the right to receive notice.

Warranty Minor term in a contract.

Writ A written command.

Wrongful dismissal Breach of contract of employment by the employer without justification and without appropriate notice.

Administration A procedure allowed under the Insolvency Act 1986, by which a moratorium is imposed by the court on creditors' actions against the company while an insolvency practitioner attempts to rehabilitate the business or realise the company's assets.

Administrative receiver A person defined by the Insolvency Act 1986 under a *floating charge* to manage or realise the assets which are the security with a view to paying out of those assets what is due to the debentureholders whom he represents.

Administrator A person appointed by the court to carry out the *administration* under the Insolvency Act 1986.

Agent A person authorised to act for another (the principal) and bring that other into legal relations with a third party.

Allotment of shares The allocation to a person of a certain number of shares under a contract of allotment. The intending shareholder applies to the company for shares. This is an offer which the company accepts by allocating shares to him.

Alternative Investment Market (AIM) AIM is a market operated by the London Stock Exchange for a broad range of companies, particularly young businesses. The market is governed by the Public Offers of Securities Regulations 1995.

Annual general meeting (AGM) Every company is required to hold a meeting of each its members each (calendar) year, at intervals of not more than 15 months, at which it is usual, but not obligatory to transact the 'ordinary business' of the company. Such business may include consideration of the accounts, declaration of a dividend and appointment of auditors. Private companies may dispense with such meetings if they pass an *elective resolution*.

Articles of association Rules governing the internal conduct of a company's affairs, such as appointment, powers and proceedings of directors, alteration of capital structure, dividends and so on. Limited companies may draft their own articles or adopt a model format provided by *Table A* of the Companies (Tables A - F) Regulations 1985.

Assignment Transfer of rights and liabilities.

Auditor A person appointed by the company in general meeting to report whether the accounts reflect a true and fair view of the company's affairs.

Bill of exchange A type of order to pay money.

Bona fide In good faith

Bonus issue A bonus issue is made when a company applies its reserves to paying up unissued shares which are then allotted to members. Bonus shares are a substitute for additional dividends which might otherwise be paid.

Business name A name used by a company other than the registered one.

Call A demand made by a company upon a member to pay an amount outstanding on his partly-paid shares. The power of the directors to make calls is defined by the articles.

Called up share capital The aggregate amount of calls for money or other consideration which members are required to pay (or have paid) in applying for shares.

Capital clause A clause appearing in the memorandum of association of a company which specifies the amount of share capital and its division into shares of a fixed amount.

Capital redemption reserve A reserve created by a company to maintain its capital structure when it carries out a purchase of its own shares. A transfer is made to the reserve from the proceeds of a fresh issue and distributable profits. The sum must be equal to the amount of the capital redeemed.

Capitalisation The conversion of profits into capital by the issue of bonus shares.

Caveat emptor Let the buyer beware.

Certificate of incorporation A certificate issued by the Registrar of Companies on the registration of a company. The certificate is conclusive evidence that the company has been registered and that all the requirement of the Companies Act in respect of registration have been complied with.

Charge An encumbrance upon an asset which gives the holder certain rights over the asset. In particular a charge gives to the creator a prior claim over other creditors for payment of his debt out of the asset.

Class rights Rights attaching to particular types of shares. They are usually specified in the articles.

Common law The body of legal rules developed by the common law courts and now embodied in legal decisions.

Compensation for loss of office A sum paid by a director when he ceases to hold office. If a director has a service contract he may be entitled to compensation for its breach by his dismissal as provided by the Companies Act 1985. The Companies Act provides that such compensation must be approved by the company in general meeting and disclosed in the accounts.

Compulsory liquidation A liquidation initiated when a creditor petitions the court.

Connected person With regard to directors' loans and substantial property transactions, this includes the director's spouse or child under 18, a company in which the director and connected persons own one fifth or more of the equity share capital.

Consideration That which is given, promised or done by a party to a contract.

Constructive notice A person may be deemed in law to know of a certain matter regardless of whether he has actual knowledge of it. In the case of companies this applies to some of the details in company registers, for example the register of charges.

Contract An agreement which the law will recognise and enforce.

Contributory A person liable to contribute to the assets of a company in a winding up. This includes present and certain past members, personal representatives of deceased members and trustees of bankrupt members.

Creditors' voluntary winding up A form of liquidation where a company does not provide a declaration of solvency. if no such declaration is made, the liquidation proceeds as a creditors' voluntary winding up even if in the end the company pays its debts in full.

Crystallisation A *floating charge* attaches to the relevant assets, for example on liquidation or if the contract so provides.

CREST An electronic system used for settling transactions in shares and other securities by the Stock Market.

Cumulative preference share A type of *preference share* where dividends which are not paid in one year are payable the following year.

Damages The sum claimed or awarded in a civil action in compensation for the loss or injury suffered by the plaintiff.

Debenture A written acknowledgement of a debt.

Debenture trust deed A deed made in connection with a series of separate registered debentures. The deed appoints a trustee to represent the interests of the holders, defines the nominal amount of the debenture stock and specifies the date of repayment, the interest rate and the rights of the trustee to enforce the security.

Derivative action A remedy available to a minority shareholder to redress a wrong done to the company. Such an action is brought where those who have committed the offence control the company, and thus, under *Foss v Harbottle* could prevent it from taking action. Any benefit obtained will accrue to the company since the claim is derived from and made on behalf of the company.

Director A person who takes part in making decisions and managing a company's affairs.

Dividend A distribution of profits to members made in proportion to their shareholdings.

Equity share A share which gives the holder the right to participate in the company's surplus profit and capital. There is no limit to the size of the dividend which may be paid except the size of the profit itself. In a winding up the holder is entitled to a repayment of the nominal value plus a share of surplus assets. The term equity share embraces ordinary shares but it can also include a *preference share* when the terms of issue include either the right to an additional dividend or the right to surplus assets in a winding up.

Ex gratia By way of favour or gift.

Ex parte Of the one part or one side.

Extraordinary resolution A resolution requiring a 75% majority at a general meeting of which 14 days' notice has been given. An extraordinary resolution is required, for example, to put the company into creditors' voluntary liquidation.

Fixed charge A *charge* attaching to a particular asset on creation. The asset in question is usually a fixed asset, which the company is likely to retain for a long period. If the company defaults in payment of the debt the holder can realise the asset to meet the debt. Fixed charges rank first in order of priority in a liquidation.

Floating charge A *charge* on a class of assets of a company, present and future which changes in the ordinary course of the company's business. Until the holders enforce the charge the company may carry on business and deal with the assets charged. It attaches to the assets only on *crystallisation*.

Fraud Using misrepresentation to obtain an unjust advantage in the knowledge that it is untrue, without belief in its truth or recklessly, not caring whether it be true or false.

Fraud on the minority Discrimination by the majority shareholders against the minority. The minority may have a remedy at common law.

Fraudulent trading Carrying on business and incurring debts when there is to the knowledge of the directors no reasonable prospect that these debts will be repaid, ie with intent to defraud the creditors. Persons so acting may be liable for the debts of the company as the court may decide.

Gazette An official publication from the Stationery Office in which certain notices must be inserted as prescribed by statute, for example the appointment of a liquidator.

General commercial company An *objects* clause of a company implying that it can carry on any trade or business whatsoever. This clause may now be used as a result of the reforms of the Companies Act 1989.

Good faith Fair and open action without any attempt to deceive or take advantage of knowledge of which the other party is unaware.

Guarantee A promise to answer for the debt or default of another.

Holding company A company which controls another, its *subsidiary* by holding the majority of its voting rights, being a member of it and having the power to appoint or remove a majority of the board of directors.

Indemnity Security against or compensation for loss.

Indoor management rule The principle which states that the outsider who deals with the directors (or apparent directors) is aware of the requirements or restrictions imposed by the articles but is entitled to assume, unless he knows or should suspect the contrary, that these internal rules have been observed. This is also known as the rule in *Turquand's* case.

Injunction An order of the court directing a person not to carry out a certain act.

Insider dealing A person who has been knowingly connected with the company in the previous six months uses unpublished price sensitive information to make a profit or avoid a loss on a recognised stock exchange or through an off-market dealer. This is a criminal offence under Part V Criminal Justice Act 1993.

Insolvency The inability to pay creditors in full after realising all the assets of a business.

Insolvency practitioner Persons acting as a liquidator, administrative receiver, administrator or supervisor of a voluntary arrangement must be insolvency practitioners, authorised by the professional body to which they belong or by the DTI.

Issue at a discount An issue of company securities at less than their nominal value. Debentures may be issued at a discount but shares may not, according to the Companies Act 1985.

Issue at a premium An issue of a share at more than its nominal value. There are special rules laid down by the Companies Act governing the treatment of the premium.

Issued share capital The *nominal value* of the shares which a company has issued.

Joint venture An informal strategic alliance between two or more persons or business for the achievement of a specific purpose. Usually limited in time, joint ventures have no legal status.

Legal person A human being (natural person) or a corporate body (artificial person) having rights and duties recognised by law.

Lien A right to retain possession of property until a debt has been paid.

Lifting the veil (of incorporation) A company is normally to be treated as a separate legal person from its members. 'Lifting the veil' means that the company is identified with its members or directors or that a group of companies is to be treated as a single commercial entity. An example of this is to prevent fraud.

Limitation of actions By statute, proceedings must be commenced within a certain period of time from the date when the action could first have been brought.

Limited liability Limitation of the liability of members to contribute to the assets of a business in the event of a winding up.

Liquidated damages Fixed sum agreed by parties to a contract and payable in the event of a breach.

Liquidator A person who organises a company's liquidation or *winding up*. His task is to take control of the company's assets with a view to their realisation and the payment of all debts of the company and distribution of any surplus to members.

Listed Quoted on a recognised stock exchange.

Loan capital A form of business finance which means that the lender is a creditor of the business either short term (eg a bank overdraft) or long term (eg a debenture redeemable in five years' time). Loan creditors are not the same as members and have no voting rights.

Maintenance of capital A principle whereby creditors are protected. This involves preventing companies from making payments out of capital and thus depleting their assets.

Market purchase A purchase by a company of its own shares under the normal market arrangements of a recognised investment exchange.

Member Shareholder of a company.

Members' voluntary winding up A form of liquidation where the directors have made a declaration of solvency and either the members have passed a resolution that the company be wound up, or the company has come to the end of a period fixed for its existence.

Memorandum of association Together with the *articles of association*, this defines what the company is and how its affairs are to be conducted. It gives details of the companies name, objects, capital and registered office.

Minimum number of members A public company must be formed with two members. The Companies Act provides that if a public company carries on business without at least two members for more than six months, the remaining member who is aware of this is jointly and severally liable with the company for the company's debts. A *private* company, however, may now be formed and operate with only one member.

Minor A person under the age of eighteen.

Minutes A written, indexed record of the business transacted and decisions taken at a meeting. Company law requires minutes to be kept of all company meetings. Minutes of general meetings should be available for inspection by members.

Misrepresentation False statement made with the object of inducing the other party to enter into a contract.

Natural person A human being with rights and duties recognised by the law as opposed to an artificial person such as a corporate body.

Negligence This may refer to the way in which an act is carried out, that is carelessly, or to the tort which arises when a person breaches a legal duty of care that is owed to another, thereby causing loss to that other.

Negotiability Quality possessed by certain documents representing claims to money which may be transferred by delivery (and in some cases endorsement).

Negotiable instrument A document which is negotiable, for example a bill of exchange or a cheque.

Nominee shareholder A person whose name appears on a company's register of members but who in fact holds the shares for somebody else. This is important in connection with *concert parties.*

Objects clause A clause in a company's memorandum of association which sets out the 'aims' and 'purposes' of the company.

Ordinary resolution A resolution carried by a simple majority of votes cast. Where no other resolution is specified, 'resolution' means an ordinary resolution.

Ordinary share A share which gives the holder the right to participate in the company's surplus profit and capital. The dividend is payable only when preference dividends, including arrears, have been paid.

Partnership The relation which subsists between persons carrying on a business in common with a view of profit. Every partner is liable without limit for the debts of the partnership. In the absence of any written agreement, matters such as profit sharing are determined by the Partnership Act 1890.

Passing off Carrying on a business in a manner which is likely to mislead the public. This normally relates to using a name which is similar to that of another business.

Per se By itself.

Perpetual succession The principle by which a change in the membership of a company or the death of a member is not a change in the company itself. A company is a separate legal person which continues unaffected by changes among its members.

Poll A method of voting whereby each person entitled to vote does so in writing, indicating the number of votes which he is casting in proportion to his shareholding.

Possession Actual physical control over property with the intention of maintaining that control.

Power of attorney An authority in the form of a deed which enables one person to act on behalf of another, if necessary by deed and, for example, convey property.

Pre-emption rights The right of shareholders to be offered new shares issued by the company in proportion to their existing holdings of that class of shares.

Pre-incorporation contract A contract purported to be made by a company or its agent before the company has received its certificate of incorporation. An agent may be made personally liable on such a contract which will be unenforceable against the company.

Precedent A previous court decision.

Preference shares A share which carries a prior right to receive an annual dividend of a fixed amount. There are no other *implied* differences between preference and ordinary shares but there may be express differences, for example preference shares may carry a priority right to return of capital. Unless otherwise stated, preference shares are assumed to be *cumulative*.

Premium The amount by which the payment for a share exceeds its nominal value. The Companies Act lays down detailed rules regarding the treatment of a premium and a *share premium account*.

Prima facie At first sight or on first impressions.

Private company A company which may not offer shares to the public, and which has not been registered as a public company.

Pro rata In proportion to the value.

Promoter Person who undertakes to form a company by making the appropriate business preparations.

Prospectus A notice, circular, advertisement or other invitation offering to the public for subscription or purchase any shares or debentures of a company.

Proxy A person appointed by a shareholder to vote on behalf of that shareholder at a company meeting.

Public company A company registered as such under the Companies Act. The principal distinction between public and private companies is that only the former may offer shares to the public.

Purchase of own shares A company may, subject to detailed rules, purchase its own shares. A private company may finance the purchase out of capital but this is closely regulated.

Quantum meruit As much as he has deserved.

Quasi contract Resembling a contract but not really a contract.

Quasi loan A payment to a third party on a director's behalf with the company being indemnified later by the director.

Quasi partnership A small, usually private company, where the relationship between the directors is essentially like that of a partnership. The courts have taken into account the existence of such quasi-partnerships when applying the law.

Quorum Minimum number required to be present for a valid meeting to take place.

Quoted company Company whose securities are listed on a stock exchange.

Ratification Subsequent validation by the members of a decision which the company did not take in general meeting at the appropriate time.

Re In the matter of.

Receiver Person who takes control of the assets of a company subject to a charge as a means of enforcing the security for the benefit of the secured creditors by or for whom he was appointed.

Reduction of capital A diminution of the share capital of a company, for example to reflect a loss in the value of its assets. The scheme needs to be approved by the court to ensure that the creditors are not adversely affected.

Registered office A business address to which all communication with a company must be sent.

Registration Process by which a company comes into being. Certain documents must be filed with the Registrar of Companies and a Certificate of Incorporation must be issued.

Secretary An officer of a company appointed to carry out general administrative duties. Every company must have a secretary and a sole director must not also be the secretary.

Securities Company shares and debentures.

Shadow director A person in accordance with whose instructions other directors re accustomed to act.

NOTES

Share A member's stake in a company's share capital.

Share premium account An account into which an excess of payment for a share over its nominal value cannot be placed.

Show of hands Method of voting in which each member has only one vote, shown by raising his hand, regardless of the size of his shareholding. This contrasts with a *poll*.

Special resolution Resolution requiring a 75% majority of votes cast and 21 days' notice. A special resolution is required for major changes in the company, such as alteration of the name or articles.

Standard of proof The extent to which the court must be satisfied by the evidence presented.

Statute-barred Inability to pursue an action because proceedings were not started within the period prescribed by statute.

Subsidiary company A company under the control of another company, its holding company.

Substantial property transaction An arrangement by which the company buys from or sells to a director of the company or of its holding company property which exceeds £100,000 in value or (if less) 10% of the company's net assets subject to a minimum of £2,000. The shareholders' approval is required.

Table A A model form of *articles* for a company limited by shares set out in the Companies (Tables A - F) Regulations 1985.

Tender Offer, particularly of goods or money.

Title Legal right to possession or ownership of property.

Tort A wrongful act.

Trust An arrangement by which the legal owner of a property has an obligation to administer it for the benefit of the beneficiary who has an equitable interest in it.

Uberrimae fidei Of utmost good faith.

Ultra vires Beyond their powers. In company law this term is used in connection with transactions which are outside the scope of the objects clause and therefore, in principle at least, unenforceable.

Unenforceable Not actionable in a court

Unfair prejudice to members Treating any part of the membership of a company unfavourably. A member may apply to the court for relief under the Companies Act.

Void Having no legal effect.

Voidable Capable of being rendered void at the option of one of the parties, but valid until the option is exercised.

Waive Give up a claim or right, such as the right to receive notice.

Winding up A process by which a company ceases to exist, otherwise known as a liquidation. May take the form of a *compulsory winding up*, a *members' voluntary winding up* or a *creditors' voluntary winding up*.

Wrongful trading The term used where directors of an insolvent company knew or should have known that there was no reasonable prospect that the company could have avoided insolvency and did not take sufficient steps to minimise the potential loss to the creditors.

INDEX

NOTES

NOTES

BPP PUBLISHING

CASES

NOTES

BPP PUBLISHING

NOTES

BPP PUBLISHING

NOTES

ORDER FORM

Any books from our HNC/HND range can be ordered in one of the following ways:

- Telephone us on **020 8740 2211**
- Send this page to our **Freepost** address
- Fax this page on **020 8740 1184**
- Email us at **publishing@bpp.com**
- Go to our website: **www.bpp.com**

We aim to deliver to all UK addresses inside 5 working days. Orders to all EU addresses should be delivered within 6 working days. All other orders to overseas addresses should be delivered within 8 working days.

BPP Publishing Ltd
Aldine House
Aldine Place
London W12 8AW
Tel: 020 8740 2211
Fax: 020 8740 1184
Email: publishing@bpp.com

Full name: ____

Day-time delivery address: ______________________________________

____

______________________________________ Postcode ______________

Day-time telephone (for queries only): ____________________________

BPP PUBLISHING

Please send me the following quantities of books:

Core

		No. of copies	Price	Total
Unit 1	Marketing (8/00)		£7.95	
Unit 2	Managing Financial Resources (8/00)		£7.95	
Unit 3	Organisations and Behaviour (8/00)		£7.95	
Unit 4	Organisations, Competition and Environment (8/00)		£7.95	
Unit 5	Quantitative Techniques for Business (8/00)		£7.95	
Unit 6	Legal and Regulatory Framework (8/00)		£7.95	
Unit 7	Management Information Systems (8/00)		£7.95	
Unit 8	Business Strategy (8/00)		£7.95	

Option

Units 9-12	Business & Finance (1/2001)		£10.95	
Units 13-16	Business & Management (1/2001)		£10.95	
Units 17-20	Business & Marketing (1/2001)		£10.95	
Unit 21-24	Business & Personnel (1/2001)		£10.95	

Other Material

	Workbook (3/00)		£9.95	

Sub Total	£

Postage & Packaging

UK : Course book £3.00 for first plus £2.00 for each extra, Workbook £2.00 for first plus £1.00 for each	£
Europe : (inc. ROI) Course book £5.00 for first plus £4.00 for each extra, Workbook £2.50 for first plus £1.00 for each	£
Rest of the world : Course book £20.00 for first plus £10.00 for each extra, Workbook £2.50 for first plus £1.00 for each	£

Grand Total	£

I enclose a cheque for £______________ (cheque to BPP Publishing Ltd) or charge to Access/VISA/Switch

Card number: [ ][ ][ ][ ][ ][ ][ ][ ][ ][ ][ ][ ][ ][ ][ ][ ][ ][ ][ ]

Issues number (Switch only): ______________________________

Start date: ____________________ Expiry date: ____________________

Signature ______________________________

BPP PUBLISHING

REVIEW FORM & FREE PRIZE DRAW

We are constantly reviewing, updating and improving our Course Books. We would be grateful for any comments or thoughts you have on this Course Book. Cut out and send this page to our Freepost address and you will be automatically entered in a £50 prize draw.

Jed Cope
HNC/HND Range Manager
BPP Publishing Ltd, FREEPOST, London W12 8BR

Full name: ____

Address: ____

____

______________________________________ Postcode ______________

Where are you studying?

Where did you find out about BPP range books?

Why did you decide to buy this Course Book?

Have you used our texts for the other units in your HNC/HND studies?

What thoughts do you have on our:

- Introductory pages

- Topic coverage

- Summary diagrams, icons, chapter roundups and quick quizzes

- Discussion topics, activities and assignments

The other side of this form is left blank for any further comments you wish to make.

BPP PUBLISHING

Please give any further comments and suggestions (with page number if necessary) below.

FREE PRIZE DRAW RULES

1. Closing date for 31 January 2001 draw is 31 December 2000. Closing date for 31 July 2001 draw is 30 June 2001.
2. Restricted to entries with UK and Eire addresses only. BPP employees, their families and business associates are excluded.
3. No purchase necessary. Entry forms are available upon request from BPP Publishing. No more than one entry per title, per person. Draw restricted to persons aged 16 and over.
4. Winners will be notified by post and receive their cheques not later than 6 weeks after the relevant draw date.
5. The decision of the promoter in all matters is final and binding. No correspondence will be entered into.

BPP PUBLISHING